*Blurring the Lines of*
Race & Freedom

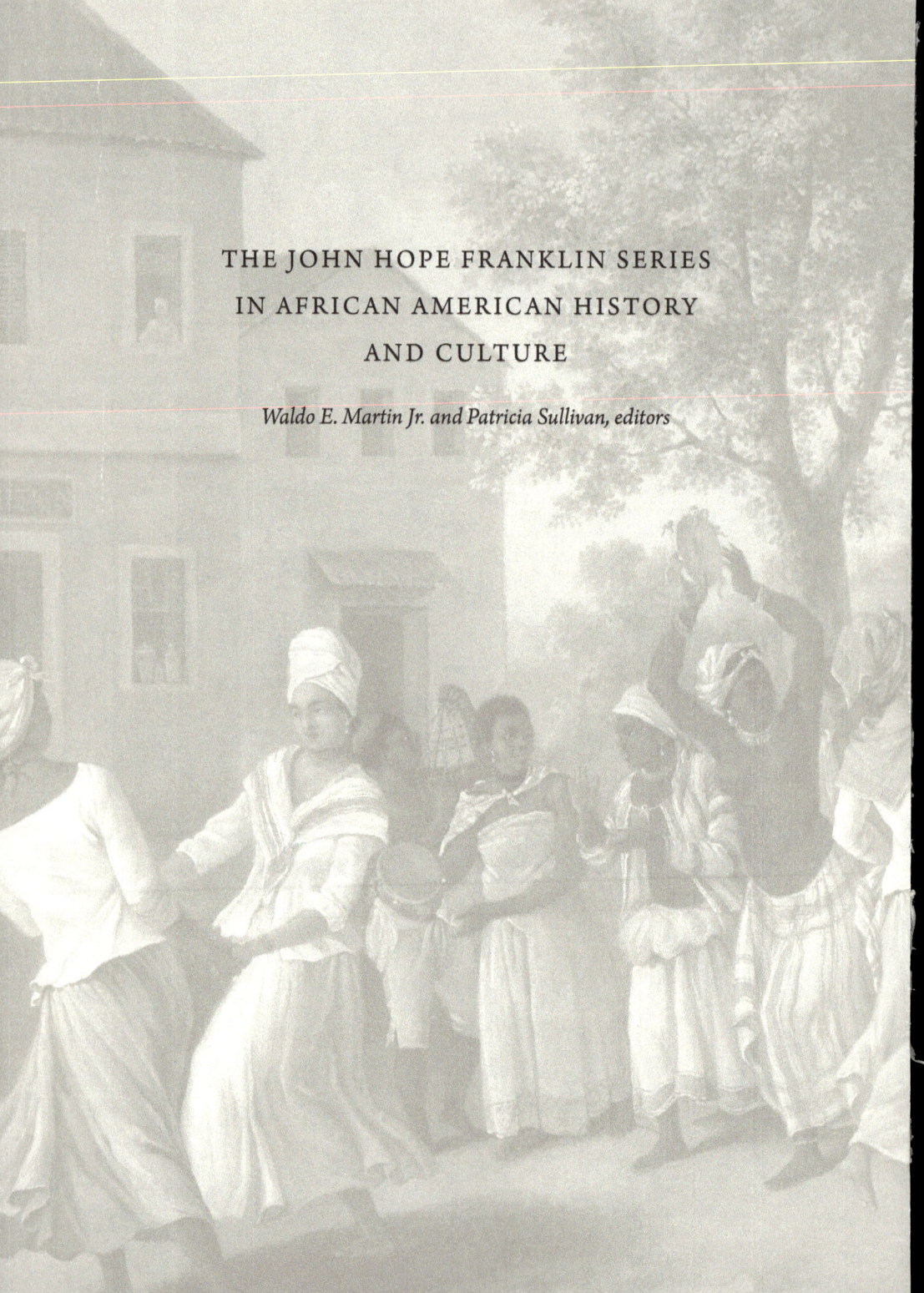

THE JOHN HOPE FRANKLIN SERIES
IN AFRICAN AMERICAN HISTORY
AND CULTURE

*Waldo E. Martin Jr. and Patricia Sullivan, editors*

# *Blurring the Lines*
—···· OF ····—
# Race & Freedom

Mulattoes & Mixed Bloods
*in English Colonial America*

A. B. Wilkinson

THE UNIVERSITY OF NORTH CAROLINA PRESS
*Chapel Hill*

© 2020 The University of North Carolina Press

*All rights reserved*

Designed by Jamison Cockerham
Set in Arno, Scala Sans, and IM Fell English, Great Primer, and DW Pica
by Tseng Information Systems, Inc.

Cover illustration: Agostino Brunias (ca. 1730–1796),
*Dancing Scene in the West Indies.* Courtesy of Tate Images.

*Manufactured in the United States of America*

The University of North Carolina Press has been a member
of the Green Press Initiative since 2003.

LIBRARY OF CONGRESS CATALOGING-IN-PUBLICATION DATA
Names: Wilkinson, A. B. (Aaron B.), author.
Title: Blurring the lines of race and freedom : Mulattoes and mixed
bloods in English colonial America / A.B. Wilkinson.
Other titles: John Hope Franklin series in African American history and culture.
Description: Chapel Hill : The University of North Carolina Press,
2020. | Series: The John Hope Franklin series in African American history
and culture | Includes bibliographical references and index.
Identifiers: LCCN 2020004240 | ISBN 9781469658988 (cloth) |
ISBN 9781469658995 (pbk. : alk. paper) | ISBN 9781469659008 (ebook)
Subjects: LCSH: Racially mixed people—United States—History. | Racially mixed
people—United States—Social conditions. | United States—Race relations—
History. | United States—History—Colonial period, ca. 1600–1775.
Classification: LCC E184.A1 W4525 2020 | DDC 305.800973/09032—dc23
LC record available at https://lccn.loc.gov/2020004240

*To* BERNE *and* MICHELLE

# CONTENTS

*Acknowledgments ix*

Introduction *1*

1  The Rise of Hypodescent in Seventeenth-Century English America *24*

2  Children of Mixed Lineage in the Colonial Chesapeake *59*

3  Mulattoes and Mustees in the Northern Colonies and Carolinas *93*

4  Mixed-Heritage Identities in the Eighteenth Century *128*

5  Mulatto Marriages, Partnerships, and Intimate Connections *163*

6  The Advantages and Disadvantages of Blended Ancestry *199*

Conclusion *235*

*Notes 247*

*Bibliography 289*

*Index 307*

# FIGURES, MAPS, GRAPHS, AND TABLES

### FIGURES

Eighteenth-century *casta* painting  15

Portrait of *Matoaks als Rebecka* (Pocahontas)  32

*Yland of Barbados*  39

*A Map of Virginia and Maryland*  47

Decision in favor of Manuel's freedom  49

Eighteenth-century tobacco label  63

*A Negroes Dance in the Island of Dominica*  113

Descriptions of a "mestizo" or "mustee wench named Betty"  115

Portrait of Ann Arnold  135

*Two Indian Men in Their Winter Dress*  161

*The Barbadoes Mulatto Girl*  172

Caribbean women  190

Man of color directing women of color with a child  207

Mulatto runaways in the *Virginia Gazette*  236

### MAPS

Atlantic World, mid-eighteenth century  xii

Colonial Americas, mid-eighteenth century  xiv

Colonial Chesapeake, ca. 1740  xv

GRAPHS

Population estimates for Maryland, Virginia,
Jamaica, and Barbados, 1650–1690  *41*

Racial descriptions of runaways of color in the
*South-Carolina Gazette*, 1732–1775  *119*

Population estimates for Maryland, Virginia, and Jamaica, 1755  *210*

Racial descriptions of runaways of color in the *Maryland Gazette*
and *Maryland Journal and Baltimore Advertiser*, 1745–1775  *230*

TABLES

Free and bound statuses among those living in colonial
Virginia and Maryland, early eighteenth century  *70*

Population estimates and percentages for Maryland,
Virginia, and Jamaica, 1755  *211*

South Carolina slave manumissions by race, age, and sex, 1721–1776  *214*

# ACKNOWLEDGMENTS

This book has been a beautiful, long struggle, and after many years I am still captivated by the lives of the people within these pages. It has been an honor to tell their stories, and I hope that those who now hold this book enjoy reading about these people as much as I have enjoyed writing about them.

My academic journey has been a long one, and I, of course, am indebted to those who have come before me and those who have mentored me along the way. To the faculty, administrators, professors, and, most important, my peers from Dartmouth College, thank you for saving this formerly struggling undergrad student from flunking out. I would not have made it this far without your friendship and guidance. At Dartmouth, it was under historians such as Colin G. Calloway that I began to look at primary sources and cultivate an interest in the past. At the University of Chicago, I was fortunate to study under Thomas C. Holt, who helped fortify my research skills in the Master of Arts Program in the Social Sciences.

A heartfelt thanks goes out to my former students and colleagues in Chicago Public Schools, Peralta Community College District (Laney College and Berkeley City College), University of San Francisco, the University of California at Berkeley, and the University of Nevada, Las Vegas (UNLV). Not only has teaching paid the bills, but sharing history, telling personal stories, and engaging in lively discussions has fulfilled me in ways beyond a mere profession. I am constantly reminded of how much of a gift the exchange of knowledge is, and I hope this book contributes to that tradition.

When I left teaching high school on Chicago's South Side and moved out to Berkeley, California, to begin a PhD program, I had little idea what I was getting myself into. Again, there were many people who helped me along the way, but Waldo E. Martin Jr. stands out above the rest. I cannot thank him enough for his advice, mentorship, and scrutiny of my scholarship. I am a better teacher and a more insightful historian because of him. During my doctoral studies, others indelibly shaped my thought on history and critical race theory: Loïc Wacquant, David Hollinger, Mark A. Peterson, Jennifer Spear, Mark Healey, Robin Einhorn, Margaret Chowning, Nelson Maldonado-Torres, Carlos Munoz Jr., and finally, Michael Omi, who has been extremely influential on my approach to social history. Lastly, I was fortunate enough to audit Leon Litwack's last History 7B class (intro U.S. survey course from the colonial period to the Civil War). Listening to those lectures and reading his work in my classes showed me how history should be done.

Of course this book would not have been possible without the generous institutional funding from the University of California, Berkeley, and UNLV. Grants from the Center for Race and Gender at the University of California, Berkeley, and the Berkeley Empirical and Legal Studies Fellowship helped get this project off the ground. UNLV's faculty travel funding and summer faculty research awards helped me finish this work. I also want to acknowledge the *Journal of Social History* and *Southern Historian* for previously publishing in article form some of the scholarship that appears here.

Much gratitude goes to the many archivists, librarians, and administrative staff across the archives and academic institutions I have studied and worked at, who have pointed me in the right direction more times than I can count. Research assistants Danielle Ford, Julian Roberts, and Shiori Yamamoto at UNLV also deserve special recognition for the many hours spent quantifying data. I am grateful to nearly everyone in the Department of History at UNLV for reading portions of this manuscript either individually or in working groups. I could not ask for a more collegial department, and I am particularly thankful to those who had a hand in helping me find a place here. A special shout-out goes to Willy Bauer, Raquel Casas, Andy Fry, Anita Revilla, David Tanenhaus, and Mark Padoongpatt, who have spent considerable time supporting me these past several years.

Finally, to my friends and family: you truly know how long and hard a struggle it has been for me to get here, and I am only here because of you. I am thankful to my ancestors and all my relations who have struggled to get us here, especially Granny, Millie C. Edwards, and Grandpa, Gil LaLonde. I love you, Grandma Evie and Aunt Sandy. I promise you'll be hearing more from me now. To Mom and Dad, I dedicate this book to you. Of course I wouldn't be here without you, but I also wouldn't be the man I am today if it weren't for how you loved me.

To all my elders who have prayed for me, to my stepparents, aunts, and uncles who have guided me, and to my friends and extended family who have encouraged me, I say thank you. To my siblings, Nic, Rachel, Lindsay, Jordan, and Alex, you can all finally come out and visit now that I'll have more time to kick back. Please bring your partners and all the nieces and nephews. Cousins, I want to see you more too. I know I have to make up some lost time with all of you (the following will show y'all where I spent it). Finally, to Fawn Douglas, who has propped me up these past few years, words cannot express what you and Sol mean to me. #teamFABS

*Blurring the Lines of*
Race & Freedom

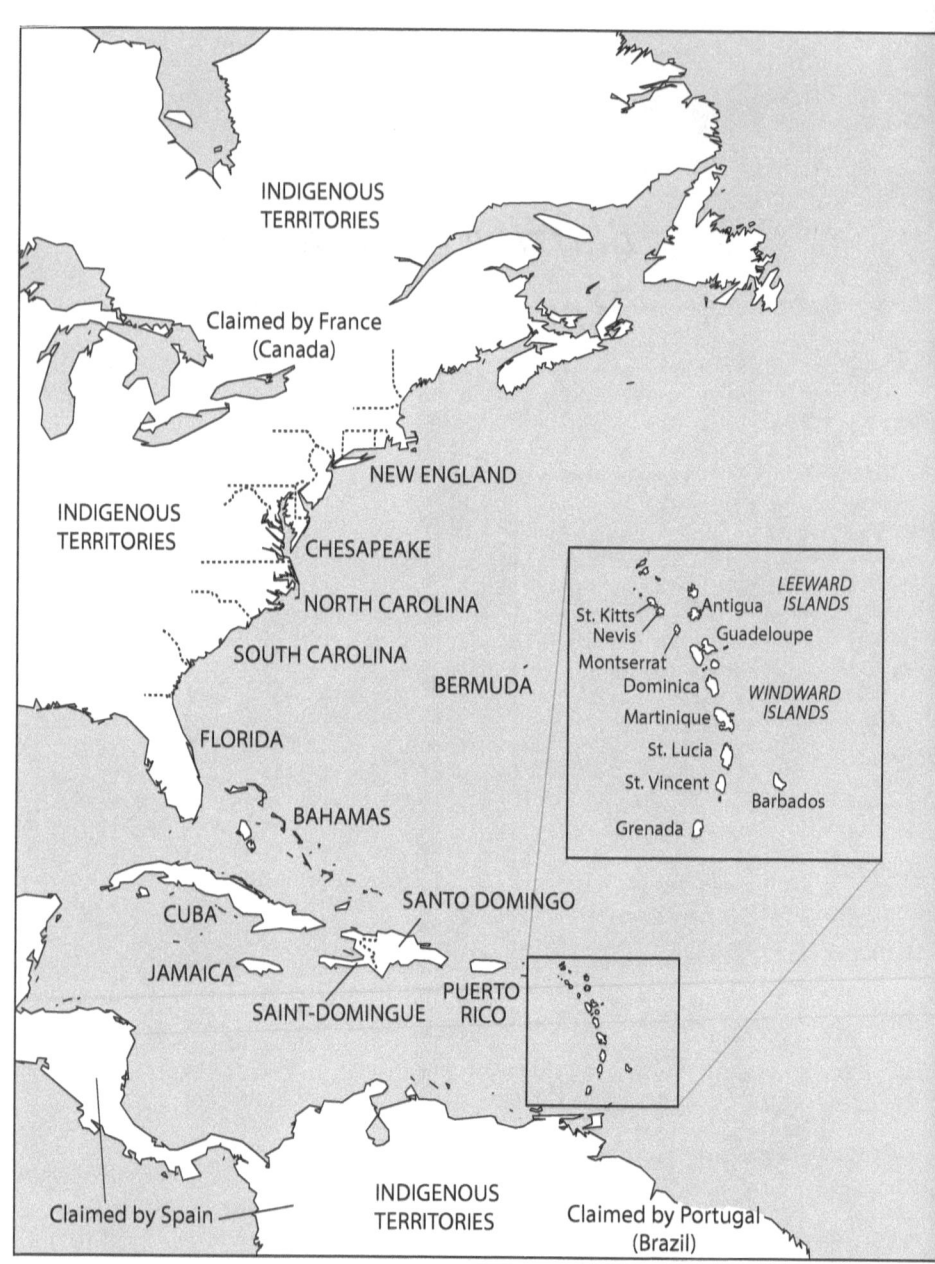

Atlantic World, mid-eighteenth century

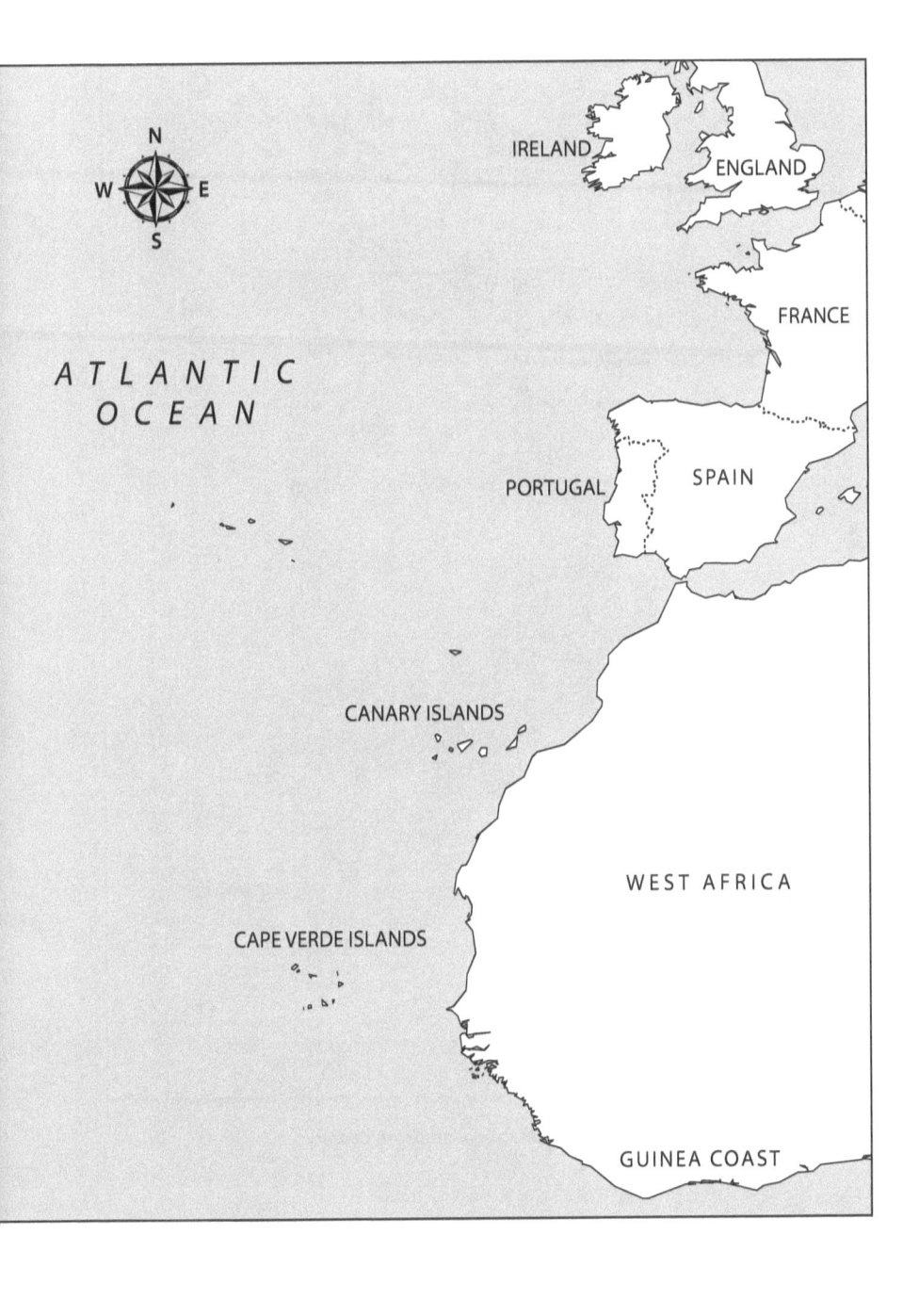

Colonial Americas, mid-eighteenth century

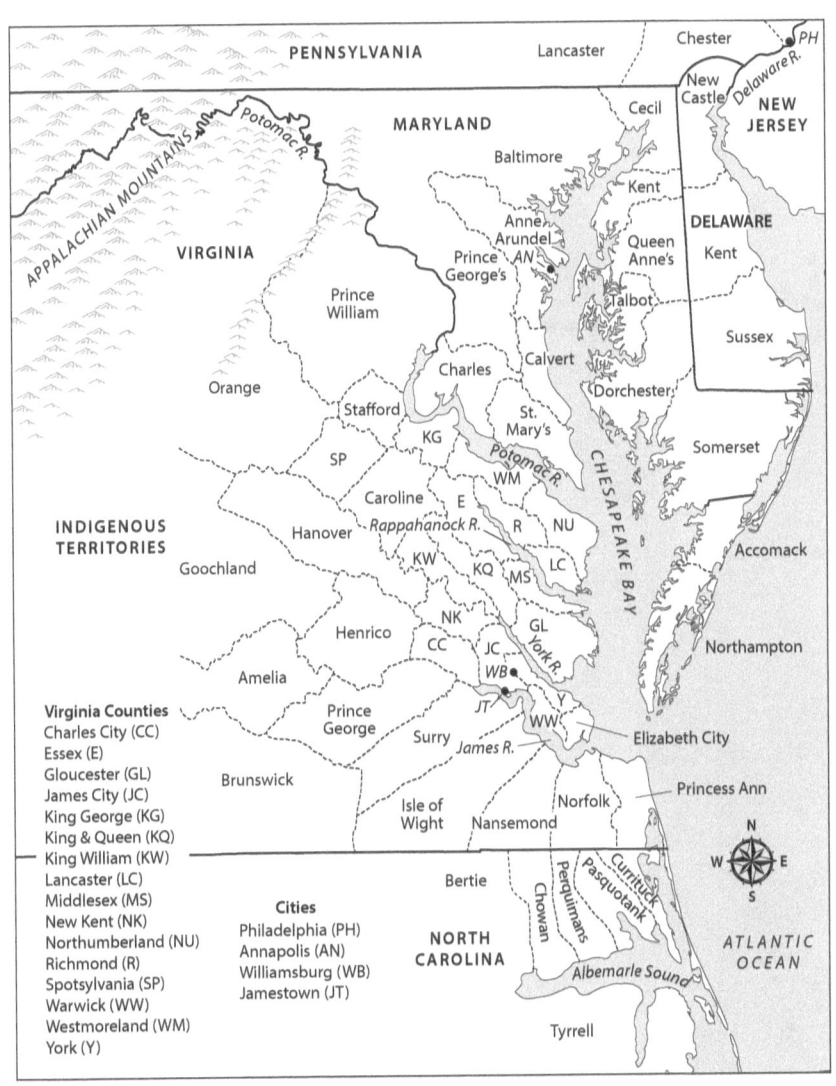

Colonial Chesapeake, ca. 1740

# INTRODUCTION

Thomas Courtney knew he was in trouble when the Maryland General Assembly called him to appear before the colony's highest court in 1692. In May of that year, Thomas traveled at least fifty miles from his country home in St. Mary's County to reach the king's provincial Court of Chancery, which convened in the bustling capital town of Annapolis. During his journey passing through lush forests and fields filled with young tobacco sprouts, Thomas wondered what the magistrates might do with him after he arrived at the council's chamber. He was likely nervous as he stepped up to testify in front of the most powerful men in the colony, including Maryland's top justices and the newly appointed royal governor of the province, "his Excellency" Sir Lionel Copley. The high court had summoned Thomas to question him about carrying out "barbarous and inhumane" acts against his servant, an unnamed "Malatto Girl." Though it is possible the "girl" may have actually been a young woman in her teens or twenties, the female servant had shown great defiance by attempting to free herself from her master on more than one occasion. Thomas confessed that he and his wife were guilty of punishing the girl for her insolent behavior, and he sought to explain why they had committed "so barbarous a Cruelty" against the "Malatto."[1]

Thomas related his side of the story to the authorities, about how his "Malatto Girl" had run away "several times" and routinely took his belongings, including supplies that she used on her journey to escape her masters. She may have reasoned that her labor contributed to the material success of the Courtney household and that her service entitled her to these items. Thomas Courtney disagreed. When left "without any hopes" of altering her recalcitrant behavior, Thomas asserted that he "was forced at last to use . . . Severity towards her in order to reclaim her" from her "Villanous Actions."[2]

When Thomas and his wife physically restrained and disciplined the girl, she was filled with dread. We can imagine she screamed when she saw the couple brandish a metal blade, quickly realizing that this form of punishment would be more severe than the beatings she had previously endured. She struggled to get away, but her "Master and mistress" overpowered her. She could not escape their grasp after they pinned her down. Then she felt a sharp, searing pain and heard a loud penetrating tear as the metal slashed through her flesh. The Courtneys succeeded in cutting the girl's ear off "close to her head." Blood ran profusely as shiny droplets fell and sprinkled the ground around her. The girl continued to cry out and squirmed to get loose, which only made it more difficult for the Courtneys to finish the job. Although we do not know for certain, perhaps she stopped struggling sometime along the way. Thomas did not recount every detail for the court, but he did admit that he and his wife decided to take the girl's other ear as well. Once again, she heard the awful sound of the knife sawing through cartilage as the second ear was "Cropt close to her head by the hands of her Tyrannicall Master and Mistress." Crimson streams flowed from both sides of her head and must have soaked into the coarse fabric of her clothing. Stains in the cloth turned from bright red to dark maroon as the blood began to clot. After the Courtneys left her, the humiliated "Malatto Girl" wept. The physical pain from her wounds eventually subsided and paled in comparison to the shame and despair she felt.[3]

This young woman's bound-labor status and mixed ancestry are critical to understanding why she resisted her masters, how her owners punished her, and how the Maryland assembly treated her and others in similar positions in the English colonies. As was typical in master-slave relationships, the "Malatto Girl" repeatedly refused to accept a subservient position in the Courtney household, and her owners felt that responding with physical violence would correct her rebellious behavior and strengthen their control. Thomas believed the girl deserved harsh discipline after repeated acts of disobedience, but he would not have done the same if she were a servant of *full* English, Irish, or other European descent. He cropped the servant girl's ears because he thought that since she was "his Slave, he might do with her as he pleased." But was the girl a slave?[4]

The "Malatto Girl" and other people of mixed ancestry complicated the legalities of bound status and confused masters about how they could treat their bondswomen and bondsmen. The girl probably had a father of African descent, but she was not legally a slave because she was "born of an English Woman." Therefore, the Maryland assembly declared that she could only be "a Servant according to a Law of this Province for one and thirty years"—a special labor position that authorities created for mixed-heritage people born to European mothers. Thomas Courtney may have attempted to hold the "Malatto Girl" indefinitely in slavery because of her father's lineage, but he could not treat her as a slave because she had an English mother.[5]

Even after Thomas's "Malatto Girl" received such a gruesome punishment, she kept fighting for her freedom, traveling to Maryland's capital in the spring of 1692 to bring a formal "Complaint" about her master to the general assembly. After Thomas gave his account to the court, the judges deliberated and decided they could not allow the "barbarous and inhumane usage of unreasonable Masters," which they recognized was "too frequently practiced in this Province." On May 24, 1692, Maryland's governor concluded that it was "Just and reasonable that the Malotta Girl of Thomas Courtneys . . . be forthwith Manumitted and Set free." Other sympathetic members of the assembly referred to this case when passing an additional "Law in favour of Negroes & Slaves to prevent the Barbarous Tyrranical and Inhumane usage of them." The provincial assembly stated that county court justices could free slaves of any master who would "dismember or Cauterize any such Slave." In this manner, people of mixed ancestry influenced not only this law but also a multitude of legal statutes in the English colonies.[6]

This book explores how the lives of mixed-heritage people with two or more ancestral backgrounds—primarily African, European, or Native American—influenced concepts of racial mixture in the English colonial Americas, including North America and the Atlantic islands of the Western Hemisphere. I argue that the position of "mixed people" among the monoracial classifications of "white," "Negro," and "Indian" complicated colonial systems of servitude and slavery and that the struggle for freedom by people of blended ancestry and their families prevented colonial elites from firmly establishing a concrete socioracial order. Mulattoes and others of "mixed blood" defied static racial categories and sometimes held middling positions in colonial socioracial hierarchies. Even though most faced discrimination and prolonged servitude, which other Europeans did not encounter, some were free or experienced advantages over other Africans and Native Americans in slavery. Bondage and freedom were inextricably linked in English America, and people of mixed descent played a key role in how colonists fashioned racial ideologies in the seventeenth and eighteenth centuries. English colonists throughout the Americas designed laws and practices that functioned to mark people of mixed ancestry as dishonorable, along with Africans and Indigenous people, and legislators in certain colonies specifically targeted Mulattoes when constructing labor systems. In response, mixed-heritage people located various methods to contest bondage, often drawing on multiple ancestries. They chose to sue in courts to achieve liberty, entered into relationships that violated colonial laws, and fought in various ways to experience greater autonomy. This resistance allowed some people of blended heritage to occupy a liminal socioracial position, and as a result, colonial officials could never relegate all people of mixed descent firmly to a bound status of servant or slave.[7]

The story of the Courtneys' "Malatto Girl" is one of countless freedom struggles that illustrates how I approach history in the following pages. This is an intellectual and legal history that delves into how people in the colonial English Empire shaped mixed-race ideologies through custom and law. I consider the development of ideas around racial mixture and people of blended ancestry largely through statutory law and court proceedings. While relying on these sources presents challenges, investigating legal institutions allows me to expose how European colonizers perceived, labeled, and positioned people of mixed descent within English provincial societies.

However, power does not operate unilaterally. Studying those who created and wielded the law not only gives us insight into the actions and intentions of wealthy Europeans but also sheds light on the mixed-heritage people and families who continuously pushed back against structures of colonial power. It is impossible to adequately analyze the ideas of the social and political elite without also unpacking the complex identities and experiences of mixed people. Thus, equally as important, this is a social and cultural history of so-called Mulattoes and other people of "mixed blood." I examine the social position of mixed-heritage people — like the Courtneys' "Malatto Girl" — in the English colonies, the legal circumstances surrounding their lives, how their masters perceived them, how they viewed themselves, and what they strove for most: freedom.[8]

More than 100 years before the founding of the United States, English societies were laying the foundation for how the nation came to think about racial mixture and people of mixed ancestry. Later understandings of ethnoracial mixture in Anglo-America are tied to how Europeans conceptualized "mixed people" in the colonial period, when authorities first identified people of mixed African, European, or Indigenous American lineage. During the colonial era, people of mixed, or blended, ancestry were assigned various racial labels and labor positions in English America — an area that included not only the provinces along the eastern seaboard of North America but also islands in the North Atlantic Ocean, such as Bermuda, and others in the Caribbean Sea. During this time, Europeans referred to "America" generally as all regions of the Western Hemisphere, and I will do the same. Europeans also used the phrase "New World," but these places were not new to Indigenous peoples who had considered them home for millennia.[9]

Several questions have helped guide this investigation. How and why did British colonists first come to conceive ideas of ethnoracial mixture? This question delves into the way Europeans perceived human difference and constructed early notions of race. Through a careful reading of the sources, it is also possible to discover how various groups saw people of mixed ethnoracial descent. But how did people of blended ancestry view themselves and their place within English colonial society? The answers to this inquiry are more difficult to uncover because people from mixed families tended to occupy lower levels of society and left few written records. Still, it is possible to determine the thoughts of traditionally marginalized groups—Africans, Native Americans, poor Europeans, women of all backgrounds, and mixed-heritage peoples—by interpreting their actions and sifting through what others wrote about them. What emerges from the sources is that people of mixed lineage knew they navigated the colonial world from a subjugated position, and many used the modicum of power they had to locate small and larger freedoms within the socioracial order. Their responses to both formal and informal restrictions on their liberty helped shape social, legal, and labor systems.

*Blurring the Lines of Race and Freedom* provides a detailed examination of the origins of mixed-race ideologies and mixed-heritage peoples, who were referred to as Mulattoes, Mustees, or people of "mixed blood" in the English colonies. I emphasize the English slaveholding provinces of North America and the Caribbean but also make broader connections with European colonies in Latin America and other parts of the Atlantic world. After looking at early English colonies in the sixteenth and seventeenth centuries, the book turns to the slave societies of the eighteenth century, where colonial records identify the largest numbers of mixed-heritage people in the British Empire. Comparing geographical regions reveals that the Tidewater Chesapeake colonies of Virginia and Maryland originated the harshest laws against intermixture and were among the first to build institutions that systematically punished mixed-heritage people. Chesapeake colonists developed a brand of racial ideology that propagated extremely negative views of mixed people, but these ideas appeared across the English provinces. While English elites were responsible for promoting racial thinking, everyday European colonists—middling and smaller planters, yeomen working in the fields, and others in the lowest tiers of society—also adopted and helped spread racial thought.

Scholarship on people of mixed lineage has grown since the publication of Joel Williamson's *New People: Miscegenation and Mulattoes in the United States*, and many historians have shown that mixed-heritage people were not "new" in the colonial United States but appeared in earlier periods. By his own admission, Williamson called his book "an 'outline' history of miscegenation and mulattoes in the United States." While I do not use the term "miscegenation," which was not coined until 1863, my book fleshes out Williamson's "outline" for Mulattoes and others of "mixed blood" in the colonial period. I expand on Williamson and other scholars who have explored how social differences between the "upper South" in the Chesapeake and the "lower South," centered in South Carolina, influenced mixture and people of mixed ancestry. I am also indebted to Kathleen M. Brown's *Good Wives, Nasty Wenches, and Anxious Patriarchs: Gender, Race, and Power in Colonial Virginia*. Her chapters titled "Engendering Racial Difference," "Sexual Regulation and the Social Construction of Race," and "Gender and the Politics of Freedom" have been foundational to my understanding of the Chesapeake—where the largest number of Mulattoes lived and where authorities constructed the first segregationist laws to prevent the birth of mixed-heritage people. In South Carolina, the Caribbean, and colonies north of the Chesapeake, there were fewer restraints placed on intermixture and mixed people. Nevertheless, slavery bound Africans, Native Americans, and mixed-heritage people everywhere, and racism affected the lives of free people belonging to these groups. My research compares regions across the English colonial Americas and probes how consistencies among provinces and their distinct social climates all played into the development of mixed-race ideologies.[10]

In recent years, there has been a rise in scholarship on this topic that pivots beyond English North America, and two works of colonial history, by Brooke Newman and Daniel Livesay, have made excellent contributions to our understanding of racial mixture, kinship, inheritance, blood, and subjecthood in the British Caribbean. These historians follow the movement of ideas and people across the Atlantic world and verify the existence of a fluid racial atmosphere in Jamaica that allowed some mixed-heritage families to achieve benefits that came with racial whiteness. They also show that the extension of rights to most free Africans, Indigenous Americans, and people of mixed ancestry as British subjects was limited. The British Crown considered European colonists and people of color to be subjects, yet colonial authorities did not award equal legal protections to the latter group. Most people of mixed descent were held in bondage, and those who were free faced numerous restrictions. I compare the experiences of mixed-heritage people in English continental America with those in the Atlantic islands and show how mixed people everywhere used family ties and links to European lineage to combat these obstacles.[11]

The dependence of colonial planters and merchants on bound labor helped fashion racial groups, but people of mixed ancestry and their families created racial middle grounds that opposed bondage and the monoracial categories of "white," "Negro," and "Indian." Throughout the colonial period, the English used the law to construct bound-labor systems that sustained commercial enterprises, including the mass production of marketable commodities. Sugar and coffee in the Caribbean, tobacco in the Chesapeake, rice and indigo in the Carolinian Lowcountry, and other agricultural crops were integral to plantation economies and the building of nascent racial perceptions. Colonial elites used racial classifications in the law to oppress and exploit Africans, Indigenous Americans, and mixed-heritage people in servitude and slavery. Colonial legal systems also interfered in the lives of poor European plebeians through legislative attempts to define, restrict, and persecute interracial families. Governing officials in both Europe and America organized the economy, labor, and law to strengthen institutions around racial domination, which also sustained negative portrayals of intermixture and mixed-heritage peoples. Thus, these mixed-race ideologies became ingrained in colonial societies.¹²

Africans, Native Americans, and people of blended ancestry and their families commonly fought colonial institutions by contesting bondage in a number of ways. Even acquiescence to colonial systems required intricate power negotiations between slave and master that included survival tactics by both parties. Although this book focuses on mixed-heritage peoples, their strivings are part of broader African and Indigenous struggles to maintain personal autonomy and communal sovereignty. People from all these groups believed themselves deserving of freedom and strove for greater liberties when already free. The resistance of mixed people—coupled with their position as a people who could sometimes claim certain British rights and privileges—complicated a fixed colonial racial hierarchy. While most remained in bondage, their actions during the colonial period prevented authorities from relegating all people of mixed descent firmly into servant or slave status.

While Mulattoes and other people of "mixed blood" straddled monoracial categories in the seventeenth and eighteenth centuries, historians have routinely lumped their stories together with those of all "Negroes," or those of full African descent. The phrase "Negroes and Mulattoes" repeatedly appears in colonial legislation, and there are times when grouping the two proves valuable for analysis. However, colonists used specific racial terms for reasons they saw as important and found mixed-race terminology useful during their time. They used words such as "Mulatto" and "Mustee" because contemporaries widely understood what they meant without further explanation.

Racial meanings and thinking changes over time, and early English colonists applied the term "Mulatto" not only to people of mixed African and European descent but also to those who had some Native American lineage. This should come as no surprise, since the struggles of mixed-heritage people in English colonial America often appear alongside those of African and Indigenous ancestry in records from Virginia, Maryland, North Carolina, South Carolina, Jamaica, and Barbados. Digging deeper into these stories provides a sharper picture of what mixed-heritage people's lives looked like beyond the U.S. "one-drop rule," according to which a person of mixed ethnoracial lineage is typically considered fully "black." While this book does not address the one-drop rule directly, I respond to Winthrop Jordan and Paul Spickard's call for historians to answer "how and why this social rule developed."¹³

Quite simply, the one-drop rule did not exist in the English colonial era and appeared much later in U.S. history. A better framework for understanding mixed-race ideologies in the colonial period falls under the notion of racial hypodescent, in which people of mixed ethnoracial ancestry are most often associated with their socially inferior lineage, and other individual factors cause their legal or social status to fluctuate by varying degrees. Mobility within this definition of hypodescent is key, since this is what accounts for the ability of mixed-heritage people to rise above their "Negro" or "Indian" parents in social status. This elevation was not always possible and was often only temporary. The factors that allowed this social flexibility incorporated labor status, occupation, patronage, religion, language, and access to other forms of cultural capital, along with actual or perceived kinship ties, especially to European heritage or racial whiteness.[14]

The prevalence of the one-drop rule in the twentieth-century United States has allowed some scholars writing about African Americans to gloss over the topic of racial mixture and speak about all people of African descent simply as "black." However, it is particularly problematic for historians to write about all those of African heritage as "black" people, because documentation clearly identifies many of these individuals as Mulatto or under other mixed labels and these titles carried real social meaning. Many times, colonists described people of mixed ancestry generally as "Negro" (they used the word "black" much less often), and those with knowledge of local racial classifications identified mixed individuals specifically using mixed-race language. Additionally, many people of blended heritage would not have personally identified as "black" or "Negro." For these reasons, hypodescent is a more accurate and useful ideological framework for analyzing attitudes concerning people of mixed ancestry in English colonial America. The concept allows us to delve deeper into various racial meanings and people's lived experiences.[15]

Mixed-heritage people's liminal position in monoracial groups allowed them opportunities to achieve social mobility that most Africans did not have. Historians usually ascribe this type of socioracial fluidity to ideas of *mestizaje*, or interracial mixture, in Latin America and the Caribbean and portray Anglo-America as having a more rigid racial caste system. Indeed, English colonists in every American province frowned upon intermixture with Africans and Indigenous people, yet affluent Spanish, French, Portuguese, and other Europeans often felt the same way. Stemming from centuries-old ideas of noble blood, various European elites publicly decried what later became known as racial mixture, *mestizaje*, or *mestiçagem*. All worked to subjugate "mixed bloods" within their respective colonial societies. At the same time, European colonists from all walks of life chose to mix with people of African or Indigenous backgrounds.[16]

I argue that when considering critical mixed-race theory in the colonial period, it is useful to think of European empires on a spectrum of racial (in)tolerance, where firm disapproval and general acceptance of ethnoracial mixture sit on opposite poles. Overlapping sentiments coexisted in any given empire, as some people despised mixture while others, perhaps reluctantly, accepted it within their societies or families. Similarities in racial views were present across European colonies. However, seventeenth-century English lawmakers in the Tidewater Chesapeake began constructing a distinctive mixed-race ideology in the colonial era that aligned with a strict form of racial hypodescent. Virginia, Maryland, and eventually North Carolina devised the greatest systematic opposition to intermixture and became the most difficult places for mixed-heritage people to live in the colonial Americas. In this book, I explain how English officials in these three provinces attempted to eradicate racial mixture and thus diverged from other European slaveholding societies in North America, the Atlantic, and Latin America, which more often tolerated intermixture.

## A SHORT HISTORY OF ETHNORACIAL MIXTURE IN THE AMERICAS

It is helpful to first frame the larger colonial history of ethnoracial mixture in the Western Hemisphere before turning to the English, or British, Empire (I will refer to England as Britain generally after the Acts of Union take effect in 1707). Several European powers visited and colonized peoples of the Western Hemisphere before English efforts began. Around the year 1000, Norse people (Vikings) located prime fishing waters off the coasts of what are now Newfoundland, Nova Scotia, and Maine. While the Norse had contact with Indigenous people, their encampments did not last, and it is unknown if they mixed with the native *skrælingjar*. Some five centuries later, Cristóbal Colón (Christopher Columbus) sailed from Spain and reached the Caribbean in October 1492. This famous voyage ushered in an era of sustained contact between people of the Eastern and Western Hemispheres and established permanent colonial settlements. An explorer to some and an invader to others, Colón initiated a trade in goods, animals, plants, foods, diseases, and people across global hemispheres. These exchanges and the intermingling of humans from places thousands of miles away from each other drastically changed cultures and created a "New World" around the globe, which included "new people."[17]

The idea that people could be of mixed blood was not new to Europeans. Indeed, the concept of hybridity was defined in Spanish and Latin dictionaries during Colón's time. According to late fifteenth- and early sixteenth-century definitions, a *hybrida* was a mixture of the tame and the wild, or someone who had one parent who was a citizen and another who was a foreigner. Even in this early modern period, Europeans imagined that bloodlines held significance when considering kinship, inheritance, religion, and nobility. At this time, the term *race* denoted those of "worthy" or "noble" blood.[18]

Indigenous peoples of the Western Hemisphere began intermixing with Europeans shortly after Colón's first voyage reached the Caribbean islands and in the decades that followed, when monarchies in Spain and Portugal funded additional trips that brought forth an unprecedented era of colonization. Sex yielded children with such frequency that the Spanish regularly employed the term *mestizo*, and the Portuguese *mestiço*, to describe people having both European and Indigenous lineage. The Iberian empires of Spain and Portugal also brought tens of thousands of enslaved Africans to the Caribbean, Central America, and South America. Beginning in the sixteenth century, Iberians used Africans to replace Indigenous workers in places where disease, warfare, and forced labor had taken millions of lives. Africans had sexual liaisons and encounters with Iberian and Indigenous peoples in the Americas as well. Their children were commonly referred to as *mulatos*, though Iberians used various terms to identify offspring mixed with some African ancestry (including *loro, pardo, mamaluco, zambo,* and *zambaigo*).[19]

Historian Jack Forbes posits that the likely antecedents for the word *mulato* in Spanish and Portuguese are *muladi* and *mulado*. These were Iberian words derived from the Arabic *mawallad*, which defined Iberian Christians who converted to Islam, and Forbes finds that this word was "pronounced *muellad* in the Arabic of Spain." These terms and their derivatives date back to the tenth century, appearing during the Moorish conquest and occupation of the Iberian Peninsula, where mixture was prevalent. Arab historians and dictionaries of the past defined the word *muladi* in another manner that stands out: "Its general significance is the child of an Arab father and a non-Arab mother." This fits the definition of Spanish hybridity by the fifteenth century, at the end of the Moorish occupation of Iberia, and also matches subsequent definitions for *mulato* during Iberian conquests in the Western Hemisphere. *Malado* and similar words appear in both Spain and Portugal and may have had overlapping definitions, as people also applied the term to servants. Perhaps not coincidentally, mixed-heritage children have a much longer history of being subjected to servitude. These definitions and the meanings behind them suggest that the word *mulato* came out of the Arabic language and the colonization efforts of the Moors in Spain from the eighth through fifteenth centuries, not from the Spanish word for mule, as some would later surmise. This does not discount the fact that the Spanish words *mulato*, as assigned to people, and *mulo*, as assigned to the animal, and their variations both conjure up ideas of hybridity.[20]

While the etymology of *mulato* may forever be obscured, the Spanish and Portuguese spread the word, along with other racial terminology and ideologies, throughout the Atlantic world. The English largely acquired their racial lexicon from the Spanish during early colonization efforts in the Western Hemisphere. Compared to the English of the sixteenth century, Iberians had developed racial beliefs based on a much longer history of contact and interaction with people outside Europe. They had been colonized for centuries by Moors from northern Africa. They had explored the west coast of Africa and the Americas since the fifteenth century. And they subjugated certain Africans and Indigenous Americans well before the English began holding slaves in the Americas. The Spanish and Portuguese pioneered the transatlantic slave trade, and the English later joined the Dutch in entering into this commerce in the seventeenth century, when traders brought Africans into the Anglo-American Caribbean and into ports along the North Atlantic coast.[21]

While European imperialism looked different in the Western Hemisphere, the process of colonization operated similarly during its initial phases. Europeans came to places in the Americas that were inhabited by Indigenous peoples, whose assistance and knowledge helped Europeans thrive. During this phase, the newcomers realized they could not easily survive without continuous supplies from Europe or aid from local Native American populations. Europeans relied on Indigenous Americans as guides, servants, slaves, and suppliers of food and other trade goods.

Generally, the first wave of Europeans who came to the Americas interacted closely with Indigenous populations, intermixed, and promoted Christianity with goals of building societies either with or alongside Native Americans. Still, early colonial interactions often turned violent as European colonists sought to exploit resources, land, and labor. Indigenous people retaliated against Europeans who forced *indios* ("Indians") to toil in mines and fields. In the sixteenth century, the Spanish and Portuguese realized that the original inhabitants of the Caribbean and other regions were dying in great numbers due to disease, warfare, and grueling labor, so they began to replace the dwindling numbers of Indigenous people with African slaves. Indigenous populations never quite recovered in the Caribbean, where they mixed in with Europeans and Africans, though their numbers rebounded in Central America and South America after massive population decline. Some Europeans had dreamed of creating utopian societies with Indigenous peoples in the Americas. However, these hopes were unattainable when imperialism was grounded in power relationships that held European "civilization" as superior and degraded Indigenous and African cultures and peoples as inferior.[22]

Iberians were the first Europeans to engage with Indigenous peoples in the Americas through a process of *mestizaje* and built integrated mixed, or *mestizo*, societies, albeit based on uneven socioracial hierarchies. Other Europeans followed these models, but the English in North America, and specifically those in the Chesapeake, initiated a socioracial order that prohibited intermixture and restricted people of mixed ancestry to a greater degree than those living under Iberian authorities. At first, English colonists lacked a clear racial lens through which to view Indigenous Americans and Africans or even themselves, but they eventually developed racial ideologies that included extremely intolerant beliefs toward mixture and mixed-heritage peoples.

Three interconnected factors of religion, gender demographics, and settlement patterns influenced how the English diverged from other European colonists, who more openly mixed with Africans and Indigenous Americans. First, Catholicism distinctly influenced the character of Spanish, Portuguese, and French colonization efforts in the Western Hemisphere, which diverged from imperial projects under English Protestantism. When compared to provinces controlled by Protestant empires—mainly the English—those ruled by Catholic powers bestowed greater rights upon African and Indigenous people in the Americas. From the late fifteenth century through the sixteenth century, Iberian empires and the Vatican set guidelines for how Catholics should treat *negros* and *indios*. Catholic monarchs and the Pope attempted to limit Indigenous bondage (though it still persisted), and they deemed African slavery an acceptable alternative as the transatlantic slave trade increased over the sixteenth century. While colonists did not always follow royal or clerical decrees, the Catholic Church officially recognized non-Europeans as people deserving of ecclesiastical rights. For example, by the late seventeenth century, the Spanish had long required that African slaves receive Catholic baptism, though many English Protestants refused to confer the sacrament upon their slaves out of the fear that conversion would open a pathway to freedom.[23]

Beginning in the seventeenth-century French Caribbean and Louisiana, Catholic doctrine guided the *Code Noir*, which officially extended marriage and other rights to African slaves, similar to laws in Ibero-America. French officials intended the *Code Noir* to protect slaves from excessive abuses, though slave owners did not always follow these guidelines. While the French Empire also exploited African and Indigenous labor and cultivated racial hierarchies based on ancestry, it differed from its Protestant counterpart by granting more liberal manumission and other concessions to people of African descent. Mixed-heritage people could exercise legal rights in Catholic colonies and experienced socioracial flexibility, but not all were allowed to move freely throughout society as equals.[24]

The gendered dynamics of European immigrants in the Americas were a second crucial factor that directed imperial practices around intermixture in the colonies. Male traders, military men, and missionary priests predominated in the French, Portuguese, and Spanish colonies, which were generally more open than the English to men mixing with women of African and Indigenous descent. Many English and other European refugees—men, women, and children—came to North America with the goal of transplanting communities and re-creating European societies in the Western Hemisphere. For instance, Puritans immigrated with whole families and established themselves in Algonquin territory, which they renamed New England. With close to even sex ratios, they aimed to reproduce Protestant institutions that would be a model not only for the Church of England but also for the rest of the world. In other English colonial regions such as the Chesapeake, early demographics leaned heavily male, but natural reproduction increased and Europeans reached gender parity by the eighteenth century without widespread mixture with Native Americans and Africans.[25]

Immigration and gender demographics in North America connect directly with the third factor that shaped intermixture, European settlement patterns, which exemplify the English model of settler colonialism that disdained mixture with non-Europeans. The Spanish and French often lived in Native American communities or regularly intermixed with Indigenous populations in rural areas and colonial towns. In North America, the Spanish founded Catholic forts and missions on the Florida peninsula and in the Southwest. The French established forts in an arc that spanned from the St. Lawrence River, through the Great Lakes and Ohio Valley and southward along the Mississippi River, through Louisiana and New Orleans. French traders, merchants, and missionaries were principally involved in fur trading in Native American villages, and people intermingled and cultures merged in colonial towns and forts. The French called people of mixed Franco-Indigenous ancestry *métis* and those of mixed African-Franco heritage *mulâtres*—a group that grew in eighteenth-century New Orleans and Saint-Domingue. Many European men under Catholic regimes in North America, Latin America, and the Caribbean had open relationships with African, Indigenous, and mixed-heritage women, which led to a certain level of social acceptance of *métis* and *mulâtres*, *mestizos* and *mulatos*.[26]

English colonists in North America did not intermix with Indigenous Americans to the same extent as the French or Spanish. Instead, they largely reproduced European households, in part because English settler societies more quickly reached self-sustaining populations and approached more even sex ratios than other colonies. European populations attained a natural increase in New England after the mid-seventeenth century, and the Chesapeake and other areas achieved sustainability by the end of the century. Some Anglo-Indigenous mixture took place where peoples frequently came into contact, though colonial social customs and Native American cultural preferences limited intermarriage. Sometimes English colonists took "Indian" wives as well as servants or slaves into their homes, and they commonly allied with Indigenous groups. While these alliances were imperfect, and disagreements often erupted into war, many English traded peaceably with Native Americans and gained permission to reside on certain Indigenous lands in North America. In the second half of the century, the English had also overtaken the Dutch colony of New Netherland and were successfully replicating Anglican societies, with a mix of other Europeans, along the Atlantic seaboard. Even though Native Americans and Africans were always present in the colonies, English officials viewed these groups as a threat to the expansion of European "civilization" and sought to keep intimate distance from non-"whites." Intermixture took place, though on a relatively small scale.[27]

While all Europeans adhered to a "white" supremacist socioracial order, many English differed from their French, Portuguese, and Spanish peers in terms of the degree to which they accepted racial intermixture and people of mixed ancestry within their colonies. By the eighteenth century, the English typically opposed open intermixture with people of African or Indigenous heritage, while this type of *mestizaje* was commonplace under the Catholic regimes. For example, the Spanish colonial model permitted exogamy—marriage outside one's group—and allowed mixed people opportunities to occupy various positions on the socioracial ladder. Non-"white" *castas* (castes), especially those with Spanish ancestry, experienced greater social mobility than those in most English provinces. These *castas* made up a significant portion of Spain's colonial population and became so large that elite Spaniards and *criollos*, or Spaniards born in the Americas, often applied the term *casta* to African, Indigenous, and mixed-heritage peoples.[28]

Artists in Nueva España (New Spain) illustrated their ethnoracial diversity in hundreds of eighteenth-century *casta* paintings that showcase families of blended ancestry. While the populace did not regularly use all of the featured racial labels, the artistic imagery portrays the prevalence of *mestizaje* and reflects the general social acceptance of mixed-heritage peoples in Latin America. Some of the classically trained artists were themselves labeled *mulato* or *mestizo*, and had African and Indigenous forebears. Families like these also existed in the English colonies, though on a much smaller scale. Painters would not create images that highlighted mixed-heritage families in the English colonies, where elites denigrated non-"whites" and societies held wide-scale contempt for racial mixture. Still, these people and the stories of their families existed in Anglo-America.[29]

As the English expanded their colonial ambitions and attempted to surpass the grandeur of the Spanish Empire, they envisioned societies where the blood of Europeans would remain separate from that of African and Indigenous peoples. Englishman Edward Long wrote from Jamaica: "Let any man turn his eyes to the Spanish American dominions, and behold what vicious, brutal, and degenerate breed of mongrels has been there produced, between Spaniards, Blacks, and Indians, and their mixed progeny." Edward felt it was the duty of all "white men" in the British colonies to raise a "race of unadulter-

This eighteenth-century *casta* painting depicts the idea of *mestizaje*, or racial mixture, in Nueva España (New Spain). Spanish colonists did not regularly use all of the racial labels applied to the sixteen panels painted here by an unknown artist; rather, they more commonly used the categories of the families pictured near the top of the painting: panel 1, "*Español con India, Mestizo*"; panel 2, "*Mestizo con Española, Castizo*"; panel 3, "*Castiza con Española, Español*"; and panel 4, "*Español con Mora [Negra], Mulato.*" (Katzew, *Casta Painting*, 42–44; Instituto Nacional de Antropología e Historia, Mexico City)

ated beings" instead of a group of mixed *"yellow offspring not their own."* This sentiment captures why many English positioned themselves in opposition to the *mestizaje* schema found in Latin America and intentionally avoided ethnoracial mixture.[30]

By the mid-eighteenth century, the British had established a presence along the eastern seaboard in continental North America—where physical separation from Native Americans had become a defining tenet of settler colonialism. Still, mixture with people of African descent was more common in South Carolina and on several Caribbean islands, where Europeans were in the minority. English settler colonialism resulted in the removal or subjugation of those who did not serve their interests. The British routinely vilified Africans and Indigenous people as "savage" and used this label as justification to expel Native Americans from their ancestral lands or enslave them along with Africans. Over the years, both Indigenous peoples and Anglo-Americans distanced their communities from one another in attempts to secure their respective survival, and this separation also limited intermixture. Even if this early form of segregation was never completely enforceable or attainable, the English largely rejected mixture with Indigenous Americans and with Africans inside their colonies. These ideas guided both English sentiment and settlement throughout most of their expanding empire. Although there were many people of mixed ancestry who lived in the English colonies, no widespread mestizo America would exist under British rule.[31]

## CHAPTER OVERVIEW

*Blurring the Lines of Race and Freedom* centers on the English colonies with the largest mixed-heritage populations, or those in the Chesapeake, the Carolinas, and the Caribbean. It is no coincidence that these slave societies—those structured on a commitment to human bondage as a principal labor source—produced the greatest number of mixed-heritage people. I also introduce evidence from other English provinces and juxtapose English mixed-race ideologies with those in French and Latin American colonies to contextualize the British story. Chapters move in roughly chronological order, primarily from the early seventeenth century through 1775, the eve of the U.S. Revolution.

The first chapter explores the origins of hypodescent ideology—the framework for understanding ethnoracial mixture in colonial America—specifically in the seventeenth-century Tidewater Chesapeake and English Caribbean. Here I examine the origins of mixed-race ideologies and people of blended African, European, and Native American descent, commonly identified as Mulattoes. Chapter 2 traces the development of English society's response to mixed-heritage people in the colonial Chesapeake from the 1690s into the early decades of the eighteenth century. This was a critical period for the establishment of hypodescent ideology in North America, as magistrates in Virginia and Maryland passed legislation that sought to prevent intermixture and strengthened institutional structures that punished people of mixed ancestry. Chapter 3 moves outward along the Atlantic coast to the north and south of the Chesapeake and compares nuanced patterns of intermixture in the northern colonies and the Carolinas. It also looks closer at African and Native American mixture in these provinces as well as different approaches that officials took when handling diverse types of intermixture and people of blended heritage.

The final three chapters focus more on people of mixed descent in terms of their culture, identity, and life struggles and how the connections they maintained with family and friends allowed relative access to freedom. When I began research for this book many years ago, I wanted to understand how people of mixed ancestry saw themselves and navigated the Anglo-American world. Putting together a picture of their lives has been difficult because most mixed-heritage people toiled in bondage and left behind few written documents of their own. I have pieced together important aspects of their lives by scouring colonial legislation, court cases, petitions, letters, newspaper articles, and hundreds of runaway slave advertisements. The fourth chapter compiles information from these materials to show how people of mixed ethnoracial ancestry self-identified in the early to mid-eighteenth century. While personal affiliations varied depending on region, social status, and individual lineage, so-called Mulattoes clearly viewed themselves like most other European colonists: as Christians and people deserving of freedom. They crafted various and situational ethnoracial identities that sometimes defied categorization. They pragmatically positioned themselves to advance their independence, which sometimes meant gravitating toward whiteness. At other times they fought for the freedoms of their darker family members under the wider racial designations of "Negro" or "Indian."

Racial identity is a theme that also influenced how people of blended ancestry chose intimate partners, and chapter 5 looks exclusively at the sexual relationships and connections that mixed-heritage people entered into in the English colonies. Available sources lean toward the most documented relationships involving free women of mixed backgrounds, which I admit may skew the view of what was typical. Nonetheless, it appears that interracial sex, whether forced or voluntary, most commonly took place between "white" men and women of color, and hierarchies of race, class, and gender were inextricably linked through these interactions. Chapter 6 presents an expansive view of how Mulattoes and other mixed people accessed freedom while recognizing that most of them still languished under the weight of bondage. Free people of color were often associated with light-skinned privilege, benefited from marginal whiteness, and retained advantages over enslaved Africans. However, any advantages that people of mixed ancestry received must always be considered alongside the disadvantages. Finally, the book's conclusion connects the freedom struggle of Africans and mixed-heritage people to the beginning of the U.S. Revolution and provides some final thoughts.[32]

## A NOTE ON RACIAL LANGUAGE

In the mid-eighteenth century a "Molatto slave" named Will ran away from his master near Philadelphia. According to his owner, Will was nearly thirty years old, "very near the Negroe complexion," and born "of a Negroe father, and Indian mother." He also spoke "both English and Dutch" and was "a sensible, cunning, ingenious fellow." Will's description shows the complexities of determining identity, ascertaining ancestry, and deciphering racial descriptors. European colonists often referred to people having both African and Native American heritage as Mulattoes in the Chesapeake colonies. In other provinces, colonists might have called Will and others like him a Mustee — a person of Native American descent who also had ties to either African or European lineage. We are not sure how Will saw himself in racial terms, but we know he was an intelligent, self-reflexive, and freethinking person.[33]

Multiple meanings exist for words such as "Mulatto," "Mustee," and other mixed-race labels, all of which are mercurial, changing over time and space, and varying between observer and observed. I use the word "Mulatto" to describe people in the colonial period who had a combination of two or more ethnoracial ancestries: African and European, Native American and European, African and Native American, and sometimes all three backgrounds. I acknowledge that individuals from other ethnoracial groups could be classified under the label. Many times, Europeans referred to "Mulattoes" and "Mustees" separately from "Negroes." However, it is also apparent that colonists often used the word "Negro" as an umbrella term for all those of African extraction, while "Mulatto" and "Mustee" were more precise terms used to designate a subcategory of "Negro" along the lines of racial hypodescent.

Because racial labels and their significance are constantly changing, it is difficult to write about race historically. For instance, the English did not regularly refer to themselves as "white" until around 1680 in colonial America. They also did not widely apply the word "black" to those of African lineage until the eighteenth century, and even then, they used the term "Negro" far more widely over the colonial period. Therefore, I place "black" and "white" in quotation marks throughout my work to avoid confusing our contemporary use of racial terms and phrases with historic definitions. Typically, I use racial language within quotes and cite words exactly as they appear in historical records, including misspelled words and those in italics (all italicized words in quotations are emphasized in the original sources). However, for ease of reading, I usually remove quotation marks from "Mulatto" and "Mustee," two words that have generally fallen out of use in the English language today. I have decided to place "Negro" inside quotation marks as a rule, as the word is still in use and is considered by many to be derogatory. When I use "Negro" along with "Mulatto" or "Mustee," however, I retain quotation marks on all the terms for uniformity. I also capitalize "Negro," "Mulatto," and "Mustee" throughout, though in the quoted sources they appear both in the capitalized and lowercase forms.[34]

I seek to use accurate and appropriate language when referring to people of mixed heritage and do not mean to uphold, revive, or reify racial terms or ideologies. I do not advocate bringing back into use the words "Mulatto," "Mustee," "half breed," "mixed blood," or other racial terms. These words are relics of the past and should remain there. Although I use the racial language of the time, I recognize that these words carried negative connotations and colonists could wield these words as slurs. Part of what follows is the history of how these words became racial epithets. Thus, when using racial labels, I try to show that people were perceived to be of mixed ancestry, even if I do not make this distinction explicit at every step along the way.

At times I discuss where the meaning of racial terminology was conflated, contested, or debated in the historical documents. In other places, I apply racial terminology without deeper analysis. Two such phrases are "mixed people" and "people of color." In recent decades "people of color" has come back into regular use with a definition similar to what it once meant so many years ago: people of discernable non-"white" or non-European ancestry. The term "mixed people" does not appear widely in written American colonial texts, though Englishman Granville Sharp used the phrase when discussing "mixed people or Mulattoes" in 1769, so it was used and may have been understood by his contemporaries. French colonists used the term *sang-mêlés* ("mixed-bloods") and more often *gens de couleur* in the eighteenth century, while the English commonly used "people of color" and "persons of color" by the end of the century, if not earlier. I will use these phrases without quotation marks in later chapters, again attempting to keep terminology in line with the use of its time. Admittedly, the expressions "mixed people" and "people of color" can be problematic for many reasons, though they accurately capture the "white"/non-"white" racial binary born out of the colonial period and can tell us some things about heritage as well.

Defining groups of people without falling into racial absolutism is a daunting task, and writing about mixed race is even more challenging because race is intangible and mixed people defy monoracial categorizations. When describing ideas of race, racial mixture, or perceptions of racialized groups, I try to represent people's ideas in their time. While I have taken great care to decipher and translate mixed-race labels and experiences from the past for an audience in the twenty-first century, inconsistencies remain because racial characterizations are largely founded on how different individuals read race in the bodies of others around them. Even in the present, ideas concerning race remain in a state of flux, though people generally understand that racial meanings often determine who is included or excluded from access to power within a society.[35]

Racial markers based on phenotype—skin tone, hair texture, and facial features—are always open to individual interpretations and do not always reflect the ancestral makeup of mixed-heritage people. One master in Pennsylvania listed various features for his "Mulatto Slave" Joe Lane, writing that the bondsman "is pretty fair [skinned], his Wool black, and much curled, [and he] has a Nose like a Negroe." Another man, Tom, was called a "Negro man" in Virginia and may have had some Native American ancestry. "His hair is of a different kind from that of a Negro's, rather more the Indian's, but partaking of both, which, though short, he frequently ties behind," stated his owner. Colonists sometimes associated people with ethnoracial mixture even though their actual ancestry remained unknown.[36]

Even the word "Indian" might refer to people from two sides of the globe. According to their owners, the "mulatto" Betty had "short *Indian* hair" in Charles Town (Charlestown), South Carolina, while the "Mulatto Slave" Amos in Virginia had "long, bushy Hair, like an East-Indian's." Did Amos have ancestry from South Asia, or what we call India today? This was certainly possible. Benjamin Manuel was born around 1725 in North America and lived in Pennsylvania. His father was "an East India man, and his mother an English woman" when newspapers described him some thirty years later as a servant. His master noted that "his complexion [is] like that of a Mulatto." There were definitely people from "East India" and their descendants in the English Americas. Some may have been labeled as Mulatto, but their numbers were extremely small, and I have nearly exhausted the cases in those I have located above.[37]

Overwhelmingly, "Indian" meant Native American, terminology I use together with "Indigenous" to signify the original inhabitants of the continental Americas and the Caribbean. Sometimes masters did not know if someone was Native American or had mixed ancestry. The master of John Moycum said the servant was an "Indian or Molatto." Another owner called his bondsman Frank a "Mulatto or half Indian man." A third man, Jacob, was called a "Mulattoe Fellow ... [who] had an Indian Father." In the following chapters I discuss how colonists applied the term Mulatto to those of Native American ancestry, and it is clear that Mulattoes were not only those of African and European parentage.

Unless someone's heritage is listed otherwise, it should always be assumed that those identified as Mulatto could have Indigenous lineage.[38]

In fewer cases, English colonists used "Mulatto" to denote skin color instead of mixed ancestry, yet they rarely used the word to simply describe skin tone and most often used "Mulatto" as a noun or adjective describing a person of mixed ethnoracial descent. In Virginia someone called Will Cooper a "Negro man . . . between a black and mulatto colour," while in Pennsylvania, Jack's owner said his bondsman was a "Negroe . . . of a Mulattoe Colour." Here, colonists described people of a "mulatto colour" as being "Negro"—whom they took to be unmixed African. Brothers Michael and Lewie were both referred to as actual Mulattoes in Virginia. Their master described Michael as a "dark Mulatto" and his brother Lewie as a "light Mulatto." The brothers were likely of mixed descent, as were most people who fell under the label. Surely not all Mulattoes were people within the first generation of perceived mixture (one "black" and one "white" parent). For these reasons I am careful not to call individuals Mulatto outside the sources, and I strive for accurate language when describing ancestral backgrounds.[39]

Despite the varied applications of mixed-race language, colonial use of certain terms was widely uniform, and colonists applied words precisely to people of mixed ethnoracial ancestry because they often knew the people they owned quite well. Saunders's master described him as "a tall well made Carolina born negro man . . . of a yellow complexion, being of the mustee breed." If we decipher Saunders's background through this description, it appears that he was of African and Native American extraction. In another instance, a master described several runaway "Negroes," including one Flora, "of a yellowish complection," who was accompanied by Statira, or Tira, "of the mustee breed." This example shows how colonists drew racial distinctions among their slaves when they could provide the information. Both women were of African descent, and while the owner described Flora's "yellow" skin tone, she confirmed that Tira was actually of African and Indigenous ancestry—being a "Negro . . . of the mustee breed" (part Native American). Communities were much smaller in the colonial period than today, and masters usually had specific lineal knowledge of their servants' and slaves' families.[40]

Descriptions based on skin color alone further complicate racial classifications and are poor indicators of ancestry. This is why we cannot assume that those described as having a "yellow complexion" were all of mixed parentage. Colonists applied the term "yellow" to the skin tones of Africans, Native Americans, and people of mixed heritage. This is why my research method avoids using descriptors based on skin color to assume someone's ancestry and attempts to precisely locate people's actual lineage only when possible. This strategic and conscientious approach also prevents me from anachronistically applying the one-drop rule to all "Negroes" and mistakenly lumping all people of African descent as "black" under a single experience.[41]

---

The current understanding that some people are of "mixed race" while others are not ignores the reality of human migration over millennia and invites us to renew our thinking on ethnicity and race. Are we not all of mixed blood (or mixed DNA)? Indeed, ample human variation has always existed in the world, and in many ways we are all of blended heritage—everyone is in fact a mixture of their mother's and father's ancestors. When understanding the concept of race as a social fallacy, the existence of interracial or mixed-race people would be an impossibility, for races cannot actually mix. Scientifically, the idea that there are pure races of people who can indeed intermix is false. Socially, however, we understand that people might be *mixed* to some degree in terms of race, ethnicity, or culture.[42]

It is often stated that "races do not exist among humans" or that "the only race is the human race." Even though "race doesn't really exist," we still routinely group people by phenotype or perhaps assume that types of people are connected to some primordial essence. While biological and cultural explanations for race, or a combination of the two, cannot be proved, real consequences emanate from these racial beliefs. Race and racial categories require examination because people hundreds of years ago treated others differently based on racial perceptions and still do today, and this treatment results in tangible, material outcomes in people's everyday lives.[43]

Ideas concerning ethnicity are also connected to notions of race; therefore, describing ethnic groups can likewise be fraught with problems. Normally, I link ethnicity with regional ancestry—where someone's ancestors or people are from in the world. Ethnic groups often share many of the same cultural attributes, but culture is malleable and people from one background can adopt things like language, food, music, and other traditions from any group. For me, the distinction here between culture and ethnicity is that one cannot change where his or her ancestors came from. Still, grouping ethnicities that correlate loosely with regions—such as Africa(ns), Europe(ans), and (Indigenous/Native) America(ns)—generalizes hundreds of diverse subsets of people who might not use a uniform descriptor to define themselves. There is no one correct way to define groups of people by ancestral background, yet I find ethnic labels more precise than racial language ("white," "black," or "Indian"). Since race and ethnicity are regularly conflated, both in the past and in the present, I often use the term "ethnoracial." Instead of more accurately describing ethnic mixture, outside of race, I speak of ethnoracial mixture, which also captures the perceived idea of racial mixing or the concept of interracial mixture.[44]

Last, I sparingly refer to people being of *full* or *partial* African, European, or Native American descent based on social perceptions, not their actual ancestral lineage. For example, I use this phrasing regarding the belief that someone's regional ancestry emerged from either Africa or Europe before his or her ancestors migrated to the Western Hemisphere. Individual colonists made these designations based on phenotype or family knowledge. Most often I simply refer to someone as European instead of *full* European, even if this person might, in theory, trace all of his or her ancestral origins to Europe. I similarly use the labels "African," "Native American," and "Indigenous American" and acknowledge these limitations, as some may read these terms with the presumption that individuals lack ancestry from other regions of the globe (something DNA tests might disprove). Although my terminology is imperfect, my intentions are to correctly describe people by using their regional ancestry or ethnicity instead of relying on racial classifications. This is not to ignore that ethnicities are also socially constructed, though arguably by the people themselves instead of outsiders applying racial labels onto groups. Finally, I recognize that science now holds that all of humanity, regardless of where someone's ancestors come from, originated from the African continent, technically making us all of African descent.[45]

# I

## The Rise of Hypodescent in Seventeenth-Century English America

In February of 1634, the "Molato" Mathias de Sousa and nearly 200 English colonists were filled with anticipation as they stood on the decks of their ships and viewed the forested lands that surrounded the Chesapeake Bay. The weary passengers did not know what the future held when they disembarked onto the shores of North America. The English Crown had given permission for them to settle in the area, but they had not yet gained approval from local Indigenous Americans to make this place their home. Still, the English priest Andrew White and Governor Leonard Calvert led the group of Anglo-Catholic colonists to found a new province: Maryland. Jesuit officials recorded Mathias de Sousa, along with other travelers, among their early headright counts, which allowed them to petition English authorities for land grants based on the number of laborers they transported to the colony. They brought Mathias and the other men and women into these lands as "the true and proper Servants of Andrew White Esq. one of the first Adventurers into this province." Like other colonists, Mathias worked for the Jesuits to help establish the colony and to improve his life. He attended the first Catholic mass in Maryland, held by Father White on March 25, 1634, and guarded the priests when they dealt with local Piscataways during land and trade negotiations. Although the visitors may have appeared strange to them, these Piscataways gave permission to Governor Calvert and the English to remain in the area. While the people who met on those shores so long ago came from different cultures, they shared similar emotions: curiosity, fear, hope, and wonder.[1]

Even though Mathias de Sousa came from a different place than most of the English colonists he traveled with, they included him among their group.

He likely knew multiple European languages and picked up words from Piscataways and other Native Americans as colonial Maryland grew. By 1641, Mathias still worked for the Catholic Church. In one instance, Father Ferdinand Pulton appointed him as the skipper of a pinnace, which Mathias used to lead an expedition across the waters of the Chesapeake Bay to trade with Susquehannocks. The two-month trip highlighted his navigational aptitude, knowledge of local geography, and ability to conduct business negotiations with Indigenous peoples. Mathias's life represents the vulnerable position that early colonists occupied as they carved out an existence on Native American lands; his journey also illustrates the general acceptance that he, as a free person of mixed heritage, received from the English in the early years of colonial Maryland.[2]

Mathias de Sousa's story, along with those of other people of mixed ancestry, reveals that English society did not feature a strict ethnoracial order in the seventeenth-century colonial Chesapeake, and some mixed-heritage people possessed social mobility and forms of equality. During these early decades of colonization, socioracial flexibility existed for certain people of blended African, European, and Indigenous descent in Virginia and Maryland, as it did in Latin America and other English colonial regions across the Atlantic. However, after the first half century of colonization, the practices of Chesapeake magistrates deviated from those of other English colonial administrators; most notably, the Chesapeake authorities began legally punishing ethnoracial intermixture and levying penalties, including slavery and prolonged servitude, against mixed-heritage peoples. From the 1660s onward, English officials sought to subordinate people of mixed descent, along with Africans and Native Americans, in a social hierarchy that favored those with solely European bloodlines.

Chesapeake authorities believed that maintaining control over the mixed-heritage population was essential to creating a well-ordered society, while people of mixed backgrounds insisted on maintaining their autonomy, often basing claims to freedom on their connection to European lineage and Christian faith. Such efforts to escape bondage moved provincial elites to begin attacking intermixture in the 1660s, which placed mixed-heritage peoples at the crux of the most significant racial laws in colonial Virginia and Maryland. In 1662, the Virginia General Assembly admitted, "some doubts have arisen whether children got by any Englishman upon a negro woman should be slave or ffree." People of mixed ancestry and their families created these "doubts" by actively fighting to achieve or maintain their liberty. Virginia's legislature reacted to freedom suits brought by people of mixed descent by passing the first slave statute that instituted heritable slavery in English America. Likewise, in 1664 colonial officials in Maryland introduced their initial provincial slave code, in large part to define the inheritance of slave status for growing numbers of children, or "the Issues of English or other freeborne woemen that have already marryed Negroes." Fears of a society that accepted these relationships, and the offspring they produced, prompted colonial English lawmakers to target intimate relationships between Africans, Europeans, and, later, Native Americans through the legal regulation of sex, marriage, and labor.[3]

This chapter examines mixed-heritage peoples in the early Tidewater Chesapeake by explaining how colonists there first came to identify people of blended ethnoracial ancestry, and it situates the origins of mixed-race ideologies in English colonial America within the wider Atlantic world. While scholars have investigated the lives of mixed-heritage people in later periods and in other regions, we know far less about those of mixed descent in English colonial America. Historians have shown that seventeenth-century colonial legislators wielded legal systems to solidify a race-based society inextricably linked with African women and natural reproduction in slavery. English officials explicitly passed laws to codify African slavery, prevent African unions with Europeans, and limit the growth of a mixed-heritage population. Previous scholarship highlights the importance of Chesapeake law in this process, especially Virginia's 1691 statue aimed at "preventing abominable mixture and spurious issue" between Europeans and those of African, Native American, or mixed ancestry. This capstone legislation represented a position that had developed over several decades of legal experimentation in both Virginia and Maryland. The ordinance itself discloses that ethnoracial mixture had often gone unchecked in earlier decades, which is why administrators enacted more severe restrictions against "negroes, mulattoes, and Indians intermarrying with the English" and penalized their children of mixed lineage. The views of these blended families contradicted those of colonial elites, and the people's disregard for these laws, coupled with lax implementation before the 1690s, was in part why Chesapeake authorities refashioned these legal codes over the years.[4]

The existence of "mixed people" in early Anglo-America was crucial to how colonists structured racial beliefs at the time, especially when provincial officials created segregationist laws and articulated a negative mixed-race ideology that coalesced around the notion of hypodescent, whereby people of mixed ethnoracial lineage were relegated to the position of their socially inferior parentage. While academics have typically identified a strict form of racial hypodescent in the English Chesapeake, evidence shows that people of mixed ancestry could, at times, elevate their legal or social position by varying degrees based on their proximity to European heritage or racial whiteness. Some colonists supported efforts to keep so-called Mulattoes connected to bondage, but ideas related to racial hypodescent operated with far more flexibility in both legal and social practice, especially in the seventeenth century.[5]

In many ways, the experiences of mixed-heritage peoples in the Tidewater Chesapeake were similar to those living in Latin America and the broader Atlantic world, where a family's status could rise through social connections and further intermixture with Europeans. While African or Native American lineage still made one eligible for slavery in the early Chesapeake colonies, the first generations of mixed people with some European ancestry could access freedom, especially from the 1630s through the 1680s. Their efforts to remain free competed with the interests of planters who favored a firm social hierarchy, and this tension prompted English authorities to establish formal regulations for enslaving people of blended heritage. In the second half of the century, the burgeoning Chesapeake gentry—composed primarily of wealthy English planters, merchants, and professionals—began to mandate harsher policies against people of partial African or Indigenous ancestry. Mainly, planter-legislators passed waves of legal statutes during the latter half of the century that promoted hypodescent and monoracial categories. These laws helped transform ideas of race into a more salient concept in the colonial Chesapeake and set the region apart from other provinces in North America, the Caribbean, and Latin America by the 1690s. Even so, mixed-heritage people and their families continued to resist subjugation, which kept them from falling squarely into a single category in the emerging racial order and allowed some to achieve racial whiteness.

## SPANISH AND ENGLISH EMPIRE BUILDING IN INDIGENOUS AMERICA

Early colonial racial formation, or the establishment of racial thought, in the Americas developed out of interactions between Africans, Europeans, and Native Americans. By the time English colonists established Virginia and Maryland in the seventeenth century, Indigenous Americans already had over 100 years of contact with Europeans in other parts of the Western Hemisphere. In North America, Native Americans had had exchanges with several groups of European explorers who anchored their ships at various points along the Atlantic coast and Gulf of Mexico in the sixteenth century. Before English settlement, sexual intermixture between Indigenous peoples and various European groups had already been prevalent in Latin America and the Caribbean, since Cristóbal Colón's first voyages in the 1490s. In North America, ethnoracial mixture took place sporadically throughout the sixteenth century, and much of it went unrecorded.[6]

The Spanish and perhaps enslaved Africans were some of the earliest to have children with Indigenous peoples in North America, likely by the 1520s. Although European explorers had landed intermittently before that time, Spanish expeditions beginning in 1521 led to a failed attempt at setting up a colony called San Miguel de Gualdape somewhere along the coastline that later became South Carolina. Florentine explorer Giovanni da Verrazzano and his men recorded traveling to the region in 1524 and possibly mixed with Indigenous peoples as they landed several times while moving northward along the Atlantic coast. While other European groups explored areas in North America or attempted to establish coastal forts in the sixteenth century, the Spanish and their African slaves intermingled most often with Native Americans during several treks into the continental interior. Survivors from Pánfilo de Narváez's expedition (1528–36), Hernando de Soto's travels (1539–42), and other journeys into North America almost certainly produced children with Indigenous women. Sustained mixture was assured after the Spanish established San Agustín (St. Augustine) in the area they called La Florida. In 1565, San Agustín became the first permanent European town in North America and became home to so-called *mestizos* and *mulatos* under the Spanish Empire.[7]

Significant Anglo-Indigenous intermixture appears to have taken place after the English attempted to found their first colony in the Americas at Roanoke Island. The colony floundered from 1585 to 1586 in the coastal region of what is now North Carolina, when the first group abandoned Roanoke and returned to England due to supply shortages. The English were not equipped to establish a colony in a place where they lacked knowledge of the environment and could not sustain themselves. The next year an effort to reestablish the colony at Roanoke also failed, although this time there would be no return voyage. Sometime between 1587 and 1590 over 100 English settlers disappeared. While no one knows for certain what became of the lost colony, scant evidence suggests that those who survived sought refuge among neighboring Chowanocs and perhaps moved in with other Indigenous groups in the continental interior. When the English at Roanoke Island could no longer wait for the delayed supply ships, the only way for them to remain alive was to move in with Native Americans, who had the cultural knowledge and technology needed to flourish in the lush forests of the area.[8]

A scene from the 1605 English play *Eastward Ho!* briefly addressed the story of the first colonists at Roanoke, as it was rumored that the stranded Englishmen had "married with the Indians." Characters in the play speak of the offspring resulting from unions with Native American women as being "English" and having "as beautiful faces as any ... in England." Around the turn of the century, the English knew that Native Americans differed from them culturally, yet they realized that Indigenous peoples were essentially the same as Europeans in their physical makeup. References to the mixed matches in *Eastward Ho!* were also gendered. The English, being patrilineal, considered only that the English men lost at Roanoke would have children by Indigenous women, not the other way around. In the play, English men passed their heritage through the paternal line on to their offspring, but the reality is that any English men and women who left Roanoke would have survived only by mixing in with Native Americans and melding with Indigenous cultures. Any children, mixed or not, would grow up acculturated to lifestyles within these Native American societies.[9]

Nearly twenty years after the Roanoke experiment fell apart, England's King James I issued a royal charter for a joint-stock company to a group of investors who sought to turn a profit from establishing a new colonial project in America. Within the same year of its 1606 charter, the Virginia Company of London outfitted three ships that set sail across the Atlantic Ocean. After a long six-month journey, the weary travelers arrived in the Powhatans' territory of Tsenacommacah (Attanoughskomouck) in the spring of 1607. The colonists decided to stay on a secluded peninsula about forty miles upstream on what they called the James River, which emptied into the Chesapeake Bay. They built a triangular fortification called James Fort along with houses that became James Town (Jamestown), the first successful English colony in America.[10]

Jamestown floundered as the colonists struggled to survive next to the Powhatans and allied tribes. English theft of "Indian corn" and militaristic policies over their initial years of settlement led to tumultuous relationships with Indigenous groups. Still, some English interacted peaceably with local Native Americans and ran away to live with them. Englishmen had sexual relationships with Indigenous women, and one report, by the Spanish, stated that forty to fifty had intermarried in the first years of the colony. Whether this number accurately counted exogamy—marriage outside one's group—the rumors of sex appear true. In 1610 the Virginia Company and Jamestown officials threatened torture and even death to English who defected from the colony, and they took a defensive position at the fort in attempts to separate colonists from Native Americans.[11]

Compared to the Spanish and Portuguese, English intermixture with Indigenous peoples occurred on a much smaller scale in their early seventeenth-century colonial settlements. Certainly, Europeans and Native Americans in the Chesapeake and other English provinces engaged in sex more than sporadic reports would suggest. Occasionally, Anglo-Indigenous unions took place, though most often when individual Europeans abandoned English colonial life and Native Americans adopted them into their communities. This may have been the case after Roanoke and during the early years at Jamestown, when colonists were desperately low on supplies and experienced a "starving time" from 1609 to 1610. Englishmen who left Jamestown for Native American villages and survived had intimate encounters with Indigenous women and fathered children of mixed descent. Indigenous people accepted mixed-heritage offspring as equals and often viewed these connections as a way of strengthening political and economic ties with Europeans. Generally, English notions of religious and cultural superiority prevented widespread exogamy within colonial Virginia. As a result of increasing warfare, segregation, and a tense social climate between the English and Powhatans, intermixture occurred infrequently. Then in 1613, during a period of heightened Anglo-Powhatan warfare, the English managed to kidnap one of the teenage daughters of Wahunsenacawh, principal chief of the Powhatans. The English referred to the adolescent girl by her childhood name: Pocahontas.[12]

Pocahontas revealed later in life that her true name was Matoaka. During Matoaka's first year of captivity, when she was around seventeen years old, the Englishman John Rolfe felt a growing affection for the teenager, who was a dozen years his junior. John offered to marry Matoaka, which she accepted, likely in an effort to quell the violence and seal peace between the warring English and Powhatans. At the time, John had doubts about joining himself in matrimony with "Pokahuntas," because he viewed the mixed marriage in terms of religious beliefs: the "unbeleeving creature" did not profess the Christian faith. Reflecting back on his state of mind before their wedding, John wrote that he was aware "of the heavie displeasure which almightie God conceived against the sonnes of Levie and Israel for marrying strange wives." The fear of wedding a non-Christian Indigenous woman forced him to contemplate the sincerity of his feelings. John further questioned how he could "be in love with one whose education hath bin rude, her manners barbarous, her generation accursed, and so discrepant in all nurtriture from my selfe." Clearly, John's concerns about Matoaka stemmed from the common European perception that the Powhatans and other Native Americans were uncivilized because they were not Christian and were nurtured outside of English culture.[13]

John was concerned not only for himself but also for the religious salvation of any children he might have with Matoaka. After much thought and prayer, he found a reasonable solution: "The Children of Christians are accompted [accounted] holye, yea although they be the yssue [issue] but of one parent faithfull." Even if the couple's future children had parents of mixed religious backgrounds, John could rest easy believing that his Christian faith would be enough to cover them in God's eyes. John resolved his "pryvate controversie" once he concluded that his doubts were caused by the "wicked instigations" and "diabolical assaults" of the devil. After "fervent prayers" John felt assured with his decision to join with Matoaka, believing that God viewed the union as acceptable. He was also further satisfied after Matoaka accepted Christian baptism and took the name Rebecca. In the spring of 1614 John Rolfe married Rebecca (Matoaka), and many in Jamestown and in Tsenacommacah hoped the union would bring greater peace after several tumultuous years of conflict.[14]

Around the time of this famed marriage, the Virginia colonists had located an agricultural resource that finally made the Virginia Company successful: tobacco. Indigenous peoples in Tsenacommacah and other regions had grown different strains of the plant for hundreds of years, but colonial production of the crop in the Chesapeake helped send Europe and other parts of the world into a craze for smoking the dried leaves of the plant. Atlantic traders imported the most popular strain of sweet tobacco from the Caribbean, and John Rolfe started growing it at Jamestown around 1611–12. Five years later, John Smith wrote that "the market-place, and streets, and all other spare places [were] planted with Tobacco, [and] the Salvages [are] as frequent in their [English] houses." During times of peace, Native American "sa(l)vages" mixed with the English in their homes and shared cultivation techniques, such as rotating crops in the fields to replenish the soil's nutrients. By the end of the decade, the Jamestown colonists were profiting from regular tobacco shipments to England. This commenced a major economic shift that spurred English desire for Native American lands and brought more than 75,000 European immigrants to the Chesapeake between 1620 and 1680. Commercial tobacco production led to the decline of the Powhatans and nearby Indigenous populations and eventually to the destruction of Tsenacommacah, while it saved the struggling colonial enterprise in Virginia by making the venture economically profitable.[15]

Nevertheless, the English Crown revoked the Virginia Company's charter in 1624 due to continuing problems, including fluctuating tobacco prices, attacks from Indigenous peoples, and high European death rates from war, disease, and endemic illness. In the 1630s, tobacco also helped spawn growth in neighboring Maryland. By the middle of the century, farmers had pushed the expansion of the tobacco economy up rivers and along the coasts of the "Two Fruitful Sisters Virginia and Mary-Land." The Tidewater Chesapeake colonies relied so heavily on the staple crop that colonists used tobacco as currency to pay for goods, services, and court fines and to purchase servants and slaves, who worked on plantations cultivating the plant.[16]

Yeoman planters gained prosperity and social mobility when they acquired enough land and laborers to grow tobacco, and John and Rebecca (Matoaka) Rolfe similarly lived off the proceeds generated from growing the crop. The year after their marriage, Rebecca gave birth to the couple's only son, Thomas (b. 1615). In early childhood, his mother and her relatives—who still visited and possibly lived with the family—spoke to Thomas in their native language. This tutelage ended abruptly after Rebecca died from illness in 1617 during the family's trip to London. Thomas remained in England and grew up under the care of his uncle, learning to speak English and observing the Christian faith. In 1635, he returned to America, where the Virginia colonists accepted him within their growing community.[17]

After nearly two decades of separation from Powhatan culture, Thomas Rolfe saw himself as an Englishman. In Virginia, he amassed large landholdings and settled an English fort in Chickahominy territory. Although Thomas lived among the English and married a colonist, he had at least some commu-

Portrait of *Matoaks als Rebecka* (Pocahontas) by Simon van de Passe, 1616. "Matoaks als Rebecka daughter to the mighty Prince Powhatan Emperour of Attanoughskomouck als virginia converted and baptized in the Christian faith, and wife to the worth[y] Mr. Joh[n] Rolff." (The British Museum, London)

nication with his Indigenous kin. In 1641, he asked the governor of Virginia for permission to visit his mother's relatives, including his aunt "Cleopatre" and "his Kinsman Opecancanough." Thomas had to petition colonial officials to visit these family members because Virginians had since strengthened segregationist policies regarding nearby Native Americans, especially after 1622, when Opechancanough orchestrated violent strikes against the English, which nearly wiped out the colony. English leaders attempted to protect Jamestown against outside assaults by cutting it off from Native Americans, and these policies impeded sexual intermingling in the province. Thomas's request to visit family also reveals the distance between him and his Indigenous relatives. Thomas may have felt conflicted as the Powhatans and English went to war again in the mid-1640s. This time, the elderly Opechancanough led his final attacks against the English.[18]

Did Thomas attempt to reach out to his fellow Englishmen and Indigenous kinfolk to strike a truce like his mother had done before him? Did he face rejection from his Powhatan family members? We are not sure, but it appears that Thomas was unable to straddle the two worlds. The English captured Opechancanough, put him on display before English crowds, and subsequently executed the Powhatan leader. The loss marked a shift in regional power from the once mighty Powhatans to the English settlers. Thomas remained loyal to the colony and held the rank of lieutenant by the end of the war. His allegiance to the English followed the culture of his upbringing. Despite his Powhatan heritage, Thomas's efforts helped expand the colonial territory of Virginia, facilitated his success as a Christian Englishman, and made him a wealthy man.[19]

Others of mixed Anglo-Indigenous ancestry resided in the colonial Chesapeake, yet acceptance into English society required cultural assimilation, which included the adoption of Christianity. In the early seventeenth century, Keziah Elizabeth Tucker was the daughter of Robin, a Nansemond man who received Protestant baptism from the English. In 1638 Keziah married the English minister John Bass, and the couple had eight children together. While some Nansemonds moved farther west, the Anglicized Bass children lived among colonists in newly formed Norfolk County, Virginia. The blended family handed down a Bible in which they recorded dozens of names, birthdays, deaths, and marriages. They took pride in their religious devotion, noting that their children were "Baptized Christian persons." Bass descendants married people from various backgrounds, and while colonists accepted some of them as "white," others held on to their Indigenous identity. William Bass, a son of Keziah and John, claimed lands for his family that had "been used by his and Their forbears since & before English governance in Virginia." With the Basses likely facing the loss of their ancestral lands to the English, a Norfolk County court granted the family's claim, recognizing that the Basses were "persons of English and Nansemun Indian descent."[20]

While the Christian faith provided the first generations of mixed Anglo-Indigenous people with the ability to rise within English colonial society, their identities were complex and they faced multiple challenges connected to race and religion. In 1644, the Englishman Giles Brent Sr. married the Piscataway Mary Kittomaquund under the Catholic faith in Maryland. Several years later Mary Kittomaquund Brent gave birth to Giles Brent Jr., and he grew up in a multicultural household. The mixed-heritage Giles Jr. could speak "the Indian tongue" and was a devout Catholic, which set him apart as an outsider among the Protestant English in more ways than one. English colonists recognized him as part of their society, as Virginia officials appointed him as a tax collector and eventually promoted him from militia captain to colonel.[21]

A man of war, Giles became a leading insurgent during Nathaniel Bacon's rebellion, when disgruntled colonists took up arms against Governor William Berkeley and others who represented established authority in Virginia. Giles participated in and led attacks against both Native Americans and other English colonists. Near the end of the rebellion, Giles reconciled with Governor Berkeley's forces and accepted a pardon in order to avoid execution. Before the revolt, English colonists respected Giles despite his Catholic and Piscataway backgrounds, although these labels may have brought him greater scrutiny. Giles married an Englishwoman, and the couple had several children, but Mary Brent later sought to separate from her husband after suffering from domestic abuse. With a career marked by violence, it appears that Giles had carried similar aggression into his household. A few months after the court sided with his wife, Giles died young at the age of twenty-seven on his Middlesex County plantation in Virginia.[22]

The Brent, Bass, and Rolfe families show that early English communities accepted some people of mixed European and Indigenous heritage in the colonial Chesapeake. Like other colonists, they faced similar challenges, yet they also dealt with issues peculiar to their circumstances as people of mixed ancestry. Even if they lived among the English, they all witnessed how war, prejudice, and English land encroachment devastated Indigenous communities. They strove to keep their lands and families intact, even as they helped English and other European immigrants supplant dwindling Indigenous populations and pushed other Native Americans west or onto smaller landholdings within the expanding colonies. Mixed-heritage men like Thomas Rolfe and Giles Brent Jr. directly participated in English settler colonialism. These mixed people, and others like them, identified with European societies, yet as Indigenous people, did they also feel an internal struggle over which communities they belonged to or held loyalties to?

## IMMIGRANT AND NATIVE BORN: THE FIRST MULATTOES IN THE COLONIAL CHESAPEAKE

Even though people of blended heritage contributed to colonial societies, many European colonists lamented interracial unions and the mixed offspring they produced. These negative racial views were rooted in aristocratic European ideas connected to blood and ancestry among nobility. In Latin America, complex and somewhat fluid soci234acial systems developed in the sixteenth century out of a foundational belief in the purity of European blood (*limpieza de sangre*) and led to the denigration of African and Indigenous bloodlines. Even before 1492, Iberians had long made efforts to keep their blood free from Moorish or Jewish ancestry in Europe, but they could not stop widespread intermixture with Africans and Indigenous peoples in the Americas. In the colonial Americas, Spaniards typically favored people of mixed Indigenous and European lineage (*mestizos*) over people of African and European mixture (*mulatos*) and those of blended African and Indigenous heritage (*pardos* and *zambos*). Indigenous people who mixed with Europeans had the leeway to rise in society, and their descendants could move closer to racial whiteness through subsequent generations of mixture with Europeans. Elites begrudgingly accepted certain Spaniards with far-removed Indigenous ancestry who climbed the soci234acial ladder, and at times those in power made concessions to *mestizos*, *mulatos*, and others of mixed descent. This allowed a number of mixed-heritage people to attain elevated positions in colonial societies.[23]

In the sixteenth century, the English also viewed blood as an early transmitter of race via family lineage, but the idea primarily applied to nobility, and some believed race could be mutable. In the following century, the English mirrored the Latin American model when initiating colonial projects in the Western Hemisphere. English colonists developed racial frameworks as they established their colonies through the seventeenth century. While European colonial empires shared similar racial ideologies, the English diverged from others. The starkest difference came in the Chesapeake, where the English founded settler societies that largely separated themselves from Native Americans. This curtailed widespread Anglo-Indigenous intermixture, but the English could not do the same with the Africans they brought into the region.[24]

The first report of the English buying African slaves in the Chesapeake occurred in 1619, when John Rolfe recorded the purchase of around "twenty Negars" coming in from English traders traveling under a Dutch flag. The ship, the *White Lion*, had taken these slaves from Portuguese traders and delivered them to Point Comfort, at the mouth of the James River. Other records suggest there may have been even earlier "non-Christians" from unknown origins in the region who could have been African. Some of the "20. and odd Negroes" who survived the long journey to Virginia may have come from the Christian Kingdom of Kongo or were possibly Kimbundu-speaking people from the Kingdom of Ndongo in Angola. Wherever the new arrivals' origins, the English in the Chesapeake brought them from Point Comfort to Jamestown, where the colonists sold the Africans again to colonial farmers who sought laborers for their tobacco fields. While people of African descent appeared early in the colonies, there were relatively few in the Chesapeake until the second half of the century, when the English began trading more Africans directly from the Guinea coast in West Africa; estimates are roughly 200 people of African ancestry out of 11,000 colonists in 1640 (about 2 percent) and 1,700 out of 35,500 in 1660 (5 percent). In the seventeenth century, European planters and servants made up most of the workers who toiled in tobacco fields, followed by smaller numbers of bound Africans and Native Americans. Death rates were high and labor was scarce over the first several decades of colonization in the Chesapeake, so small planters commonly worked tobacco fields side by side with their families, servants, and slaves. These conditions created an atmosphere where people intermixed with some frequency.[25]

Interactions between Europeans and Native Americans informed how colonists developed ideas around race and mixture with Africans. Most English colonists viewed Indigenous peoples as culturally inferior even though they often encountered Native Americans on equal footing. The English recognized the strength of groups like the Powhatans and others both in and surrounding Tsenacommacah, but these relationships changed in relation to shifting axes of power over the years. Although some of the first Africans in the Chesapeake gained freedom and built successful lives for their families, the English in seventeenth-century America encountered small numbers of Africans in subjugated, relatively powerless positions of bondage. This played a key role in shaping European racial perceptions of superiority and inferiority but did not prevent English sexual intermingling with Africans, which likely started in Virginia by the 1620s. Colonists caught Hugh Davis "defiling his body in lying with a negro" (gender unidentified) and also fined Englishman Thomas Key "for getting his Negro woman with Childe" around 1630. A decade later authorities whipped a "negroe woman" after she became pregnant by Robert Sweet, a European man. Apparently, magistrates did not assign greater punishments to interracial "fornication" and reprimanded the offending parties "according to the laws of England." Still, it is likely that some early colonists had strong feelings against mixture with non-Christian Africans based on English traditions of social hierarchy. These beliefs helped structure nascent understandings of race, the foundation upon which colonists built ideas against intermixture.[26]

While people of mixed African and European ancestry were native born in Virginia by the 1630s, some of the earliest people who immigrated with the

English into the Chesapeake were referred to as Mulatto—a term the Spanish and Portuguese had long used to identify people of mixed African and European lineage. Those of blended heritage, along with other Europeans and Africans, sometimes traversed the Atlantic or came to North America from the Caribbean and other places in the Americas. Mathias de Sousa was a product of this Atlantic world, labeled a "Molato" among the initial group of Maryland immigrants that the Anglo-Jesuit priest Andrew White "brought into the province" in 1634. In late 1633, the priest and other colonists set sail from England aboard the *Ark* and the *Dove*—the first two ships sent to establish the colony of Maryland in the Chesapeake. Where Mathias joined the group of travelers is unknown, though Andrew White's journal provides some clues. Before crossing the Atlantic, the *Ark* and the *Dove* stopped for supplies at an island off the "Coast of Affrique" (Africa)—perhaps part of the Cape Verde or Canary Islands—where "40 or 50 Portingalls" (Portuguese) had been "banished... for crimes committed by them." Mathias may have been one of these men, for in English documents he is called Mathias Tousa, Mathias de Sousa, and Matt das Sousa, which all point to Iberian origins.[27]

More than a century before the English established colonies in the Americas, Iberian explorations and invasions of people around the Atlantic rim initiated regular ethnoracial mixture on both sides of the ocean. In the early seventeenth century, an English traveler in West Africa met both Europeans and Africans who called themselves "Portingales" and also noted that "others of them are *Molatoes*, betweene blacke and white." This "Molato" reference was anecdotal and did not assign any inferior or superior position to the people, but it did figuratively position them between "blacke and white." The English adopted the term "Molato" and eventually constructed its racial meaning around this time, but in the 1630s the label did not necessarily restrict Mathias de Sousa in the Chesapeake. If the English encountered Mathias stranded on an island off the coast of Africa, they may have presented him with an opportunity to escape exile in exchange for his service. If Mathias did not come directly from Europe or Africa's coastal islands, he joined the colonists' voyage in the Caribbean, where the *Ark* and the *Dove* also made stops before arriving in the Chesapeake.[28]

After several years of service with the Jesuits, Mathias de Sousa worked independently as a freeman, and his experiences with the English in America resembled those of others who labored in the Chesapeake after they paid off their debt for travel to the colonies. On March 23, 1642, the Maryland General Assembly counted Mathias in the colony's rolls at a session where legislation was "passed by all" freemen in attendance, showing that he may have participated in the legislative process. Nonetheless, free status did not preclude Mathias from further bound labor, and later that year he wound up back in the service of his peers after struggling to pay off local debts. Such readmission to service was common at the time, and no one threatened him with extraordinary bondage or used racial terms to differentiate Mathias from other English colonists in the records. In fact, documents listed him only once as "Molato," in a report describing his initial arrival to the Chesapeake. By all accounts, Mathias operated like other European immigrants, as he contracted his labor, traded with Native Americans, testified in court, and appeared in the colonial general assembly, where he may have voted as a freeman.[29]

As seafarers in the Atlantic carried people of blended ethnoracial ancestry like Mathias de Sousa to the Chesapeake, the term Mulatto spread throughout other European empires. The English picked up *"mulato"* from the Spanish—just as they had done with the word *"negro"*—and from the early to mid-seventeenth century the label mainly characterized people of mixed African and European lineage. Most European travelers coming to the English colonies probably encountered the expression, and Mulattoes themselves, in Barbados—the main entry point into the Americas for countless ships that made the voyage across the Atlantic. The English established the Caribbean colony in 1627 and experimented with tobacco, cotton, indigo, and other crops before achieving economic success with sugar production by the middle of the century. Though a small island not more than 170 square miles, Barbados established English imperial power in the Americas by becoming the largest sugar-producing colony in the world from the late seventeenth century to the early eighteenth century. A diverse labor force of English, Irish, and Scottish servants along with enslaved Africans led to regular intermixture and a substantial mixed-heritage population. While distance separated Anglo-American colonies in North America and the wider Atlantic, many English laws, customs, words, and ideas concerning people of mixed ancestry traveled between provinces.[30]

By the mid-seventeenth century, English records in Barbados, Bermuda, Maryland, and Virginia identify people of mixed heritage as Mulatto, most often when settling questions about freedom and bondage. Bermuda—once known as the Somers Islands and located 700 miles east of the Carolina coast and several hundred miles north of the Caribbean—had a plantation economy and served English trading vessels that stopped there to resupply when traveling across the Atlantic. From the 1640s to the 1660s, Bermuda authorities bound out "Malatto" children for lengths of service ranging from around twenty years—similar to other European children—to thirty years. Others were customarily held as slaves. The length of service depended on which parent had European ancestry and whether they could, or would, advocate for their child's freedom. By 1655, the Somers Isles Company lamented that European fathers were not claiming the "divers Bastardes, children begotten by some man or other upon the Companyes negroe weomen." Two years later in Barbados, John

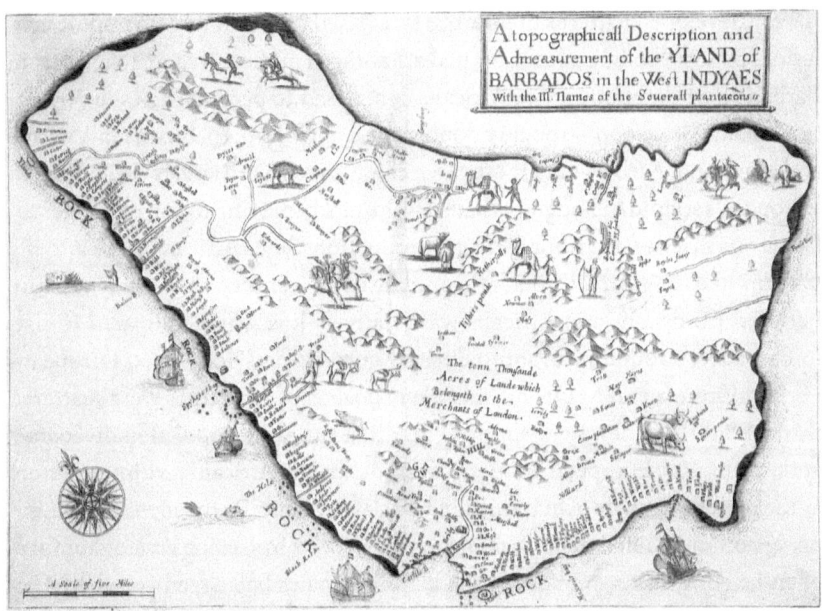

*Yland of Barbados*, ca. 1657 (north points to the top left). This colonial map of Barbados labels dozens of plantations, and details both Europeans and Africans, including runaway slaves. (Ligon, *True and Exact History of the Island of Barbadoes*)

Lee, an English lieutenant, freed two Mulattoes who were possibly his children. On his deathbed, John requested that officials put a girl, Betty, in school and apprentice a boy, Cullee, as a cooper, which would help aid their future prosperity. Across the English colonies, parents' involvement, labor status, and socioeconomic power determined the length of service authorities assigned to mixed-heritage children.[31]

Barbados was the first English colony to develop a significant mixed-heritage population, followed by Jamaica and the provinces of Virginia and Maryland—where the highest levels of ethnoracial mixing occurred between Africans and Europeans in colonial North America. The most successful planters and merchants in these places used their wealth, influence, and political backing from the English monarchy to establish their authority at the top of a hierarchy that subordinated poor Europeans and placed those of African and Indigenous American descent on the lower tiers of colonial society. People subjugated in servitude and slavery occupied similar social spheres, working and living together in the same spaces, largely on sugar and tobacco plantations. Within this atmosphere, sexual intermingling between various groups occurred regularly, if not inevitably, especially before the crystallization of racial systems that stigmatized intimate intermixture.[32]

Each English colony that attached itself to the plantation economy and slavery developed patterns of intermixture based on its own demographic evolution. By 1650, no English colony had ethnoracial mixture that matched that in Barbados, where about 13,000 Africans comprised 30 percent of a total population of almost 43,000 — roughly double the number of inhabitants in Virginia and Maryland. At this point, these three colonies were still largely committed to European servitude, though Barbados was quickly moving toward a greater reliance on African slave labor for sugar production. Since Africans came into the Chesapeake irregularly through the middle of the century, the level of mixture between Europeans and Africans was relatively low when compared to that in Barbados. Around 1650, approximately 700 Africans and 22,500 Europeans lived in Virginia and Maryland, and likely dozens of Mulattoes were scattered throughout the Tidewater counties. After that time, the population diversified with continuing European immigration and growing African slave importation, as the region began its own transition to a slave society. By the 1670s the Chesapeake colonies joined their Caribbean counterparts in seeking greater numbers of enslaved Africans, yet both Barbados and Jamaica had already reached African majorities by this point. Diverse populations facilitated regular intermixture, as seen in a 1683 Barbados census that counted 326 Mulattoes. In 1690, African and European populations in the Chesapeake reached around 11,500 and 65,500, respectively, leading to an increase in the number of mixed-heritage people in the region.[33]

By the turn of the century, both statistics and qualitative documentary evidence show that hundreds of mixed-heritage people lived in the four English colonies with the largest slave populations: Virginia, Maryland, Barbados, and Jamaica. Others were spread throughout the English Atlantic provinces in Bermuda, the Carolinas, and the Leeward Islands and in places with racially diverse communities. They were especially concentrated in colonial ports and could be found in the northern cities of Boston, Newport, New York, and Philadelphia as well. Most English colonists in these areas had regular contact with people of mixed African, European, and Indigenous ancestry, or they knew that people called Mulattoes lived in their local communities.[34]

While the label of "Mulatto" differentiated one from other European colonists, a person's ethnoracial background was never the sole marker of his or her place in the social order. The concept of race emerged within protoracial English colonial societies in the seventeenth century, where embryonic racial thinking existed, in part, because the provinces lacked established institutions that structured and upheld firm racial categories. The process of racial formation in colonial America was long, uneven, and uncertain as people from divergent backgrounds simultaneously imagined multiple racial ideologies. While European travelers carried ideas between provinces, the inhabitants of each region advanced unique approaches to the emergence of mixed-heritage peoples.

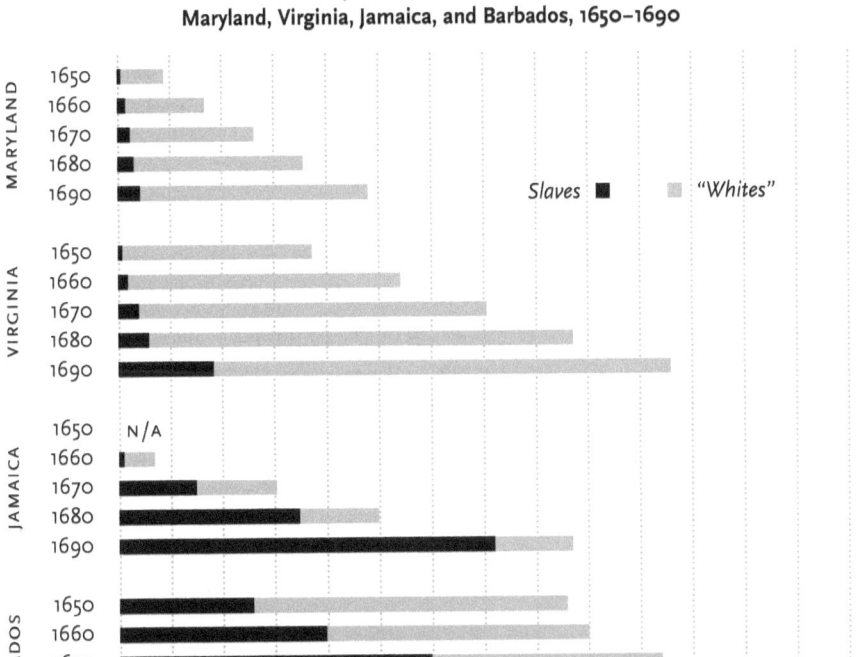

Population estimates for
Maryland, Virginia, Jamaica, and Barbados, 1650–1690

*Sources*: Susan B. Carter et al., *Historical Statistics*, 13–14, 33–34, 52–53, 60–63; Dunn, *Sugar and Slaves*, 87, 155, 312; McCusker and Menard, *Economy of British America*, 151–53; Livesay, *Children of Uncertain Fortune*, 24; Newman, *Dark Inheritance*, 17; "Trans-Atlantic Slave Trade - Estimates," Slave Voyages, www.slavevoyages.org/assessments/estimates.

As in Latin America and the Caribbean, English colonists distinguished between people based on intersections of gender, religion, ancestry, occupation, language, and a number of other criteria. These factors helped shape common understandings of human difference, as colonists developed race consciousness in the Anglo-Atlantic world.[35]

Reflecting the experiences of those in Latin America, some people of African, Indigenous, and mixed descent moved in colonial English communities with varying degrees of autonomy and social mobility. In this manner, early English societies resembled the rest of the Americas, where people of African or Indigenous ancestry might achieve successes similar to those enjoyed by other European plebeians. Though the colonial Chesapeake paralleled its

Caribbean counterparts in early decades, over time, English societies in Virginia and Maryland began to develop a distinct brand of hypodescent that diverged from that in places such as Barbados and Jamaica.

In the first half of the seventeenth century, Mulattoes could obtain equal status with other English in the Chesapeake, but as their numbers increased and Africans became more strictly associated with slavery, their free position grew precarious. This is exemplified in the life of Elizabeth Key, one of the first people of mixed African and European ancestry born in the Chesapeake, around 1630. Little is known about her mother, only that she was an enslaved "Negro woman" belonging to the Englishman Thomas Key, who lived to the southeast of Jamestown. Since Elizabeth's father was also her mother's master, her conception could have been the result of assault or coerced sex, since masters routinely held power over their female slaves. After his "Moletto" daughter's birth, Thomas planned to travel back to England and left Elizabeth in the care of a friend, Humphrey Higginson, who was also her godfather. Thomas instructed Humphrey to raise Elizabeth and provide for her food and clothing in return for her limited service. Thomas made clear that Humphrey should not consider his daughter a common servant or "dispose of her to any other." According to court testimony, Humphrey agreed to care for Elizabeth and "promised to use her as well as if shee were his own Child."[36]

Thomas Key saw his mixed-heritage daughter as English and believed she would be able to claim that birthright, though he understood that not everyone shared this view. Thomas knew that Elizabeth's diverse lineage and connection to a "Negro" slave mother placed her future on shaky ground, since African ancestry opened the possibility for her to fall from temporary servitude into lifelong bondage. Fearing for his daughter's freedom in Virginia, Thomas also directed Humphrey to "carry the said Molletto for England" and provide what she needed to begin a new life "for her selfe" if Humphrey ever decided to return to their home country. However, after Thomas's death, Humphrey abandoned his obligation as guardian and returned to London without his goddaughter in the mid-1650s. Around 1655, Elizabeth appeared as a "maid servant" with two children on the Northumberland County estate of John Mottrom—a wealthy Virginian who died that year. The administrators of the estate who could gain from its sale saw an opportunity to capitalize on Elizabeth by claiming her as a slave.[37]

Based on her English lineage, Elizabeth considered herself a free woman and accordingly took her case to the Northumberland County court, where at least six witnesses gave testimony in January 1656. These witnesses largely corroborated her story, and several points swayed the jurists assigned to the case. First, they noted that Elizabeth Key "hath bin long since Christened... and that by report shee is able to give a very good account of her fayth." Next, they determined "That Thomas Key sould her onely for nine yeares to Col. Higginson with severall conditions to use her more Respectfully then a Comon servant or slave." Finally, the twelve-man jury found that "by the Comon Law" of England "the Child of a Woman slave begott by a freeman ought to bee free." These three factors helped establish Elizabeth's liberty: Christian faith, the understanding that she had been legally bound out as a servant, and free English paternity. "For theis Reasons wee conceive the said Elizabeth ought to bee free," declared the jury. Local officials and community members believed that her direct connection to English culture and lineage proved more important than her African ancestry. Elizabeth was overjoyed upon hearing the news but was disheartened after the administrators of John Mottrom's estate appealed the case to the Virginia General Assembly. After several months, however, a special committee upheld the county court's initial decision: Elizabeth would remain a free woman.[38]

Elizabeth Key and other mixed-heritage people had connections to European lineage that allowed them to rise above other African and Indigenous people, and Elizabeth's story demonstrates a unique departure from racial hypodescent: both local and provincial courts awarded Elizabeth the status of her English father instead of her African mother. Elizabeth also went on to marry William Greensted, her lawyer and the father of her two children. This was the first documented marriage between a European man and a woman of African descent in the Chesapeake. As with previous examples of blended Indigenous and European families, Christian baptism and marriage indicated social acceptance and a relaxed socioracial hierarchy. At least two dozen people acknowledged Elizabeth's claims to English rights: her father, her partner/lawyer, people in her community who testified on her behalf, and jury members who decided in her favor. Virginia's governor and members of the general assembly also considered her a free woman. Granted, court officials may have simply followed English common law instead of their personal beliefs. However, the general assembly also doubled as the colonial legislature, which meant that it had the power to write racial slavery into legal codes. The assembly could have designated people of mixed heritage as "Negro" but chose not to set this precedent.[39]

Nevertheless, others doubted Elizabeth's free status and referred to her racially as "black" rather than "Moletto." Not surprisingly, those who stood to profit from keeping Elizabeth enslaved argued that her mother's African lineage should confine her to lifelong bondage. Clearly, the prospect of capital gain backed more rigid hypodescent ideology and promoted hard racial lines. Elizabeth's proclaimed owners described her as the "Negro wench named Black Besse," using negative gendered and racial terminology that associated her only with African slavery and ignored her English heritage. Furthermore, court testimony revealed that John Key, the English son of Thomas Key, had also called his half sister Elizabeth "Black Bess" in the past. John's language was intentionally derogatory, for after hearing his comment, a Mrs. Speke "Checked him & said Sirra you must call her Sister for shee is yor Sister." When Mrs. Speke chastised him, "John Kaye [Key] did call her Sister." While John used a racial term as a pejorative verbal jab to describe Elizabeth, he still recognized their kinship through the same father. Mrs. Speke also recognized the familial connection between the two siblings and demanded that the brother respect his physically darker sister, even if she had African ancestry.[40]

The discrepancy in social views regarding Elizabeth Key's background reflects the incipient stage of Anglo-American racial thought and competing mixed-race ideologies present in the mid-seventeenth-century Chesapeake. Some colonial Virginians applied a strict form of hypodescent to Mulattoes based on partial African ancestry, referring to them as "black" or "Negro." Others recognized multiple factors when judging the social position and labor status of mixed-heritage people, including ties to European culture and lineage. Elizabeth Key's story illustrates the colonial acceptance of more lenient notions of hypodescent, where racial divisions were not always evident and Mulattoes could occupy positions similar to those of other European indentured servants, free Africans, and Native Americans who adopted Christianity.

### MIXED-HERITAGE PEOPLES AND THE LEGISLATIVE ORIGINS OF RACIAL SLAVERY

The timing of Elizabeth Key's lawsuit in the mid-1650s is significant because it was one of the last times that Virginia authorities rejected hypodescent and recognized the rights of a mixed-heritage person based on a connection to English paternity. In the years following Elizabeth's case, other people of blended ancestry brought similar suits against their masters, sparking the passage of a series of laws that mark a shift in notions about mixed people. English colonists' racial attitudes were in flux in the early to mid-seventeenth century, although discrimination against Africans and Indigenous Americans was characteristic of the slave trade and European imperialism. The English initially enslaved Africans and Native Americans by custom, and the absence of slave law benefited mixed-heritage people with partial European ancestry. This lasted into the second half of the century, when officials in Barbados, Virginia, Maryland, and Jamaica created legislation that linked labor status to racial background. The emerging gentry and planter classes supported formal slave laws as their labor preferences moved from European servitude to a greater reliance on African slavery. These statutes were the basis for a legal construction of race, which contributed to hardening racial ideologies that promoted hypodescent and adversely influenced thoughts on ethnoracial mixture. In the 1660s Chesapeake legislators joined other English colonies in the Atlantic in legal attempts to elevate people of full European lineage and subdue those of African and mixed descent.[41]

In 1662, mixed-heritage children provided the impetus for what became one of the most significant pieces of slave legislation in American history, a law that is critical for understanding attitudes toward ethnoracial mixture and people of blended ancestry within the development of racial systems. Virginia legislators introduced their first official slave code as follows: "WHEREAS some doubts have arisen whether children got by any Englishman upon a negro woman should be slave or ffree, Be it therefore enacted and declared by this present grand assembly, that all children borne in this country shalbe held bond or free only according to the condition of the mother." Lawmakers wrote this legislation to address the status of mixed-heritage offspring born to free English fathers and African slave mothers. By shifting the inheritance of slave status from the paternal to the maternal line, Virginia colonists broke with English common law and likely drew upon the Roman slave code of *partus sequitur ventrem*. Virginia's civil law was now clear: regardless of paternal ancestry, slave women could not give birth to free children. This act bound future generations of African descendants to perpetual bondage and implicitly condoned the sexual exploitation of slave women. The statute also opposed the decision in Elizabeth Key's case by providing that masters could legally enslave mixed people of European lineage without fearing they would be forced to grant these people's freedom. When colonial magistrates formally attached heritable slavery to one side of a person's ancestral line, they instituted a racial system based on hypodescent ideology.[42]

Maryland followed Virginia in passing legislation to prevent ethnoracial mixture at a time when planters were making larger investments in African slave labor. In 1664, the Maryland General Assembly questioned whether children born "of such weomen of the English or other Christian nac[i]ons ... allready marryed to negros or other Slaves" should be bound or free. Officials also discussed the length of service they should assign children "borne of such marryage." Initially the lower house of the assembly agreed to thirty-year terms for the mixed-heritage offspring of such families but harsher policies were set in the final bill. Governor Charles Calvert and the majority of Maryland's councilmembers agreed that "all negroes or other slaves" imported into the colony would serve for life and further decided that "all Children born of any Negro or other slave shall be Slaves as their ffathers were for the terme of their lives." Unlike authorities in Virginia, those in Maryland worried about the bound status of children born to African men and European women and the number of lawsuits that "may arise touching the Issue [children] of such woemen" who married slaves. This caused them to stand by English common law, in which inheritance followed the paternal line, so they legally passed down slavery in the same manner.[43]

Maryland's magistrates sought to prevent children of mixed descent from accessing freedom through their European mothers, in part because they understood that mixed-heritage children born within wedlock were free. Before this statute, Chesapeake authorities disciplined Africans and Europeans who engaged in extramarital sex according to regular laws of "fornication" and "bastardy," both religious crimes. In 1662 Virginia doubled these fines for interracial couples. The Englishmen behind these laws initiated the idea that sex and marriage across racial lines was evil or inherently wrong, and legal institutions in North America pushed this philosophy for the next 300 years.[44]

As increasing numbers of mixed-heritage children motivated Chesapeake legislators to impede interracial relationships, men in power were also seeking to increase the number of marriageable European women in the region. For the greater part of the century, English officials realized that the majority-male population and skewed sex ratio in the Chesapeake led to a dearth of available European brides. Limiting unions between African men and European women reduced male competition for free European women, who were highly sought after as marriageable partners. Maryland's high court openly lamented that "freeborne English women forgettfull of their free Condicon and to the disgrace of our Nation doe intermarry with Negro Slaves." To prevent such unions, authorities enslaved "freeborne" European women who married African slave men. This severe penalty went beyond all other sanctioned legislation in the English provinces throughout the colonial period.[45]

By the mid-1660s Maryland, Virginia, Antigua, and Bermuda had all passed some type of legislation against ethnoracial mixture or people of blended ancestry, but local officials did not always police these laws, and those who continued to intermix often avoided prosecution. In the Chesapeake and the Atlantic islands, some elites disapproved of intermixture between Europeans and people of African or Indigenous descent, yet many quietly accepted the practice and tolerated it. From 1662 to 1691, only one legal case appeared in York County, Virginia, in which a European woman was charged with "fornicacōn & Bastady w[i]th a negroe slave," even though additional intermixture took place without prosecution. During this time, York County administrators reprimanded local churchwardens for poor enforcement of misdemeanors in their districts. Meanwhile, authorities in Antigua and Bermuda also passed legislation against ethnoracial mixture that lacked heavy enforcement. The two most populous colonies in the English Caribbean—Barbados and Jamaica—altogether ignored the issue in their statutes.[46]

By the late seventeenth century, many Caribbean colonies already con-

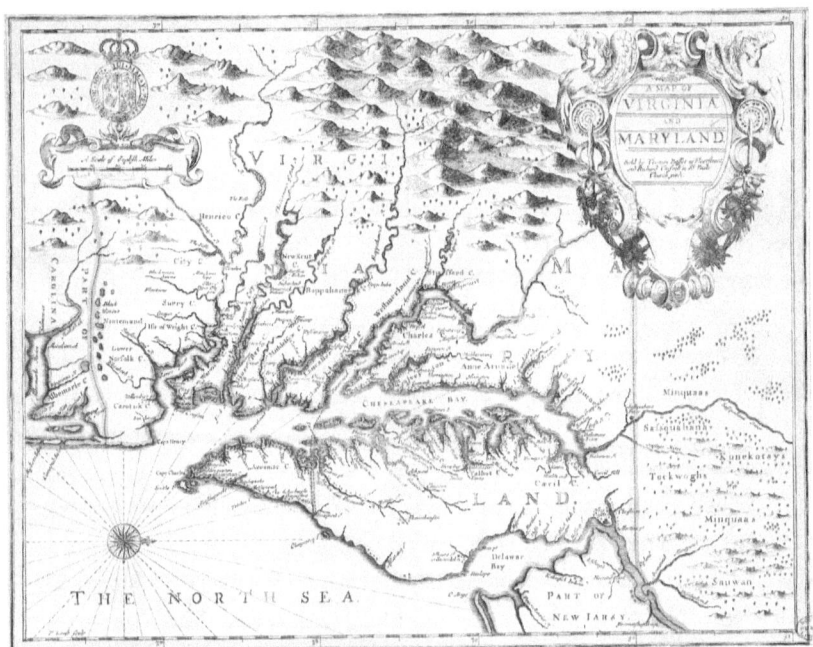

*A Map of Virginia and Maryland*, ca. 1676 (north points to the right). Details in this colonial map show plantations, towns, and churches as well as Indigenous villages and other settlements along major waterways in the Tidewater Chesapeake. (Norman B. Leventhal Map and Education Center, Boston Public Library)

tained African majorities and significant mixed-heritage populations, which made legislative efforts to prohibit intermixture futile. Europeans were in the minority on these island colonies and, even if elites outwardly frowned on the practice, they could not stem the tide of mixture. In contrast, Virginia and Maryland administrators hoped they could contain sex with a proportionally smaller number of Africans and Native Americans — many of whom pulled away from the coasts, leaving a growing European majority in the Tidewater. To English officials in the Chesapeake, legislation that promoted segregation furthered their goals as the region began to set itself apart from its peers when it came to handling interracial liaisons.[47]

In addition to taking actions to prevent exogamous relationships between Africans and Europeans, Maryland officials sought to condemn the mixed children of these couples to slavery or prolonged servitude. Even though Maryland law stated that children were slaves like their fathers, bound status was also customarily passed down through the maternal line. Maryland legislators used a combination of de jure and de facto tactics to capture most Mulattoes in lifelong bondage. Also, while European women who married slave men before the 1664 legislation remained free, one clause operated ex post facto and ordered children already born to married African and European couples to "serve the Masters of their Parents till they be Thirty yeares of age." While this sentence stopped short of outright enslavement, it legally positioned children of blended heritage between freedom and slavery.[48]

Historians have typically highlighted the thirty-year servitude penalty for Mulattoes in Virginia's 1691 act against "abominable mixture and spurious issue"; however, administrators in Maryland and Bermuda appear to have been the progenitors of this policy. Although no existing law appears, Bermuda authorities sometimes assigned thirty-year indentures to Mulatto children born on the island as early as the 1640s. Two decades later, in 1664, Maryland was the first to legally punish some people of mixed ancestry with servitude lasting three decades or more. Maryland lawmakers set a legal precedent that extended servitude for mixed-heritage offspring beyond the terms set for European children, which Virginia and other colonial officials adopted in future legislation. Colonial mandates that assigned mixed people to lengthy terms of servitude or slavery legally reinforced hypodescent and encouraged the public's perception of these people as subordinate laborers along with African and Native American slaves.[49]

Despite restrictive legislation in the Chesapeake, some people of mixed heritage found pathways out of bondage through legal loopholes that were accessible only to those of blended ancestry. While slaves of full African descent also located routes to freedom, their successes diminished in the latter half of the century when compared to those of mixed people, who retained access to liberty through European lineage. Even so, since only certain segments of the mixed-heritage population remained free, their labor status remained uncertain within the evolving colonial socioracial order. An example of this is seen with Manuel, a Mulatto in midcentury Virginia who was shipped to the colony and perhaps had Iberian connections. Evidence suggests that he was born in the early 1640s, and William Whittacre claimed to have purchased the "Mulata named Manuel . . . as a slave for Ever" from Thomas Bushrod sometime before 1664. The Englishmen who bought and sold Manuel intended to hold him permanently in bondage, but Manuel believed he could obtain his freedom and brought his case to the provincial court. In September 1664, the Virginia General Assembly granted Manuel's request by judging him a servant and ordered him "to serve as other Christian Servants Do." By proving his Christian faith and freeborn status, Manuel gained his independence and William Whittacre lost a slave.[50]

Manuel's story shows that even as Chesapeake laws strengthened around slavery, Mulattoes continued to find ways to escape bondage. In the first decades of English colonization, some slaves of African descent gained freedom by proving their adherence to Christianity, but mixed-heritage peoples had the

In September 1664, the Virginia General Assembly decided in favor of freedom for "a Mulata named Manuel." He was freed from servitude a year later in September 1665. ("The Bland Manuscript," in U.S. Library of Congress, *Thomas Jefferson Papers*, 232)

added advantage of a European parent who could make that religious claim more plausible. Like Elizabeth Key in the preceding decade, Manuel's European ancestry aided his freedom request. At the same time, Manuel's non-European lineage led his master to believe he could claim him as a slave, a common practice for owners of mixed-heritage servants. While Virginia court justices treated the "Mulata named Manuel" favorably, others were not as fortunate in the years to come. If he had sued for his freedom a few years later, it would have been difficult to gain independence, for Virginia officials declared in 1667 that Christian baptism no longer assisted slaves who sought manumission. This closed a door to freedom for those of African descent, though room remained for certain people of blended heritage to obtain liberty.[51]

Manuel, and others who petitioned for their freedom, irritated many Chesapeake planter-legislators, who responded by passing bills that supported a racial order based on hypodescent. These authorities realized that the law could subordinate Mulattoes under those of full European ancestry. Their actions were part of wider efforts to shore up the slave system and avoid social instability. Chesapeake elites had reason to worry in the 1670s and 1680s, when servants, slaves, poor immigrants, and small planters initiated several conspiracies and revolts. When these groups banded together and pressured those in power — as they did during Bacon's Rebellion and other insurrections — officials took actions that widened sociracial gaps between Africans and Europeans. It is no coincidence that lawmakers began regularly using the term "Mulatto" in colonial legislation around this time and placed people of mixed ancestry on the "Negro" side of the racial divide. The growth of the mixed-heritage population in the Chesapeake went hand in hand with the rise in African slave importation, and both added to the fears of larger planters who used racially based legislation to maintain control over these groups.[52]

Statutory laws do not provide a complete picture of how people operated on the ground, yet they serve as useful signposts for identifying the progression of colonial racial ideologies and often reflect the issues that magistrates were responding to at the time. In 1672 Virginia's assembly addressed runaway slaves who were "out in rebellion" or living free away from their masters and directed that Europeans could use violent force with "any negroe, molatto, Indian slave, or servant for life" who resisted capture. In 1678 Maryland followed Virginia and declared that "Negroes and Mulattoes" could not gain manumission based on Christian baptism. Four years later in Virginia, all "Negroes, Moors, Mollatoes or Indians" who were not Christian before they were purchased or brought from outside the colony were to be "adjudged, deemed and taken to be slaves to all intents and purposes." In most of these statutes, the language identified Mulattoes and other Africans and Native Americans as slaves. Authorities often lumped "Negroes and Mulattoes" together in slave legislation, but these pairings gloss over a significant portion of mixed-heritage people in the Chesapeake who lived as free and whose experiences differed dramatically from those of the enslaved.[53]

In the last decades of the century, Chesapeake officials strengthened a legal system that helped replicate hierarchical orders seen in Europe, as colonial professionals, merchants, and large planters sought to create a new noble class based on aristocratic English notions of rank and prestige. Even though the provincial gentry had few familial connections to English nobility, they built on the idea of regal bloodlines and extended the concept of race as a national identity to their experience in the Americas. As Iberians relied on similar beliefs in *limpieza de sangre* to fashion a sociracial hierarchy in Latin America, colonial leaders in the English Empire likewise crafted ethnoracial divisions. The process appears most legibly in the Chesapeake, where administrators attempted to institute and police racial lines, in part because so many people intermixed without shame.[54]

## SITUATIONAL MULATTO PRIVILEGE IN
## THE LATE SEVENTEENTH CENTURY

People of African descent, including those of mixed ancestry, resisted increasing legal constraints in the early Chesapeake and found ways to secure liberty. Still, distinctions between "Negroes and Mulattoes" existed in social practice, even when they were not explicitly stated in law. The sale of two Iberian Mulattoes in Virginia shows how certain slaves of mixed ancestry gained privileges that the English did not usually grant to other Africans at this time. "A Spanish Mullatto, by name of Anthonio," entered Middlesex County via the Rappahannock River on March 5, 1678. His bondage suggests that his father may have been a Spaniard and his mother an African. John Endecott, an English trader from Boston, sold Anthonio in Virginia and claimed, "I hav[e] full power to sell him [Anthonio] for his life time, But at ye request of William Taylor, I doe sell him But for Tenn years." William Taylor served as a witness to the indenture and appears to have helped negotiate the sale. Anthonio also likely pushed for his eventual manumission, perhaps based on his Christian faith and partial European ancestry or a combination of the two. At the expiration of his service, the contract declared the "Mulatto, Anthony, to be a free man to goe wherever he pleaseth." Furthermore, Anthonio probably understood colonial slave law and was not the only Spanish Mulatto to make the leap from slavery to servitude.[55]

Countless examples of slaves moving between Ibero-American and Anglo-American colonies display how creole peoples, cultures, and racial ideologies were transferred between European empires. Anthonio's contract records his name both in Spanish and as the Anglicized version, Anthony, which marks his transition into English colonial society. The document concludes with Anthonio's own signature at the bottom, showing that he consented to the premises of the agreement. This was unique, as literate slaves did not normally participate in their bills of sale, but Anthonio took an active role in legally confirming his future freedom as a servant. We lack his exact words, but Anthonio communicated with those who traded him, perhaps in more than one language. He probably knew Spanish and could speak at least some English. Anthonio was a creole person in terms of his ethnoracial mixture and a creole culturally because he was able to operate within multiple colonial spheres in the Atlantic world. Having journeyed from various ports across the Atlantic, slaves like him were often multilingual and versed in multiple cultures and understood the legalities of their bondage. A direct connection to European lineage often granted mixed-heritage people access to important cultural tools that they could employ to acquire freedom.[56]

Following trade networks that connected empires across the Atlantic, slaves such as Anthonio often came to Virginia through the Caribbean on New England merchant ships. A second Anthonio appeared on one of these vessels only two months later in Middlesex County. This Anthonio found similar circumstances when Ralph Wormeley paid twenty pounds sterling to another Boston merchant, John Saffin, for the man's labor. Ralph purchased the "mulatto Serv[an]t" for ten years, after which time the bondsman would "be free & wholly at his owne dispose." This contract only referred to Anthonio as a servant, but its extended term suggests that he had been a slave at some point. Both Anthonios may have used their skills to negotiate labor contracts that were shorter than the lifetime bondage assigned to most African slaves. Even though ten years was a longer term than typical European servants endured, the length of these Mulattoes' indentures exposes an intermediate labor status that mirrors their blended backgrounds. A space in between freedom and slavery represented a loose form of hypodescent, seen throughout the colonial Americas, in which many Mulattoes were limited by their African ancestry yet not totally condemned by it.[57]

While some Chesapeake Mulattoes obtained access to freedom, a great number were born to enslaved mothers, and their owners held them under strict maternal hypodescent in slavery. Hundreds of enslaved African and Indigenous women gave birth to mixed-heritage children in the seventeenth century—the product of rape, coercion, and willful intercourse with European men. A sample of seventy-five people listed in Maryland estate inventories from 1674 to 1687 shows that Mulattoes accounted for 15 percent of all servants and slaves. Most appear to be children or adolescents of African mothers. Additional Mulatto slaves and servants appear in bills of sale, inventories, wills, and other documentation with increasing regularity by the end of the century. In the mid-1680s, Frank was a "mallatto . . . slave for life" on the plantation of John Wallop in Accomack County, Virginia, where he carried out the daily tasks surrounding tobacco planting and cultivation. Frank also handled some of the corporal punishment of John's other laborers, including European servants. Frank's father was likely European and his mother an enslaved African woman. His life resembled the existence of other African slaves, though his European background perhaps situationally elevated his status on the plantation.[58]

Even though mixed-heritage slaves lacked the same liberties as free Mulattoes, both groups often experienced greater privileges than African slaves. In Lancaster County, Virginia, Robert Griggs freed several slaves in his 1684 will: one was listed as "Molatto" and several others as "Negro." Robert manumitted the "Negro" slaves after a period of bondage, insisting that they first complete lengthy thirty-five-to-forty-five-year terms of service under his "Molatto Woman named Molley"—the only slave that Robert immediately freed. He also bequeathed to Molley a "heifer and three Barrells of Corne upon her freedom," a yearly supply of clothing, and a "house and ground to live and plant upon." Robert further instructed that she could remain there with her husband. While Robert did not disclose why he gave Molley preferential treatment, the "Molatto Woman" likely benefited from a direct link to European ancestry. It is quite possible that she was Robert's daughter, niece, half sister, or other family relation. Personal connections between slaves and their owners often influenced individual manumissions, and masters sometimes favored mixed-heritage slaves with whom they also shared bonds of kinship.[59]

While most enslaved Mulattoes inherited their labor status customarily from African mothers, by law, some children of mixed ancestry in Maryland inherited slavery through their African fathers or European mothers who were enslaved by legislation that prohibited interracial unions. In 1681, provincial officials decided to reconsider this type of bondage after the marriage of an African slave named Charles to an Irish woman, Eleanor Butler. The couple decided to marry, knowing their union would legally extend Charles's lifetime bondage to his wife, Eleanor, and possibly to their future children. Governor Charles Calvert held Eleanor in servitude but lost her labor after the marriage, when she became the property of her African husband's owner. In the weeks following the couple's 1681 wedding, Governor Calvert and the Maryland General Assembly changed the existing law, announcing that any "White woman serv[an]t . . . in Matrimony with any Slave" would become free. The story of "Negro Charles" and "Irish Nell" represents how those who disobeyed colonial authority also influenced legislative action.[60]

The Butlers' and others' resistance to colonial power protected Mulattoes with European maternal ancestry, ensuring that not all of them would be slaves for life in Maryland. Still, magistrates remained acutely aware of the mixed-heritage sons and daughters that European women brought into the colonial world. While they were no longer willing to enslave European women who married African slave men, Maryland legislators continued to bemoan the "diverse Inconveniencys Controversys & suites [that] may arise Touching the Issue or Children of such ffreeborne women." Officials attempted to resolve legal tensions by formally moving to *partus sequitur ventrem* and decided that "all Children borne of such ffree-borne women [in matrimony with any slave] . . . shall bee ffree." The amended law held wide implications, especially for people of mixed heredity and their descendants, who gained the free status of their European mothers. Unfortunately for the Butlers and other families, the legal modification did not operate ex post facto, and several of Charles and Eleanor's "mallattoe" children fell into slavery because their parents married before the revision. However, the family's opposition to colonial authorities made it possible for countless mixed-heritage children to attain freedom in the future.[61]

Family members who experienced years of servitude keenly recognized the rising sentiment of racial hypodescent at work in the colonial Chesapeake and made efforts to facilitate paths out of bondage for their children of mixed lineage. The Bass family exemplifies how families in the Tidewater Chesapeake managed to protect children of blended ancestry from extended terms of service. (They had no apparent relation to the Nansemond Bass family.) In the early 1660s John White held "A negro man Servant and an English woman Servant" in bondage in Virginia. Like many laboring couples, the two became intimately involved in the household of a common master, and their relationship produced a "Mallatto" child named Sarah Bass sometime around 1664. John later moved to Maryland, and on August 13, 1672, he appeared with Sarah in the Somerset County court to record the girl's age, labor status, and length of service. In a society based on rank and status, it must have been a daunting experience for the young Sarah to stand before the court justices and "Acknowledge herselfe to be . . . almost eight yeares of age." Her master and guardian may have reassured her that their appearance in court was merely a formality. Court officials determined that Sarah would "serve the said John White" until she was twenty-one, a typical term for servant children at the time.[62]

Before leaving Virginia, John White acknowledged that he would care for Sarah Bass and recognized that a "Cowe & Cowe Calfe" belonged to the young girl as her property. John verified that Sarah would inherit the "female increase" of the two cows, while he maintained use of the "male encrease." While John appears as the main actor in this story, the presence of Sarah's parents is visible in his actions. Even though Sarah's parents had limited autonomy, they likely worked out this arrangement with their master. Livestock would assist Sarah's future independence, granted that John fulfilled his obligation to protect the child's freedom and personal property. A parent's role was vital to the future success of mixed-heritage youth because children could not easily advocate for their own freedoms.[63]

While colonial records often lack African voices, all parents fought for the rights of their mixed children, and the actions of some free African men reveal these struggles. Anthony "Tony" Longo was one of several African men who had a sexual relationship with a European woman on the early Eastern Shore of Virginia. He was also one of the earliest Africans in the colony to gain his freedom, as a teenager in 1635. By the mid-1650s, he had married a woman named Hannah, and although her race went unrecorded, she was possibly the European mother of his children, a "Mallatto" son and two daughters. Hannah likely passed away by 1669, leaving the elderly Tony to care for his three children — a difficult task because he was nearly sixty years old and had slipped into poverty after working many years as a tenant farmer. At this advanced stage in life, Tony may have relied on his children for material support as much as they depended on him as a father.⁶⁴

In the English colonies, poor parents risked losing their children to servitude in wealthier households, and after Tony petitioned for tax relief, the Accomack County court took his children away from him. Officials bound out Tony's three children and apprenticed his "Mallatto" son, James, to a man with far more power, the wealthy Edmund Scarborough. Interestingly, Tony's children received twenty-four-year indentures, three years longer than most European children. This appears to be as punishment, for the court noted, "the lazy and evill life of the said Anthony Longo and that his children are vitious and lazily bred." Authorities felt that James and his sisters were "like[ly] to prove no better then their slothful father if [they] continewed with him." But were these accusations true?⁶⁵

In earlier decades, Tony had farmed land, traded with other colonists, and had regular interactions with his European neighbors. Despite this, European hostilities and racial animosities shown toward free Africans increased since Tony received his freedom in the 1630s. By around 1670, colonial society had changed and often dramatically for African-descended people. By this time, Tony appears to have fallen out of favor with local officials, and his history of resisting authority, more than his lack of industry, likely led to his family's poverty. Sitting magistrates feared that African fathers like Tony would be a bad influence on their mixed-heritage children and opted to place them with European masters. This was probably not the result Tony expected when he simply sought tax relief, or perhaps a possibility that he was intending to avoid.⁶⁶

James Longo followed his father's independent spirit and ended up more successful on Virginia's Eastern Shore. Like his father, James escaped bondage early, which may have been the result of his master Edmund Scarborough's death combined with his father's petition to Governor Berkeley to annul his son's service contract. Tony asked the court for the "liberty to keepe his children and not to bee disposed of [them] according to the court's order." The court budged somewhat on his petition and allowed the eldest Longo daughter to return to her father, and she assisted Tony until his death in 1670. After James became free, he acquired the carpenter's trade and worked diligently to save money. In 1681 he purchased 200 acres of land in Accomack County from John Washbourne, which would have cost upward of 5,000 pounds of tobacco. James later built John a brick chimney and worked on other building projects in his community, sometimes bartering for livestock, corn, and tobacco, the currency of the day. As was common, he sued others for debts in court, and his peers also sued him. Based on a glimpse of his life that comes through in court records, James's European neighbors accepted him in the community, and while all did not treat him fairly, his affluence surpassed that of his father at a time when life generally became more difficult for those of African descent.[67]

While the Mulatto James Longo had regular interactions with European colonists, he also maintained ties to those of African ancestry in his community. James took in a mixed-heritage child, Sarah, into his home to raise her until she turned twenty-one. Sarah was born out of wedlock to a European servant named Dorothy Bestick, who had a relationship with a "Negro Slave" named George Francis on a nearby plantation. The parents could not pay the fine for bastardy and fornication of 1,000 pounds of tobacco, so James and another neighbor put up the fee. Whether James was motivated by personal gain or connected by friendship with one of Sarah's parents is unknown. James likely recalled the painful experience of how he and his sisters had been taken from their father and placed in servitude years earlier. Perhaps this motivated him to pay for Sarah's indenture so that he could keep the young girl close to her family and protect her from those who might misuse her.[68]

By the late seventeenth century, parents met increasing difficulties in navigating Chesapeake legal systems that sought to keep their African, Native American, and mixed-heritage children in bondage. William Catillah was another "Malattoe boy" in Virginia, who had a livestock inheritance stipulated in his indenture. The contract made clear that when William turned fourteen years old, his master was obligated to deliver a young heifer along with all its offspring "to run and be for the use and behoofe of the s[ai]d Malattoe boy." William's family, like others, appears to have made this agreement with his master to ensure that he would have the resources needed to become self-sufficient at the end of his service. Up through the 1680s Chesapeake courts regularly indentured children of blended ancestry until they reached twenty-one years of age, but William's master claimed an unusually long thirty-year contract. At the time, Virginia officials could only legally assign this lengthy term to children of Native American descent. Could the "Malattoe" William Catillah have been Native American?[69]

In the Chesapeake, colonists most often identified those of mixed African and European heritage as Mulatto, but the word sometimes referred to those of mixed Indigenous and European ancestry. Chesapeake colonists rarely used the term *"mestizo,"* and Virginia officials legally recognized some people of Native American descent as Mulatto in 1705. Here lawmakers drew a formal line of hypodescent at one-eighth African or one-half Indigenous lineage — stricter than society had practiced in the seventeenth century. After further intermixture with Europeans, Mulatto families would legally become "white."[70]

In the seventeenth-century Chesapeake, mixed-heritage families could cross over into social whiteness and avoid racially discriminatory laws by continuing to mix with Europeans over multiple generations. This practice occurred in Latin America and the Caribbean and can also be found in colonial North America. Thomas Rolfe and his descendants were the earliest documented family to achieve this type of status through multigenerational mixture in the Chesapeake. Thomas's wife was likely an Englishwoman, and in 1675 their daughter Jane married Robert Bolling, an Englishman from an esteemed family. Jane and Robert Bolling's only son, John, was born the year after their marriage, and he had several children who married in with families of elite English planters. Hence, the grandchildren and great-grandchildren of John Rolfe and Pocahontas/Matoaka/Rebecca were not only accepted into English colonial society, but they reached its upper echelons. Although this may have been an exceptional case, intermarriage allowed other families with Native American antecedents to blend into colonial English society and effectively become "white." Some of the blended English-Nansemond children of John and Keziah Bass appear to have married further with Europeans and lost their "Indian" status, while others in the family continued to mix with people of African and Indigenous descent.[71]

Also telling is that seventeenth-century records rarely attached ethno-racial labels to certain members of the Nansemond Bass family and never classified descendants of the Rolfe-Bolling family by race. These people often lived as English and therefore did not have to racially pass for "white"—they were free, and many in their communities were already aware of their "Indian" origins. The increasing privileges associated with whiteness, and degradation of blackness, assisted efforts by colonial officials to hinder the social acceptance of mixed-heritage people and eventually led to the idea of racial passing in following centuries.[72]

Chesapeake authorities attempted to reduce the growing number of free mixed children born of second-generation intermixture with Europeans because the offspring of Mulatto and European couples did not always carry racial labels in their communities. The children of the "moletto" Elizabeth Key and her European husband William Greensted apparently did not inherit their mother's racial classification. As for many in the Bass and Rolfe-Bolling families, extant records from Northumberland County never identified the Greensted children by race. Even though William Jr., John, and Elizabeth Greensted were of one-fourth African descent, they all freely participated in Virginian society as other European colonists did from the 1650s through the 1680s. William Greensted Sr. bequeathed lands to his children on Virginia's Northern Neck, and officials granted them their property. Elizabeth the younger married a European man, whose family accepted her as a daughter-in-law and provided for her orphaned brothers after their parents' deaths. In 1679 William Jr. and John Greensted served with other "able men" in their local militia and mustered with firearms and ammunition to help protect the colony. The brothers went on to own several hundred acres of land where they could plant tobacco like their neighbors. In 1686 William Jr. also served on a six-person jury in Northumberland County with other men in his community.[73]

Evidence surrounding the Greensted family shows that their peers accepted them as other European colonists, revealing that mixed-heritage people of predominantly European ancestry did not experience the same restrictions as those with greater proportions of African lineage. Their children by Europeans were more likely to find social acceptance and equality. Even though they achieved economic security on par with their European peers, this does not discount that people of mixed ancestry still faced varying degrees of racial discrimination in the seventeenth-century English colonies. While the Key-Greensteds, Rolfe-Bollings, and other families demonstrate how hypodescent diminished after successive generations of exogamy with Europeans, overall this racial ideology strengthened as new policies punished an increasing number of mixed people in the Chesapeake.

While the children of Mulattoes might obtain racial whiteness after another generation of intermixture with Europeans, Chesapeake legislators moved to thwart this type of recognition in the 1690s. However, in the decades before these acts, many people of mixed lineage had enjoyed freedoms and avoided tightening regulations. Even though Chesapeake authorities used formal legislation to prohibit mixture between ethnoracial groups, intimate relationships involving sex and marriage produced hundreds of mixed-heritage people over the seventeenth century and thousands throughout the colonial period. Provincial legislation ultimately limited personal autonomy and stigmatized people of mixed descent for centuries in English colonial America and later in the United States. Regardless, people of blended ancestry challenged the emerging racial order and continued to cross what some had imagined as racial boundaries. As a result, Chesapeake authorities could never legally define all mixed-heritage people distinctly in a single category as slave, servant, or free.[74]

# 2

# Children of Mixed Lineage in the Colonial Chesapeake

On September 15, 1690, Roger Rise brought his servant woman, Elizabeth Sparrow, to the Norfolk County court in Virginia. The year before, the young woman became pregnant while working in Roger's home. Roger paid for Elizabeth's service for a limited number of years and may have grown upset when her work slowed and labor pains interrupted her regular household chores. Elizabeth named her newborn daughter Mary, and after giving birth the mother spent time nursing and attending to her infant's needs while performing normal duties such as preparing meals, doing needlework, and completing other household tasks. Like many servant women during the time, she may have also worked in the tobacco fields—planting, hoeing, and harvesting the crop under the sweltering sun. Like most masters, Roger was not happy about having to provide for an unwed servant woman with a young child in his home, especially when it took away from her labor. Colonial masters viewed this scenario as a financial burden, which is why Elizabeth may have ambivalently celebrated her daughter's birth. She knew that having a child while remaining indentured brought consequences: extra time would be added to her service term. In addition, Elizabeth was a European woman who was "delivered of a Bastard Child begotten by a negro." Some colonists may have distastefully looked down on Elizabeth holding her "Molato" newborn Mary. Would the mother and daughter face other ramifications as well?[1]

When colonial authorities summoned Elizabeth to appear in Norfolk, she anticipated legal repercussions for her crime of "bastardy" but was probably less aware of what would happen to her mixed-heritage daughter. The county court justices ordered her to pay 1,000 pounds of tobacco to Roger as compensation for the work she missed due to her pregnancy. This was a hefty sum, and there was only one way a poor woman in her position could pay: with her labor.

Hence, the court added two more years of service to Elizabeth's previous contract. The justices then fined her another 500 pounds of tobacco for bastardy because she was an unwed mother. Again, she could not pay this amount, so the justices directed the sheriff to "take her Into Custody and give her twenty Lashes on her bare back well Laid on." Luckily for Elizabeth, Roger interceded on her behalf and paid the fine to spare her from the "Corporal punishm[en]t." For paying this expense, the court granted her master another year of Elizabeth's service—resulting in three additional years added to her indenture. Finally, the court assigned her "Molato" daughter, Mary, to live and work for Roger until the girl reached the age of twenty-one.[2]

Despite being born into servitude, Mary Sparrow was fortunate to have been born in 1690. The Norfolk County court's punitive actions would have been the same if her father had been a European man instead of African, but a drastic legal change came in 1691. In fall of that year, the Virginia General Assembly declared that all children resulting from such "abominable mixture" would serve nearly an additional decade, until their thirtieth birthday. The following year, Maryland's assembly stipulated a similar penalty, sentencing children of blended ethnoracial ancestry to thirty-one years of service. Considering the relatively low life expectancy at the time in the Chesapeake, thirty or thirty-one years of servitude constituted the greater part of most people's lives. Around the turn of the century, most mixed-heritage children were slaves like their African or Indigenous mothers and others were sentenced to serve thirty-plus years under the masters of their European mothers. These laws and others in the following decades effectively gave mixed children a legal status between freedom and slavery.[3]

Chesapeake legislation is central to understanding racial hierarchy and the early development of mixed-race ideologies in English colonial America. Magistrates in Virginia and Maryland consciously engineered legal systems to punish parents and children of blended families as a method of stemming the tide of intermixture. Those in power also openly scorned mixed-heritage children and worked to legislate the labor status of these so-called Mulattoes as servants and slaves to profit from the tobacco economy. This harsh regulatory practice first appeared in the 1660s, and following generations of English colonial lawmakers made resurgent efforts to denounce sex and marriage between disparate ethnoracial groups in the 1690s and early 1700s. Colonial Chesapeake governments originated some of the harshest penalties against people of mixed ancestry in the Atlantic world, which set the region apart from other English provinces.[4]

This chapter demonstrates how colonists in the Chesapeake uniquely crafted racial thinking already present in the English Empire, how legal institutions affected those of mixed ethnoracial heritage, and how "mixed people" and their families responded to these legal challenges. While the Chesapeake stood out among other English provinces throughout the colonial period, the 1690s and early 1700s were a transformational time for developing anti-intermixture legislation. Stabilizing these legal policies was challenging, but during these decades officials consolidated power and instituted provincial laws that created a legal legacy that would carry on for three centuries. At first, county magistrates experienced problems disseminating and enforcing laws that punished intermixture and people of mixed descent. Shifting mandates often led to legal confusion at local levels, where lower officials were responsible for enforcing these statutes. Colonial courts also struggled to police those who lived in the continental interior, distant from English authorities stationed in eastern Tidewater counties. Therefore, county administrators haphazardly applied the law to families of blended ethnoracial lineage and often sentenced mixed-heritage children to irregular terms of servitude. Over time, Chesapeake societies formalized legal and other institutional structures, which led to increased prosecution. Although uniform regulation remained a challenge, masters trapped thousands of freeborn mixed people in indentures during the colonial era.[5]

Chesapeake records reveal that despite segregationist laws, many colonists continued to freely intermix, particularly those who lived on the fringes of colonial society. These blended families and mixed-heritage people increasingly used the courts to fight for their independence. In the 1690s, mixed children born to English mothers encountered stricter legislation in Virginia and Maryland and found it more difficult to locate pathways to freedom than previous generations had. As county courts began to condemn these children of blended ancestry to lengthy terms in bondage, adults born decades earlier also fought to retain their liberty. The most successful Mulattoes could prove a tie to European maternal lineage in court or had European mothers or family members who were active in preserving their freedom. Nevertheless, negative portrayals of interracial sex and marriage, coupled with legislation that subjugated people of mixed heritage as bound laborers, confined those identified as Mulatto to lower positions within the socioracial order. This fostered a strict form of hypodescent, in which people of mixed ancestry were most often associated with their socially inferior parentage.[6]

Legal codes and court cases illustrate the concerns of wealthy planter-politicians and their efforts to confine mixed-heritage families and children to the lower ranks of society, but the elite could not have accomplished these goals without the support of middling and lower-class Europeans. Hypodescent ideology became prevalent in the colonial Chesapeake when those who wielded power formed a loose, informal coalition with lower-class Europeans. Large planters were most concerned with controlling labor, while plebeian colonists and immigrants wanted access to capital and opportunities for social mobility.

Into the eighteenth century, the greater part of the European yeomanry remained indebted or subservient to the colonial gentry and many surrendered class mobility in exchange for another emerging category: racial whiteness.

The creation of "white" identity produced material, social, and psychological benefits for European colonists, which encouraged them to uphold a racial caste system. English immigrants and colonists at varying socioeconomic levels united in the Chesapeake to create and sustain institutions that promoted European or "white" superiority over "Negroes," "Indians," and "Mulattoes"—people of African or Native American ancestry. This process galvanized the shift from a protoracial to a racial society in the English colonial Chesapeake by the early 1700s. While Europeans bonded across class divides, racial divisions also buttressed elite authority and protected the wealth of large tobacco planters. Colonial Chesapeake assemblies passed laws in the last decade of the seventeenth century and first decades of the eighteenth century that substantiated the development of a provincial aristocracy and also firmly established hypodescent in English colonial North America. While hypodescent strengthened during this time, statutes still left openings for some people of mixed heritage to occupy a middle ground between slavery and freedom. Though success was often fleeting, people of blended ancestry and their families employed all possible legal means to locate paths to independence for themselves and their descendants.[7]

## COLONIAL TOBACCO, LABOR, AND THE SOCIORACIAL STRUCTURE

Tobacco drove the economy of the colonial Chesapeake during the seventeenth century and helped reshape the landscape of Tsenacommacah, which the English rebranded as Virginia. Unlike New England's colonial villages that replicated the motherland, colonists erected few towns in the early Chesapeake. Instead, Europeans in Virginia and Maryland expanded in a pattern similar to that in the Caribbean, where individual plantations spread along coastal areas and up rivers into the continental interior, and these waterways provided transportation by boat or ship. Plantations contained several dwellings scattered on plots of land held by a "freeholder" who employed or owned laborers who resided year-round on the grounds. Workers constructed buildings and roads, served as domestics, raised crops and livestock for commercial export, and the colonial enterprise added to the wealth of the owner.[8]

Despite market booms and busts over the century, tobacco became the backbone of colonial Chesapeake growth; it structured settlement and work patterns in the region and propelled a mixture of slave, servant, and free labor. Colonists also grew a multitude of other crops: cereal grains such as wheat, bar-

This eighteenth-century tobacco label depicts key aspects of Virginia's plantation system, including tobacco cultivation, use, export, and the relationship between master and slave. (George Arents Collection, New York Public Library)

ley, and oats and an array of vegetables, though mainly corn. For meat and milk products, they raised cattle, pigs, sheep, and poultry and hunted wild game. Most colonists still pursued the dream of owning a plot of land so they could grow the one crop that offered the highest prices and greatest social mobility: tobacco. By the 1670s, colonists raised tobacco with great efficiency, but overproduction led to falling prices and economic depression in the final decades of the century. During this time, opportunities decreased and many Europeans remained in poverty. The flow of servants immigrating into the Chesapeake from Europe slowed, and fewer people were able to acquire land and workers, although wealthy planters maintained access to both.[9]

The decline of English servitude in the 1670s Chesapeake coincided with a shift to more expensive African labor and the strengthening of sociuracial structures that crystallized in subsequent decades. By the end of the century, large planters who could afford the high price of slaves, purchased all that Atlantic traders made available. As the tobacco market stagnated, smaller planters were unable to assume the high costs associated with slave labor and lost some of the economic and political influence they had enjoyed in earlier decades. Those already established in tobacco production continued to purchase slave labor, expand landholdings, and further augment their political power. This resulted in the emergence of a multigenerational gentry who controlled colonial legislatures through business ties and governing influence. In the 1690s and 1700s the elite continued to strengthen its hold over colonial society with legislation that restricted the mobility of others in terms of both class and race. When constructing legal statutes, planter-legislators identified which people of mixed ancestry could be enslaved and sought to ensnare more of the freeborn in bondage through indentured servitude.[10]

Colonists modeled general assemblies and county courts after English institutions, yet they had few legal precedents for subjugating Africans and Native Americans, and this led to challenges when they decided to legislate against sex and marriage in an ethnically diverse America. At first, colonists followed English common law and applied routine punishments to Europeans who had extramarital sex ("fornication") and conceived children outside of wedlock ("bastardy") with Africans and Native Americans. Across the colonies, English officials believed that "fornication," "bastardy" and "illegitimate" offspring disrupted well-ordered societies, and they responded to these perceived threats by shoring up marriage laws in the eighteenth century. Throughout colonial America, both the Catholic and Protestant Church permitted marriage between Europeans, Africans, and Native Americans who had accepted Christian baptism. Although the Anglican Church never outlawed racial exogamy, colonists began to look down on these relationships as racist sentiments grew. Unable to invalidate ecclesiastical standards, colonial magistrates in several provinces chose to magnify penalties for interracial sex under criminal law. Moved by economic motivations, wealthy planters sought to keep mixed-heritage offspring in bondage and away from the inheritances of European fathers, so they crafted laws that disciplined "whites" who engaged in intimate affairs with "Negroes" and "Indians." This legislation further helped to fashion early provincial ideas about racial difference.[11]

As the slave trade increased in the Chesapeake, powerful planter-politicians created economic and social incentives for Europeans to attach racial ideologies to people of African, Native American, and mixed ancestry. It was no coincidence that English colonial law and society supported racial ideologies that coalesced around a systematic commitment to African bondage and, to a lesser degree, Native American slavery. English authorities supported racial labels in colonial legislation and generally characterized people within society into four main categories: "white," "Negro," "Indian," and "Mulatto." While not all colonists employed race as the primary condition upon which to judge others, legal systems used racial classifications as a tool to help determine one's labor status. And people of mixed ethnoracial backgrounds were subject to both enslavement and long-term servitude.[12]

By the turn of the century, race operated simultaneously with sex, religion, occupation, and other intersecting factors that influenced a person's position within colonial society. None of these categories operated (or operate today) on their own or merely through institutions. Rather, individuals and institutions both pushed racial thinking. It would be a mistake to believe that the gentry alone held these notions. The folk—everyday people who constitute society—also sustained beliefs that allowed racial ideas to thrive. While elites initially advanced notions on race to maintain and grow their wealth, European colonists on multiple levels of society embraced racial ideologies that elevated their position, either materially or psychologically.[13]

## "THE DESIGN OF PREVENTING SUCH MUNGRELL MARRIAGES" AND "SPURIOUS ISSUE"

Despite laws aimed at preventing interracial intimacies in the colonial Chesapeake, people from diverse backgrounds continued to have sex and conceive children both in and out of wedlock. A number of African men married European women in the seventeenth century, and these couples often remained in a state of slavery or servitude. Not far from the Potomac River in Westmoreland County, Virginia, an Englishwoman named Hester married an African man, James Tate. The couple lived in bondage, although in different households, and their offspring also grew up in servitude. In 1690, the county court bound the Tates' oldest son, James Jr., to serve his mother's master "untill he bee free as is according to Law," which was twenty-one years old at the time. The following year, the court indentured three more of the Tate children in the same manner, although this time the "Mulatto Children"—Jane, Elizabeth, and William—were "bound apprentices" to their father's owner. Apprenticeships were intended to be reciprocal contracts in which a master cared for a child through adolescence while teaching him or her a valuable trade or craft so the child could then make a living as a free adult. In return the child served the master and his family until he or she reached maturity. But until what age would the younger three Tate children serve?[14]

Typically, masters freed English girls from apprenticeships at eighteen and boys at twenty-one, and while it is known that the latter was James Jr.'s term, the precise length of service for his siblings went unrecorded. The justices of the Westmoreland County court sentenced the three youngest Tate children "to serve untill they ... bee free according to Law," but that law had recently changed. The court decided the case of Jane, Elizabeth, and William Tate in November 1691, a month after Virginia officials made a significant alteration in childhood indenture law. In October, Virginia officials had decided that mixed-heritage children, both boys and girls, would serve until they were thirty years old, around a decade beyond the normal term set for European children. The legal length of indenture for the younger Tate "Mulatto Children" could have been longer than their eldest brother's twenty-one years of service, but this is not certain, since officials did not routinely record the exact length of servitude in the court decisions.[15]

The Tate children and hundreds, if not thousands, of other Mulatto children were affected by Virginia legislation after 1691, which instructed officials on slavery, intermarriage, and illegitimate mixed-heritage offspring. The ordinance grouped "Negroes" and "Mulattoes" together a total of seventeen times. This figuratively and formally linked people of blended ancestry to their African lineage. Virginia magistrates also went further than they had before in discussing racial boundaries by including a comprehensive section of legislation that addressed mixture in three important areas: marriage, sex, and child birth. Legislators called "for prevention of that abominable mixture and spurious issue [children] which hereafter may encrease in this dominion as well by negroes, mulattoes, and Indians intermarrying with English, or other white women, as by their unlawfull accompanying with one another." Referring to mixed-heritage children as "spurious" equated all Mulattoes with illegitimacy, even if they had been born within wedlock.[16]

Disdain for ethnoracial mixture grew in the Chesapeake, and the following year Maryland officials reissued anti-intermixture codes. In 1692 Maryland authorities strengthened previous legislation against "any freeborn English and white woman that shall . . . intermarry with or permit herself to be begotten with child by any Negro or other Slave." This law once again called mixed unions a "disgrace" but also included more derisive language that defined interracial relationships as "evill." Legislators increased existing penalties, adding seven years of servitude for any woman of European descent who married or had a mixed-heritage child by a "free Negro or Slave." Any free African man who married a European woman would "forfeit his freedome and become a Servant . . . during his natural life." These efforts to regulate certain relationships further promoted the idea that racial divisions and boundaries should exist, specifically between "white" women and "Negro" men. In this way, the rising gentry pushed to racially stratify society, similar to class structures in England.[17]

Once again, Chesapeake officials used legislation to prevent courtship across perceived racial lines and continued to articulate racial segregation in the English colonies. The purpose of these statutes was clear by the early 1690s: Virginia and Maryland authorities no longer wanted any English, or other Europeans, to marry those outside the "white" race. Colonial administrators identified Europeans as "white" in law and placed them above those labeled "negroe, mulatto, and Indian"—whom officials viewed in an inferior position. Statutory laws encouraged people to think of themselves as belonging to static racial groups, which also encouraged them to self-segregate. This legislation identified exogamy as deviant and criminal and supported the belief that endogamy—marrying within one's own group—should be the accepted norm. Yet there was nothing natural about the construction of racial boundaries; otherwise, they would have formed organically without legal mandates. Chesapeake laws were the strongest proclamations against interracial relationships in the Americas and denigrated the families of mixed-heritage peoples. Still, not everyone adopted racial thinking to the same extent, especially Europeans, Africans, and Native Americans who formed intimate bonds with one another.[18]

To catch those who violated anti-intermixture laws, Chesapeake legislators rewarded European colonists who notified authorities of existing interracial relationships and mixed-heritage births, thereby cultivating ideas of racial difference. In 1691, the Virginia legislature ordered that "if any English woman being free shall have a bastard child by any negro or mulatto," she would have to pay fifteen pounds sterling one month after the child was born. If she could not pay this fine, she would "be taken into the possession of the Church wardens"—administrators of the local church parish. The churchwardens then sold the woman to a colonial master for a five-year indenture in Virginia (Maryland assigned seven). As we have seen, the servant woman's current master often paid the fee to receive extra years of service from her, for it was impossible for poor servant women to pay these fines on their own. The churchwardens split the money three ways: one-third went "toward the support of the [colonial] government"; one-third went "to the use of the [church] parish"; and one-third went "to the informer" of the crime—most often the master, though anyone might receive the reward for notifying officials. It did not matter whether a European mother was bound or free when considering the fate of her mixed newborn, as the provincial legislature ordered the "bastard child [to] be bound out as a servant by the said Church wardens untill he or she shall attaine the age of thirty yeares."[19]

Planters used the two institutions of provincial government and the Anglican Church in tandem to persecute European women and their mixed-heritage offspring. For example, in Lancaster County, Virginia, the court issued an extra five years of service to Catherine McCollins for having a "mulatoe Child born of her body begotten by a negroe." Catherine was a servant to Elias Edmonds, so he received, or kept for himself, one-third of the fee for turning her in to local administrators, then paid the Crown and church parish the other two-thirds for her extra time. The court required that the "mulatoe Child ... be bound by the s[ai]d Churchwardens until it arrive to ye age of thirty yeares." Hence Elias also benefited from the child's labor over the next three decades. These thirty-year sentences, aimed at deterring intermixture and profiting the master, drastically affected the lives of mixed-heritage people and their families.[20]

Virginia and Maryland lawmakers borrowed from one another and experimented with multiple regulations when crafting punitive actions against European women and their children of blended ancestry. Maryland's law of 1664 was the first to extend thirty years of servitude to certain mixed-heritage children, though it was repealed in 1681. Ten years later Virginia officials assigned the same number of years to Mulattoes born to "white women." Both provinces were unique among other American colonies in their prolonged efforts to enact strict penalties against children of both African and European lineage, but why the trial and error? Chesapeake officials went through this repetitive legislative process because each generation of colonists found it difficult to achieve what the former could not: preventing interracial mixture and subjecting all children of mixed ancestry to lifelong bondage without enslaving their European mothers.[21]

As in previous decades, local cases involving European women influenced the decision-making of colonial legislators in the 1690s. On January 12, 1692, Margaret Ruston, a servant woman belonging to Edward Pye, appeared in the Charles County court of Maryland and admitted "shee had a bastard Child." Margaret and the father of her child may have had the same master but came from divergent backgrounds; she was a European servant and he was a "negroe slave." After Margaret's confession, the court instructed the sheriff to take "Margarett Ruston into his Custody & Carry her to ye whipping post and there to strip her from ye waist upwards and on her bare back to give her twelve lashes." Anxiety, fear, anger, pain: many of these feelings pulsed through Margaret's body as authorities brought her to the "whipping post" and administered her sentence, which was typical for women convicted of bastardy at the time.[22]

A local planter, William Dent, had witnessed this type of corporal punishment before, and this time he watched the justices decide Margaret's case just before he brought an unrelated legal issue about one of his servants to the same county court. William had inherited large tracts of land, servants, and slaves from his father in Charles County. He was familiar with the racial intermixture that commonly occurred in his neighborhood and the Mulatto slaves who appeared on nearby plantations, if not also on his own. William also served on the Maryland General Assembly, and a few months after he watched Margaret receive her sentence, he served on a committee responsible for rewriting legislation "concerning Negroes and Slaves." In the spring of 1692, William worked with Daniel Clark, a colleague of his from Dorchester County. Together, they drafted a bill that addressed intermixture and children of blended heritage.[23]

Maryland's planter-legislators had complained for years of "Vexatious and unnecessary" lawsuits that stemmed from blended families and their children fighting their subjugated legal status. Laws from previous decades contradicted each other regarding the bondage of mixed-heritage children birthed by "white" women. Were these children legally enslaved like their fathers or free by the womb of their mothers? Masters, mixed families, and the children at the center of the debate often ended up in court to determine their legal status. Maryland's assembly tasked William and Daniel with straightening out the inconsistencies. In May 1692, the two men appeared before the governor and the other assembly members to recommend a new approach.[24]

While many of William and Daniel's fellow assemblymen agreed with their proposal, others found their revisions problematic and voiced concerns over seemingly harsh measures. William and Daniel suggested a hefty fine of 10,000 pounds of tobacco for those found guilty of conducting marriages between those of African and European descent. They also requested a similar fine for masters who either encouraged or allowed African slaves to marry "white Women" servants. To prevent these interracial unions, they further threatened the wealth of masters by proposing that the law free enslaved men who were permitted to marry "white Women." This would help ensure that slave owners would not let their African bondsmen and European bondswomen "intermarry."[25]

While not all of these suggestions appeared in the final statute, William Dent and Daniel Clark clearly argued why such legislation was needed: they devised the bill with "the design of preventing such Mungrell Marriages." For some time, the word "mongrel" stood as a pejorative term for mixture in the English language, and the architects of this bill openly conveyed their distaste for such unions. In the draft, William and Daniel urged their elite peers to require "all white Women that shall Marry to Negroe Men to be Servants during the Life of the Man whom they Marry." Assembly members asked whether they were willing to oppose the "Laws of England" and enslave "white" women. Some also questioned whether "any white Man or Woman that shall Begett or have Begotten a Bastard Child by a Negroe shall be Compelled to Serve Seven years only . . . [or] during Life." William and Daniel proceeded strategically when devising the legal language, specifically when suggesting perpetual bondage for "white Women" who married "Negroe men." They consciously avoided the harsh language of Maryland's previous legal code that enslaved European women and suggested not using "the word Slavery . . . in the Act . . . although it may hap[pi]ly Amount to Slavery in Effect." In other words, William and Daniel proposed to enslave "white Women" without calling it slavery.[26]

William and Daniel also wanted to create a division in status between freeborn mixed-heritage people and those of full African descent. The assembly reported that William and Daniel believed it was "reasonable to make a Distinction between them [Mulattoes] and Negroes, and not to Equalize them in point of Servitude." This is why the two men suggested a mandatory thirty-one years of servitude for the mixed-heritage "Bastard Children born of white or

**Free and bound statuses among those living in colonial Virginia and Maryland, early eighteenth century**

| | No Service (Freeborn) | 4–7 Years of Servitude Immigrant Transatlantic Voyage Indentures | Extra 5–7 Years of Servitude Free Mothers of "Mulatto" Children | Child Servitude until 18-21 Years Ages Vary for Females and Males | 30–31 Years of Servitude "Mulatto Bastards" | Life (Slavery) |
|---|---|---|---|---|---|---|
| "White" Female | ● | ● | ○ | ○ | — | — |
| "White" Male | ● | ● | — | ○ | — | — |
| "Indian" Female | ● | — | ○ | ○ | — | ○ |
| "Indian" Male | ● | — | — | ○ | — | ○ |
| "Mulatto" Female | ○ | — | ○ | ○ | ● | ● |
| "Mulatto" Male | ○ | — | — | ○ | ● | ● |
| "Negro" Female | — | — | — | — | — | ● |
| "Negro" Male | — | — | — | — | — | ● |

● Typical position
○ Possible position, depending on individual circumstances
— Rare position, never or in exceptional cases

*Sources*: Hening, SALVA, 3:86–88; Browne, AOM, 13:546–48.

*Note*: In addition to social custom, Virginia and Maryland authorities mandated these terms of service by the late seventeenth century and instituted them further in the eighteenth-century Tidewater Chesapeake. Note that mothers who had bastard children within servitude typically were subject to another one to two years of service. "Negroes," "Mulattoes," and "Indians" were enslaved according to the condition of their mothers. Mulattoes were the only group that regularly received thirty- or thirty-one-year contracts, depending on the status of a free mother. "Indians" here include those living inside the colonies, as most living outside the realm of the English provinces were free and not subject to English laws, though colonists brought some into the colonies as servants and slaves.

English Women." Under this proposal, William and Daniel implied leniency, because children of enslaved African fathers and free European mothers would not face slavery. At the same time, these children could not avoid extended servitude, for the assemblymen acknowledged that the parents were too poor "to Maintain them." In a room full of planter officials, suggesting that children of mixed descent serve their masters until thirty-one years of age—one year more than in Virginia—was a persuasive tactic. The assembly supported this part of the bill and passed it into law.[27]

As Virginia had done the year before, Maryland's assembly constructed legal incentives for European endogamy within a legal code that prescribed strict discipline for mixed-heritage children and their European mothers, who engaged in sexual relations with African men. When authorities passed the bill into law on May 26, 1692, they plainly stated their intentions: those who entered into interracial marriages "shall undergo the paines and penalties by this Law." Maryland's assembly was "willing" to accept the plan to punish children of mixed ancestry born to unwed European mothers by making them "serve to the Age of 31 years." Interestingly, they lowered the penalty on children born to married African men and European women to twenty-one years of servitude, similar to the length of time assigned to other European children born out of wedlock. The mixed-heritage offspring of enslaved African women inherited their mother's condition for life, the same as most Mulattoes throughout the colonies. However, officials had reservations about the "severity" of enslaving European women who married "negros or other Slaves" and rejected William and Daniel's suggestion to enslave "white Women." Colonial assemblies were both motivated by and limited in creating legislation based on what personally benefited them, what they believed was fair, what held under the "Laws of England," what would prevent excessive litigation, and what they believed would help structure a well-ordered colonial society.[28]

Maryland's legislation addressed the "inconveniencies" and "controversies" that children of blended ancestry brought up in provincial courts, but it did not solve every issue with their labor status nor did it solidify strict racial hypodescent. One of these "controversies" took place in St. Mary's County, where Thomas Courtney and his wife punished their "Malatto Girl" for repeatedly running away by cutting off her ears "close to her head" (see introduction). For "so barbarous a Cruelty," the same provincial court in 1692 "Manumitted Courtneys Mallatto Girle" and drew up an act to protect slaves who might be similarly abused by "unreasonable Masters." The decision came directly after the court passed the law assigning thirty-one years to mixed-heritage offspring, which left another legal loophole open for some mixed people to escape slavery. Although most Mulatto children were at a legal disadvantage compared to those who had two parents of European lineage, compared to those of full African descent, mixed children with European maternity retained clear advantages. In terms of legal status and socioracial hierarchy, many Mulattoes occupied a middle ground between their free "white" mothers and enslaved "Negro" fathers.[29]

Mulattoes' intermediate position between freedom and slavery resulted from mixed-heritage families who negotiated power with colonial elites. While most in the wealthy planter class favored slavery and extended servitude, people of blended ancestry and their families continually pushed provincial magistrates for liberty. Mixed families found places where they could use the law in their favor and their resistance influenced future legislation. By the late seventeenth century, Chesapeake officials had debated the status of mixed-heritage peoples on multiple occasions and carefully reorganized legal bondage for Mulattoes, leaving fewer avenues to freedom. Not all lawmakers sought to punish children of mixed ancestry for the actions of their parents, but the majority of Chesapeake magistrates eventually agreed with passing these mandates.[30]

As Chesapeake authorities moved forward with plans to prohibit intermixture by castigating interracial families, many parents were pained to learn their children would suffer in bondage. It was agonizing for parents to see courts place their children in service for thirty years or more, as they realized these lengthy terms far exceeded those of other servants. Unless a woman had multiple bastardy offenses, her sentence usually did not exceed a decade, and only convict laborers from Europe or slaves received that much time. Compared to punishments for people of full European lineage, thirty-plus-year sentences went far beyond other contracts and placed an exceptionally high burden on people of blended ancestry, who had committed no offense other than being born of racially mixed parentage.[31]

### PUNISHING "MALLATTO BASTARDS" AND MIXED-HERITAGE FAMILIES

For colonial Chesapeake officials, instituting legislation that prohibited interracial mixture and punished mixed-heritage children was a long and uneven process. Over the colonial period, Maryland and Virginia legislators struggled to enforce laws intended to stem intermixture and grappled with how to legally position mixed offspring. Disseminating and upholding provincial decrees was difficult, as administrators took months or years to implement—or sometimes never fully implemented—laws in outlying colonial areas, where European settlement was sparse. Counties near the provincial capitals of Jamestown and Annapolis might quickly receive copies of new legislation, but wider circulation into places farther away was often slow. People on the provincial fringes were commonly unfamiliar with legal codes years after colonial assemblies had passed certain mandates. Sometimes colonists willfully ignored new laws or purposely evaded them by moving beyond the reach of colonial authorities. Even within more settled counties, provincial statutes, especially against ethnoracial mixture, faced enforcement problems. Neighbors often had close personal ties and depended on each other for survival. Many times colonists chose not to turn in their peers to authorities, and some were involved in mixed relationships themselves.[32]

In some areas, local county and parish officials brought few European women up on charges of giving birth to a "mulatto bastard" and irregularly prosecuted offenders, but over time, more masters bound out children of mixed ancestry and their mothers throughout the Tidewater Chesapeake. In the late seventeenth and early eighteenth centuries, county courts began to regularly bind mixed children in servitude, which coincided with the growth of immigrant, slave, and native-born populations. The uptick in "mulatto bastard" prosecutions around this time also reflects the fact that both Virginia and Maryland reorganized efforts to enforce legal statutes against ethnoracial mixture and mixed-heritage people in the early 1690s.

The legal suits in the years that followed Virginia's and Maryland's early 1690s laws show that county courts haphazardly executed the legislative orders throughout the decade. In January 1693, Edward Pye brought his servant Margaret Ruston back to court in Charles County, Maryland. Like other masters, Edward sought compensation for the productive value lost during his servant's pregnancy. He requested that officials reconsider what she owed for "haveing a bastard Child in ye time of her Servitude," even though she had already received twelve lashes the year before. It is possible that Edward returned Margaret to the court after he learned of William Dent's recent legislative accomplishments with the general assembly. After all, William was the assemblyman from Charles County, and Edward hoped he could profit from the new law that added seven years to the labor contracts of "white" female servants who had bastard children with "Negro" men. This time, the county court recorded that it was uncertain about how to handle this case because "the Child of Margaret Ruston is a Molatto." Fortunately for Margaret, the magistrates upheld their initial ruling of 800 pounds of tobacco in damages or an extra year of service, a term that was already assigned to her master. Regarding her child, she asked the county court "to have ye s[ai]d Child with her"; in other words, she wanted custody.[33]

Charles County justices were reticent about applying extra penalties to Margaret's mixed-heritage child because they were unaware of the specifics contained in the new legislation, and she had given birth before the law had gone into effect. Therefore, the court withheld judgment as to whether the

"Child ought to serve ye s[ai]d Edward Pye" or should remain free with the mother—Margaret had already satisfied her master for the damages he claimed to have incurred from her pregnancy. Court officials admitted they had to "advise themselves of & upon . . . ye old Lawes Concerning Negroes & Slaves" before they could make an informed legal decision. Although nothing about Margaret's case appears in the record for the court's next meeting in March, when the magistrates should have made their judgment, the justices did charge another woman, Anne Hasellwood, "for haveing a molattoe bastard child." It appears that the county magistrates chose not to pursue Margaret any further, since they could not apply recently updated statutes to her past offense. While authorities did not follow the newly enacted law for Margaret and her child, Anne Hasellwood's case, and others like hers, illustrates that officials were in the process of strengthening punitive legislation against mixed-heritage families.[34]

After the Maryland General Assembly reinforced penalties for Mulatto bastardy offenses in 1692, it took several years for some county courts to begin handing out harsher sentences. In 1694 and 1698, the Charles County court brought Mary Fountain up on charges of "haveing a Bastard Child." Court records initially did not reveal the ancestry of either child, but later documents identified the second as a "Mollatto" son named Thomas. Mary may have also given birth to another "mollatto Bastard Child" a few years later as a "servant woman." The omission of the "Mollatto" label was common in court records and shows irregularities in the application of early racial law. Many local officials still viewed bastardy as the greater offense.[35]

In January 1701, the Charles County court opened an extensive case into Mary Fountain's bastardy offenses and ordered her to show up at the next court session in March. She appeared as requested, confessed her guilt, and "submitted hirself to the Court" for punishment. The justices then commanded the sheriff "to take Fountain into his Custody and Carry hir to the whipping post and there to Strip hir from the waste upwards and to Give hir thirty nine Lashes well Laid on . . . her bare Back for hir offence to allmighty God." Thirty-nine lashes was a substantial penalty for such a crime, and it is probable that the justices were responding to the fact that Mary was a repeat offender. At the time, the court did not assign her mixed-heritage child Thomas to service, but a few years later, in 1704, authorities mandated that he would serve in her master's family until the boy reached "thirty One yeares of Age." The gap between his birth and the time the court assigned his indenture appears in other cases as well, perhaps indicating that masters only later learned that they could contract the mixed children of their servants to longer terms.[36]

While colonial magistrates were directly responsible for creating legislation that targeted families of mixed ancestry, local officials, who were familiar with the women they prosecuted, may have been reluctant to follow the full extent of provincial laws. When the Charles County court assigned Thomas Fountain to a thirty-one-year indenture in 1704, nine out of the ten county justices had already served on at least one of the courts where his mother, Mary, had been repeatedly brought up on charges of Mulatto bastardy. William Dent headed at least two of the court sessions, which indicates that these men were familiar with the histories of these ethnically blended families. Although county justices were hesitant to severely discipline Mary in the 1690s, with William leading the court in the 1700s, the same men imposed harsher penalties on her and her family. Individual justices who presided at the provincial level held greater influence and carried news of recently developed regulations back to the county seats. This transmission of information assisted broader systemic efforts to tighten legislation based on racial hypodescent.[37]

County courts in Virginia were similarly uninformed about current legislation surrounding families of blended heritage, or they purposely refused to apply new laws. Officials in Lancaster County, Virginia, admitted that they misplaced a colonial statute in 1702, after John Hutchins turned in his European servant woman Catherine Cassity "for haveing a Mulatoe Child." More than a decade after the law was issued, authorities did not have the ordinance readily available. Still, they were aware that Catherine's offense stipulated more severe discipline because she had given birth to a child out of wedlock to a man of African or Native American descent. The justices released Catherine, but she did not escape punishment indefinitely. The court instructed the county clerk to search for the legislation so that she could be "condemned accordingly" the following year.[38]

Catherine's case shows the disconnect between colonial laws issued in provincial capitals and their implementation at county levels. Additionally, a gap existed between racial ideologies held by elites and those on the ground among common folk. Catherine and her child's father had little problem engaging in a consensual sexual relationship even though they did not share the same ethnoracial background. When the Lancaster County court returned to Catherine's case after locating and reviewing the 1691 law, the justices assigned her an extra five years of service. Her master, John Hutchins, could keep Catherine and her child for those years or might later sell them to another freeholder, but he was responsible for initially paying the Crown and parish for the servant's labor where the "offense was Committed." These arrangements benefited all parties involved except for the servant and slave families who endured extended bondage.[39]

Although court justices assigned Catherine Cassity an extra five years of service to John Hutchins in May 1703, there is no record that her child was indentured at that meeting of the court, again, a common practice that has several plausible explanations. First, infant mortality was relatively high, and many children died before a court could legally contract them to a master, which is why some quietly disappear from the records. Second, officials sometimes ignored, misinterpreted, or were unaware of applicable legal statutes and assigned children to the free position of their mothers. Finally, it was typical for planters and officials, such as churchwardens, to customarily indenture children without official contracts. This meant that masters could hold children until thirty or thirty-one years of age or until eighteen or twenty-one, perhaps out of benevolence or a sense of justice. Surely, some mixed-heritage children escaped punitive thirty- or thirty-one-year legal indentures through informal agreements made between their parents and masters. In later decades, members of the Cassity family appear in Lancaster County records as free Mulattoes, suggesting that at least one of Catherine's children survived into adulthood and achieved freedom for posterity.[40]

To avoid the courts, Catherine Cassity, and possibly the father of her child, may have worked out a verbal agreement with John Hutchins to provide for her son or daughter, for some parents dealt personally with their masters to circumvent prolonged bondage for their mixed-heritage children. Mothers and fathers could arrange directly with their masters or other planters to secure freedom for a child. These parents made larger, often unrecorded, sacrifices to help their mixed offspring escape legal prosecution. Even when in court, officials did not always write down the terms of these indentures and sometimes left no record at all, making it difficult to assess the conditions of individual agreements and the number of mixed people who fell under these circumstances.

While it is difficult to determine the number of freeborn "mulatto bastard" children who lived under indentures, statistical analysis of surviving documents, coupled with what is known about lost records, makes it clear that Chesapeake colonists held thousands of mixed-heritage people in servitude over the colonial period. Legal papers show dozens of similar cases by the end of the seventeenth century, and colonial evidence leaps into the hundreds for cases in the eighteenth century, reaching over 1,000 individual cases in Virginia and Maryland. Despite the loss or destruction of county records over time, there are nearly 150 surviving documents of Mulattoes in Maryland held under thirty-one-year indentures out of around 250 servants described as having mixed ancestry. The overall totals were surely higher, as this data lacks information from several counties, including Calvert and St. Mary's, which contained significant numbers of mixed-heritage people. In neighboring Virginia, even though court orders from around twenty colonial counties have been burned or destroyed over the years, documents from over 800 individuals of mixed ancestry remain intact from the remaining thirty or so counties.[41]

Existing records reveal that local courts prosecuted the greatest number of blended-heritage families living in counties nearest the provincial capitals and that Virginia surpassed any other colony holding freeborn people of mixed lineage in bondage. While documentation is incomplete, the oldest Chesapeake counties, which established the earliest colonial societies, recorded the most cases. Virginia authorities along the James River, in southern Virginia, and on the Eastern Shore regularly assigned extra years of servitude and prolonged indentures to scores of European women and their "mulatto bastard" children. Again, legislators also allowed planters to customarily bind these children to prolonged thirty-plus-year service indentures. In Maryland, court justices bound hundreds of Mulattoes to thirty-one-year contracts, mainly in the counties between the Chesapeake and the Potomac River, not far from the capital in Annapolis. When accounting for counties with missing records, along with mixed children who were customarily indentured, it is apparent that children of blended ancestry made up a small number of total births yet comprised a significant portion of bastardy lawsuits: by modest estimates, at least 10 percent of the cases in the Tidewater Chesapeake.[42]

As Chesapeake county courts increasingly monitored intermixture, many colonists disagreed with legislators and administrators who attacked blended-heritage families, and many couples resisted legislation that attempted to prevent Africans from forming households with Europeans. In 1693, the grand jury in Elizabeth City, Virginia, tried Ann Wall, a European woman, "for keeping company with [a] Negroe man under pretense of marriage." The birth of a mixed-heritage child named John confirmed Ann's relationship to the "Negroe man," who possibly went by the name of Juan or Swann—which Ann and her children took as their surname. A few years later, Ann gave birth to a second child, Thomas, and over several months authorities pursued her for "haveing a Mallatto bastard Child borne & begotten of her body by a Negroe." By late 1695 the court demanded that Ann be taken into custody and punished as the "Law directs" for having "two Mallatto bastards." Officials sentenced Ann to serve her master, Peter Hobson of Norfolk County, an additional five years and moved further to prohibit Ann's interactions with her African partner.[43]

There is little doubt that the English Ann and her African husband Juan/Swann had voluntarily entered into an intimate relationship, for there were far more deterrents than motivations for Ann to join with a "Negroe man." Upon Ann's second bastardy conviction, the county justices further required that she leave the county after she finished her servitude. If Ann returned to see her de facto husband, the justices directed that she would be "banished" to the island of Barbados. This was an unusual ultimatum that rarely appears in the records yet shows that some Chesapeake authorities would go to great lengths to separate interracial families.[44]

Virginia's laws, and the people responsible for them, wreaked havoc upon families of blended ancestry and their mixed children by creating instability in their lives. Ann Wall Swann's impending exile would have estranged her not only from her husband, but also from her two boys, John and Thomas. Court magistrates also penalized the children for being identified as "two Mallatto bastards" and assigned the brothers to serve their mother's master according to law—for thirty years. John and Thomas Swann might have eventually been without their mother, and if another master held their father, the brothers could be denied regular contact with both their parents. These methods of castigation and destruction of exogamous relationships kept mixed-heritage families from easily unifying within the same household. These couples risked legal separation from each other and their children simply for operating as husband and wife. Ann, her husband Juan/Swann, and their children John and Thomas make up just one of countless families who were never able to freely live together under their own authority. In this way, colonial governments damaged relationships, strained kinship bonds, and created a harsh existence for mixed families in the Chesapeake.[45]

Mixed-heritage families routinely fought to remain together, and when their options were exhausted, some ran away from their masters with their children. Susanna Grimes, a European woman, "ffledd from ye hand of Justice" and her master, Colonel Hollyday, when she took her daughter Elizabeth out of Prince George's County, Maryland. Susanna probably knew that she and her "Malatta Childe" faced legal penalties, which induced the servant to run away sometime after giving birth to her baby girl on October 15, 1700. The mother decided she would not allow her child to grow up in bondage, so she took supplies and headed east, making a daring escape that took them through miles of fallow tobacco fields, cold waterways, and thick forests.[46]

In their attempts to gain freedom, Susanna and Elizabeth may have received help along the way or sought to remain undetected until she reached neighboring Anne Arundel County. Susanna perhaps believed she had traveled far enough from her master to set up a new life for herself and her mixed-heritage daughter. Unfortunately, her worst fears were realized in the summer of 1704, when suspicious authorities captured Susanna and her three-year-old child. Sheriffs passed the mother and daughter from one constable to another, carrying the captives back to servitude in Prince George's County. There "Susanna and Elizabeth [were] Sold according to [the] Act of Assembly"; the mother was assigned seven years of service and the daughter thirty-one. Because their owner, Colonel Hollyday, had since died, the court auctioned the pair off to a new master, who paid 2,800 pounds of tobacco to purchase their indentures. Parents such as Susanna agonized over the bondage they and their families faced, yet these women understood that their lowly social position promised little recourse in the courts. Susanna saw escape as the last best chance to keep her mixed-heritage daughter out of extended bondage, and in hopes of achieving greater independence for her family, she willfully took the risks that came with fleeing servitude.[47]

### INTERRACIAL MARRIAGE PETITIONS AND "WHO SHALL BE ACCOUNTED A MULATTO"

Even by the end of the seventeenth century, beliefs surrounding racial mixture in the Chesapeake were still in flux, as colonists held opposing views about whether the law should penalize families of blended heritage. In the spring of 1699, some European residents sent a "grievance" to the Virginia General Assembly from Surry County, across the James River from Jamestown and Williamsburg (which became Virginia's new capital that year). The residents continued to witness relationships between people of African, European, Native American, and mixed ancestry, which prompted them to request "that the Law for prevention of Marriages with Negroes Mulattoes and Indians be inforced and Strengthened by an Additionall Clause." Five years later, colonists from neighboring Prince George County, Virginia, mirrored this complaint, claiming that current "Laws now in force for prohibiting Negroes, Mulattoes, and Indians from marrying with any *English* hath not had its desired effect." Clearly, these colonists were upset that racial exogamy went unpunished on the southern shore of the James River. Although Virginia's assembly "rejected" both petitions and explained that laws in place "already Sufficiently provided" for impeding mixed marriages, it also promised to reconsider the requests when issuing future legislation. While the names of the petitioners are unknown, the plea likely originated with established colonists, not the poor or newly arrived immigrants.[48]

Exogamy continued regularly in the Tidewater Chesapeake because European colonists from immigrant, servant, and otherwise impoverished backgrounds usually cared less about ethnoracial differences than did their upper-class peers. It took time for newly arrived immigrants to imbibe the prejudices held by longtime European colonists living in the Americas. Newer European immigrants and servants were more likely than their American-born counterparts to openly engage in consensual relationships with "Negroes, Mulattoes, and Indians." This does not discount the fact that many European colonists, from the non-elite to the wealthier classes, feared that mixed-heritage children might gain equal rights as English Crown subjects and opposed extending full protections to people of African and Indigenous descent.[49]

Even as some English colonists protested against interracial mixture, others objected to laws that restricted Africans, Europeans, and Native Americans from intermarrying. Normally, lower-class people who mixed disapproved of these statutes, but they lacked the resources to file formal petitions. The same week that burgesses rejected the Surry County plea to strengthen opposition to exogamy, another group made the opposite request of the general assembly. In 1699, George Ivie, who came from a leading family in Norfolk, Virginia, petitioned the colonial government to repeal the law that punished interracial marriage. George was not alone, as a number of other community members joined him in denouncing legislation that prohibited "English people's marrying with Negroes, Indians and Mulattoes." This protest demonstrates that there were still multiple views across the class spectrum regarding racial mixture at the end of the seventeenth century.[50]

While not everyone felt disparagingly about intermixture in the colonial Chesapeake at the turn of the century, these views did not win major concessions from the general assemblies of Virginia or Maryland. Similar to their dismissal of other requests, the Virginia legislature did not respond to George Ivie's petition. While institutional power structures further cemented racial categories and prevented intermixture, there were always outliers who either engaged in mixed relationships or were loyal to neighbors and friends who challenged segregationist laws. These actions took place even as legal systems increased social stigma, informal policing, and racial polarization, which all helped restrict intimate relationships that crossed perceived socioracial boundaries.

When considering where the racial boundary between "black" and "white" fell during this period, officials literally drew the line at the Mulatto—a dividing line that always remained blurred. The larger of the two Chesapeake colonies became the first to officially define people of mixed ancestry, in October 1705. When deciding who could legally hold political office in the province, the Virginia General Assembly declared that no criminals and no "negro, mulatto, or Indian" could "bear any office, ecclesiasticall, civill, or military, or be in any place of public trust or power." This fell in line with previous legislation that equated non-"white" racial backgrounds with criminality. The assembly further used the legislation to clear up "all manner of doubts" as to "who shall be accounted a mulatto," stating "That the child of an Indian and the child, grand child, or great grand child of a negro shall be deemed, accounted, held and taken to be a mulatto." This meant that a person of mixed European and Indigenous ancestry could make his or her descendants "white" after a second round of intermixture with another European. However, families with one African ancestor would have to mix exclusively with other Europeans for at least four generations to clear the "Negro" from their legal bloodline. Colonial legislators rarely stated exactly who was a Mulatto, and when they did, the classification remained poorly defined because race itself is intangible. The Virginia

General Assembly designated who was and who was not a Mulatto in order to erase all "doubts" about racial marginality, but the law was not largely disseminated, or widely known, so social interpretations continued to allow for socio-racial flexibility.[51]

In the Virginia Mulatto clause, magistrates portrayed a distinct picture of the racial order: European, then Native American, and then African, with mixed people, or Mulattoes, falling in between. The general assembly outlined a racial scale when it portrayed "Indian" blood as more soluble than "Negro" blood, capable of losing its taint after only two generations of mixture with other Europeans yet requiring twice the amount of mixture for erasing the African. A person having three-fourths European descent and one-fourth Native American ancestry would be free to have all the rights of other Englishmen and Englishwomen within the colony, whereas one needed fifteen-sixteenths European lineage to overshadow one-sixteenth African heritage to receive all rights and privileges in the province. While this mandate reveals the absurdity of attempts to define mixed-race categories, it becomes clear that we cannot assume that the term "Mulatto" applied only to those of African and European descent, as the first legal definition also included people of Native American ancestry.[52]

Virginia's 1705 law demonstrates how authorities stigmatized African blood and relied on stronger hypodescent ideology to place those having at least one African great-grandparent lower on the racial ladder. Europeans viewed blood running through the veins of Africans as potent yet soluble; the lineage could eventually be washed out through further intermixture with Europeans. Ironically, while many Europeans felt they belonged to the more superior race, they also believed that Africans' essence held sway over European blood through intermixture: "whites" were superior, but their "black" blood negatively dominated in Mulattoes. Thus, it took several generations of racial mixture with Europeans to remove the stain of blackness. This type of racial thinking reveals the relative fluidity of hypodescent during the colonial era. In many English provinces, including in the Chesapeake, society could accept people of remote African descent as "white." From this perspective, "Mulattoes" were merely a different type of "Indian" or "Negro" who could take a step closer to whiteness with each successive generation of mixture with "whites." What later became known as the one-drop rule did not yet exist in the colonial era, for people of remote African heritage could and were in fact deemed "white."[53]

While some European colonists racially positioned "Indians" and "Mulattoes" between "whites" and "Negroes," others wanted to equally debase Africans, Native Americans, and people of mixed ancestry. When colonists from Prince George County, Virginia, asked for stricter anti-intermarriage laws in 1704, they also proposed that "Mulattoes and Indians be Pr[o]hibited from keeping Christian Servants." Virginia's high court received this petition and noted that the request would "be considered when the Revisall of Laws comes under consideration." The following year, the House of Burgesses adopted this suggestion to its revised laws, further limiting the rights of "Mulattoes and Indians" along with those of "Negroes."[54]

Virginia's "act concerning Servants and Slaves" in 1705 constructed its most comprehensive slave code, setting the standard for generations to come in the Chesapeake and neighboring provinces. The general assembly condensed individual, fragmentary statutes from the latter part of the seventeenth century into an expansive doctrine that committed the colony to racial slavery, hypodescent, and ethnoracial hierarchy. English colonists farther south also passed comparable piecemeal legislation until they composed more comprehensive slave codes in Barbados (1661), Jamaica (1684), and South Carolina (1691). All of these provinces affirmed African slavery as the focus and future of their labor systems and cemented their status as slave societies. Although some added "Indians" and "Mulattoes" to subsequent statutes, none prohibited or penalized intermixture like the Chesapeake colonies. In 1705, Virginia's legal code went into great detail about people of mixed ancestry, listing "mulattoes and other slaves" in subjugated positions with "Negroes." Lawmakers pulled language directly from the 1691 statute restricting ethnoracial mixture and included a clause that sought "a further prevention of that abominable mixture and spurious issue [children], which hereafter may increase in this her majesty's colony and dominion." The law was essentially the same, except it now directed administrators to issue thirty-one-year instead of thirty-year indentures to mixed-heritage children born to free Christian "white" women.[55]

While the updated Virginia legislation again disciplined "white men and women" who intermarried with "negroes or mulattos," this time the assembly dropped "Indians" and reopened the door for European and Indigenous marriages. Interestingly, while officials allowed European intermixture with Native Americans, they did not want European colonists mixing further with people of blended ancestry, perhaps to prevent their descendants from eventually achieving or claiming racial whiteness. The general assembly justified the decision to punish "mulatto" and "white" unions by stating that the problem of intermarriage and "unlawful coition [sex]" would increase within the colony if legislators did not pass these regulations. As the elite planter class again marked racial mixture as undesirable, they revealed that fears of continued European intermixture with people of blended heritage prompted them to tighten racial hypodescent under the law.[56]

## "BORN FREE OF THE BODY OF A WHITE WOMAN" — GETTING FREE FROM SERVITUDE

Seeking their freedom, mixed-heritage people went to Chesapeake courts in the 1690s and early 1700s to face powerful masters who wielded the law, and the most successful plaintiffs had one thing in common: a European mother who proved free maternal ancestry. Sarah was a "Molotto Servant" in Virginia, who sued her master, Thomas Harwood, for release from her labor contract in 1694. Like other free Mulattoes, Sarah was the "Daughter of an Englishwoman," and she came before the York County court "alledging herself to have [already] Served to ye age of twenty one years." Sarah stated that she was born around 1673, likely to a single mother out of wedlock. Authorities contracted her to Thomas until her twenty-first birthday, just as they had done with other children born to poor European women. The law promised Sarah eventual freedom through her mother's English ancestry, yet her father's African or Indigenous heritage classified her as a "Molotto." Like many masters, Thomas probably attempted to take advantage of Sarah's socioracial background to hold her in bondage past the term of her indenture.[57]

Early 1690s legislation that extended the contracts of Mulattoes may have instilled a sense of urgency in Sarah to remove herself from servitude. Even though these laws were not supposed to operate ex post facto, this did not stop dishonest masters from trying to hold mixed-heritage people longer than their legal terms of indenture. Unfortunately, Sarah was unable to provide evidence of her age, which left her vulnerable to further service. While county officials might reject Sarah's request or decide her plea was premature, the young woman may have simply wanted to guarantee her forthcoming freedom. Even if Sarah and her lawyer lost her suit, they at least established her free birth in the county court record. This ensured her eventual release from bondage before Virginia officials might further erode the rights of all Mulattoes.[58]

People of mixed heritage often lived in uncertainty while in servitude, specifically in the Chesapeake, where statutes changed every decade. Could the next wave of legislation wipe out their tenuous freedom? This was the case for Lewis Mingo, who in August 1713 asserted that Henry Wharton was holding him past his indenture term in Charles County, Maryland. Lewis, whose court records refer to him as both "Negro" and "Mulatto," argued that his "mother was a white woman" and that he had served past the thirty years required of Mulattoes indentured under Maryland law. His attorneys convinced the justices of the same, and Lewis won his case.[59]

Nevertheless, Henry Wharton appealed the county court's decision, basing his claim on a legal technicality dating to the previous century. Henry and his lawyers argued before the provincial justices in Annapolis that Lewis was "a slave by virtue of an Act of Assembly in force when he was borne," which passed slavery through the paternal line. This referred to Maryland's 1664 law that enslaved children by the status of their African fathers, regardless of whether they had freeborn mothers. Henry asked the provincial court to overturn the lower court's decision. His lawyer insisted that since Lewis's parents were "lawfully married according to the rights and ceremonies of the Church of England," he should have legally been a slave like his father.[60]

Lewis retained two lawyers to defend his freedom in Maryland's highest court. His legal counsel asked the magistrates to reaffirm the lower court's judgment, but after deliberation, Maryland's justices "Reversed, annulled, and altogether held for none" the original ruling, overturning his initial victory. The justices instructed Lewis to return to Henry. The inability of Lewis and his legal team to counter the appeal served a mighty blow to his psyche. The colonial system clearly shaped the trajectory of Lewis's life: he served over three decades as a servant, became free for several months, and was then ordered back into lifelong bondage.[61]

Most surviving freedom lawsuits brought by Mulattoes around the turn of century are from the Tidewater Chesapeake, and those who secured liberty figured out how to navigate a legal system that the colonial elite designed to operate against them. In Virginia, William Lloyd, and later his son Thomas, held the "Mulatto Woman" Ann Redman in bondage. In October of 1697, Ann made a complaint in the Richmond County court that Thomas illegally held her as a slave even though she was "born free of the Body of a White woman Servant Named Jane Redman." As the daughter of a "White woman," Ann should have been indentured only until she was eighteen or twenty-one years old, but she filed her complaint at age twenty-seven, claiming that her freedom was long overdue. In her petition, Ann associated with her maternal ancestry, noting that her mother was an "English Woman" and a "Reputed Christian." This was a tactical move that attempted to link Ann to English rights of free birth through the Christian faith. Nowhere did she or her lawyer mention the presumed African or Native American heritage of her father, for it might have compromised her case. The strategy worked, and the court found in Ann's favor and declared that she "be free and Clear from the Service of the said Thomas Lloyd."[62]

Why did it take Ann more than five years after her indenture expired to bring her case to court? First, not all free Mulattoes were aware of the laws that made them free. Some may have believed they had to legally serve for a longer period of time. Still, many knew their family's origins and were well aware of when they should legally become independent. Oftentimes those born of free mothers lacked the resources to take their masters to court when held past their indenture term. They required money and social connections to secure legal representation. Also, mixed-heritage people were required to have proof of their age and free birth before they could gain liberty through the courts. Even then, people of mixed ancestry who could verify free European maternity did not always have a sure path to freedom. The power dynamic always tilted in favor of the master class, which had written colonial laws with the design to keep people under the yoke of bondage. Even with the law on her side, it was not easy for a "Mulatto Woman" to overcome this power differential and win a case against her European master.[63]

Mulattoes who reached the age to qualify for freedom did not always have their European mothers present to speak for them in court, and although these mixed-heritage people held a freeborn legal distinction, planters could easily retain them in bondage or move them as chattel to another owner. This may have been the case with Edward Buss in Westmoreland County, Virginia, when he petitioned the court "for his freedome" in 1702. Unsure of his labor status, court officials identified Edward as a "Mulatto Serv[an]t or slave" — terms that were often used interchangeably. At the September court, Edward alleged that "hee was born of an English or white woman [and] had liberty." Nonetheless, the court found "no Sufficient evidence" to prove the claim and required him to "return home to his said Master." At least for the time being, Edward remained bound, though he was determined to continue his pursuit of freedom. Although Ann Redman's and Edward Buss's lawsuits had opposite outcomes, they represented an obvious pattern: it was becoming more difficult for mixed-heritage servants and slaves to secure freedom by the early eighteenth century.[64]

While court cases do not record what these individuals felt when they heard the justices' decisions, we can imagine various responses from those who received news that dictated their future. Ann may have gone through a period of shock or disbelief that she had defeated her master in court. Edward may have known his legal suit was a long shot at liberty, but he may have also been surprised that he lost his case. At the commencement of long, difficult journeys out of bondage, it is likely that many seeking their freedom could not hold back tearful reactions. We do not know exactly when tears came, but they surely represented immense joys and years of bottled-up frustrations.

The time and effort it took people of mixed heritage to bring their freedom suits to court demonstrate that it was an arduous process. Mulattoes had a greater chance of winning independence than most slaves, but their liberty was not guaranteed. Those in bonds were typically poor, and most resided on isolated plantations far away from county and provincial courts. Servants and slaves had to muster great emotional strength when taking a master to court, since they could face retribution in the form of physical, psychological, or sexual abuse. The legal process was slow, and if they lost their case, they had to remain with their master. People living in captivity had to weigh the risks involved in securing legal representation and gathering evidence. This usually included securing witness testimony, since it was particularly difficult for mixed-heritage people to furnish tangible proof of their freedom. Family members knew the details of former agreements, but they often did not have copies of the contracts, which officials drew up during infancy or in early adolescence, if they did so at all. Even if churchwardens or masters recorded dates of birth or indentures, they held the documents and could easily destroy or manufacture them. Again, Mulatto indentures lasted longer than any other labor contract in the colonial period, making these servants especially susceptible to lifelong bondage. Considering the many obstacles blocking freedom, it was easy for planters to keep mixed-heritage servants past the designated time stipulated under the law.[65]

Colonial officials did not intend for the legal system to benefit everyone equally, but this did not stop people of blended ancestry from repeated attempts to gain equality. Even though the Mulatto Edward Buss failed in his first lawsuit, he refused to relinquish his dream of one day becoming a freeman. Edward continued his efforts to piece together a case for his liberty, and after several years he achieved this goal. When he finally became a freeholder, like others, he farmed his own corn and tobacco in Westmoreland County. Even though some colonists still mistreated him, Edward probably decided to remain in the area because of strong ties with nearby friends and family. Despite his past as a slave, he went on to effectively sue other men in the same county court that had once ruled against his freedom. Edward overcame greater obstacles than most on his journey to becoming a small planter in colonial Virginia during a time when it was more difficult for others of mixed heritage to achieve similar success in the Tidewater counties.[66]

Into the eighteenth century, European colonists increasingly policed racial intermixture and mixed people in the Chesapeake because it could expand their and their neighbors' wealth. This was the case for the colonists who benefited from pursuing Elizabeth Taylor for "Bastardizing" in Prince George's County, Maryland. In 1711, Elizabeth, a European woman, confessed that "Negro George" was the father of her "Mallatto Girle called Sarah"—one of at least three mixed-heritage children of hers. The court gave Elizabeth one year of additional service under Thomas Wainwright, her and George's master.[67]

A few years earlier, Elizabeth had given birth to another baby girl, Mary, but the courts treated the two sisters differently. Mary had a European father, so the court contracted the girl only until age sixteen, indicating one of the privileges held by those identified as "white." In contrast, the same county court assigned Mary's mixed-heritage sister Sarah to a thirty-one-year indenture under James Gibbs, which split the family members between masters. By 1714 Elizabeth ended up in the same household as her second "Mallotto Child," albeit under a seven-year contract to a different master, William Marshall. A friend financially assisted William by putting up 3,400 pounds of tobacco for the purchase of Elizabeth's and her child's indentures. In this manner, European men worked together to bind out children of mixed ancestry.[68]

Elizabeth exercised what autonomy she had by choosing her own sexual partners, but operating outside the boundaries of Christian doctrine and colonial law brought punishments that tore her family apart. Multiple penalties did not stop Elizabeth from having yet another "Mallato Bastard"—a boy whom William Marshall kept with her other child. Even though some siblings were kept together, there was little guarantee that their mother would be with them beyond adolescence. Elizabeth moved several times between masters, and they could sell her indenture to another owner at any time. William already held two of her children, each to thirty-one-year contracts, and he was under no obligation to purchase the woman after her contract expired. The future for these blended families was volatile and uncertain. Where would Elizabeth go after she had served out her time? Would she be forced to leave her young ones behind when she embarked upon a life of freedom or continue working for her former master so that she could remain close to her children? Authorities often controlled where family members would go, but sometimes these impoverished mothers had to make these agonizing decisions with little choice.[69]

While the indenture system concerning "Mallatto bastards" was not formally slavery, it operated in much the same way by repeatedly binding women and their children to years of involuntary service. George and Elizabeth Taylor may have tried to keep their young children together, but they were incapable of removing themselves from bondage. Parents in this situation worried that they would not live long enough to ensure that their children attained freedom from extensive thirty-plus-year indentures. Life expectancy in the early eighteenth century had increased over the previous century, yet it was relatively low for the laboring classes. Those doing heavy physical labor might expect to live past forty years and even into their fifties or beyond, but for people of blended ancestry, this still meant they would spend the better part of their lives in bondage under servitude.[70]

Couples in blended families, such as George and Elizabeth Taylor's, perhaps held an optimistic view, hoping their children and posterity might one day escape bondage, but they also may have realized their sons and daughters had little power to defend against prolonged service. Some parents may have been relieved to know that the law did not declare their mixed-heritage offspring slaves, but they also knew that the intersections of race and gender worked against their daughters in servitude. Enslaved African mothers knew that, regardless of the father's background, their children had little chance of achieving free status. African men may have sought out free female partners, hoping that the mother's freedom would pass on to her children. Free European and mixed-heritage servant mothers held advantages over the enslaved.[71]

Sometimes European mothers went to court on behalf of their mixed children to reduce their offspring's servitude or to keep them from falling into slavery. In the summer of 1703, twenty-three-year-old Jonathan Glover brought a legal suit "about his freedom" against his master, Samuel Luckett of Charles County, Maryland. Although his father was presumably of African or Indigenous ancestry, Jonathan was not a slave. Sometime after his birth in February of 1680, he had been indentured to Samuel and had since been held under this contract as a servant. Sarah Smith, Jonathan's English mother, gave testimony about the birth of her son, whom court records listed as a "Mollatto." With the help of his mother's testimony, Maryland officials "Confirmed" Jonathan's freedom on August 10, 1703. For individuals of mixed heritage with ties to European lineage, having a "white" mother who could legally speak in the courts on your behalf was a vital asset. If Sarah Smith had been a woman of African or Native American descent, her right to speak in court may have been limited. If she had been a slave, her son's legal status would have followed her condition and Jonathan would have been enslaved for life.[72]

The intersecting vectors of race, class, and gender determined social mobility for people of mixed ancestry in the English colonies because the labor status held by one's parents directed one's life trajectory. Not all people recognized as Mulatto were considered the same, as the lives of those with a European father often differed greatly from those having a European mother. Depending on the mother's labor status at the time of birth, a mixed-heritage person might be deemed fully free, bound as a servant for a period of time, or tied to slavery for life. As in Jonathan Glover's case, a maternal tie to whiteness literally meant the difference between bondage and freedom. Even in the eighteenth-century Chesapeake, English authorities allowed certain Mulattoes to benefit from European ties to liberty, while other people of mixed heritage were pushed toward the common slave status of their African parentage. This situational and fluctuating form of hypodescent appears in other English provinces, Latin America, and European colonies throughout the Atlantic world.

Chesapeake authorities maintained profits and power in plantation economies by preying on people who were legally vulnerable in colonial society: Africans, Native Americans, poor Europeans, women of all backgrounds, and people of mixed ancestry. Individuals who belonged to more than one of these groups—based on race, class, or gender—often experienced increased disadvantages. African and Indigenous women faced the most pervasive marginalization in colonial society, as "Negro" and "Indian" women consistently transferred servant and slave status to their offspring and further progeny. "White" women provided an escape point through which some people of mixed African or Native American descent could slip into freedom, which is why planter-legislators committed so heavily to exploiting generations of mixed-heritage people born to European servant women. Servant girls and young women of mixed ancestry were also among the most susceptible to indenture laws, which resulted in a cycle of multigenerational servitude for blended families in the Chesapeake.[73]

Although mothers of blended heritage had little authority in servitude, they strategically used the modicum of power they had in attempts to ensure their children would eventually be free. Here the Banks family of Virginia provides a solid multigenerational example. In the summer of 1683, the York County court sentenced Elizabeth Banks, a European servant, to thirty-nine lashes "for fornication & Bastardy w[i]th a negroe slave." The justices also mandated that she "serve her said Master," James Goodwin, extra time for the offense. Elizabeth's mixed-heritage daughter Mary went on to serve the Goodwin family like her mother before her, probably until eighteen or twenty-one years of age, which was customary for most children at the time of her birth. When Mary appeared at the York County court in 1702, officials described her as a "Mallatto & Servant to Martin Goodwin," and although she was free, the young woman was there to "bind over her Daughter Hanah Banks a Mallato."[74]

While Mary appeared before the county justices in a subordinate position, her free status gave her more influence than African slaves and most other mixed-heritage servants had. Her familiarity with the Goodwin family perhaps allowed her to secure special conditions in her daughter's indenture to Peter Goodwin. First, the contract assured that her daughter Hannah would receive only twenty-one years instead of a thirty-plus-year indenture. Second, Hannah's contract stipulated a number of terms that her master guaranteed to uphold. The court "Ordered that he, the said Peter Goodwin, See the Child Baptized into ye Christian faith." Peter also had "to teach or Cause to be taught ... ye Lords Prayer & the tenne Comandments" to the young girl. Finally, the court "further Ordered" Peter "to pay his Said Servant Hanah Banks three Barrils of Indian Corne and Cloathing according to Law" upon her release. While masters usually had to pay standard "corn and clothes" to servants at the end of their term as part of their "freedom dues," indentures rarely stated such explicit provisions for children of mixed descent. Did the Banks family suffer like others of mixed ancestry under servitude, or did these women use their European lineage and years of dedicated service to negotiate the system with the Goodwins?[75]

Hannah Banks was a second-generation "Mallato" who had an indenture that resembled other European children's, which obligated her master to rear her in what most colonists considered a respectable and virtuous Christian life. Additionally, the promise of release at twenty-one years along with "Corne and

Cloathing" ensured that when the young woman came of age, she would start her adult life as a free woman with some material security. Perhaps most important was that this contract ensured the promise of freedom by a recording in a court of law. The county court documented her free status, which guaranteed Hannah's release from bondage in the future and might prevent her master or his heirs from breaking the agreement.[76]

The Banks family occupied a space in between freedom and slavery, and while many of them served the first part of their lives in bondage, they also kept themselves from falling into the perpetual servitude that many women of blended ancestry faced in the colonial Chesapeake. Virginia and Maryland courts contracted mixed-heritage women respectively to an additional five or seven years of service when they began having children in their late teens and twenties. Their daughters, who were indentured to thirty- or thirty-one-year indentures, often repeated the cycle because they could not marry while in servitude. Thus, Chesapeake legislation funneled women of mixed heritage and their families into multigenerational bondage, or de facto slavery.

This is why the Banks family was both ordinary and exceptional at the same time. They were like many poor European families who worked as servants over multiple generations in the colonial Chesapeake, and they were extraordinary because they were a blended family that somewhat successfully fought to maintain freedom. Authorities could have applied extensive indentures to Mary Banks and her daughter Hannah in 1702 or when Mary came back to the York County court in 1704. What the justices did then added further mystery to the family's story.[77]

A little over a year after she first appeared in the York County court, Mary Banks gave birth to another "Mallatto" daughter, whom she named after the baby's European grandmother, Elizabeth. Mary appeared in the county court in early 1704 when the infant was "about three or four Months Old" and "Acknowledged" that she had given birth to another "Bastard Child." Martin Goodwin paid her fine, which exempted her from the lash, so she agreed to serve him one year—far less than the five years assigned to European women who had a mixed-heritage child.[78]

Elizabeth's indenture, dated February 24, 1704, declared that Mary did "freely & voluntarily give" her daughter to Martin Goodwin "in Such Service or Employm[en]t," yet it is unclear how long "Martin Goodwin [and] his Heirs" would hold this younger daughter. Elizabeth's contract also specified that the Goodwins would "Employ" her "untill She be free According to the Law & Custom of ye Country for all Mollatto Bastards." At the time, Virginia law stated thirty years, although only fifteen months earlier, Elizabeth's sister Hannah received nearly a decade less, perhaps by a special arrangement. We know what the "Law" mandated, but the "Custom" that these families operated by in York County is less known. Also missing from the contract was any language about freedom dues or Martin's responsibility to bring Elizabeth up in the Christian faith, though the indenture did state that Martin "promised" to give the servant girl "Sufficient Dyet & Clothing." Perhaps Martin offered other verbal assurances, or Mary implicitly relied on the Goodwin family to protect her daughter. Nonetheless, they both signed the contract in their own way, Martin Goodwin with his full signature and Mary Banks with "her mark," an X that reflected her limited literacy. It is easy to see the hierarchy in the Banks and Goodwin families, yet few mixed-heritage women signed contracts to prove their children were free.[79]

Over the colonial period, legislation created in the 1690s and solidified in the following century captured thousands of Mulattoes in the Chesapeake in extended servitude or kept them enslaved their entire lives. By the early eighteenth century, county courts across Tidewater Virginia and Maryland were legally indenturing "Molatto Bastards" to thirty or thirty-one years, and masters were also holding Mulattoes past the lawful age, drawing up false indenture papers, and selling mixed-heritage servants as slaves. Mulatto boys and young men often had a gendered advantage because mixed-heritage women who gave birth fell into a type of serial servitude. To be sure, countless Europeans also dealt with cruel masters, oppressive indentures, and multigenerational service. However, Chesapeake officials typically assigned those of full European ancestry to eighteen or twenty-one years of service for the same bastardy offenses. While the success of European servants was by no means guaranteed, the privileges that came with whiteness often aided their upward social mobility in ways that the law denied to women of African, Indigenous, and mixed backgrounds. The legal institutions that Virginia and Maryland colonists developed were foundational for subjugating people of blended ethnoracial ancestry and influenced social perceptions of mixed peoples and their treatment for centuries.[80]

Into the eighteenth century, racial hypodescent strengthened for people of mixed ancestry in the Chesapeake, as European colonists, from yeomen to elite planters, associated Mulattoes with their African or Native American lineage. As Virginia and Maryland planters shifted to a greater reliance on African slave labor, especially in coastal areas, colonial society moved further against the freedoms of mixed-heritage families and their children. An established group of gentleman planters and assemblymen emerged who claimed power in the region by purchasing slaves in larger numbers than in decades past. They had a financial interest in keeping the descendants of all Africans in bondage, whether in slavery or in servitude. The consolidation of power among the emerging gentry inhibited the ability of smaller planters, European immigrants, mixed-heritage families, and servants and slaves to thrive in the Chesapeake. These poor classes with few opportunities sometimes responded by migrating or fleeing outside of Tidewater Virginia and Maryland and further inland into Indigenous territories or they moved into neighboring provinces and other colonial regions. All English colonies, from New England to the Caribbean, contained mixed-heritage peoples and various forms of hypodescent ideology, all of which evolved in nuanced ways.

# 3

# Mulattoes and Mustees in the Northern Colonies and Carolinas

South Carolina planter and assemblyman James Gilbertson had lived in the colony for more than thirty years when on August 16, 1720, he set up some notable provisions for one of his female slaves and her children. "My will is that my Molato Woman Ruth shall be free immediately after my Decease," James stated in his last will and testament. Ruth was likely the child of a European father and an enslaved mother of African or Native American ancestry. We are not sure of her connection to James beyond slave and master, though it would have been unlikely that he would openly acknowledge a familial relationship, if there were any. James left one-third of his estate—including his enslaved "Negroes and Indians"—to his wife, Mehitable, and the other two-thirds to Anne, their "only daughter." In addition to declaring Ruth's freedom upon his death, he stated that her "three female Children, Betty, Molly, and Keatty shall be free att the age of One and Twenty Yeares." He also gave Ruth a "feather Bed w[hi]ch the Indians did Cutt up"—perhaps a reference to an outside Indigenous raid on James's plantation or to an internal revolt led by his disgruntled Native American slaves. Last, he made provisions for Ruth to live on his "plantation during her natural life." If she was aware of her master's plan, Ruth may have had mixed emotions when James finally passed away. Perhaps she mourned her master's death or was overjoyed knowing that the event signaled emancipation for her and her children.[1]

Why James Gilbertson made special arrangements in his will for the "Molato Woman Ruth" is shrouded in mystery, though the two could have been connected in any number of ways. It is possible that they were directly related by blood. James may have been Ruth's father and thus the grandfather of her children, Betty, Molly, and Keatty. This legal manumission could also reveal a brother freeing his half sister and his three nieces. Or Ruth may have been more intimately connected to James through a sexual relationship, and he was fulfilling an agreement to free his concubine and their children. It is also possible that James had no direct connection to Ruth through kinship. He may have been carrying out a promise for another friend connected to the woman or was simply freeing the loyal slave who had served him faithfully over many years. All of these scenarios played out in countless stories of families across the colonial Americas and explain the motivations behind masters freeing mixed-heritage women and children in colonial Carolina.[2]

We do know that Ruth, a woman of mixed ancestry born around the turn of the century, carried some type of favor with her master and that a European man with great status in his community wielded power, even from the grave. James liberated this enslaved family by simply putting ink to paper, but would officials uphold the document? Ruth and her three girls waited months for authorities to approve James's will before they became free. During this time, they patiently watched other enslaved "Negroes and Indians" on the 1,000-acre plantation spread manure and prepare the fields, plant corn and irrigate rice, and bring in the harvest. A full year had passed when on Tuesday, January 9, 1722, magistrates in Charlestown's court ruled "That the Molatto Woman named Ruth have her living on the Plantation, according to the Will of the said Gilbertson." When Ruth heard the news, we can imagine that she rejoiced and embraced her daughters.[3]

Ruth, Betty, Molly, and Keatty were an exceptionally lucky enslaved family, for the other families of "Negroes and Indians" on the same plantation would remain confined to a life of drudgery. These slaves often intermixed with one another, but the stories of blended African and Indigenous people are less known. After James Gilbertson's death, day-to-day routines continued for those in bondage, but evidence shows that many slaves of mixed African and Native American ancestry also fought for their freedom and were just as eager to secure their liberty as "Molato" slaves such as Ruth.[4]

This chapter investigates the emergence of mixed-heritage people in English colonies outside of the Chesapeake and Caribbean from the late seventeenth century to the early eighteenth century. By then, English colonists had gained control and established several colonies in three northern regions: New England (Massachusetts, New Hampshire, Rhode Island, and Connecticut), near the Hudson River (New York and east New Jersey), and surrounding the Delaware River (Pennsylvania, Delaware, and west New Jersey). South of the Chesapeake, the English set up plantation systems in a place they called Carolina, which developed into two provinces: North Carolina and South Carolina. All English colonies passed discriminatory policies toward "Negroes," "Indians," and "Mulattoes," although they instituted laws and customs to varying degrees of severity. In each province, colonists developed diverse attitudes toward ethnoracial mixture and people of mixed ancestry. While overlapping mixed-race philosophies existed among neighboring English provinces, in the continental colonies and in the Caribbean, administrators in certain regions carried out strict legal forms of hypodescent, holding mixed-heritage children to laws similar to those governing their lower-caste African or Indigenous parents.[5]

The demographics of each colony and the culture of its inhabitants influenced which people intermixed and how authorities reacted to that mixture. Fueled by increased voluntary European immigration and the forced importation of African slaves, the Chesapeake had the greatest amount of ethnoracial mixture and the heaviest regulation of blended families. Though the northern regions had the lowest numbers, bound and free mixed-heritage people and their families worked on country farms and in urban settings such as Boston, Philadelphia, and New York City. South of the Chesapeake, a closer examination of the Carolinas reveals how plantation economies shaped wide-scale intermixture and the experiences of mixed people. Early North Carolina was an extension of Virginia, yet its colonial development was slow and mixture often went undetected by officials. Farther south, the Carolinian "Low Country"—so named because of the region's many rivers and estuaries that create hundreds of miles of coastal wetlands—emerged as an offshoot of colonial Barbados, with less direct immigration from Europe than the provinces farther north. The Lowcountry's main city, Charles Town (Charlestown), became the primary English port for African slave importation into North America and the main trade hub for thousands of Native American slaves trafficked through the continental southeast. Indigenous slavery existed in every English colony and resulted in significant intermixture with African peoples. In South Carolina, this group of blended heritage grew so large that it received its own name: Mustee.[6]

The archetypical mixed person in the English colonial empire appears to have been African and European, and while these Mulattoes are prominent in historical records, significant intermixture between Africans and Native Americans produced so-called Mustees throughout the British colonies. Colonial naming practices were not uniform, and people of blended African and Indigenous or European and Indigenous ancestry most often fell under the labels of "Mustee," "Mulatto," "half Indian," or "mixed blood." They lived in every colony, usually in some type of bondage, and often appeared in Indigenous communities as well. "Persons of Mixt Blood" were often born out of a shared sense of struggle with "Negroes" and "Indians" under colonial slavery, servitude, and subjugation. Bondage fueled mixture in all regions, from New England to the Caribbean. Colonists in Massachusetts were the first to enact a slave statute in the English colonies, intended to enslave Indigenous war captives as well as Africans. While bondage in northern settler societies with relatively fewer slaves contrasted with the slave societies of other regions, the trade in human captives brought intermixture everywhere.[7]

By the mid-1660s, Barbados, Virginia, and Maryland had all passed statutes that specified "Negro" slavery, and most colonies included "Indians" and "Mulattoes" in their slave codes by the early eighteenth century. While English colonies in the Chesapeake and Caribbean developed societies based on racial slavery over time, South Carolina incorporated African and Indigenous peoples into a slave society from its outset in the 1670s. By 1708, the province had an African majority and contained more enslaved Native Americans than any other English colony. South Carolina officials did not prevent these groups from intermingling and did little to prohibit ethnoracial mixture in the colonial period. By comparison, North Carolina sat on the outskirts of merchant centers and had fewer slaves and a proportionally higher European population. As North Carolina's slaveholdings grew, its colonists appropriated laws from Virginia that punished blended families and individuals.[8]

Even though economic and cultural differences emerged across various English colonial regions, societies in all areas embraced mixed-race ideologies under the framework of racial hypodescent — as European colonists from one province to the next perceived people of blended ancestry as a dishonorable group along with Africans and Native Americans. Negative portrayals of interracial mixture and mixed-heritage peoples expressed in one colony traveled with people between regions over land and sea. North Carolina exemplifies this diffusion most clearly, as its lawmakers in the eighteenth century adopted Virginia and Maryland's strict hypodescent ideology from the previous century. South Carolina resembled the Caribbean, and like in the northern provinces, colonists there never policed intermixture to the same extent as in the Chesapeake. Regardless of their location, people of blended heritage had to understand local variations in custom and law if they were going to secure freedom. No matter where they lived, people of mixed ancestry strove for independence from bondage and for greater autonomy.[9]

## "INDIANS, NEGROES, & MELATTOES" IN THE NORTHERN ENGLISH PROVINCES

The majority of mixed-heritage people lived in colonial slave societies that had large African populations, but some resided in places with far fewer slaves, such as the northern English colonies. Seaports and farmlands that surrounded cities north of the Chesapeake had significant ethnic and racial diversity, with English, Dutch, German, French, Swiss, African, and Native American populations. Even if on a smaller scale than on plantations of the Caribbean and in southern colonies, intermixture took place with regularity in the largest port cities of Philadelphia, New York City, Newport, and Boston. Notably, these cities were in northern provinces, where higher European populations and more equitable sex ratios generally limited ethnoracial mixture. In addition, prejudice and religious differences prevented widespread European liaisons with Africans and Indigenous people. Nevertheless, sexual intermingling took place with Native Americans outside of colonial settlements, most often between European fur traders in Indigenous-controlled regions to the west, which the English referred to as the "backcountry." Northern colonists never prohibited exogamy with Native Americans, though Christian conversion, marriage, and adherence to ecclesiastical law were required for permissible relationships. Native Americans also partnered with Africans, which was common beginning in the seventeenth-century. Though often unrecorded, the number of African and Indigenous relationships may have exceeded that of African and European liaisons and produced numerous people of "Negro" and "Indian" descent.[10]

In the years when Africans began trickling into the Chesapeake, the English were establishing colonies in what would become New England. In 1620, English religious separatists from the Anglican Church, known as Puritans, founded the Plymouth Colony on the lands of Algonquin-speaking peoples near the Massachusetts Bay. While Plymouth was the first successful English colony in the area, both before and after its establishment several other English colonies failed in the region. With the help of Wampanoags and other Native Americans, the Puritans overcame many hardships, and these religious refugees founded other settlements such as the Massachusetts Bay Colony. Ecclesiastical disagreements led to internal splits and spawned other colonies nearby such as Rhode Island and Connecticut. New Englanders tended to immigrate with whole families, which led to stable sex ratios and a self-sustaining population by the mid-seventeenth century. In the 1630s during the Great Migration of Puritans and other English into the region, disagreements with local Indigenous groups broke out into open conflict, which set the stage for legal slavery.[11]

Despite relatively peaceful negotiations between the English and Native Americans during their initial encounters, the expansion of New England led to conflict and bondage for Indigenous peoples in the Northeast. In the mid-1630s, the English and their Indigenous allies went to war against the Pequots, decimated their villages, and took hundreds of prisoners into their homes and sold others overseas. In order to legitimize the enslavement of Native American captives taken in "just warres," the Massachusetts Bay Colony became the first English province in America to create slave law in 1641. New Englanders were adept farmers, fishermen, and ship builders, and their seagoing vessels carried "Indian" captives to colonies throughout the Atlantic. Furthermore, New England's agricultural and merchant marine economy became immersed in intercontinental trade between Europe, Africa, and colonies throughout the

Americas, which included trade in African and Indigenous slaves, who were purchased largely by Caribbean planters. By the 1640s "negars" who went unsold in the Caribbean trickled into New England provinces on African slave-trading vessels. The Pequot War and King Philip's (Metacom's) War (1675–76) were high points in the "Indian" trade, with thousands of Native Americans taken captive and sold into servitude or lifelong bondage. By the end of the century, New England ships carried salted cod, cereal grains, rum, and bound captives to slave societies engaged in lucrative tobacco, sugar, and other crop production. English colonists north of the Chesapeake were not wholly dependent on slave labor themselves, but they relied on slavery and the trade surrounding its sustenance.[12]

While the English readily found marriageable European partners in New England, they occasionally engaged in sex with Africans and Native Americans, two groups who often joined with each other. In Salem, the Essex County court fined the "negar servant" Katherine for two cases of bastardy, the first in 1650. In the second case, three years later, an English servant, James Thomas, was named the father and ordered to pay eighteen pence a week to Katherine's master for child-rearing expenses. Nearly twenty years later in Massachusetts, "Indian" Jasper and "Negro" Joan gave birth to a mixed-heritage child, for which the Suffolk County court convicted them of fornication. The same year, in 1672, English servant Christopher Mason confessed to the same court that he had gotten "Negroe Bess with Childe," for which the justices gave both parents twenty lashes. Intermixture occurred regularly in Boston and surrounding towns such as Roxbury, where English servant Elizabeth Parker gave birth to a "Mollato" son, Silvanus Warro Jr., named after his enslaved African father. In Plymouth Colony, Hannah Bonny, a European woman, was "well whipt" after giving birth to a similar "bastard child" in 1685. The "Negro" father, Nimrod, was also "sentanced to be severely whipt" and had to "pay 18 *pence* p[e]r weeke" to Hannah "towards the maintainance of the s[ai]d child for a year." If Nimrod or his master could not pay the child support, the court ordered the "negro to be putt out to service . . . from time to time" so he could raise the money. These were normal penalties for crimes of fornication and bastardy, as authorities cared less about interracial mixture and more about religious piety. Still, a lack of punishment for intermixture did not mean social acceptance or the absence of racial animosity.[13]

Many Englishmen and Englishwomen in the northern colonies believed in African and Native American inferiority, looked down on ethnoracial mixture, and extended racial hypodescent into eighteenth-century laws meant to preserve their investments in bound laborers. In 1703 Massachusetts legislators made it difficult for masters to "set at liberty" their "mulatto and negro slaves" by mandating that slaveholders post expensive bonds to ensure freed people would not become a public nuisance. Many northern colonies copied this policy. Rhode Island officials monitored the province's sizable population of African slaves, some of whom were of mixed descent. These people sought independence, and officials noted in 1714 that "several Negro and Molatto Slaves, have Ran-away from their Masters and Mistresses." Runaways boarded ferries that took them to neighboring colonies and they freely passed through the countryside and towns by telling locals that they were carrying out the business of their masters. To prohibit this practice, magistrates issued a law that forbade boatmen from transporting any slave out of the colony and required traveling slaves to carry a pass written by his or her master. Free "Negro and Molatto" people may have also carried papers to ensure their safe passage while traveling in New England provinces.[14]

Lawmakers often grouped "Mulattoes" with "Negroes" and "Indians" throughout the English colonies, but northern provinces (societies with slaves) had fewer legal restrictions than slave societies, and many African, Indigenous, and mixed-heritage people were able to attain liberty. For instance, in 1703 a constable in Hartford, Connecticut, was instructed to arrest a "mallatta servant" named Abda, probably upon her master's request. However, another European man, Joseph Wadsworth, opposed the officer and protected the woman so that Abda remained free. Cases involving the freedom of Indigenous and African-descended people continued throughout the century. In 1739, a Mustee man named Caesar argued in Connecticut that "he ought not to be holden in Service as a Slave," because the English took his Indigenous mother, Betty, captive during King Philip's War. Legally, Betty should have been a servant and freed after ten years, which would make her son Caesar free, even if his father was an enslaved African. Masters typically used African ancestry to figuratively erase free Native American heritage. Even though Caesar's parents were married, his father's slavery did not pass on to him, and a local jury decided in favor of his independence based on his mother's free status. When compared with those in the Chesapeake, South Carolina, and the Caribbean, colonists in New England may have been more likely to free those in bondage, because slavery was not as integral to the labor system there. Other "Negro," "Indian," "Mulatto," and "Mustee" servants and slaves sued in colonial courts and also won their freedom in the provinces along the Hudson and Delaware Rivers.[15]

Like other English colonies, New York and New Jersey—while under Dutch rule in the seventeenth century—went through a period during which colonists practiced slavery customarily and some people of African descent moved freely within a protoracial society. People of mixed ancestry had visited the region before the Dutch founded New Netherland beside Algonquin-speaking communities, near what became the Hudson River and surrounding islands. In 1613, the Mulatto (*malaet*) Juan Rodriguez traveled with the Dutch and traded metal weapons with local Indigenous people before New Netherland was established as a colony in the following decade. He eventually married in with local Rockaways, among whom he had several children, and may have been the first non-Indigenous inhabitant of Manhattan.[16]

Like other Europeans, the Dutch also accepted the idea of blood "intermingling" in the bodies of mixed-heritage people. Around the mid-seventeenth century, Dutchman Jacob Steendam expressed this view in a poem written to his son of blended ancestry:

> Since two bloods course within your veins,
> Both Ham's and Japhet's intermingling;
> One race forever doomed to serve,
> The other bearing freedom's likeness.

Jacob came to New Netherland after living on the west coast of Africa, referred to as Guinea, where he had intimate contact with the local people. The Dutch were prominent in the transatlantic slave trade at the time and intermixed with African and mixed-heritage women in Africa, on Atlantic ships, and in the American colonies. Mulatto men and women on the Guinea coast often acted as intermediaries in trade, and these cultural brokers had more power on the African continent than in the Americas. The ability to negotiate between multiple cultural worlds also appeared in the American colonies, as people like Juan Rodriquez learned Algonquin languages and translated for the Dutch so that they could trade with Native Americans.[17]

The plantation labor for slaves in Dutch colonies in the Caribbean and Brazil (before the Portuguese annexed it in 1654) was generally harsher than in New Netherland; this pattern also applied to the Delaware River valley, where a variety of European ethnic groups lived with a small number of Africans. In these early North American colonies, slavery and servitude were at times indistinguishable, though nonetheless harsh, and people of African descent could sue Europeans in court. Around midcentury, the free Mulatto Anthony Jansen was a landowner and merchant in New Netherland. He and his Dutch wife, Grietse Reyniers, were involved in several legal suits, though it is not clear whether Anthony's race provided impetus for these disputes. In 1654, Anthony won two months' wages in a case against William Strengwits, a European man. Around this time, the Dutch renewed efforts to expand into the Delaware Valley, where they competed with Scandinavian settlements. Beginning in 1638, Swedes and Finns set up several forts in the Delaware Valley, where they traded with Native Americans and expanded on Indigenous lands. These colonists also brought a small number of Africans into their communities until the Dutch overtook them in 1655. A medley of people continued to intermix after the English displaced Dutch power in 1664. New Netherland became New York and

New Jersey, and over the next several decades the colonies of Pennsylvania and Delaware also took form under English rule.[18]

Like the other northern colonies, Pennsylvania and Delaware legalized slavery but diverged from New York and New Jersey by eschewing large slave importation. Colonial leaders in Pennsylvania favored European labor and aggressively sought to limit slaveholding in the colony by placing heavy taxes on slave imports, though Africans had resided in the Delaware Valley since the mid-seventeenth century. People of mixed heritage were living and working in the region before William Penn and the Society of Friends (Quakers) came to the area and founded Pennsylvania in the early 1680s. Indigenous and African followers of the Protestant faith could marry with Europeans, and while exogamy was not frequent, it did occur. In 1677, a colonial court held in Upland on the Delaware River recorded a "molato woooman Called Swart anna" in a fornication case with Richard Ducket, a European servant. Their child proved the crime, and although Richard claimed he had the "Intention to marry" the swarthy-complected Anna, the law forbade him from doing so while still in servitude. When Richard promised to take care of his mixed-heritage child "as soon [as] he [was] free," the court absolved the father of his "offence." Richard's remorse and his master's approval helped earn the pardon. If Anna wanted to marry the father of her child after his service ended, she was legally able to do so, and it appears that their child would have been free. Outside of the Chesapeake, lax laws regarding interracial marriage were characteristic of most English colonies at the time.[19]

While slavery grew in all northern colonies and the restrictions placed on slaves increased in the eighteenth century, religious faith in some areas may have fostered greater access to liberty for some slaves, including those of mixed heritage. In September 1703, the Mulatto Antonio Garcia sued in the provincial court of Pennsylvania for his freedom. English privateers had captured the "Spanish vessel" he traveled on and made him a slave. His captors first carried him to Barbados and then Jamaica before bringing him to Philadelphia. "Protesting that he was born free, of free parents, had ever lived so, and could not be now made a slave by his capture," Antonio asked the council in Philadelphia to consider him a "prisoner of war." The justices ordered him to return with sufficient evidence of these facts. Several months later, he presented the court with an affidavit from a witness who attested to his liberty, "with many other arguments for his being a freeman & a Christian." His captors, who claimed the "Mulatto for [a] Slave," could offer "nothing to the Board" in response, so the magistrates declared Antonio a freeman. While there were certainly other "Negroes" who found routes to independence during this time, it would have been more difficult for them to claim "free parents" as the Mulatto Antonio did. By this time, laws stated that Christianity did not grant freedom to enslaved

Africans and Native Americans. Still, the culture and custom of the region was also important, for if Antonio had remained in the English Caribbean or had gone to a colonial slave society in North America, his fate might have been much bleaker.[20]

Mixed-heritage people who sued for freedom in eighteenth-century Pennsylvania or New England may have had a greater chance of success than someone doing the same in other English colonies, because of the role religion played in these societies. William Penn Jr. and other prominent Quakers made up the majority of justices who sat on the provincial council that released Antonio Garcia. While most Friends in the Delaware Valley did not call for an end to slavery until later in the century, their pacifist leanings mitigated the harshness of the institution in Pennsylvania, northern Delaware, and western New Jersey. The Quakers' faith, like that of some Puritans in New England, appears to have created a social climate that was more accepting of liberty for those who had been illegally enslaved. In 1700, a freedom petition of "a Negro and his wife, who were unjustly held in Bondage," encouraged Puritan judge Samuel Sewall of Massachusetts to write one of the first antislavery pamphlets arguing against African slavery, *The Selling of Joseph*. Samuel's Puritan sensibilities guided his thinking and also that of some of his contemporaries in New England. Colonists did not organize a movement to abolish slavery, but some people of religious faith in the northern provinces argued that slaves should be treated with humanity. These sentiments reflected regional views on slavery and perhaps also on interracial mixture.[21]

North of the Chesapeake, the English did not heavily police intermixture, though they still carried ideas of racial hypodescent. In Samuel Sewall's antislavery tract, he argued that Africans did not belong in Massachusetts because "there is such a disparity in their Conditions, Color & Hair, that they can never embody with us, and grow up into orderly Families, to the Peopling of the Land." While Samuel believed that all people had an "equal Right unto Liberty" because "God . . . hath made of One Blood, all Nations of Men" (Acts 17:26), he did not take into consideration African intermixture with Europeans, writing that Africans "remain in our Body Politick as a kind of extravasat Blood." According to Samuel, "Negro" blood would always exist outside of the "white" body, politically and perhaps physically. Five years later he opposed the colony's only anti-intermixture statute that, like in Virginia, attempted to prevent "Spurious and Mixt" offspring and stifle exogamy between Europeans and any "negro or molatto." Samuel successfully implored his colleagues to remove "Indians" from the bill, perhaps because Anglo-Indigenous mixture was somewhat common in New England. He also worried that such a law would "promote Murders and other Abominations," likely abortion or infanticide of mixed-heritage children.[22]

Social custom and relatively lower numbers of slaves in the northern colonies limited African-European mixture, but racial animosities grew as slave importation into the English colonies grew in the eighteenth century. During this time, New York and New Jersey approached becoming a slave society as African importation and slavery rose in both urban and surrounding rural areas. European immigration and reproduction kept the rate of Africans between 11 and 15 percent of New York City's population, though colonists responded by passing legal restraints on both slaves and free people of African and Indigenous descent. This may have forced some free families to relocate. Born to Swartinne, an African woman, and Johan de Vries, a Dutch sea captain, the mixed-heritage Jan de Vries was a teenager living in New Amsterdam, New Netherland, when the English took control of the colonial Dutch city. In 1679 Jan married a woman from Albany, Adriaentje Dircks, and the couple baptized four children in New York's Dutch Reformed Church in the 1680s. Possibly seeking to escape taxes or prejudice, they moved to Tappan, New Jersey, where they held lands that their descendants resided on well into the following century. In 1704, the New Jersey General Assembly responded to families like the de Vrieses by prohibiting any free "Negro, Indian or Mulatto" from owning "any House or Houses, Lands, Tenements or Hereditaments" in the colony. While royal authorities later overturned the policy, New York magistrates attempted to enact the same act and passed similar restrictions. Many of these laws came after the New York City slave insurrection of 1712, and officials passed another round of regulatory legislation after another revolt in 1741, where "whites" were implicated in plotting with dozens of "Negro" slaves to burn down the city.[23]

A spate of fires shook New York City in March and April of 1741, and the conspiracy trials that followed reveal colonial fears of unchecked mingling between Africans and Europeans. Two of the prime suspects implicated in the rebellion were an African slave, John Gwin (Caesar), and an Irish woman, Peggy Kerry. The couple "pretended to be married," and around age twenty-one, Peggy gave birth to "a Babe largely partaking of a motley Complexion." One court justice called Peggy "a Person of infamous Character, a notorious Prostitute, and also of the worst Sort, a Prostitute to Negroes." Regardless, John had an attachment to Peggy and their mixed child, as he paid for their room and board, perhaps with money and goods that he stole. Though he was implicated in the fires, a jury found him guilty of theft, for which he was hanged on May 11. Authorities gibbeted his body and then put it on display. Weeks later, Peggy was also found guilty, along with other "whites" who had supposedly conspired with "Negroes" in a plot by the downtrodden to overthrow the provincial government. On June 12, the hangman took Peggy's life a month after her partner's, and their child of blended ancestry became an orphan. Elite anxieties surrounded interracial alliances, intermingling, and mixed people, because mixture represented a disorderly society where the lower classes might join to overturn existing colonial hierarchies.[24]

Peggy Kerry and John Gwin's infant was not the only mixed-heritage orphan in the colonies, for social stigma and poverty drove other parents to abandon their Mulatto sons and daughters. The product of an interracial liaison, Lemuel Haynes was orphaned after his birth on July 18, 1753, in West Hartford, Connecticut. His father was an African man and his mother a "white woman," possibly a Scots immigrant servant or a woman from "respectable ancestry in New-England." Either way, Lemuel's mother was shamed by his birth and avoided him later in life. At five months old, he was bound out as a servant until age twenty-one to David Rose, who brought him to Massachusetts. His new family took care of him as one of their own; even neighbors said that Mrs. Rose "loved Lemuel more than her own children." The Rose family brought Lemuel up in the Christian church, and he eventually went on to become a minister who served predominantly "white" congregations. His success story is one of the few recorded for Mulattoes in colonial history, as most ended up in bondage.[25]

In the northern regions, people of mixed ancestry appeared in towns, larger cities, and rural areas surrounding metropolitan centers, where they served as domestics, worked as artisans, and labored in the fields. Over 40 percent of Pennsylvania's "Negro" and "Mulatto" slave population lived in Philadelphia, and in the second half of the century their numbers grew, especially as Quakers began advocating for abolition in following decades. Mixed people also resided in adjacent areas. In nearby Chester County, a "Mulatto slave" called Guy, also known as James, may have worked in a trade or labored like other northern slaves who raised corn, wheat, and other grains. This work might not have been as physically demanding as on tobacco, rice, or sugar plantations, but masters still subjected enslaved men and women to the same punishments and humiliations. Like slaves in other regions, James also sought freedom and left his master, and his journeys took him through Pennsylvania, Delaware, and Maryland. James also spent time in several jails, including in Philadelphia around 1755–56. There he may have run into a "Mulatto Fellow" named Timothy Jeffries, a freeman whom authorities had locked up around the same time for stealing ten yards of fabric. Whether Timothy lived in Philadelphia or was just passing through is unknown, but he was put to work in the city after authorities sold him as a convict laborer. Another "mullatto servant," Sarah, performed "all sorts of Housework" for a New York City merchant. Her master called Sarah "a handy Wench" and noted that she "speaks good English and some Dutch." These stories were typical for urban servants and slaves, who regularly served in the homes and workshops of middling and upper-class Europeans.[26]

In the northern colonies, both slaves and free people of African, Indigenous, and mixed heritage met discrimination in their communities and had to strive to overcome negative stereotypes regarding their character. When discussing Spanish privateers and pirates attacking English vessels on the Delaware River in 1748, Pennsylvania governor Anthony Palmer argued that the colonists should resist "the Insults of so despicable an Enemy—Crews of Negroes, Mulattoes, & the very Dregs of Mankind." English officials portrayed these groups as perpetual outsiders in the colonies and leaned on notions of racial hypodescent, placing people of mixed ancestry on the lowest tiers of society. Legislators in Massachusetts set a nine o'clock curfew for all "Indians, negro and mulatto servants and slaves," supposedly to curtail the "great disorders, insolences and burglaries . . . committed in the night time." New Hampshire and other colonies with extremely few slaves enacted similar laws. In this manner, colonists admittedly took "Espesial care to keep Indians, Negroes, & Melattoes in Good Order." Just as patrols in slave societies kept people of African and Indigenous descent in check, colonists in northern cities formed groups of night watchmen to "Inform of the Breach of Law" by non-"whites." European conceptions of "Indians, Negroes, & Melattoes" as liars, thieves, and criminals fueled prejudice and numerous provincial statutes, which impeded these groups' progress and prosperity in all English colonies.[27]

Free and enslaved African-descended populations in the colonies north of the Chesapeake were small compared to those in other English regions, and relationships between "Negroes" and "Indians" often produced children who grew up with diverse cultures. African-Indigenous people routinely appeared in court cases concerning bastardy, fornication, and slavery in English provinces and in colonial runaway slave advertisements. Wan was "half Indian half Negro" and lived in Perth Amboy, New Jersey. He spoke English and a local "Indian" language. English records sometimes referred to people as "half Indian," which portrays a way of colonial thinking where someone is not considered whole or as possibly a sum of various racial parts. Native Americans traditionally viewed group belonging differently and placed value on kinship ties and cultural aptitude. Wan could speak the language of his "[Indian] country," and his Indigenous ties likely followed his maternal lineage. While African intermixture with Native Americans was prevalent in northern colonies, the greatest amount took place in the Carolinas.[28]

## NORTHERN AND SOUTHERN CAROLINA AND THE "INDIAN" SLAVE TRADE

Beginning in the mid-seventeenth century, English colonists started traveling south from Virginia through tangled brush and marshlands to reside in the Albemarle region, which eventually became known as North Carolina. Dozens of Indigenous groups were already established in the area and had lived on these lands for millennia. In the 1580s, the English failed in their first attempts to establish a permanent colony at nearby Roanoke Island after they ran out of supplies. Survivors from the first groups of English colonists left behind at Roanoke presumably mixed in with neighboring tribes after supplies ran low and the colony collapsed (see chapter 1).[29]

Several decades after the English established Jamestown in 1607, more colonists began to leave Virginia to seek better opportunities than those offered under English rule. Europeans who migrated south onto Yeopim lands, near the Albemarle Sound, tended to mix in with Native Americans more freely than those in the Tidewater Chesapeake. One English traveler to the region spoke of the English traders who traversed the swamps to conduct trade in the area: "These men have commonly their Indian Wives, whereby they soon learn the Indian Tongue, [and] keep a Friendship with the Savages." Colonists across the provinces consistently held disparaging views of Indigenous people and of Europeans who intermixed with "Indians." Some of the traders who married "Indian Wives" abused these women and dishonored their commitments. Others adopted Native American ways and engaged in more reciprocal relationships within these communities.[30]

In Indigenous villages, women prepared food for European traders, taught these men local "Affairs and Customs," and engaged in sexual relationships, which sometimes resulted in the birth of mixed-heritage children. Many colonial traders remained temporarily and left behind their Indigenous families when they returned to colonial society. However, Nathaniel Batts, the first recorded Englishman to remain near the Albemarle Sound, supposedly left his European wife behind in Virginia and married a Native American woman. Though her name and background are lost to history, Nathaniel traded with Yeopims in the 1650s and purchased land from them on the Pasquotank River in 1660. An English missionary later described this region as a place "peopled with English, intermixt with the native Indians to a great extent." By the end of the century, many poor indebted farmers, religious dissenters, and runaway servants and slaves found sanctuary within or beyond the murky swamplands that divided southern Virginia from Indigenous lands that the English came to call Albemarle and then Carolina.[31]

In 1663, England's King Charles II issued the official charter for Carolina, which laid claim over Native American lands from the Albemarle Sound to Spanish Florida. Under the royal charter, colonists left Barbados in 1664 and landed along the southeast Atlantic coast at a place they called Cape Fear, where they attempted to establish Charles Town. The colonial enterprise failed, much like Spanish, French, and other English efforts along the coast in the preceding century. Several years later a renewed effort brought three shiploads of English immigrants to the area via Barbados. The first ship, *Carolina*, arrived at the Seewee Bay in March of 1670. This expedition overshot its original destination of Port Royal, but local Native Americans directed the foreigners to the banks of a nearby location where the English founded the second city of Charles Town (Charlestown) on a waterway they renamed the Ashley River. This Charlestown established a successful English colony, trade hub, and North America's main station for importing Africans and exporting Indigenous slaves.[32]

Two separate colonial regions emerged within the province of Carolina: one on the banks of the Ashley River and waterways feeding Charlestown Harbor in the south and the other surrounding the Albemarle Sound in the north. In northern Carolina, the geography of the outer banks and shallow seaports made it difficult for large ships to navigate, which stifled imperial trade, direct African slave importation, and large-scale European immigration. The first English immigrants to southern Carolina brought enslaved Africans, and further slave importation grew in the colony faster than in the Albemarle. Charlestown quickly became interconnected with England's mercantilist trade economy, especially in the Caribbean, while colonists viewed the northern part of Carolina as a backwoods haven for people fleeing the authority of Virginia's government. In the latter seventeenth century, Chesapeake debtors, fugitives, religious dissenters, runaway servants and slaves, and others hid in the secluded marshlands of northern Carolina. Many of these refugees traveled south through the treacherous terrain of the Great Dismal Swamp, and sought to remain outside the empire's purview. The motley group of migrants who passed through the swamps settled near rivers that flowed into the Albemarle Sound and sometimes mixed with native Yeopims, Pamlicos, Chowanocs, and each other.[33]

Compared to the Chesapeake and other English colonial regions, social divisions in seventeenth-century northern Carolina were not as pronounced along lines of race, class, and gender, which facilitated intermixture at a time when nearby Chesapeake provinces began legislating against it. One English report asserted that there were "a great many idle & poor people" who lived in a "loose way" in northern Carolina. According to colonial administrators, this group of "very mutinous people" was dangerous because they did not follow elite cultural norms nor did they recognize the traditional English sociracial order. In 1677, one official claimed that "Indians, Negros, and women" made up a third of those who unified to overthrow the governor appointed by the Crown. The Albemarle's isolated location allowed people to find relief from the constraints of colonial Chesapeake governments and operate outside of strict English social hierarchies. The region remained a protoracial society until the early eighteenth century, when larger planters consolidated power, passed laws that supported racial division, and started policing ethnoracial mixture. It was not until 1715 that lawmakers issued legislation to prohibit intermarriage and interracial sex. Before that time, relationships between Africans, Europeans, and Native Americans went unpunished in northern Carolina.[34]

Separated by hundreds of miles, North Carolina and South Carolina developed into two vastly different types of English settlements by the turn of the century, yet diplomatic relations with Native Americans were vital to each site. In all continental colonies, the English understood that their survival depended on maintaining peaceful relations with powerful Indigenous confederacies. Like in other provinces, tensions between groups regularly boiled over into open conflict in North Carolina and South Carolina as European settler colonialism exacerbated a litany of issues. The English in South Carolina further pressed Native American societies by intensifying the trade in Indigenous slaves, which fed the growth of plantation communities.[35]

The English regularly enslaved Native Americans in North America, where captives served as domestics in colonial households, worked on local plantations, and were sold to meet labor demands in the Caribbean. This practice was nothing new. Since the late fifteenth century, the Spanish had enslaved Indigenous peoples of the Western Hemisphere, and many European groups relied on other forms of forced labor in the following centuries. While the English did not enslave Native Americans on the same scale as Africans, the practice was widespread, as the English traded Indigenous people as human chattel in all colonies, from Massachusetts to the Caribbean. European empires did not invent "Indian" slavery, for Native Americans had long abducted outsiders, mainly women and children. They also forcibly took Europeans and Africans from the colonies. However, this type of bondage differed from chattel slave systems because this captivity typically was not heritable and people were adopted into Indigenous communities. In both Native American and European societies, captive women gave birth to children of mixed lineage.[36]

The European traffic in "Negroe & Indian Slaves" was racially based and allowed the English to expand their power within the exchange economy of the larger Southeast. The English in the Lowcountry gained power through a mix of trade negotiations, military pressure, and expansion as officials parceled out lands surrounding Charlestown to colonists for plantation agriculture fueled by African and Indigenous labor. Europeans and their slaves cleared trees for fields, experimented with multiple crops, and raised cattle along the low-lying rivers and waterways that fed into Charlestown Harbor. Colonists also persuaded Indigenous allies to reside on the outskirts of their territory. These "Settlement Indians" secured the plantations against raids by enemy "Indians" and returned runaway servants and slaves to their masters. In return, the English engaged in a mutually beneficial trade with allied Native Americans, offered them protection, and exchanged European goods such as glass beads, cloth, alcohol, and metal items including pots, pans, axes, guns, and bullets. The top two items colonists sought in return were animal pelts and slave captives, and the magnitude of the "Indian trade" led to conditions for large-scale African-Indigenous intermixture and set South Carolina apart from other provinces.[37]

While all English colonies enslaved people of Indigenous descent, the "Indian trade" in South Carolina was the largest in the empire and created demographic conditions that spurred ethnoracial mixture from the late seventeenth century into the eighteenth century. In the northern colonies and the Chesapeake, the English enslaved Indigenous people in relatively small numbers, but early South Carolina was exceptional, as the colony exported tens of thousands of Native American captives to provinces throughout the Atlantic. Between 1670 and 1715, the English—with the help of their Indigenous allies—likely transported 30,000–50,000 Native American slaves through the Southeast. This was more than the number of African captives brought into the colony through Charlestown Harbor in the same time frame. Though many "Indian" slaves remained in South Carolina, colonists transported others to provinces farther north or to Barbados, Jamaica, Bermuda, and the Leeward Islands. On the Atlantic islands, Indigenous peoples mixed with the hundreds of thousands of Africans transported from across the Atlantic, but what happened to the thousands of Indigenous slaves who remained in South Carolina?[38]

## "NEGRO, INDYAN AND MALLOTA SLAVES" IN THE CAROLINIAN LOWCOUNTRY

Before European colonization, Native Americans generally conducted warfare with less frequency, killed male war captives, and traded women and children, who were usually integrated into the community. After colonization, Indigenous peoples increasingly raided and traded their enemies, along with furs, to pay for the European goods on which they depended. Instead of killing men in battle or through ritual torture, capturing and trading them as slaves became more profitable. The English realized that enslaving Indigenous men skilled in warfare in South Carolina posed a threat to the province, so they shipped these captives to other colonies throughout the Atlantic, where they mixed in with local populations. Colonists often traded Native American women and children internally within South Carolina. Unlike captivity within Indigenous communities, English societies rarely incorporated Native American women as equal members. European traders kept these women as concubines and sold others to work as domestics or in plantation fields. Some of these Indigenous women found consensual relationships, mostly with enslaved African men.[39]

The Native American slave trade restructured Indigenous societies, influenced slave communities on plantations, and resulted in significant mixture inside colonial South Carolina. Various backgrounds of slaves listed in late seventeenth-century probate records highlight ethnoracial hierarchy and unequal power relationships inherent within colonial systems of bondage. One of the first colonists on the Ashley River, John Smyth, accumulated a variety of bound laborers, whose descriptions reflect the ethnic diversity on early Carolina plantations. An inventory of Smyth's property in 1682 records the following laborers:

> Two white servants by name Thomas Pindar [and] Samuell Hermitage having nineteen months to serve . . . £8
> one serv[an]t: by name Morgan Jones for ditto time being sicke . . . £2
> three Negroe men: Sambo: Smart & Tony . . . £52
> one Negroe womoan named Doll . . . £16
> one Malatta by name Marea & four Pickaninys} Nanny, Will, theata & pegge . . . £26
> three Indian Girles Named Betty Ginny & Sarah . . . £15
> one Indian boy named Hercules . . . £2

Servants and slaves from various parts of the globe interacted with each other in Charlestown and on surrounding plantations. Europeans under limited servitude were recorded along with those of African and Native American heritage, who went without defined terms of service because they were bound for life. The "Indian" boy and girls reflect the tendency for women and children to remain as slaves on Carolina plantations.[40]

Although the English purchased a variety of people from their Native American allies, documents rarely record the specific tribal affiliations of Apalachees, Choctaws, Guales, Mocamas, Timucuas, and Westos and people from dozens of other groups who mixed in with African slaves. John Smyth's workers intermingled both socially and sexually, as the "one Malatta by name Marea" reveals. Marea is listed with the other African children, described as "Pickaninys," not the "Indian" children, hinting that she was an enslaved child of some African descent; her mother may have been the "Negroe womoan named Doll." Perhaps one of the "white servants"—Thomas Pindar, Samuell Hermitage, or Morgan Jones—or even John Smyth was the father. While it is unclear whether Marea was born in South Carolina, she was one of the first mixed-heritage children recorded there. Many others followed in the years to come.[41]

South Carolina's economy was linked to other island colonies in the Atlantic as the slave system became an integral part of the intercolonial trade. Much like in the northern colonies, seventeenth-century plantation owners near Charlestown raised livestock, grew cereal grains, and collected timber for export to places like Bermuda, Barbados, and Jamaica. Carolinian beef, pork, and corn fed laborers who lived and worked on the islands, while wood was used for buildings and fires to boil sugarcane and process molasses. This production required labor, and since plantation owners saved costs by not having to pay enslaved workers, they viewed African and Indigenous people in bondage as the most valuable commodity in the colonial world.[42]

The English moved enslaved Africans and Native Americans through Charlestown, and some slaves transported across the seas were of mixed ancestry. In 1679, Carolinian Henry Woodward gave specific instructions for an employee to secure the purchase of six young slaves from either Bermuda or Barbados: "three Negro lads, two Negro girles all of them if possible under the age of twenty one years of age, [and] one Nigro girl or Molottoe girl native born about [the] same age." Henry insisted that the African men come from "different Countreys" so they would not all know the same language. This might prevent quick alliances and stem rebellion while also encouraging them all to learn English as a common language. But why did Henry request a "Nigro girl or Molottoe girl" who was "native born" in the Americas? Colonists preferred American-born slaves as domestics because they could already speak English and were acculturated to European ways through their upbringing in the Americas. Mulattoes were creoles—those who were acculturated to life in the colonial Americas—which Henry knew when he requested the delivery of a "native born" girl.[43]

Other mixed-heritage children born in colonial North America were the result of intimacies between European traders and Native American women, and these connections took place along a spectrum of forced, coerced, and consensual relationships. Richard Prize was a European "Indian Trader" who moved goods through Charlestown and bartered with Native Americans in the "backcountry." He owned a few Indigenous slaves and freed two of them in 1707, a woman called Fortuna and a girl named Jeany. Richard also had a long-term connection with at least one other "Indian woman," an unnamed slave with whom he had two children, Elizabeth and Sarah Prize. He gave the mother of these children "her liberty and freedom from Slavery," and it appears that their girls were already free. Richard recognized his daughters not only by giving them his surname but also by bequeathing his small estate to them.[44]

In his will, Richard Prize assigned his friends James and Elizabeth Paretree as guardians of Elizabeth and Sarah, his mixed European and Indigenous daughters. Clearly, he wanted the girls to acculturate to European ways; even though their Native American mother was still living, Richard appointed the Paretrees as executors of his will and requested that the couple raise his girls "up in ye fear of God." The Paretrees would make sure his daughters learned the Christian faith, a standard obligation of English godparents. Did Richard's arrangement to remove Elizabeth and Sarah from their Indigenous mother's care dishearten the unnamed mother and her two daughters? Around this time, another Englishman, John Lawson, traveled through Native American villages in the Carolinas, and noted the strong matrilineal bonds that mothers had with their children. John lamented that it "seems impossible" that European men would ever be able "to get their Children (which they have by these *Indian* Women) away from them; whereby they might bring them up in the Knowledge of the Christian Principles." Through a connection to their European father, Elizabeth and Sarah received their freedom, an inheritance, and Christian instruction under European caretakers. However, this meant separation from Indigenous kin, and the girls likely lost attachments to their mother along with her language, religious traditions, and other forms of Indigenous culture.[45]

Slavery weakened traditional knowledge systems that Indigenous and African peoples passed down to their children over generations, yet colonial spaces also provided fertile ground for diverse cultures to amalgamate and flourish in new ways. Despite the cultural erasure that occurred through slavery, the plantation also became a repository where slaves shared ways of life and tools of survival within their communities, especially within the slave quarters, away from the master's view. In the early 1700s, the wealthy landholder William Duckenfield sold his estate in the Chowan precinct of North Carolina, which included 4,000 acres of land near the Albemarle Sound and twenty-three "Negro Indyan and Mallota Slaves named . . . Sambo Bess Kate Totty Virginia Mall Hannah old Hannah Nany Tony Nany Peggy Squire Roetty Cheshire Squire Mustapha Robbin Nat Jack Tom Ned and Sukee." The agreement, which also included other "Goods Cattle and Chattles," revealed the ancestry only of Nat, "an Indyan Boy," since William turned him over immediately at the signing of the contract. It is impossible to know Nat's specific ethnic heritage or that of his peers, but the bill of sale repeatedly used the phrase "Negro Indyan and Mollatta Slaves" to note the diversity among this group.[46]

The twenty-three individuals formed a mixed community that combined various African, European, and Indigenous traditions, which can be seen throughout the slave societies of the Carolinas, Chesapeake, and Caribbean. These people's everyday struggles went beyond the daily toil in the fields common in plantation work. The enslaved tended to each other when sick, eased emotional pains, and shared traditional remedies to heal the wounded. People within these communities played music, danced, shared food, told stories, laughed, cried, and mourned in death. At times they fought, but they also loved each other, shared intimate relationships, and experienced the joys of childbirth and the heartaches of rearing children in bondage.

Slaves realized that others like them lived free not too far away from the plantations they labored on: free "Negroes," "Mulattoes," and nearby "Indians" fueled the dreams of the enslaved. Near the Albemarle Sound, the populations of Chowanocs and other Indigenous groups that occupied the area greatly de-

*A Negroes Dance in the Island of Dominica.* Slaves and free people of color labored and communed in the island colonies of the Caribbean as well as in the slave societies of North America. (Agostino Brunias, 1779, The British Museum, London)

creased from disease, warfare, and other disruptive forces caused by the colonial expansion of North Carolina. In the eighteenth century, English authorities supported legislators who encouraged the growth of large plantations under a hierarchical society that was committed to slavery and the subjugation of African, Native American, and mixed-heritage people. A major conflict arose in 1710, when several hundred immigrants of Swiss and Germanic descent moved farther onto lands south of the Albemarle Sound. Tuscaroras and several nearby Indigenous groups pushed back against this growing European presence and attacked in September 1711. Over the next two years, South Carolinian soldiers, along with Yamasees, Catawbas, Cherokees, Creeks, and other Indigenous allies, ventured north and attacked the Tuscaroras and their allies, taking perhaps 1,000 to 2,000 captives back to South Carolina to sell as slaves. The province of North Carolina was saved because the English paid handsomely for those taken in battle, putting captives to work as domestics and plantation laborers while selling others overseas out of Charlestown.[47]

The Tuscarora War (1711–13) led to further intermixture both inside and outside the English colonies. The defeated Tuscaroras who avoided capture agreed to peaceful terms with the English and vacated areas next to the growing North Carolina province. They retreated north and eventually joined the five nations of the Haudenosaunee (Iroquois), becoming the sixth tribe of the confederacy. Throughout the war, the English had attempted to persuade these

Tuscaroras to return all runaway African slaves living with the tribe. Many Native Americans received rewards from the English for returning runaway slaves, but the Tuscaroras refused to give up escaped Africans who had aided their war effort. These Tuscaroras may have adopted the Africans after moving north as a way to rebuild dwindling populations. While some Indigenous peoples returned African slaves to the English for bounties, others accepted them into their societies, just as captured Native Americans merged with Africans in colonial slave communities.[48]

The influx of Indigenous captives into South Carolina meant that most enslaved communities were not exclusively African, and colonial officials understood that mixture took place within the slave quarters. Like New Englanders after the Pequot War, South Carolina's legislators, in the summer of 1712, reaffirmed the right of European colonists to hold, buy, or sell "negroes, mulatoes, mustizoes or Indians" in slavery—unless those in bondage could otherwise prove their freedom. Officials passed this law as European traders brought in hundreds of captive Choctaws into the colony and anticipated others from the Tuscarora War. Colonists in South Carolina called people of mixed African and European ancestry Mulattoes, but rarely used "mestizo," or "mustizoe," as a racial category. The word appears in a handful of statutes and other colonial records, but it was not regularly used in English North America. However, as Indigenous slaves began to widely intermix with Africans and Europeans in South Carolina, these relationships brought a wave of mixed-heritage children who fell under a new racial category: Mustee.[49]

## THE MUSTEES

While the English never fully adopted the term "mustizoe" (*mestizo*) from the Spanish as they had other racial terms, they shortened the word to "Mustee" in the eighteenth century. An early English description of Mustees mirrors the accepted definition for *mestizoes* in a travel narrative by Woodes Rogers, who had sailed the Atlantic and Pacific Oceans from 1708 to 1711. Captain Rogers described various types of mixed-heritage people in Guayaquil, in present-day Ecuador, which he visited during his travels along the west coast of South America. "The *Mustees*," he wrote, "[are] begot by *Spaniards* on *Indian* Women." He differentiated "*Mullattoes*" as the product of "a *Spaniard*, or any *European*, on a Negro Woman." By the early eighteenth century, colonists in the Carolinian Lowcountry routinely used "Mustee" to describe slaves. On more than one occasion, editors of the *South-Carolina Gazette* replaced the word "mestizo"— printed in an original runaway ad for a slave—with "Mustee" in subsequent issues. The English used and understood the word in the Lowcountry, and it appeared in other colonial regions as well.[50]

> RUN AWAY from the subscriber about ten days ago, a young mestizo wench named BETTY, well known in *Charles-Town*, and is supposed to be harboured by her husband free *Quaco*. Whoever delivers the said wench to me shall receive FORTY SHILLINGS reward, and whoever gives information of her being harboured or entertained, shall, on conviction of the offender, receive a reward of TWENTY POUNDS. WILLIAM SCOTT.

> RUN AWAY from the subscriber, a mustee wench named BETTY, well known in *Charles-Town*, and supposed to be harboured by her husband free *Quaco*. Forty shillings reward will be given to the person that brings her home, and the sum of TWENTY POUNDS on proof of her being harboured. SUSANNAH JONES.

The top runaway slave notice lists Betty as "mestizo" on January 10, 1761. Several weeks later, her description was changed to "mustee" in the bottom advertisement, dated February 28, 1761. (*South-Carolina Gazette*, Accessible Archives Inc.)

While colonists in the Chesapeake and northern colonies did not adopt the term "Mustee" widely, some people were familiar with the word even if they were uncertain about its definition. In 1705, Virginia's attorney general, Stevens Thomson, said, "I am told the issue [child] of a Mulatto by or upon a white Person has another name ... that of Mustee." Stevens was unsure about the proper designation for people of one-fourth African ancestry, what he considered a "Mustee." By his definition, the child of a "Mulatto" with a "white Person" was not subject to the same laws as a "Negro" or even a "Mulatto." Someone had to explain to Stevens what the term "Mustee" meant, showing that it was unclear to him and not widely used by others in Virginia. The following year, New York passed a law promoting the baptism of "Negro," "Indian," and mixed-heritage slaves and reassured slaveholders that baptism would not set "any of them at Liberty." The governor and assembly declared "That all and every Negro, Indian Mulatto and Mestee Bastard Child & Children ... born of any Negro, Indian, Mulatto or Mestee, shall follow ye State and Condition of the Mother," who was usually a slave. They did not define "Mestee," but trade merchants and others carried these racial terms between port cities across the Atlantic. One English traveler in early eighteenth-century North America explained that people of mixed heritage "born of a *Negroe* and an *European* are called *Molattoes*; but such as are born of an *Indian* and *Negroe* are called *Mustees*." While the English used the term "Mustee" variably, this definition is most accurate, since Native Americans living in the colonies frequently partnered with Africans in bondage and colonists consistently identified their children as such.[51]

By most English accounts, colonists applied "Mustee" as a racial label for a person of mixed African and Indigenous lineage but also sometimes for people of mixed European and Indigenous ancestry. At times, colonists employed "Mulatto" and "Mustee" interchangeably or used various racial classifications to describe the same person. On August 7, 1706, on the Eastern Shore of Virginia, an Accomack County court recorded "a Malatta or Mustee bigg with a bastard Child." The woman, named Priss (Priscilla), was free and had become pregnant several months earlier in neighboring Somerset County, Maryland. She would have been punished if it were not for Edward Bagwell, an "Indian" who paid to have her bound under him. It is possible that Edward was the father of Priss's child or another relation and sought to protect his family member from court penalties. Before the end of the year, Priss gave birth to a boy named William. Some years later, William was called "an Indian who was born in Accomack of the body of a free Negro called Priscilla." Even as racial terms shifted between "Negro," "Malatta," and "Mustee," it appears that Priss was of mixed African and Native American descent. All three designations could be accurate by her ancestry, as authorities interpreted her racial appearance in multiple ways. The officials who labeled her son William an "Indian" in one record and a "Mulatto" in another show that colonists might refer to those of Indigenous descent as Mulattoes, especially when they were mixed with African heritage. Racial descriptors changed depending on the perspective of those creating the record and the local terms that were commonly used by contemporaries.[52]

As for others of mixed descent, several factors could determine a Mustee's status as free, servant, or slave; conversely, a Mustee's particular life situation could reveal clues about lineage missing in colonial documents. One case in point was recorded in the summer of 1717, when English traders from South Carolina bought a "Mustee Boy" at a Cherokee trading post. Although Carolina traders purchased him along with other "Indian Slaves," John Barnwell paid the commissioners of the "Indian Trade" for the unnamed boy to serve for nineteen years beginning on July 10. John put down a payment of ten pounds sterling with the promise of eventually "setting free and discharging the said Boy." He also had to enter into a bond for £500 if he broke the terms of the agreement, with instructions that the "Boy shall not be exported or carried off or shipped from this Province, during the Term." Finally, John was obligated "to educate the said Boy, Christian-like, and cause him to be instructed in a good Trade." Judging from these conditions, it is probable that this "Mustee Boy" was of blended European and Indigenous lineage, as it would have been rare for the commissioners to issue such strict instructions to protect the liberty of a person of mixed African and Indigenous heritage. The boy likely avoided slavery through a process that assimilated him into English society because of his European ancestry, like Elizabeth and Sarah Prize. Most Mustees of African descent were not so fortunate.[53]

The sex ratio of "Negroes and Indian Slaves" on South Carolina plantations contributed to a regular pattern of intermixture between African men and Native American women. While rates of slave importation varied over colonial regions, the English consistently brought more African men than women into Charlestown. Also, English colonists enslaved larger numbers of Indigenous women and children than men in the Lowcountry. While these groups did not always intermix, certain trends are reflected in the sources. In his 1712 book, John Norris explained English labor preferences when discussing how to set up a fruitful plantation in South Carolina, writing that an English farmer could acquire 150 acres of land in the province and set up a small plantation for £150. The top two expenses would be "Two Slaves": "a good *Negro* Man" for forty-five pounds "and a good *Indian* Woman" for eighteen pounds. They, along with animal livestock, would make "a good Breeding Stock" that would provide "profitable Returns with their ... Slaves encreasing." Potential planters who followed these instructions encouraged African-Indigenous intermixture, and the resulting children were known as Mustees.[54]

John Norris's vision for successful large plantations promoted mixture between African men and Native American women. In his book, someone asks what a man would need to "become a Gentleman Planter" in South Carolina. The response: he should first obtain 1,000 to 1,500 acres of land and then spend around £1,500 to purchase building materials for a house, food supplies, livestock, and slaves. A list of estimated prices shows that slaves were the largest expense—a little over £1,100. John again suggested that certain racial groups were best suited for different types of work. He specified that aspiring plantation owners should buy "Three *Indian* Women as Cooks for the Slaves, and other Houshold-Business [and] Three *Negro* Women ... each, to be employ'd either for the Dairy, to attend the Hogs, Washing, or any other Employment they may be set about in the Family." John went further to divide labor along the lines of race and gender for household chores, tending livestock, and field work: "Fifteen *Negro* Men, and Fifteen *Indian* Women" were "to be employ'd in Planting." These slaves would clear and fence fields and then plant, hoe, and reap subsistence crops, which included corn, peas, potatoes, and pumpkins. The largest portion of land would be devoted to rice and bring in the most money.[55]

Successful planters in South Carolina were familiar with the plantation economy, the aptitude of their laborers, and the transatlantic and continental slave trades. John Norris displayed his knowledge of the Lowcountry system when he recommended the types of laborers that potential planters should purchase. After years of massive Native American slave raids and in the midst the Tuscarora War, he suggested that new planters buy an even mix of African men and Native American women to work the rice fields. Africans carried technical knowledge of rice cultivation across the Atlantic, which was financially beneficial to colonial planters. Based on their experience growing the crop in West Africa, African slaves taught their European masters how to effectively prepare fields and irrigate, cultivate, harvest, and process rice for export. Native American women also had agricultural skills that aided the growth of rice, which surpassed meat and timber products as a staple export in the early eighteenth century. At this time, Africans disembarked ships that came into the Charlestown Harbor, and Indigenous captives poured into the city. Mixture between these groups resulted in numerous children of blended ancestry.[56]

Procreation among ethnically diverse slave populations was a blueprint for a successful plantation in the Carolina Lowcountry, and owners facilitated conditions that allowed for mixture between slaves of African and Indigenous descent. Wealthy South Carolinian planter Robert Daniell owned more than 1,000 acres of land on the Wando River, lands on the Pamlico River in North Carolina, and property in Charlestown. It was typical for Lowcountry planters to reside in Charlestown during the hot, humid months to avoid malaria and other diseases and then return to their plantation estates during the milder seasons. These absentee planters placed overseers of all backgrounds in charge of the daily operations of their plantations. Some masters in early colonial South Carolina allowed a system of task labor in which overseers assigned slaves a set amount of work to complete, and they could tend to their own crops and socialize the remainder of the time. Robert and his overseers may have negotiated work requirements with his slaves, who came from a variety of ancestries. When he left most of the estate to his wife, Martha, in 1718, Robert included all his slaves, "whether Negroes, Indians, Mustees, Or Mulattoes, both Male and female." While Robert used distinct racial and gendered language to describe his slaves, he made little attempt to separate them on his plantation because his family profited from the natural increase of slave families.[57]

In South Carolina, intimate relationships between Africans who came from various places across the Atlantic and Indigenous people from continental North America led to a unique phenomenon: Mustees became the largest group of mixed-heritage people enslaved in the colonial Southeast. There were certainly many types of mixed people, yet Mustees of blended African and Indigenous descent surpassed enslaved Mulattoes of mixed African and European ancestry. This fact is illustrated most clearly in South Carolina's runaway slave advertisements, where the number of Mustees surpasses the number of Mulattoes by nearly three to one. Compared to the Chesapeake, where Afri-

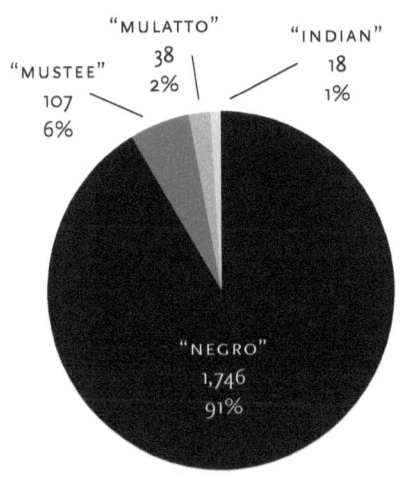

**Racial descriptions of runaways of color in the *South-Carolina Gazette*, 1732–1775**

*Sources*: South-Carolina Gazette, 1732–75; Windley, *Runaway Slave Advertisements*, 1–347.

*Note*: This data includes the first recorded runaway attempt of each individual and excludes repeat attempts by the same slave, where identifiable. Two "Mulattoes" were specifically described as "half Indian" or "of the Indian breed" and thus counted with "Mustees."

can and European Mulattoes were most numerous, the propagation of Mustee children in South Carolina resulted from natural intimacy and sex within slave quarters. Native American women most often procreated with African men on plantations and this surpassed all other types of ethnoracial mixture in the colonial Lowcountry.[58]

It is impossible to determine exact figures, but the number of Mustees reached into the hundreds by the middle of the century and perhaps into the thousands by the end of the colonial period. While it is difficult to identify their specific ethnic backgrounds, most could trace their ancestry to the African slave trade and Native American slave raids in the Southeast before 1715. It was then that the Yamasee War, fought by a pan-Indigenous alliance of Creeks, Yamasees, and other tribes, checked English power around Charlestown and interrupted the lucrative "Indian" slave trade. Beginning in 1715, this pan-Indigenous alliance led a series of coordinated attacks against South Carolina plantations. Indigenous assaults killed dozens of abusive European "Indian traders" who had used their power to run up huge debts in "Indian" country and manipulated Indigenous communities. Native American attacks inhibited but did not totally end the trade in "Indian slaves," and the English already held thousands of Native Americans in bondage by this time.[59]

English records rarely identify the specific origins of slaves with Indigenous ancestry, but many birth dates of Mustees fall in the years after major conflicts brought massive numbers of Indigenous captives into South Carolina. For example, colonist Mary Thomas deeded a three-year-old "Mustee Boy" named Jemmey to her grandchildren in Charlestown on August 31, 1721. This placed the child's conception around 1717, after major conflicts during the Yamasee

War and the decline of the "Indian" slave trade. Jemmey's mother likely came to South Carolina in the preceding years. There is no indication of Jemmey's ethnic background beyond some Native American lineage, but most Mustees in his position had an Indigenous mother and African father. At three years old, Jemmey would be bound "for ever." If he was removed from his mother and father, who would care for him? What would he know of his family's traditions without their guidance? When he became aware of his position as a slave and realized other free Native Americans lived nearby, would he attempt to join them? While we do not know how the "Mustee Boy" Jemmey felt, others who grew up in similar bondage clearly yearned to be free.[60]

Many of the "Mustee children" living on Lowcountry plantations in the 1730s and 1740s originated from Indigenous groups such as the Tuscaroras to the north, Choctaws to the west, and Apalachees, Guales, Mocamas, and Timucuas from regions to the south in Florida. Not long after English wars with Tuscaroras, Creeks, Yamasees, and other groups, a "Negro Man" named England had a relationship with an Indigenous slave woman in South Carolina, which produced two Mustee children: Prince, born around 1717, and his brother, Prosper, born about 1720. England worked as a bricklayer and taught his sons the trade before they reached adulthood. The enslaved family worked together putting up buildings at various plantations around Goose Creek, just north of Charlestown. Prince and Prosper's mother may have been sold away or was deceased when the boys came of age. As young men, they questioned their captivity and whether or not they would die as slaves. When Prince was around twenty-two and Prosper was about nineteen, they planned to escape slavery with their aging African father.[61]

England and Prosper ran away first, but Prince was either captured or prevented from leaving by his master, Joseph Wragg, who had the young man chained around one leg to prevent his flight. Determined to join his family, Prince found a way to break or remove his chain. He then stole one of his owner's stallions and rode off to find his brother and father in freedom. This ethnically blended family passed down skills, traditions, and resilience that culminated in the refusal to accept lifelong bondage. Even the brothers' names, Prince and Prosper, suggest that their parents believed the boys were destined for something greater than the life of a common slave. England and his wife cultivated a spirit of resistance in their children, and this determination enabled the family to push toward independence.[62]

Indigenous slaves routinely engaged in sex and committed relationships with enslaved Africans, as evidenced by the term "Mustee Negro," which appears in English records throughout the colonial period and is used to describe a particular type of mixed-heritage people. Diana was a "Mustee Negro" born in the midst of the Tuscarora War, and she may have picked up her recalcitrance from war captives who raised her. From her early to mid-twenties, she ran away from her master in South Carolina on at least four separate occasions. During her fourth recorded attempt, she brought along a "little Negro Boy" by the name of March. Even if he was not her biological son, she cared for the boy as a mother would. March was unable to successfully run away by himself, and Diana gained little advantage in her escape by carrying the child with her. If the boy was her son, the father was probably African, as newspapers identified March as "Negro," which perhaps meant that he had predominantly African lineage.[63]

South Carolina runaway advertisements used the term "Mustee Negro" to describe people of blended heritage more precisely, just as they revealed other distinct pieces of information about their lives. "A stout mustee negro" named Paul spoke "very good English," although he had a speech impediment "with a kind of stuttering." His master noted that Paul had survived smallpox and the marks pitted his body to the extent that the scars gave him a "black" appearance. After first referring to Paul as a "mustee negro," his owner then called Paul a "negro fellow" and offered a ten-pound reward to any "white person" who would return the runaway. Masters used racial descriptors loosely at times, which shows the malleability of these categories. The phrase "Mustee Negro" functioned as a subcategory under the umbrella term "Negro," but using specific racial terms helped colonists better identify escaped slaves and heightened the chances of their capture and return.[64]

Indigenous slaves and their descendants remembered the freedom of their ancestors, which inspired hundreds, if not thousands, to run away from their owners during the colonial period. Born around the time the Tuscarora War ended, one so-called Mustee Wench lived near the Stono River in South Carolina. She did normal housework such as cooking and washing laundry, but she was especially well trained in eighteenth-century textile production. Her master, James Mackewn, explained the steps the twenty-year-old slave took to make fabric from sheep's wool. First, the young woman cleaned and straightened the wool, then spun it into yarn, and finally with her skilled "needle-work" crafted the fabric into clothing, blankets, and other important items typically found in colonial homes. Though brought up in slavery, this mixed-heritage woman wondered why her owner benefited from her skills and profited from the work she produced. Friends and family may have encouraged her to reclaim her autonomy as an Indigenous woman.[65]

Most slaves in this Mustee woman's position knew there were "Indians" living free nearby; the young woman likely saw them and perhaps interacted directly with some of these Native Americans. "Settlement Indians" who lived in villages outside of Charlestown provided a reminder that most Indigenous people were born free. This made it difficult for the unnamed woman of mixed ancestry to understand why she did not deserve the same independence. The defiant "Mustee Wench" voiced her opinions directly to her master James and openly challenged his authority. The woman's loose tongue and acts of defiance earned her harsh physical "correction." When she could take no more, the Mustee plotted and ran away on May 14, 1733. James warned the Charlestown community to be on the lookout for the runaway: "her Back will shew the Marks of her former Misdeeds." Slave owners gave these detailed descriptions of runaways to increase the likelihood of recapturing valuable property, but this Mustee woman had a good chance at achieving her liberty. Even her master knew that others might mistake her for a "Free Wench" because she was skilled, could speak "good English," and physically resembled an "Indian."[66]

When discussing pecuniary interests and their slaves, assemblymen in South Carolina disclosed how they viewed Mustees and Mulattoes in the context of a racial order. In the 1710s, the South Carolina General Assembly was concerned with two separate enemies of the colony: "pyrates who frequently infested" the Atlantic coast and "Creek Indians" who attacked the English along with Yamasees and other Native Americans. The colony had taken on heavy debt to deal militarily with these threats, and in the late 1710s sought to raise £70,000 through taxes on landholdings and "on all negroes and Indian slaves, mustees and mulattoes" who belonged to slaveholders residing in the province. In this manner, magistrates routed tax money raised from slaves of African and Native American descent to fight outside enemies that challenged British authority. Officials assessed taxes on all bound men, women, and children "without any manner of difference or distinction of age or sex." However, the assembly noted some exceptions. Since "an Indian slave [was] reputed of much less value than a negroe," they would only be taxed at "half the value." Authorities further clarified any doubt on "what ought to be rated on mustees, mulattoes, &[et]c." by declaring that "all such slaves as are not entirely Indian shall be accounted as negroe" for tax purposes. South Carolina's colonists, like those in other provinces, applied hypodescent more rigidly to people of African ancestry than Indigenous peoples. Moreover, "Negro" slaves occupied the lowest position on the colonial racial ladder, yet African lineage added value to slaves who were also part "white" or "Indian."[67]

The variations in evaluating slave prices reflected age, gender, and ethnoracial background throughout the colonies. Most Indigenous slaves were women and children, and Europeans valued them less than the average African male or female. John Norris also considered this value when he noted that both "Slaves and [Live]Stock" would yearly increase for masters on South Carolina's plantations, "provided God blesses his endeavours, and gives Health and Life to his Slaves, till the Young ones grow up, as the Old decay." Unlike concerns that planter-legislators had about African-European mixture in the Chesapeake, African-Indigenous coupling went unregulated because these relationships financially benefited slave owners. Slave demographics within the plantation system explain how the number of blended African and Native American people increased in the Lowcountry, which is also connected to how the racial classification "Mustee" became as widely known as "Mulatto" in colonial South Carolina.[68]

## LEGISLATING ACROSS PROVINCES: "CHILDREN OF SUCH UNNATURAL AND INORDINATE COPULATIONS"

English authorities everywhere monitored the growing numbers of free "Negroes," "Indians," "Mulattoes," and "Mustees" in their communities, legislated against their daily liberties, and passed laws to limit manumissions in the eighteenth century. However, officials in English societies with slave majorities—South Carolina, Barbados, Jamaica, and the Leeward Islands—did not legally prohibit free mixed-heritage people to the same degree as in the Chesapeake and North Carolina. In this vein, the northern colonies also granted allowances to certain people of mixed descent, like South Carolina and the Atlantic islands, but for different reasons. Namely, the mixed-heritage population did not reach a critical mass in societies with smaller numbers of slaves, so officials in these areas never passed a substantial body of anti-intermixture legislation or thirty-one-year indentures that policed interracial couples and their children of mixed ancestry.[69]

The divergence between the two Carolinas provides an excellent comparison to help us understand why English provinces avoided or welcomed restrictions that targeted free people of blended heritage. Each colony rose from its progenitor: South Carolina followed the culture of Barbados (and laws from Jamaica), and North Carolina copied many of the policies of Virginia. European immigrants brought with them loose and strict notions of hypodescent, which they later transformed into legislation. The Chesapeake colonies were exceptional in the way they made ethnoracial mixture illegal and administered people who violated intermixture laws. In the Caribbean, a lack of legislation in these areas allowed relatively open mixture and led to the emergence of free communities of color, some of which attained prosperity. All these colonies contained large amounts of slavery and servitude, and most mixed people were trapped within these systems of bondage. While free people of blended ancestry faced obstacles everywhere, over time policies in the northern Albemarle diverged from those in the southern Lowcountry.[70]

In the early eighteenth century, ideas, customs, and laws that had existed for decades in the Chesapeake spread into surrounding North Carolina, Pennsylvania, and Delaware, as these colonies received thousands of Chesapeake migrants in search of arable land for agriculture. While Pennsylvania and Delaware passed some legislation against "free negro and mulatto" people in the mid-1720s, colonists never reissued and irregularly followed these statutes. Both colonies adopted the Chesapeake mandate that assigned thirty-one-year indentures to mixed-heritage children born to European women, though administrators did not widely apply this law. The majority of slaves and servants found in Pennsylvania and Delaware remained in counties bordering Maryland, and their overall numbers were always comparatively small. Legislation protected the rights of masters to bring indentured and enslaved Mulattoes into the Delaware Valley colonies from the Chesapeake, but a solid faction of magistrates in Pennsylvania and Delaware avoided creating slave societies and did not push as many laws against free people of African and Indigenous descent. Virginia's southern border was a different story, as North Carolina officials also mandated thirty-one years of labor to free mixed-heritage children born to unwed European servant women in the colony's comprehensive servant and slave codes of 1715.[71]

Cases of European colonists holding Mulattoes in bondage for personal gain are found throughout the English Empire, but in North Carolina this took place before authorities had even passed formal legislation. For example, in 1713, North Carolina justices demanded that a Captain Jenkins "deliver to the provost Marshall a Mellatto Boy" after the captain pretended the boy's parents bound him by indenture. In this case, the court stepped in to protect the unnamed boy's right to freedom and ordered "that he may be Sent to his said parents againe."[72]

Kidnappings, followed by illegal indentures and slavery, were common for children of mixed ancestry, which is why blended families often fought to protect their loved ones. In 1716, Sarah Williamson and her mixed-heritage child came to the attention of the North Carolina General Assembly when the justices referred to the indenture law they passed the previous year concerning "Women having Mulatto Children." Like in the Chesapeake, "any White woman" in North Carolina who had "a Bastard child by a Negro, Mulatto or Indyan" could be heavily fined, "publickly whipped," and "sold" for up to four years "to her Master or Owner for her Offence." Local church officials assigned Sarah to serve five years, however, insinuating that some colonists in North Carolina were following Virginia's laws passed in the previous decade.[73]

Mirroring the Chesapeake colonies, North Carolina's courts and church authorities reinforced the connection between race and bondage by routinely subjugating European women and their Mulatto children to extended servitude. In the case of Sarah's mixed-heritage son, one of the Currituck precinct churchwardens had assigned the boy to serve his mother's master for "the full Term and Space of thirty One Years." Sarah considered this a hefty sentence for her "Mellatto" son born out of wedlock. She understood that her son's African or Indigenous ancestry made him particularly susceptible to bondage and decided to bring a suit against her master in court.[74]

Thomas Swan represented the Williamson family in court and argued that both the mother's and son's indentures were invalid because of inconsistencies in how the churchwarden issued the contracts. First, the county court was never aware that these contracts had been made, since it did "not appear that the said Sarah was Lawfully in Court" to answer for her supposed crime. No one could prove "how and after what manner the said Sale was made." Justices also could not determine the length of time Sarah's child had to serve because it did "not Appear of what Age the Child was at the time of the said Sale." Additionally, Thomas argued "there was no Law or Act of Assembly in force in this Government [of North Carolina] at the time of passing the said Order Warranting the Sale of the said Sarah and her Child." For all these reasons, Sarah's lawyer asked that their contracts "be Sett aside and held Invalid." The assembly agreed and granted her plea, which restored "Sarah and her Child ... to the liberty they had before."[75]

Sarah Williamson's case demonstrates that even though North Carolina had not officially adopted legislation against interracial mixture when Sarah and her child were indentured, the churchwardens were operating customarily by Virginia law against "abominable Mixture." This dispute took place in Currituck, a coastal county in North Carolina bordering southern Virginia. The colonists who governed the area may have excused their illegal actions by contending that they operated under Virginia's legislation. The lines between written legal codes and customary practice, as well as provincial borders, were blurred during the colonial period.

Sarah's resistance to the unjust contracts forced upon her family speaks to both the vulnerability and privileges that certain Mulattoes had when their mothers were European. Some colonial men knew that existing power dynamics allowed them to assign illegal indentures to children of mixed heritage. Even if caught, they risked little punishment, so they had nothing to lose by breaking the law. Servant women and their families were often poor and illiterate, and many did not have access to the legal system. Sarah and her son were surely not the only ones in this position, but they were fortunate enough to secure representation in court. While colonial elites subjugated servant women based on race, sex, and social status, European women maintained advantages that came with whiteness. At times this allowed them to protect their children of mixed ancestry.[76]

After 1715, North Carolina joined Virginia and Maryland to become one of the main three colonies to consistently legislate against thousands of freeborn "Mulattoes" along with free "Negroes" and "Indians." Legislators in these colonies sought to overturn the legal distinction between mixed-heritage people born free and those born in bondage. They limited things such as gun ownership, participation in militias, and marriage with Europeans, among a long list of other privileges granted to European colonists. In Maryland, "no Negro, or Mulatto Slave, Free Negro, or Mulatto born of a White Woman, during his Time of Servitude by Law, or any Indian Slave, or Free Indian Natives" could testify in court cases involving "any Christian White Person." Several colonies, including Virginia and North Carolina, followed with similar laws.[77]

By the 1720s, Virginia, Maryland, and North Carolina all crafted tax policies that put extra financial burdens on free families of African, Indigenous, and mixed lineage. The North Carolina General Assembly declared "That all free Negroes, Mulattoes, and other Persons of that kind, being mixed Blood," boys and girls, men and women, were taxable starting at twelve years of age, the same as any adult male. This law also included "any White Person . . . married with any Negro, Mulatto, Mustee, or other Person being of mixed Blood." Virginia issued similar tax policies for "free negroes, mullattos, or indians . . . male and female, above the age of sixteen years." Maryland followed its neighbors with taxes for "all Female Mulattoes born of White Women, and Free Negro Women" above sixteen years old. Authorities in Maryland specifically used the phrase "Mulattoes born of White Women" to differentiate them from Mulattoes born of "Negro Women," who were usually enslaved. Paternity and maternity mattered for Mulattoes, but legislators in the above three provinces attempted to subjugate them all the same.[78]

Other colonies with large slave populations curbed the rights of free mixed-heritage people but stood apart from Virginia, Maryland, and North Carolina in important ways. The most conspicuous difference is that officials in South Carolina and the Caribbean rarely or never prohibited interracial marriage and sex. Moreover, while unwed European women who gave birth to mixed-heritage offspring could be punished, legislators never legally penalized Mulatto children. In 1717, South Carolina's assembly did acknowledge "the issues or children of such unnatural and inordinate copulation" between any "white woman" and "negro or other slave or free negro" and copied this language — along with much of the rest of the law — directly from Maryland's 1715 statute. However, South Carolina's legislators intentionally veered away from issuing the same thirty-one-year indentures to these freeborn mixed-heritage children. Instead, their ordinance stipulated that the offspring would serve until eighteen or twenty-one years, respectively for girls and boys — the same length of service assigned to European children. Overall, South Carolina's legislation remained aligned with that of Caribbean societies. Indeed, provinces with slave majorities typically allowed free people of mixed ancestry greater independence.[79]

As in Latin America and other island colonies in the Atlantic with more fluid racial systems, Europeans in colonial South Carolina took a more liberal stance on the rights of free mixed-heritage people, though these freedoms were always relative and not the full rights granted to other British subjects. Like South Carolina, the Caribbean colonies also had slave majorities, and while the number of mixed people increased over the years, this group paled in comparison to the African population, which rapidly expanded with the growth of the transatlantic slave trade. In places where Europeans were in the minority, they could not afford to totally alienate free people of mixed descent, yet they did limit some rights such as voting.[80]

Legislator-planters in South Carolina and the Caribbean were also aware that European men widely consorted with African, Indigenous, and mixed-heritage women and certainly did not want to restrain their own sexual independence by passing anti-intermixture laws in places where European sex ratios were skewed toward men. European fathers also may not have wanted to impede the rights of their mixed-heritage children. Still, these men did not often recognize their mixed offspring, and most people of blended ancestry remained enslaved like their mothers. In South Carolina, many mixed slaves were Mustees born to Indigenous mothers and African fathers, who had little chance of gaining freedom. Since the number of Mulattoes and Mustees who inherited liberty from maternal European lines was relatively small, South Carolina officials, like those in the Caribbean, probably did not seek to heavily legislate against freeborn mixed people.[81]

In short, free people of mixed heritage had greater autonomy in South Carolina, the Atlantic islands, and the northern colonies and were more likely to fall into extended legal servitude and experience fewer rights in Virginia, Maryland, and North Carolina. Perhaps with the exception of those in port cities, European colonists did not view free mixed-heritage populations as significantly large enough to threaten free labor systems in New England, New York, New Jersey, Pennsylvania, and Delaware. North Carolina followed the Chesapeake and stands out as exceptional because its policy makers also repeatedly sought to encourage racial separation and control intermixture. By the 1720s, Virginia, Maryland, and North Carolina had implemented racially discriminatory legislation that was stronger than anywhere else in the British Empire. These three colonies had great control over interracial families and free people of blended ancestry and maintained the sharpest legal forms of hypo-descent in the eighteenth century. European colonists came to view people of mixed lineage in a largely negative light, regardless of their position in society. But how did these "mixed people" perceive themselves?[82]

# 4

## Mixed-Heritage Identities in the Eighteenth Century

In the summer of 1723, a group of "molatters" met in secret somewhere in Virginia to discuss their wretched condition in the British colony. From these conversations they decided that one in their group would write a letter to the new bishop of London with several requests. The author self-identified as a "poore SLave" and described the complex bonds of kinship that many enslaved Mulattoes shared with the people who owned them: "it is to bee not[e]d that one brother is a SLave to another and one Sister to an othe[r]." Some of the petitioners were the products of sexual liaisons between bound women of African or Indigenous ancestry and European masters. The legitimate European children of these master-fathers inherited and owned their half siblings of mixed ancestry. The anonymous author from Virginia revealed that he or she was a product of such a family: "as for mee my selfe I am my brothers SLave but my name is secret." This statement, written by the hand of a mixed-heritage person in bondage, reveals a perspective that was rarely recorded in colonial history. These words also capture the paradoxes and complexities of race, identity, ancestry, kinship, and power relationships found in countless families of mixed lineage in the Americas.[1]

Like the letter's author, the other Mulattoes in the group also identified themselves as slaves and believed their European ancestry should grant them freedom. Even though some of them may have legally been in servitude, their experiences reflected the lives of those in lifelong bondage in the English colonies. The letter writer explained the need for communal secrecy surrounding their petition, stating that those in their group "dare nott Subscribe any mans name to this [letter] for feare of our masters." This is the only gendered language that suggests these "molatters" were predominantly male, although women may have been represented as well. The group worried that if they disclosed their identities they would "Swing upon the gallass [gallows] tree." The threat of hanging for simply engaging in conversations about freedom was real.[2]

Over the previous year, European colonists in Virginia alleged that slaves were planning to "kill murder & destroy" them. Fears that those in bondage would attempt to "cutt off their masters, and possess themselves of the country" led authorities to interrogate, torture, and deport those suspected of plotting rebellion. Officials sold some of these slaves in Barbados, where harsh labor conditions on sugar plantations often equated to a death sentence. The Virginia General Assembly responded with increased measures to discipline recalcitrant slaves, including capital punishment for those who plotted insurrection. Legislators also stripped the franchise from free people of color and restricted other rights, since "free negroes and mulattoes were much suspected" of aiding slave conspiracies. If caught, authorities might find the secret group of "molatters" guilty of conspiracy simply for advocating emancipation for people of mixed descent. They knew the letter itself was contraband, and if intercepted, it could lead to torture, execution, or sale away from family and friends. The group of "molatters" was willing to take the risk, for they believed that their European ancestry and Christian faith entitled them to preferential treatment among slaves and to similar rights as other British subjects.[3]

While most historical documents tell us how European colonists viewed mixed-heritage people hundreds of years ago, this message written by the group of "molatters" gives us direct insight into how people of mixed ethnoracial backgrounds viewed themselves and their situation in the eighteenth-century colonial Chesapeake. This letter and other evidence show that they closely identified with their Christian heritage and relied on connections to their European lineage when seeking liberty. Still, there were multiple ways that people of blended ancestry thought about the world around them and their place in it. While we might wonder how mixed people self-identified in terms of race or ethnicity, they may have thought about identity in different ways and probably would not have used modern-day classifications.[4]

There was no single term that so-called Mulatto, Mustee, and other mixed people used for their personal affiliation. Mixed-heritage self-identification depended on a multitude of factors linked to cultural upbringing, labor status, regional location, and physical appearance and was also characterized by occupation, religion, kinship networks, and interpersonal relationships. Among friends and relatives, people of mixed descent intimated their allegiances more through their actions and less through words. Some probably saw themselves occupying a racial middle ground, while others counted themselves among the monoracial groups of "Negro," "Indian," or "white." These portrayals were often situational and might change when speaking before a magistrate at court proceedings, where people emphasized certain ancestral ties over others. People of blended ancestry—or their lawyers—often used mixed-race language when petitioning for their freedom. This did not mean that mixed individuals commonly applied these labels to themselves, nor did they believe in their inferiority vis-à-vis those of full European descent. Indeed, mixed-heritage people often pushed to present themselves as equals in British colonial societies.

Europeans created colonial racial groups and referred to people of two or more ethnoracial backgrounds as "Mulatto," "Mustee," and "people of color," and sometimes used the terms "half breed," "half Indian," "half black," "mixed people," "mixed blood," or "Persons of Mixt Blood" in the eighteenth-century British colonies. These words often had negative connotations associated with a "corruption of blood." Europeans generally distrusted mixed-heritage people and viewed their loyalties as "unintelligible." In other words, European colonists often could not ascertain whom mixed people identified with. Some considered wealthy free people of color, who distanced themselves from "Negroes," as loyal to the Crown and worthy of special privileges. However, colonists knew that most slaves and free people of mixed ancestry aligned themselves with other African and Indigenous people and feared these alliances during rebellion. This is why the numerical growth of free people of color in many areas caused anxiety among European colonists.[5]

This chapter examines the socioracial identities of mixed-heritage people and displays how they contested colonial classifications and bound labor positions. Instead of focusing on racial labels to understand personal identity, it is more useful to examine how mixed people in British America viewed their position within colonial societies based on their labor status as slave, servant, or free. They understood that provincial communities, buttressed by "white" supremacy, stigmatized people of "Negro" and "Indian" backgrounds and legally attached them to bondage. People of blended ancestry and their families evoked identities that strengthened their claims to liberty and steered away from associating with lineage that would do the opposite, especially while filing freedom suits. When seeking independence, mixed-heritage people might implicitly acknowledge a connection to African descent, yet many chose to foreground their European lineage or Native American roots. As a means of survival, some imbibed more disparaging colonial views about "Negroes," "Indians," and those of "mixed blood" and attempted to disassociate from these groups in favor of whiteness. Still, most mixed people in the Atlantic world found ways to honor their ancestry from many parts of the globe. Those who maintained these cultural affiliations are clearly evident in runaway slave and servant advertisements, which began to regularly appear in several British colonies in the 1730s.[6]

Runaway servant and slave advertisements illustrate the complex ancestries of mixed-heritage people and reveal that they had an additional tool that helped many reach freedom: racial ambiguity outside monoracial categories.

Physical descriptions of mixed bodies in newsprint confirmed the prevalence of intermixture in slave societies and reaffirmed the idea of racial mixture in the colonial public consciousness. Runaway ads further showcase how colonists viewed people of blended ancestry and present the benefits that came with lighter skin. These sources reveal how people raised in the British colonies recognized racial differences between "whites," "Negroes," "Indians," "Mulattoes," "Mustees," and other people of "mixed blood."[7]

Descriptions of runaways taught European immigrants and native-born colonists how to racially identify mixed people; in short, they helped figuratively create and sustain the idea of mixed race. Along with legal statutes, these advertisements reiterated the belief that people of mixed ancestry were properly placed in bondage. Although mixed-heritage people might pass as free, newspaper ads affirmed their position in the minds of readers among the lowest ranks of society. Thus, runaway ads became a conduit through which colonial society imagined, reimagined, and understood people of mixed lineage. Masters, professionals, and officials used this mass media tool to tie "Mulattoes" and "Mustees" to "Negroes" in bondage, which further disseminated notions of racial hypodescent, in which colonists regarded people of blended heritage closer to their socially subjugated African and Indigenous parentage.

When running away, slaves of mixed descent were acutely aware of how to culturally perform as free people and utilized their racial liminality to manipulate perceptions of identity and remain out of their master's grasp. This did not necessarily mean they had to pass as "white" but rather that they had to imitate freedom. People of blended ancestry associated with various parts of their lineage, shifted identities, and relied on the cultural knowledge of their ancestors when it benefited them. While they held multiple views about themselves, who their people were, and where they belonged in the British colonial order, most people of mixed African, European, or Indigenous heritage believed that they, like others, had a right to liberty.[8]

## CHRISTIAN MULATTOES: "RELEESE US OUT OF THIS CRUELL BONDEGG"

In the first half of the eighteenth century, mixture between Africans, Europeans, and Indigenous Americans occurred throughout the English colonies of the Western Hemisphere, and mixed people lived in every province. The largest populations of mixed-heritage peoples appeared in Jamaica, Barbados, Virginia, Maryland, North Carolina, and South Carolina. Authorities enslaved and policed people of blended ancestry in all of the British colonies, though the northern colonies, where numbers were relatively low, tended to have fewer restrictions on free people. Colonists in Jamaica, Barbados, and South Carolina maintained more relaxed standards—especially for more affluent free people of color—which reflected a culture where mixture was normalized, even if not formally acceptable. Officials in Virginia, Maryland, and North Carolina heavily stigmatized intermixture and administered the strongest forms of legal hypo-descent.[9]

Labor status was the single largest factor that determined how people of blended heritage encountered everyday life. Whether people saw themselves as "white," "Negro," or "Indian" or recognized a combination of various ethno-racial backgrounds, servitude and slavery limited their autonomy and colored their self-perceptions. Those born free who entered into apprenticeships or labor contracts envisioned what greater independence would be like after they completed years of service. Nevertheless, most Mulattoes and Mustees grew up under the dark veil of bondage and would never experience freedom in the American colonies.

Like those under servitude, enslaved men and women of mixed descent imagined living independently and had plenty of inspiration. They listened closely to the stories of elders born free in Africa or in Indigenous American territories, who shared tales about their lives and those of their ancestors. Bondsmen and bondswomen also knew and interacted with "free negroes and mulattoes," who authorities complained were "idle and slothful" and often proved "evil examples to slaves." Many English authorities throughout the colonies saw free people of color as a threat. They regularly legislated against "free negroes and mulattoes," who might inspire slaves to demand the same autonomy or, worse, to revolt and upset the socioracial hierarchy.[10]

Additionally, many people of mixed ancestry had European family members who reminded them what life was like outside of captivity. To the dismay of many English elites, lower-class Europeans continued to mix with people of African and Indigenous lineage, and these families did not stigmatize racial mixture or their mixed-heritage children. These sentiments are conveyed in the story of a "Molato" woman named Rose, who came of age in early eighteenth-century Maryland. The paternal side of Rose's family came on ships from Africa, likely through the Caribbean, for her father, Domingo, was labeled a "Negro." Her maternal line was from England, as her mother, Mary Davis, immigrated to the Chesapeake from London. Mary and Domingo likely began their relationship in the 1670s and were married at a place called Hunting Creek in Calvert County, Maryland, located between the Chesapeake Bay and the Potomac River.[11]

As a first-generation immigrant, Mary Davis did not carry the same racial prejudice against Africans as did many English colonists born in the Americas, and although she might have found an Englishman with whom she could marry and start a family, she accepted the African Domingo as her husband. In 1677,

Mary and Domingo had a son named Thomas. Several years later, when living in neighboring St. Mary's County, Mary became pregnant with another child. On August 11, 1684, she gave birth to a daughter named Rose "on a plantation called Topp of the Hill," which is likely where she worked at the time. Mary described Domingo as a "servant" in legal testimony, though she may have tactfully been trying to distance her children from their father's slave status. While colonists sometimes used the words "servant" and "slave" interchangeably, the family lived in extended bondage. Like her parents, Rose was legally bound sometime after birth, and Henry Damall later held her indefinitely as a slave. Around her thirty-first birthday, Rose appeared in Anne Arundel County, filing a freedom suit against her master.[12]

In 1715, the Davis family and their attorney took an interesting legal approach when presenting Rose's background in court: they argued that she was a servant rather than a slave because she was "a Baptized Mullato Desended by the Mother of Christian Race." This argument attempted to meld her racial classification with her religious affiliation. Therefore, Rose claimed the "benefit by Law" given to other people of mixed ancestry in similar "unhappy circumstances"—an allusion to other Mulattoes who became legally free after thirty-one-year indentures. Noting Rose's suffering under what would become lifelong bondage, her lawyer asked the court to grant her "a free manumission from the said servitude." Rose identified herself as a Christian of English lineal descent and believed she was entitled to the same rights as other servants and subjects under the British Crown.[13]

Mary Davis supported her daughter's plea with a message she wrote in the family Bible. Mary could not attend court in person, so she gave the book that included her statement to her son, Thomas. He delivered his mother's words to the court, hoping they would prove his sister's right to freedom. Even though Rose and her family members lived separately, probably under different masters, they remained in contact and supported one another. In Mary's statement, she repeatedly noted that both of her children were raised as Christians, received baptism, and had godparents. A Catholic priest had baptized Rose, her godfather was a man named Henry Wharton, and her apparent namesake and a family friend, Rose Hunt, was her godmother.[14]

In the family Bible that recorded births and baptisms as evidence, Mary detailed her children's connections to the Christian faith with hope that these facts would guarantee her daughter's liberty. Her testimony highlighted links to fellow Christians and told stories of their familial ties to those in "old England." After describing Thomas's baptism and godparents, Mary said that "this is here Inserted to satisfy any whome it may Consern that my said son Thomas came from a Christian Race by his Mother." After providing similar information about Rose, she once again stated: "This is alsoe Inserted that you may

Know she, my said Daughter, Came of Christian Race by her Mother." Mary attempted to associate race with religion and national origin to help free her daughter (Thomas may have already been free). Some sixty years earlier, Elizabeth Key had used similar arguments, and courts in Virginia had granted her plea (see chapter 1). Both Elizabeth and Rose, women of African and European descent, claimed freedom as their birthright through English and Christian heritage.[15]

Unfortunately for Rose, early eighteenth-century racial thought in the Chesapeake grouped Mulattoes along the lines of hypodescent, closer to their African lineage regardless of English ancestry or Christian upbringing. This is partly why on March 13, 1716, the county court decided that "Rose the Molato" would "serve During Life as a slave." After "mature Deliberation," the justices rejected the argument that mixed-heritage people who belonged to a "Christian Race" deserved freedom. No doubt Rose and her family were devastated by the heartbreaking verdict.[16]

In their decision, Anne Arundel magistrates dismissed Rose's religious-racial self-identification, downplayed her mother Mary's English ancestry, and instead underscored her father Domingo's African origins. In short, officials refused the assertion that a "Molato" could claim the liberties that normally came with "white" English lineage. While Mulatto apprentices sometimes had protections included in their indentures that obligated masters to provide education or Christian tutelage, most did not, and these contracts contained fewer benefits in the Chesapeake over time. Rose's lawsuit does not mention an indenture, and often there was none written. To decide her case, the justices appear to have considered laws from the previous century, though they stretched the legislative limits. Mary and Domingo were married during a time when Maryland law enslaved Englishwomen according to their husband's slave status. Even though Rose was born after the law was overturned, Mary appears to have been kept as a slave for life. Thus "Rose the Molato" inherited her African father's slave status via her European mother. Any children Rose might have would carry the same inheritance of slavery. Thomas's freedom may have been in jeopardy as well.[17]

Maryland court justices were predominantly Protestant by the early eighteenth century and were perhaps less likely to free mixed-heritage people who were Catholic. The court could have decided in favor of Rose's freedom, finding that a thirty-one-year Mulatto indenture was sufficient. However, the decision appears to have mirrored circumstances that befell other racially mixed Catholic families in Maryland, like that of Eleanor "Irish Nell" Butler, her husband, "Negro Charles," and their "mallattoe" children. Charles and Eleanor's marriage in 1681 also made Irish Nell a slave like her African husband, and their children followed their parents into slavery. Culture shaped self-image, and many

In 1748, a Boston newspaper advertised the sale of this portrait by John Greenwood, which is believed to be among the earliest of a woman of African descent in English colonial America. The woman, Ann Arnold, appears as a wet nurse, and the attached poem reminds the viewers, "Nature her various Skill displays / In thousand Shapes, a thousand Ways; / Tho' one Form differs from another, / She's still of all the common Mother; / Then Ladies, let not Pride resist her, / But own that NANNY is your Sister." This both notes Ann's difference from European colonists and insinuates that she is still a "common Mother" and a "Sister," perhaps even related to her master's family. While her background is not explicitly stated, Ann may have had a mixture of European, African, or Native American ancestry. (Adams and Pleck, *Love of Freedom*, 33; Museum of Fine Arts, Boston)

Catholics held close to their religious faith while living among Protestants. The Catholic ceremonies, which these families observed—reflected in marriage rites, prayers, and baptism—added another layer of marginalization to mixed-heritage identity. Still, descendants of these families continued to seek freedom based on their "white," or European, maternal lineage.[18]

Mulattoes in the eighteenth-century Chesapeake were aware that hypo-descent ideology operated within colonial society, yet they still claimed their European ancestry and Christian identities to fight against those who held them in bondage. On Sunday, August 4, 1723, perhaps after a church meeting, an anonymous mixed-heritage slave began to write a letter that reflected recent discussions among a group of "molatters" in Virginia. Recently, news had reached the colony that Edmund Gibson had been appointed bishop of London for the Anglican Church of England, and the group believed it was an opportune time to seek relief from the "Cruell Bondegg" they and their families suffered under in the Chesapeake. The self-identified slave opened the letter with the following:

> To The Right Raverrand father in god my Lord arch Bishop of Lonnd[on] this com[e]s to sattesfie your honour that there is in this Land of verJennia a Sort of people that is Calld molatters which are Baptised and brouaght up in the way of the Christian faith and followes the wayes and Rulles of the Ch[u]rch of England and sum of them has white fathers and sum white mothers and there is in this Land a Law or act which keeps and makes them and there seed Slaves forever.

These opening lines lay out the general experience of most mixed-heritage people in Tidewater Virginia. The language is self-reflexive, as the writer explains the group's position as a Christian people of mixed heritage. This was a morally persuasive petition meant to move the bishop's heart, or his "Lordships brest," to action. "Take Sum pitty of us who is your humble butt Sorrowfull portitinors [petitioners]," begs the author in a supplicating tone that carries throughout the letter. Christian references are prominent throughout the text. The writer says the group speaks for the sake of Jesus Christ "who has comma[n]ded us to seeke first the kingdom of god and all things shall be addid un to us" (Matt. 6:33). Here, people of mixed ancestry were directly quoting biblical scripture. Rose Davis, along with her mother and lawyer, made similar references to Christianity in her freedom suit.[19]

While the group of "molatters" recognized their mixed ancestry, they portrayed themselves foremost as Christian and emphasized their connection to European lineage. They left out any direct mention of African or Indigenous ancestry, thus distancing themselves from any heredity associated with slavery. They knew that their affiliations with Christianity and whiteness were most likely to influence the bishop in granting their freedom. Moreover, while the group described its members' mixed heritage, they did not identify themselves as Mulattoes using first-person language. They acknowledged that they are "Calld molatters" by others while maintaining a focus on their religious upbringing and European ancestry. The letter writer also did not make a distinction between Mulattoes with European mothers and those with European fathers, suggesting that servants held to thirty-one-year indentures in Virginia commonly had the same experience in bondage as slaves: lifelong servitude regardless of which parent had African or Indigenous ancestry. This freedom plea, along with what we know about generational servitude, shows that there was little difference in the lived experience of the two types of Mulattoes. All believed that they, along with their "seed" (offspring), were "Slaves forever."[20]

The Virginia "molatters" letter and other documentation make clear that European masters traditionally held free people of blended ancestry in indefinite servitude. The anonymous writer stated that "there is in this Land a Law or act" that kept Mulattoes of "white fathers" and those of "white mothers" in bondage as "Slaves forever." This was legally inaccurate concerning the children of free European mothers; however, it was true in social practice. Coincidentally, the Virginia General Assembly had updated indenture laws earlier that spring, which made it easier for masters to hold greater numbers of free mixed-heritage children in prolonged indentures. Legislators extended thirty-one years of servitude to the children of "any female mullatto, or indian." This benefited masters who bound free people of color beyond the first generation of intermixture. Through this act, "every such child" of any Mulatto or Indigenous woman—who was herself "by law obliged to serve 'till the age of thirty or thirty-one years"—would automatically serve the same amount of time as the mother.[21]

Virginia's indenture statute of 1723 upheld a form of serial servitude already widespread in British colonies, yet it was even more damaging for the thousands of mixed-heritage people in the province because the law no longer mandated that churchwardens had to record binding children under formal indentures as stated in the preceding acts of 1691 and 1705. This legislation surely followed customs that were already in place, but it was far more dangerous for people of blended ancestry than previous laws. The edict absolved masters from official involvement with the church or county courts when establishing the thirty-one-year work contracts for children of mixed descent. Without any record of these indentures, there was little in the way of stopping perpetual bondage for free mixed people, which bolstered racial hypodescent.[22]

Written indentures signed by a master and recorded by county or church officials left a paper trail that could protect Mulattoes from extended service or slavery, but without contracts mixed-heritage families lost valuable legal proof that asserted their children's free birth. Despite the shift toward customary indentures, Virginia's court records still provide evidence of binding out scores of mixed people. Authorities in Maryland and North Carolina similarly held hundreds of Mulattoes in bonds. While thousands of freeborn people of blended heritage lived in the colonies, it is unknown how many were informally held without indentures in slavery.[23]

The "molatters" may not have known what was taking place in other colonies, but they understood their situation in Virginia, which is why they went over the heads of local church and provincial officials by writing directly to the archbishop in London, asking for equal entry into the Anglican Church family. They understood this plea as their birthright as British subjects. Their first request from the archbishop was for him to secure the help of King George I and authorities to "Releese us out of this Cruell Bondegg." Next, they appealed for adequate opportunities to become better Christians. They knew they were "commandded to keep holey the Sabbath day" but lamented that they "hardly know when it comes for our task mast[e]rs are has hard with us as the Egypttions was with the Chilld[r]ann of Issarall god be marcifll unto us." Some in the group did know what day it was and may have gathered with others on Sundays to craft the letter under the cover of church meetings. They used biblical stories to highlight the drudgery of plantation labor, showing they were not merely acting as Christians to win freedom. In fact, they presented a deeper understanding of their faith by displaying intimate knowledge of the "Bybell."[24]

Even though the anonymous letter writer was marginally literate and others within their group may have been unable to read the Bible firsthand, they shared Christian scripture with each other in the slave and servant quarters through storytelling. This mingled European religious culture with African and Indigenous traditions in America. People of mixed ancestry in slavery, like others in bondage, discussed the hypocrisy of their Christian masters and others who condoned their ill treatment. This was one reason why many Indigenous people and African-born slaves rejected European spiritual beliefs in the colonial period. In comparison, mixed-heritage people who had a connection with their European lineage and grew up with the religion of their ancestors were more likely to accept Christianity. Many yearned to draw closer to the faith of their forefathers and foremothers. The Virginia "molatters" acknowledged "the Redemption of our Savour Christ" and further lamented that they were "in Ignorance of . . . Salvation" because they were "kept out of the Church" by their masters. They also sought to legitimate their romantic relationships in Christian marriage. Like other Christian believers, they did not want to live in sin. They also noted the "Severity and Sorrowful Sarvice [Service]" their owners deployed upon them and said they were continually "hard used" in work. They explained that their masters "doo Look no more up on us then if wee ware dogs."

This group of mixed people sought to make the top church officials aware of the conditions they lived under in bondage.[25]

The final plea that the group of Virginia "molatters" requested concerned the education of their children, especially regarding access to Christian instruction. They pleaded that their "childarn may be Larnd [Learned] the Lords prayer the creed and the ten commandements and that they may appeare Every Lord's day att Church." These parents wanted their offspring to identify as they did: as Christians. They hoped that literacy and Christianity would strengthen their children's freedom claims even as they recognized their own scholastic shortcomings. Indeed, the author apologized for his or her grammatical limitations by noting, "my Riting is vary bad." Still, the group hoped that high officials in Britain would extend learning to their descendants so their progeny could achieve more than they had in life. "Our desire," they wrote, "is that godllines Should abbound among us and wee desire that our Childarn be putt to Scool and . . . Larnd to Reed through the Bybell." If British officials would "grant and Settell one thing," this would be their only request. These slaves contested hypodescent by claiming English religion and were willing to forgo liberty if their descendants could continue on as an educated and Christian people.[26]

The Virginia "molatters" letter is unique because there are few, if any, detailed writings that exist from self-identified people of mixed ancestry in the colonial period. This is also one of the few surviving letters written by any slave in this era, and it suggests that European parents, family members, or friends may have taught people of mixed lineage how to read and write—or they learned from free people of color. This was a known practice in the Caribbean, where elite British planters sometimes freed their mixed-heritage children, left them large inheritances, and even sent them to school for formal educations. In sharp contrast, this letter writer represents the most prevalent position for Mulattoes in the British Americas: lifelong bondage. By 1723, Virginia contained more people of mixed descent, identified as Mulatto, than anywhere else in North America or the Caribbean. This letter shows firsthand that people of blended ancestry in this position believed that their Christian devotion and European lineage should make them and their families free.[27]

For mixed-heritage people, identifying as Christian was not synonymous with choosing a "white" identity, though they realized the power of their European ancestry and avoided direct attacks on racial slavery. This is clear when considering that the letter writer did not argue for universal abolition or for the freedom of African slaves. The group understood the colonial politics of race and perhaps knew that requesting the abolition of slavery would undermine any chance to achieve liberty for themselves as Mulattoes. They only put forth the argument that they were wrongly enslaved as a people of mixed descent who could claim European heritage.

Since the seventeenth century, "Negroes" and "Mulattoes" in the English colonies relied on Christianity during freedom petitions, and while some may have amplified their devotion to aid manumission efforts, most practiced the faith of their own accord or at the behest of family, friends, and missionaries. Family members baptized "Mulatto" children more regularly than "Negro" children in Barbados, even though they were far less numerous. In port cities such as Boston and Philadelphia, mixed-heritage children also appear in almshouses and church baptismal records. Other examples of Christianity come to light across the British provinces, even in rural areas. Remote colonial locations had fewer churches and ordained ministers, which prompted groups like the Society for the Propagation of the Gospel in Foreign Parts (SPG) to send missionaries to these areas. The SPG actively sought to spread the Christian faith among people of African and Indigenous backgrounds throughout the Americas, with the goal of converting "heathens and infidels." While the SPG reports may have at times exaggerated their progress in propagating Christianity, the missionaries traveled to the Carolinas and "backcountry," where ethnoracial mixture occurred regularly, and ministered to diverse communities made up of African, European, Indigenous, and mixed-heritage people.[28]

From the mid-1730s through the 1740s, the Anglican reverend John Fordyce worked with the SPG to expand the Church of England's presence in South Carolina. Reverend Fordyce proselytized to those of African, European, and Indigenous descent in Prince Frederick's Parish, northwest of Georgetown, where he administered Christian baptism to hundreds of people, including those of mixed ancestry. In one report to SPG officials, he described a family he baptized that consisted of "one *Negroe* woman, and six of her Children *Mulattoes*." The family had been observing Christianity before the arrival of Reverend Fordyce, who explained that the woman and her three oldest children "could read well, and repeat the Church-Catechism; and two of the remaining three could repeat the Creed and the Lord's-Prayer." If this woman was like most Christians, she prayed daily, thanking God for life and her children. One can imagine the mother reading the Bible to her young ones and teaching them how to pray. These spiritual practices were a mainstay in this family, whose identification with Christianity was central to their everyday lives.[29]

Slaves and free people of color often combined elements of Christianity with other spiritual practices and syncretized African, Indigenous, and European religious traditions. Body modification through ritual scarring and tattooing was typical in many African and Indigenous American cultures, and Europeans also sometimes took part in the practice. James Nisbet, a "Mulattoe" servant in Richmond County, Virginia, was surely an ardent believer in a Christian god, for he had a tattoo of Jesus, the "Saviour on the Cross . . . imprinted on his Left-Arm." His decision to have this religious symbol inscribed into his flesh reflected a lifetime commitment to the faith. In Dinwiddie County, Virginia, a "dark mulatto man" named Jemmy was "very fond of *singing hymns* and *preaching*" the Christian faith. African American religious practices combined European and West African customs in the Americas and reflected the amalgamation of cultures and peoples.[30]

Slaves from various backgrounds saw themselves reflected in biblical stories and Christian teachings, which encouraged the resolve of many to be free. Just as the group of Virginia "molatters" compared their plight to "the Chilld[r]ann of Issarall" under Egyptian slavery, the preacher Jemmy made a personal exodus. The "mulatto man" left his master and went to Williamsburg, where he gave up the common slave name Jemmy and changed it to a Christian name: James Williams. Thousands of slaves similarly exercised their autonomy by adopting surnames while still enslaved, during escape, or after manumission. Dropping a slave name, usually assigned by a master, and choosing one's own name was a rite of passage for former slaves. Selecting a Christian name, singing hymns, preaching from the Bible, and getting Jesus tattooed on one's arm were all ways that mixed people fashioned themselves according to their own religious beliefs.[31]

### MULATTOES LIKE "ALL VIRGINIA NEGROS"

Religious faith helped all people get through the harsh realities and struggles that surrounded colonial life, work, and death. African, Indigenous, and mixed-heritage peoples were most susceptible to exploitation, whereby physical, psychological, and sexual abuse at the hands of masters and overseers shaped their lives under systems of bondage. Threats of violence led to emotional pain, frequent stress, and periods of depression. Within this colonial atmosphere, people of African and Native American lineage fought to hold on to their traditions. They carried their unique cultures—Mandingo, Igbo, Choctaw, Tuscarora, and many others—over generations and merged them with European customs in the colonies. Cultures survived, transformed, and helped combat the effects of settler colonialism. Parents and elders passed down music and the rhythms of life, words and language patterns, and traditional and other religious beliefs, including veneration of the ancestors and the importance of kinship ties and community networks.[32]

Families of African, Indigenous, and mixed descent carried the agonies and traumas of bondage over multiple generations, yet they also passed down strength, perseverance, and survival techniques to their progeny. Many blended families exemplify both the good and bad of slavery and servitude, and several were recorded on Virginia's Eastern Shore in Northampton County. In 1682 a "muletto Girle" named Jane Webb was born "the daughter of a white woman,"

Ann Williams, and a "Negro" man named Daniel Webb. Born out of wedlock, Jane grew up in servitude until around 1700. Sometime after, she partnered with "a Certaine Negro Slave" named Left, who served a man named Thomas Savage. Whether she fell in love with her husband or was drawn to him for more practical reasons, Jane said she had "a strong desire to Intermarry with ... Left." The couple had several children who moved in and out of servitude and slavery over the years, but the family always maintained that they were free people.[33]

While people of mixed heritage often petitioned for freedom based on their European lineage, in private many of them associated with African and Native American ancestry and identified with these groups. This is apparent in Jane's choice to marry Left, whereby she committed herself and her family to their African heritage and identity, which had become synonymous with slavery. Over the years, Jane and her family often stood helpless against their master and other colonial elites who frustrated their attempts to remove themselves from bondage. Their master, Thomas, deceptively kept Left in slavery after he had promised to release him, and he illegally bound several of their children in prolonged servitude.[34]

The Webb family understood that independence would support their social mobility and challenged those in power to obtain and maintain it. While Jane fought for her children's freedom in the mid-1720s, witnesses testified that they overheard her say, "if all Virginia Negros had as good a heart as she had they would all be free." Colonial officials saw these words as inflammatory because if "all Virginia Negros" rose up to take their liberty, it would come at the expense of Europeans in power. In the eyes of the planters, free people of mixed ancestry who sympathized with African slaves posed a serious threat to the existing power structure. This is why the colonial court condemned Jane's "dangerous words tending to the breach of the peace" and gave her ten lashes for such incendiary language. Just the thought that mixed people would choose their African ancestry over European interests drove fear into the hearts of Virginia's planter-elites, who ran the colony. In the early 1720s, authorities had reportedly uncovered plans for more than one slave uprising and viewed those who allied with enslaved "Virginia Negros" as rebellious actors. The master class knew that not all free Mulattoes favored their Christian or European identity over loyalty to their African kin. Not only did Jane choose a husband of African descent, but she also verbally identified with the plight of the enslaved and stood with them in solidarity.[35]

Jane Webb passed a spirit of resistance and Christianity on to her children. She gave most of them Christian names, and one of these sons, Abimeleck, was likely named after a king in the Bible. Like his mother before him, Abimeleck revealed a defiant spirit. In 1750, the Northampton County court found him guilty of "combining with sundry Negros in a conspiracy against the white

People of this county." The charges appear to have been stronger than his actions, since they were based on comments Abimeleck made about the potential for a successful slave insurrection. While discussing a local planter's injustices against the enslaved, Abimeleck had privately commented to another laborer that with "godalmightys assistance or blessing" those held in bondage could take over the county "in one nights time." Someone leaked the contents of this conversation to officials, and the court gave Abimeleck thirty-nine lashes for his insolent words. He also had to post a £100 bond to ensure his proper behavior in the future.[36]

Like other Africans, Native Americans, and marginalized groups in colonial society, mixed-heritage people who publicly expressed their true emotions about those in authority risked punishment. Still, they expressed personal dissatisfaction with unjust masters, labor systems, and legal institutions. When their candor reached the ears of Virginia's magistrates, Jane and her son Abimeleck both bore the consequences of corporal punishment. If anything, this retributive treatment pushed mixed-heritage people, both slave and free, to view themselves as united with other African and Indigenous slaves. Mixed people's lack of political power and legal protection strengthened their identification with other subjugated people of color.[37]

Many colonial elites viewed free African, Indigenous, and mixed-heritage people as a threat to the socioracial order, and the exclusion of these groups from having the same rights as other British subjects characterized their position inside the empire as nominal denizens. While free persons of color sought equal liberties with other "white" subjects, colonial legislators routinely blocked their full participation in colonial society. The year after rumors of slave conspiracies circulated in Virginia, the general assembly declared in 1723 that "no free negro, mullatto, or indian" could vote for members of the provincial assembly or in "any other election whatsoever." Free people of color had voted for local officials in the English provinces, but colonial magistrates passed laws against the practice in several other provinces as well, including North Carolina (1715), South Carolina (1721), and Jamaica (1733).[38]

British administrators who oversaw the colonies questioned the revocation of voting rights for free people of color. Richard West, legal counsel to the British Board of Trade, wrote of Virginia's 1723 voter restriction: "I cannot see why one *Freeman* should be used worse than another meerly upon account of his complexion." Richard asked the board to review "putting such limits and Conditions upon those persons." A dozen years after its passage, the British Board of Trade looked more closely into the statute and asked Virginia governor William Gooch to justify the decision in 1735. The governor's response explained why the assembly passed a law "depriving free Negros & Mulattos of the priviledge of voting at any Election of Burgesses to serve in the General Assembly, or at any other Elections." He put forth that "Free-Negros & Mulattos were much Suspected" to have been involved in a planned slave insurrection just before the passage of the act. Jane Webb (and, later, her son Abimeleck) had exposed these allegiances.[39]

Fears of joint rebellion by "Negro" and "Mulatto" slaves and free people of color helped officials justify policies of racial hypodescent. Although Virginia elites could not prove that "free Negros & Mulattos" were involved in the conspiracies of the 1720s, Governor Gooch considered the "Insolence" of these free people as sufficient evidence to label them coconspirators. Jane Webb's seditious words may have exemplified a veiled threat to revolt but it was also a public display of solidarity. Her marriage proved her partnership with an African man, Left, and also with the slave community. This is why Virginia's government not only prohibited "the Meetings of Slaves" but also "thought it necessary . . . to fix a perpetual Brand upon Free-Negros & Mulattos by excluding them from that great Priviledge of a Freeman, well knowing they always did, and ever will, adhere to and favour the Slaves." Governor Gooch believed these loyalties would "forever be the Case." In the Chesapeake, free Mulattoes often associated with slaves, but this was less likely when their class position was elevated, usually from the inheritances of wealthy European fathers, which was more prevalent in South Carolina and the Caribbean.[40]

In defending this early form of disenfranchisement in Virginia, Governor Gooch also pointed out that the number of free people of color who were eligible to vote was so small that it was "scarce worth while to take any Notice of them." The irony is that European colonists repeatedly took "Notice" of the relatively small free population of color because fears of their growing numbers pushed discriminatory legislation. Besides this, Governor Gooch noted that Virginia law already prohibited "free Negros & Mulattos" from serving on juries or as witnesses in legal cases. They "are as much excluded from being good and lawful Men" that he compared them to the serfs "of Old by the Laws of England." The governor argued this was also a matter of class, not just race. Many British colonists viewed "free Negros & Mulattos" as a criminal caste and supported continued subjugation of free people of African, Indigenous, and mixed descent by actively passing legislation that excluded them from colonial society.[41]

Throughout most of his diatribe, Governor Gooch grouped "Negros & Mulattos" together and further admitted that colonial officials of the past had acted "with design" to make free people of African heritage understand "that a distinction ought to be made between their Offspring and the Descendants of an Englishman, with whom they never were to be Accounted Equal." Of course, this view reflected an elite English perspective, for many free people of African, Indigenous, and mixed heritage considered themselves equal to Europeans.[42]

When Governor Gooch justified the Virginia assembly's decision to legally deprive "Free Negros & Mulattos" of the vote and other rights, he also revealed critical insight into how these people viewed themselves:

> This [disenfranchisement], I confess, may Seem to carry an Air of Severity to Such as are unacquainted with the Nature of Negros, and the Pride of a manumitted Slave, who looks on himself imediately on his Acquiring his freedom to be as good a Man as the best of his Neighbours, but especially if he is descended of a white Father or Mother, lett them be of what mean Condition soever; and as most of them are the Bastards of some of the worst of our imported Servants and Convicts, it seems no ways Impolitick, as well for discouraging that kind of Copulation, as to preserve a decent Distinction between them and their Betters, to leave this Mark on them, until time and Education has changed the Indication of their spurious Extraction, and made some Alteration in their Morals.

William Gooch perceived "the Nature of Negros" as inherently depraved, an essence that was passed down through the family line, including to those of mixed heritage. He disdained free Africans who took pride in their liberty and specifically pointed out people of mixed African and European lineage who believed that their "white" parentage made them just "as good . . . as the best of" their European "Neighbors." The governor subscribed to the elite British notion that everyone held a natural station in society, inscribed at birth. This is why he discussed Mulattoes with the "worst" or lowest sorts of European immigrants such as servants and convicts and ranked them near African slaves.[43]

Governor Gooch elucidates the strict hypodescent philosophy that came to define the eighteenth-century Chesapeake, arguing that free "Mulattoes" should be considered alongside free "Negroes" because it would "preserve a decent Distinction between them and their Betters." In other words, hypodescent squashed any calls for equality and kept free people of African or Indigenous descent subjugated in the colonial hierarchy. In this sense, Virginia officials justified segregationist law and enforced "white" supremacist policies in response to free Africans and mixed-heritage people who asserted their rights as British subjects. While Governor Gooch readily acknowledged that the legal system would "Mark" Mulattoes and keep them in a subjugated social position, below those of full European descent, he conveyed that their morals might improve with "time and Education." In actuality, governors, general assemblies, and other administrators structured colonial societies that provided people of African, Indigenous, and mixed heritage with few opportunities for advancement, because they passed and upheld legislation that oppressed people of color.[44]

While Governor Gooch's views are transparent, what did the people that he spoke of believe about where they belonged in the social order? If free Mulattoes considered themselves equal to European colonists, did this mean they sometimes considered themselves above their African counterparts? This is a complicated question. As we have seen, mixed families such as the Webbs considered themselves the same as "all Virginia Negroes," or at least some showed camaraderie with them. On the other hand, hostilities existed between lighter-skinned "Mulattoes" and darker-skinned "Negroes." These long-standing tensions, defined as colorism, were born out of this colonial period.

### COLORISM AND THE "APPROACH TOWARD WHITENESS"

Throughout the Americas, European colonists came to equate lighter skin with social advancement, and Africans, Native Americans, and mixed-heritage people also imbibed this philosophy at times. This gave birth to colorism: the privileges, prejudices, and animosities associated with skin-color hierarchy within non-"white" communities. While Europeans connected racial beliefs to people of African or Native American ancestry, communities of color also fostered ideas about race. Colorism is an extension of this racism, for many Europeans with lighter or "white" skin viewed themselves as superior to those of African and Native American descent with "black" or "tawny" skin. By the eighteenth century, people from various ethnoracial backgrounds displayed favoritism toward those with light skin, and this sometimes led to an air of superiority among mixed Mulattoes who believed their European blood elevated them above African "Negroes." These sentiments were not universal and were often situational, but favoritism and jealousies related to variations in skin color or the perception of having "white" blood could drive wedges between individuals in communities of color.[45]

Sometimes the free mixed-heritage children of wealthy men, commonly found in South Carolina and the Atlantic islands, avoided consorting with "Negro" slaves, and this social distancing intertwined with class. William Gooch noted the "Pride" of manumitted slaves in Virginia, especially when they were "descended of a white Father or Mother," even if they were lower class or of a "mean Condition." Certain wealthy people descended from both European planters and slaves may have been ashamed of their African heritage, which linked them with bondage and poverty. Some included the mixed children who were sent from Jamaica when young for schooling in Britain. One English planter in Jamaica derisively called it a "strange manner in which some of them [Mulattoes] are educated." After returning to the island years later, these elite children of "mixed complexions" became aware of "their future misery" in the Caribbean upon realizing that they originated from African slaves. This English planter may have only been slightly embellishing when he wrote that the mixed-heritage "Miss faints at the sight of her relations, especially when papa tells her that black *Quasheba* is her own mother."[46]

Evidently some mixed people found it difficult to relate to their "black kindred." This may have been why David Williamson went to Britain to study law and mathematics. Born in Kingston to Jamaica's attorney general and an African woman, he claimed, "I never associated with men of colour, although one myself, because I always found them very ignorant." In freedom and in slavery, there were greater incentives for mixed people to associate with "whites." In Bermuda, when the mixed-heritage servant Doll Allen asked the general court for the "freedome" to seek out her own contract of indenture, she based her claims on her European "fathers Right," "her birth among Christians," and noted that "it hath pleased God to sett a distinction betweene her and heathen Negros." In later periods, some people of mixed ancestry openly shunned those in African communities and even persecuted "Negroes" in order to curry favor with "whites." This type of behavior fostered social friction between people of color with "light" and "dark" skin tones.[47]

One report describing colorism appeared in 1733, when the *Pennsylvania Gazette* published an op-ed piece ostensibly penned by a free African man who was scathingly critical of free people of mixed heritage. The anonymous author writes under the pen name Blackamore and blasts *"Molattoes,"* whose "Ambition seizes many of them immediately to become *Gentlefolks*" who desire to enter into elite "white" social circles. The author claimed to be "an ordinary Mechanick" of African descent, who presumably would have been a dark-complected free "Negro." However, it is more plausible that he was a European colonist, none other than the gazette's editor, Benjamin Franklin. The famous writer used a variety of pen names in his early career, and historians believe the influential colonist used the pseudonym Blackamore in this case. Benjamin Franklin witnessed interactions between various people of African descent in Philadelphia, and the account provides information that appears to come from scientific observations that are consistent with other sources. The piece also rang true enough for the *South-Carolina Gazette* to carry the article on its front page two years later. Regardless of its origins, the op-ed offers accurate insight into the relationships between "Negroes" and "Mulattoes."[48]

Similar to Governor Gooch, Blackamore felt that free Mulattoes attempted to rise too quickly above their "natural Sphere" in society by imitating the European gentry. Class was at play as well as race here, for he generally observed that Mulattoes found themselves "to be some *new Gentleman*, or rather *half Gentleman*, or *Mungrel*"—a negative reference to their mixed heritage. Blackamore illustrated the example with a story of a mixed-heritage acquaintance, described under the pseudonym Jack Chopstick, writing that "the vain Fool thrusts himself into Conversation with People of the best Sense and the most Polite." Apparently, Jack sought to socialize with the elite after he "got a little Money," which "exceedingly alter'd" his self-perception. Blackamore sarcastically quipped, "we below cannot help considering him as a Monkey that climbs a Tree, the higher he goes, the more he shews his Arse." While Jack lacked the formal upbringing of a gentleman, money allowed the mixed-heritage man a modicum of social mobility, and through this rise, he pursued social connections with the urban elite.[49]

At its core, the tension between "Negroes" and "Molattoes," according to Blackamore, was linked to socioracial hierarchy as well as the advantages and disadvantages attached to class and color. Blackamore explained, "I pray I may always have the Grace to know myself and my Station" in life. Here the author defers to his European social "betters," but he also admonishes those free people of color who would consider themselves equal to Europeans in colonial society. Blackamore also praised the *"true Gentleman"* who could "take a Walk, or Drink a Glass, and converse freely, if there be occasion, with honest Men of any Degree below him." The author disparages people of mixed heritage while lauding the European gentry, indicating that he was Benjamin Franklin or another European colonist who sought to uphold the existing socioracial order by knocking down nouveau riche Mulattoes. Some mixed people accumulated wealth in the British Caribbean and in urban centers in North America. In rural areas, too, certain "Mulattoes" distinguished themselves from other "Negroes" and prospered after inheriting estates from European fathers. Class antipathies and color prejudice existed beyond "black" and "white" as free people of color worked to achieve success and maintain confidence in the face of colonial societies that marked them as inferior.[50]

Mixed-heritage people were in a unique middling position in which they experienced prejudice from Europeans and Africans, which is another reason why some socially distanced themselves from "Negroes." "Their Approach towards Whiteness," wrote Blackamore, "makes them look back with some kind of Scorn upon the Colour they seem to have left." Even if Blackamore was indeed Benjamin Franklin, he was nonetheless correct: certain Mulattoes were "terribly afraid of being thought Negroes, and therefore avoid[ed] as much as possible their Company or Commerce." Instead, some people of blended ancestry preferred to cultivate relationships with "whites" because they believed that having European benefactors could move them closer to the social benefits linked to whiteness. Whether these advantages were perceived or real, sometimes individual "Negroes" and "Mulattoes" developed bitter feelings toward each other because of light-skinned privilege and dark-skinned discrimination in colonial societies.[51]

Sometimes pride and fear moved mixed-heritage people to disengage from others of African descent, and dark-skinned "Negroes" responded with similar disdain for "Mulattoes." The free people of mixed ancestry who looked down on slaves and resented being affiliated with those in bondage received similar animus in return. In response, "the Negroes, who do not think them [Mulattoes] better than themselves," often gave those Mulattoes "Contempt with Interest," wrote Blackamore. "And the Whites" did not respect people of mixed heritage simply because they were "nearer Affinity in Colour." Colonial elites did not accept mixed-heritage people as equals, which made it impossible for them to craft an identity on par with "white" colonists. Blackamore summed up the situation for certain mixed people: this "Generation of Molattoes ... are seldom well belov'd either by the Whites or the Blacks." However, this is where Benjamin Franklin may have showed his hand in the text, for evidence overwhelmingly shows that most "Molattoes" were accepted within African communities during the colonial period.[52]

While some people of mixed lineage disassociated themselves from "Negroes" or felt ostracized by other people of color, this type of mutual alienation usually took place among smaller, wealthier groups of mixed-heritage people whose ancestors had mixed with Europeans over multiple generations. Hostilities between "Mulattoes" and "Negroes" may have been exacerbated in cities where small groups of free people of blended ancestry were able to form communities of their own. Cities such as Philadelphia and Charlestown, where newspapers published Blackamore's op-ed, were two locations where sizable free African and mixed populations grew during the colonial period. Even if Blackamore was not an "ordinary Mechanick" of African descent, his views accurately reflect how some wealthy mixed-heritage people operated in colonial cities, although this did not represent the masses of mixed people.[53]

Later in the eighteenth century, Charlestown, New Orleans, and other urban centers were known to contain a middle socioracial class between "black" and "white" that amassed considerable wealth and molded itself after the gentry. In a sarcastic fashion that Blackamore carries throughout his commentary, he concluded, "there are perhaps *Molattoes* in Religion, in Politicks, in Love, and in several other Things; but of all sorts of *Molattoes*, none appear to me so monstrously ridiculous as the *Molatto Gentleman*." The derisive claim presented the way many European colonists viewed free mixed-heritage people: Mulattoes with some wealth were socioracial imposters who tried to rise in society without proper training, merit, or the "blood" to become the equals of true "whites." Many of Jamaica's planter-legislators felt similarly when they stripped Mulattoes of the franchise in 1733, citing "their corruption of blood."[54]

Like many Africans and Native Americans, people of blended heritage did not readily accept inferiority, nor did they simply defer to those who had more money, power, or political influence. While it is impossible to determine the line at which self-confidence becomes arrogance, some "Mulattoes" absorbed "white" supremacist ideals and believed that their European lineage elevated them above "Negroes." Class often exacerbated these sentiments, yet even those from modest backgrounds felt they deserved similar rights to other British colonists. Certainly, mixed-heritage people from lower socioracial levels who reached for equality did not all attempt to subjugate other groups in their efforts to gain social acceptance and respect.[55]

When people of African, Native American, or mixed descent replicated a culture equated with success, this did not necessarily mean they wanted to become "white"; rather, it meant they sought to achieve the same freedoms that Europeans enjoyed. Mixed-heritage people, like others, took on forms of elite European culture to strengthen access to greater privileges through connections to patrons in their communities. Blackamore noted that the "whites" regarded these attempts to cultivate close relationships "as too bold and assuming, and bordering on Impudence." In short, "Whitefolks" were not generally "fond of the Company of *Molattoes*." These views echoed those of Governor Gooch and European gentry in the Chesapeake, the Carolinas, the Caribbean, and Latin America, all expressing concerns that Mulattoes overstepped socioracial boundaries.[56]

English colonists from various classes saw people of African, Indigenous, or mixed descent as secondary subjects within the British Empire. This is why many Europeans urged lawmakers to legally prevent "Negroes," "Indians," "Mulattoes," and "Mustees" from equal participation in colonial societies. Free people of blended ancestry combated these efforts by attempting to achieve economic success and stability for themselves and their families. Still, the majority of mixed-heritage individuals were enslaved throughout the colonial period, and most of them were left with only one method to attain freedom: escape.[57]

### ASSOCIATING WITH "NEGROES" AND "INDIANS"

When legal avenues to freedom were closed, some "Negro," "Mulatto," and "Mustee" slaves fled from their masters in search of the fruits of liberty. However, successful escape was difficult, as slave owners instituted a variety of safeguards to capture and return runaways. With the growth of print technology in the eighteenth-century, colonial newspapers provided masters with a tool that broadened the reach of information concerning escapees beyond word of mouth or local postings. While few newspapers operated routinely in the British Caribbean by the middle of the century, editors in colonial North America were consistently printing runaway advertisements by the 1730s.

Owners provided physical descriptions to help retrieve thousands of bound men, women, and children. These ads often recounted a runaway's ancestry, family relations, and other people they associated with, which revealed clues about personal identity.[58]

Despite the routine bias that came from a master's pen, colonial advertisements relayed accurate physical descriptions, ages, heights, clothing, and other details, such as where slaves were running to and with whom they kept company. Free and enslaved Africans harbored runaways of all backgrounds, including mixed-heritage people who escaped from their masters. In 1734, the master of a slave named Franke reported that the "young Molatto House-Wench" ran away from Johns Island, just southwest of Charlestown, and that she was "without doubt harbour'd by some free Negroes or Slaves." People of mixed lineage sought sanctuary among those with whom they felt most comfortable, who were often of African descent. Cudjoe was "a short well set Mustee Fellow" who ran off from a South Carolina plantation in the spring of 1743. He remained hidden through the summer months with the suspected assistance of "some Negroes" who were old acquaintances. Bondsmen and bondswomen of blended ancestry were subjected to the same arduous labor as African slaves, wore the same clothes, spoke the same dialects, and had the same desire for freedom. They shared common struggles that brought them together in community, which is why those of African descent risked severe punishment to conceal mixed-heritage escapees.[59]

Throughout the colonies, people of color who sheltered runaways needed to be confident that those they took in were loyal to their communities, just as runaways had to trust that their peers would not expose their whereabouts and turn them over to authorities for hefty rewards. This trust was important for runaways who hid out in densely populated urban areas, where larger communities of color resided. One master believed that his seventeen-year-old "Mulatto wench" Venus was possibly "harboured by other slaves in the kitchens and quarters in and about" Williamsburg. In Pennsylvania, the runaway slave John Poole, also "call'd Molattoe Jack," may have sought a change of clothes and other help from "several negroes about the city of Philadelphia . . . that he was acquainted with." Metropolitan anonymity often allowed people of color to move freely in cities. Hugh Jones was a "mulatto Man" who made a living by treating the ailments "among the Negroes and slaves of Charlestown." However, around 1753, South Carolina magistrates suspected Hugh of being a runaway and a "sham Doctor." Officials labeled him "as a vagabond and Idle person" who had "often been seen gaming among the Negroes on the Sabbath Day." While it is uncertain if Hugh was a better doctor or gambler, it is clear that he spent his time among other people of African descent. Multiple people were likely aware of the whereabouts of runaways residing in places such as Charlestown, Williamsburg, Philadelphia, New York City, Boston, and other cities, which is why secrecy was key in these urban communities of color.⁶⁰

Family members were trustworthy hosts during escape, and mixed-heritage people sought refuge among relations with whom they felt most secure. Isaac was "an outlawed Mulatto Fellow" in Virginia, who was supposedly "harbored by Colonel *John Snelson's* Negroes . . . among whom he has a Wife." If Isaac went there or somewhere nearby, he risked capture to see his partner, or he may have found solace with "his Brother *John Kenney*, a Mulatto Slave." In 1744, brothers George and William Hugill also ran away from their masters in New Castle County, Delaware. Allegedly, the "two Mulatto Men" stole wigs for disguises and guns for protection, seemingly willing to risk their lives for one another.⁶¹

Familial relations influenced mixed-heritage people's self-identity, and parents were especially influential in how their children created a sense of self. Harry was a "Mulatto Fellow" born around 1751 who grew up traveling throughout the Chesapeake with his master, Theodorick Bland. Although his slave appeared faithful at times, Theodorick came to realize that Harry was loyal to his own family first. When he was around twenty-two or twenty-three years old, Harry left his master in Dinwiddie County, Virginia. Theodorick knew that Harry probably went first to see his mother, "an old Negro Woman" who lived 100 miles or more north in Fairfax County. "Scars . . . on his Arms and Back" from previous beatings testified to how much Harry risked to visit the woman who brought him into the world. His devotion to his mother showed that Harry likely associated with his African roots. Mixed-heritage slaves believed they were entitled to the same liberties as their European fathers but many ran away from master-fathers to pay respects to their African mothers.⁶²

Although master-fathers seldom publicly revealed their paternal ties to mixed-heritage slaves, thousands of Mulattoes who appear in colonial records disclose the existence of widespread European paternity. Isaac Bee was a "Mulatto Lad" who likely had a European father. In his late teens he ran away from his master in Mecklenburg County, Virginia. Like others in his situation, Isaac felt he had "a Right to his Freedom, because his Father was a Freeman." People of mixed ancestry seem to have worried less about establishing personal relationships with absent European fathers and were more concerned with the freedom they believed was their birthright. In their eyes, independence was their inheritance.⁶³

Family and friends routinely provided support for mixed people to escape their masters, and sometimes this encouragement came from Indigenous parents. Mary was a "young mulatto or mustee" servant who lived in Santee, South Carolina, and was separated from her mother, who lived on a Stono plantation. According to her master, Mary "was inticed away by her mother, an Indian wench, named Sarah." Mary's owner figured they could not find the servant because her mother or some other "evil-minded, malicious, villainous persons, of a mean degree," aided her escape and concealed her. With this assistance, Mary disappeared from her master for at least a year or more. Native American parents in the Carolinas imparted traditional knowledge to their children and helped younger slaves resist bondage, evade capture, and remain hidden.[64]

The sale of servants and slaves over long distances frequently separated families, but when kinship bonds were disrupted, surrogates often raised young slaves of mixed African, European, or Indigenous heritage. In October of 1743, "two Mustee Fellows" ran away from their master, Rene Peyre, in St. James Parish, South Carolina. Rene said an "Indian Wench" around forty years old had also joined the two young men. She may have been their mother or aunt or a stand-in for one of these relations. Regardless, the two men shared a special familial bond with the woman whom they took the chance to escape with. The eighteen-year-old Billey did not have any outstanding physical features, though his skin was "more of an *Indian* Colour," but the twenty-one-year-old Tom would have been easy to spot, towering over other colonists at six feet, nine inches, tall. Perhaps Tom and Billey could travel faster and cover more ground without the forty-year-old woman, yet they remained devoted to this Native American elder. She certainly had skills and wisdom that aided the young men during their journey. They were seen using a gun to hunt for food, and the woman could prepare wild game and gather edible plants to eat. Like many Indigenous women, she could also identify medicinal herbs and knew remedies that could heal wounds and treat sickness. In short, she carried wisdom beyond the young men's years, which was invaluable to their collective success on the run. Tom and Billey were connected to this "Indian" woman, and their reciprocal relationship illustrates how people of mixed descent with Native American lineage honored this part of their heritage by associating with others like them.[65]

People of blended ancestry relied on teachings from multiple sides of their diverse ancestries. Like the Mustee Tom, the slave Sampson was another "very big Negroe man" who also had "some Indian blood in him," and he utilized cultural knowledge during an escape from his master in the western part of New Jersey. Sampson affiliated with his Indigenous roots, for he partnered with an "Indian woman" and passed down their culture to their son, Sam, who was born in the mid-1730s. Sam favored his mother and looked "much like an Indian, except in his hair," which had the curls of his father. On September 20, 1747, Sampson and his son left their master, Silas Parvin, in search of freedom. The runaways took rugs, which they used to sleep on, or perhaps they traded these items for food, clothing, or other goods that might aid their escape. Sam was between twelve and fourteen years old, and Sampson was around fifty. At this age, Sampson felt the aches and pains of a lifetime of toil, and even though his body was "very lame," he was armed with a "gun and ammunition." He was a "hip shot" and excellent marksman, which meant that while Sampson might have moved slower than other men, he could still defend himself and his family against anyone who might interfere with their safety. We do not know who taught Sampson how to shoot, but evidence suggests he learned a number of skills and customs from other Africans and Native Americans who reflected his mixed heritage.[66]

The people Sampson aligned himself with and the culture they shared were apparent when he took his liberty. Their master, Silas Parvin, described Sampson and Sam as "well clothed" in European dress when they escaped, though like many young slaves, the boy walked barefoot. Silas also believed they would have changed clothes and "dressed themselves in Indian dress, and gone towards Carolina." Sampson, and possibly his wife, also passed their language down to Sam, for the father and son could "both talk Indian very well" and could use the unidentified Indigenous language to communicate exclusively with each other. Despite the harsh effects of slavery and settler colonialism, Sampson's family kept their Native American culture alive by passing down traditions from one generation to the next. If they headed south toward the Carolinas, it is possible that Sampson was trying to reach his people and perhaps attempted to reunite with a tribe, village, or other family members. Their African heritage also allowed them to rely on other Africans for aid and shelter among the enslaved or free people of color. This father and son of African and Indigenous lineage, therefore, had access to multiple communities. Slaves like them, sometimes referred to as Mustees, had unique advantages to escape bondage and benefited directly from being able to rely on multiple ancestries.[67]

Mixed-heritage servants and slaves of Native American descent had a cultural edge over their African peers when Indigenous friends, kin, or tribal groups had knowledge of the land and resources that could help secure their escape into "Indian" country. At times, Native Americans invaded the British colonies directly and helped slaves escape from plantations. In 1753, the governor of South Carolina, James Glen, complained that Senecas, Nittewegas, and Shawnees "frequently come into our Settlements sculking in the Woods and Swamps" and cause the colonists much trouble by "carrying off ... our Slaves as had the least Tincture of Indian Blood in them." This shows that when some Native Americans raided European settlements they actively sought out Indigenous slaves, including those of mixed ancestry. Attacks that captured "Indian" and "Mustee" slaves tied in with larger conflicts between the English, French, Haudenosaunees (Iroquois), and other Indigenous groups. Native Americans who raided the English also took European and African captives, who could be ransomed, sold, or incorporated into existing clan systems. These raids on European settlements targeted women and children for adoption and prized those already familiar with Indigenous practices: "Indians" and "Mustees."[68]

Native Americans seized enslaved people who showed even the smallest trace of "Indian Blood" on South Carolina plantations as a tactic to strengthen their communities and challenge European power. Indigenous tribes strategically incorporated new people into their clan systems to replace those lost to disease, warfare, and captivity by others. Some groups may have even looked to recapture their own people from the English. They also realized that slaves with Indigenous ancestry were more likely to be knowledgeable of general Native American customs. These abductees had less figurative cultural distance to travel and thus required less time to become integrated into the given Indigenous group. Many of these captives could immediately contribute to village life with useful knowledge and skills.[69]

Indigenous peoples sometimes agreed that they would return "any Negro or Mullatto" runaways to South Carolina authorities, but in at least one 1751 treaty, Cherokees did not specify the return of "Indian" or "Mustee" slaves. Native Americans carefully negotiated agreements with the English, and many groups resisted or refused to return absconded slaves back to English plantations. For some slaves of Indigenous lineage on Lowcountry plantations, Native American raids liberated them from European colonial bondage. Indeed, these people may have preferred captivity that led to equality over continuing to live under chattel slavery.[70]

## CRAFTING IDENTITY: "MISTAKEN FOR A WHITE MAN" AND "PASS[ING] FOR AN INDIAN"

Mulattoes, Mustees, and other people of mixed heritage reflected the commingling of peoples from various backgrounds in the Atlantic world, and their ethnic diversity and cultural fluency allowed them to identify with multiple groups. This can be seen with language, a key component to group acceptance and identity formation. We have seen that people of blended ancestry sometimes spoke English and an Indigenous tongue. Mulattoes, no doubt, learned words from dialects spoken in West Africa via enslaved mothers. Those who were multilingual often revealed origins from several groups. Around the mid-eighteenth century, Galloway was a "Mullatto *Indian Slave*" living in New York City, and Tom, a "Mulatto Negro," resided farther north in Dutchess County along the Hudson River. Both men could speak English and Dutch fluently. Since the previous century, there were bilingual Dutch Mulattoes in New Netherland and later in New York, New Jersey, and surrounding areas. Immigration patterns into the Hudson River and Delaware River valleys influenced language and identity. In Chester County, Pennsylvania, an unnamed "Mulatto Man Slave . . . [of] a whitish Countenance" was fluent in both English and Swedish. Although English settlements overtook early Dutch and Swedish powers, the people and their cultures remained. The languages these slaves spoke reflected the ancestral lines and continuing influence of non-English colonists on people of mixed ancestry.[71]

People of blended heritage who were native born or came to reside in the British provinces through immigrant families mirror early European settlement patterns from various parts of the globe. Like other colonists, they adopted cultural attributes from the people around them and mixed in with local populations. In Philadelphia, a "young Mulattoe Servant" named John Miller learned to speak German while growing up in the mid-eighteenth century when an influx of Germanic peoples came into Pennsylvania. People from central Europe mixed in with the English and people of African and Indigenous descent. One "Mulattoe servant man" named George Huntziger grew up in rural Pennsylvania during the 1740s and 1750s. His last name suggests that he had German ancestry. George not only was a fluent German speaker but also read the language and spoke it better than English. Farther south, twenty-two-year-old Antoine was fluent in both English and French. He perhaps used his multilingual abilities to escape from the *Friendship* when the vessel docked in Charlestown Harbor. Antoine's master called him a "*French* Mulatto," and many such creole slaves grew up in the Caribbean and spent extensive time traveling the Atlantic Ocean.[72]

Non-Anglo immigrants experienced similar types of marginalization as people of color in English colonial society and may have been more open to mixture with Africans and Native Americans. For example, many Irish who traveled to America as servants and lower-class laborers commonly intermingled with people of color in the English colonies. Moses Williams was "half Indian and half Irish" and had "a swarthy Complexion." This "Indian Mulatto" was a runaway servant in Maryland and later in western New Jersey, and he spoke "good English," having been born in the provinces. Under British colonial rule, the Irish experienced nativism similar to the racial prejudices African and Indigenous peoples faced. The Irish also competed with groups of color in the colonies and discriminated against them, but commiseration, companionship, and relationships existed across subjugated groups, which produced mixed-heritage people. Moses may have encountered both acceptance and rejection from multiple communities for these reasons. Outside the colonies, Indigenous communities often considered mixed people to be full members depending on matrilineal ties or cultural proficiency.[73]

Throughout the colonial period, the English classified mixed Indigenous and European people as "half Indians" or "half breeds"—often a derogatory racial term meant to negatively mark people of blended ancestry. The designation of "half" indicated a subordinate status because one was not considered a "full blood"; in other words, one was split and not whole. Which "half" did Moses Williams choose to identify with? Did he consider himself Irish after his mother, a "white Woman," or did Moses affiliate more with the background of his father, an "Indian"? Colonists might have applied the term "half Indian" to someone with some Native American lineage regardless of their other parentage. Charles, a "servant Negroe man," was given that title when he ran away from his master in eastern New Jersey. Charles may have identified with multiple ancestries, but colonists might still have viewed this "half Indian" as "Negro"—the more widely used racial label in the colonial period, which often identified mixed people according to hypodescent ideology. Charles, an African and Indigenous man, and Moses, an Irish and Indigenous man, may have felt like they were caught somewhere between worlds. They surely thought about the two worlds of liberty and bondage as each acted on a shared desire to escape from his master to freedom.[74]

Mulattoes also historically claimed Spanish and Portuguese identities to avoid bondage in the British colonies. Free and enslaved Iberians lived in the English provinces, especially in the Caribbean and Lowcountry. In the mid-eighteenth century, Francis de Sorogosa resided near the Salkehatchie River, north of Beaufort, South Carolina, and owned Jack, a "mulatto man slave." Jack spoke Spanish and knew "the back settlements" well. When a wealthy landholder acquired him, Jack ran off and lived freely in the region, eluding capture. His owner publicized that the twenty-four-year-old "mulatto man . . . may call himself a Spaniard, and pass for free." Jack may have viewed himself as a Spaniard and felt he had the right to style himself as such, or it could have been a ruse. These American creoles were multicultural and multilingual and had the tools to shift between identities and communities when it suited them. Jack could operate among the English, Spanish, and Native American societies in the region. This adaptability made it difficult for his master to retrieve him.[75]

Jack was not the only mixed-heritage person to claim an Iberian identity in the Anglo-American colonies in order to "pass for free." Frank was another "Mulatto fellow," who was "a native of Portugal," born there around 1752. Sometime later, he ended up in Philadelphia. While Frank could have been born in Portugal, it is also plausible that he crafted this story, or identity, and that he originated from somewhere else. The proximity of North Africa and the Moorish influence in the Iberian Peninsula had produced centuries-old intermixture, which made it difficult to decipher someone's exact lineage. People with ancestral ties to Iberia, North Africa, and the Mediterranean tended to have somewhat darker features and skin tones than most northern Europeans. This may have led to some in colonial Anglo-America to designate people from these areas as Mulatto. Surely, some people in the colonial Americas were of African and Iberian descent, but pinpointing exactly where and when that mixture took place is often impossible.[76]

In many ways, this is where perceptions of race mattered more than someone's actual ancestry, for some people of mixed heritage knew that drawing on Iberian connections could secure freedom. Therefore, they crafted identities to their advantage in order to convince others that they deserved liberty and "white" privilege. James Johnson was known in Berks County, Pennsylvania, as "a Mulattoe Servant Man, who passes for a Portugee." It is not known whether James had Portuguese ancestry or if he fashioned himself as such. Regardless, he cultivated a relationship with a "white Woman" named Catherine. The two informally married, and any children they had might have been accepted as "white" in the colonies.[77]

By the early to mid-eighteenth century, successive generations of mixture had taken place between Africans, Europeans, and Native Americans, which produced a number of people who could racially pass as "white" persons. In 1734, one Virginia master said his bondsman Godfrey Smithers possessed "a much fairer Complexion than usual among Mulattoes, and [he] may be mistaken for a white Man." Two years later, a Virginian slave named Daniel was said to be "whiter than Mulattoes commonly are" and relied on his European ancestry as a means to escape. It is possible that Daniel recognized himself as a "white" man by his European lineage. Some mixed-heritage slaves used their European features and light skin to temporarily pass in society as "white" people, which allowed them to travel freely without being suspected as runaways.[78]

The rise of newsprint and the publication of hundreds of runaway slave advertisements in the eighteenth century provide the first definitive instances of racial passing in colonial North America. However, not all people of blended ancestry could racially pass for "white," and it is clear that more slaves attempted to "pass for free" in the colonial period. Newspapers featuring mixed-heritage people show how racial ambiguity helped some bend the lines of race to ease escape. The following advertisement from New Kent County, Virginia, illustrates how runaway notices in the *Virginia Gazette* presented the "light" bodies of mixed people:

> RUN away from *Eltham*, on *Sunday* the 10th of *January*, a light Mulatto fellow named OTHO, about 5 feet 9 inches high, freckled in the face, has light grey eyes, and brown hair, which he wears tied behind, his skin under his clothes is very white, and had on, when he went away, a blue cloth waistcoat, and a coat of the same, with a red velvet cape. I expect he will endeavour to pass for a white man. All masters of vessels are

forewarned from harbouring or carrying the said slave off at their peril. I will give FIVE POUNDS to any person who will deliver him to me, or secure him in any gaol [jail] and give notice thereof.
BURWELL BASSETT.

This was the typical format of a runaway advertisement, with an atypical description, since the majority of masters described their slaves as "Negro." Burwell Bassett claimed ownership over the "light Mulatto fellow named OTHO" as his human property, provided details about Otho's body, then offered a financial reward to anyone who would return the bondsman. If it were not for the "light Mulatto" racial label, Otho's physical description would have matched that of other Europeans: "white" skin, freckles, gray eyes, and brown hair long enough to tie up in a ponytail. So what actually made Otho different from any other European colonist?[79]

The category "Mulatto" held racial meaning for the people who read Otho's description, and this advertisement taught others about racial mixture over the sixteen consecutive weeks that it was published from February through June of 1773. The ad appeared, along with others, in two Virginia newspapers, and the words reinforced existing racial understandings, teaching colonists how to view the bodies of mixed-heritage people. Older colonists taught younger people and newer immigrants that a person could appear "white" but was, in fact, still a Mulatto. Even though Otho had multiple European ancestors over several generations, as a slave he could not claim total whiteness or freedom because his mother had presumably not been a free woman when she gave birth to him. Otho's only option to begin a life in liberty was to make the choice to "pass for a white man," at least until he believed he could stop running and settle down. Burwell did not say how long his slave would take on a "white" identity, and Otho may not have known either, but both men knew that physically appearing "white" could facilitate the transition into freedom.[80]

Masters believed that mixed-heritage people who racially passed were impersonating "whites" while hiding an essential "Negro" or "Mulatto" character. Slave owners did not believe their slaves had a valid claim to whiteness and portrayed light-complexioned runaways as racial imposters. In Charles County, Maryland, Jane Brent wrote that her "Molatto Slave" Harry's complexion was "so fair ... that he has oftener been taken for a white Man than what he is." Even though Harry *appeared* to be "white" to others, to his master he *was* a "Molatto Slave." But what if Harry believed that he was a "white Man"? Did he have a right to make this racial claim?[81]

Colonial understandings of race were infused with cultural attributes and labor status, especially servitude and slavery. Harry's speech revealed that he had been brought up among those of enslaved African ancestry. According to his owner, Harry spoke "Negroish" and sounded "almost like a Negro." Not all slaves who simply looked European could easily hide their African or Native American heritage during an escape attempt, even if they looked "white." Speech, mannerisms, and other customs connected to Indigenous, African, and creole African communities made it difficult to easily pull off a racial transition into whiteness.[82]

Making the decision to live as "white" was not the only type of racial passing that mixed-heritage people took part in; others chose to identify primarily as "Indian." "A mulatto Negroe" named Tom attempted to pass himself off as an "Indian" in mid-eighteenth-century Pennsylvania. In 1751, Tom was thirty-seven years old, "short, well set, [with] thick lips, flat nose, [and] black curled hair." Tom's master was informed that his slave intended "to cut off his hair, and get a blanket, to pass for an Indian." He also may have attempted to alter his clothing and make himself "Indian stockings" to wear. Although it is not apparent whether Tom had Native American lineage, he was familiar with John and Thomas Nutus, two "Indians at Susquehanna," and Tom inquired directly about how he could run away to join them. While it is possible that he had Susquehannock or other Indigenous ancestry, perhaps Tom believed he could construct a Native American identity, which would aid his escape and possibly ease his acceptance into a Susquehannock community. He certainly would not have been the first person of African descent to reside with Native Americans. Whether he was of Indigenous ancestry remains a mystery, but if Tom's plan was successful, he may have permanently chosen to identify as "Indian."[83]

It is not always possible to distinguish between mixed-heritage people who displayed an interest in joining Indigenous communities out of a desire to unite with their kinfolk and those who had little intention of living among Native Americans. James Dyson, also known as Jem, knew that presenting himself as an "Indian" might allow him to move around more freely in colonial society. After escaping from slavery, he was suspected of changing his appearance and clothing so that he could "pass for an Indian." James was five and a half feet tall and described by his master as a "Mulatto waiting man" between twenty-eight and thirty years old. The runaway wore his long black hair tied or braided and had "curls on each Side of his Face." After his escape, James was "seen with his Hair combed out straight" while wearing "an Indian Matchcoat." Some believed he only intended "to make his Escape in that Disguise." His master thought that since James was a "light Mulatto" he would "probably pass for a Freeman" and make his living as a shoemaker. It is unclear whether James had Indigenous ancestry, but if he did not, he put on the act of "Indian" to pass as free.[84]

While it is difficult to ascertain the actual lineage of many people of mixed descent, their claims to Indigenous heritage should not be entirely dismissed simply because their masters discounted them. Certain runaways may have

*Two Indian Men in Their Winter Dress.* These men wear two different types of matchcoats. "Fig. 1. *wears the proper* Indian *Match-coat, which is made of Skins, drest with the Fur on, sowed together, and worn with the Fur inwards, have the Edges also gashed for Beauty Sake. On his Feet are* Moccasins. *By him stand some* Indian *Cabins on the Banks of the River.* Fig. 2. *wears the Duffield Match-coat bought of the* English," and this outfit also contains Indigenous elements such as moccasins. (Beverly, *History of Virginia*, 3:142)

donned a Native American facade as a disguise to escape bondage, while other evidence shows that some people of blended ancestry spoke Indigenous languages, wore familiar "Indian" clothing, and escaped to live with other Native Americans. These people knew their backgrounds, or parts of their family tree, and embraced indigeneity or sought to reconnect with their cultural roots by shaping Indigenous identity anew.

Understandably, slaves of mixed ancestry often downplayed their African heritage in colonial society to avoid prejudice and the bondage associated with "Negroes." Tactical passing as "Indian" or "white" to flee from bondage did not necessitate that one permanently lived as such. The emotional toll of severing cultural and kinship ties to family dissuaded most people from long-term racial passing. Those who could pass more often relied on a type of temporary passing, where they crafted a racial persona as "Indian" or "white" for a shorter period of time to successfully escape. Afterward, most runaways in the British colonies likely aligned themselves with free people of color, where culturally they felt most comfortable.[85]

Deciding to temporarily or permanently pass was an option available to some individuals of mixed ancestry, but only certain family members could travel across somewhat flexible racial divides as they blurred lines of identity over multiple generations. These mixed-heritage people moved into colonial

European communities, started families after they settled into a new area, and might have avoided talking about their ancestral origins to their children. Their neighbors might tacitly understand the family was "colored," or they might not be racialized at all. These families on the racial middle ground met varying levels of prejudice, but they also socialized with other Europeans and married into these communities. After further intermixture with Europeans, their descendants might not even know that they were anything but "white." In terms of building successful lives, it is understandable that these people might only relate with their European ancestry. The identities they crafted were no less valid than those of the people who were more closely affiliated with the dark side of the so-called color line.[86]

European masters created the idea of racial passing in the colonial period when they denied the notion that people of mixed heritage could control their own identities by recognizing multiple ancestral lines or by connecting with a lineage of their own choosing. The expression of passing as "white" or passing as "Indian," with the assumption that someone must actually be "Negro," followed the standard reasoning of racial hypodescent. Mixed people with malleable identities in the racial borderlands rejected hypodescent ideology and found multiple ways to position themselves in colonial societies. While we may never have a complete picture of how individuals so long ago associated with their ancestry, it is clear that many marginalized people of color—Africans, Native Americans, and those of mixed descent—valued their cultures, often crafted their own personas, and fought for their independence.

The stories of runaway slaves and servants give us additional insight into the personal backgrounds of mixed people. However, most runaways were men, and piecing together their lives often leaves a lopsided gendered view of mixed-heritage identities. Earlier in this chapter, women who fought for the future of their children and their children's children illustrated how identity formation followed familial lines. Children often form a sense of self based on parental models, but as they become adults, other relationships take precedence in their lives, namely intimate relationships. Marriage, domestic partnerships, and sexual interactions open up a wider view of how mixed-heritage people perceived themselves in the colonial period and allow us to reframe women of blended ancestry at the center of the freedom struggle.

# 5

# Mulatto Marriages, Partnerships, and Intimate Connections

In November 1742, justices in Prince George's County, Maryland, brought Elizabeth Graves up on charges of "intermarrying with a Mulatto" named Daniel Pearl. The court prosecuted Elizabeth because she was a woman of European ancestry who joined in matrimony with a mixed-heritage man, who likely had European and African or Native American ancestry. At the same court session, the grand jury also presented a European man, William Marshall, for the offense of "intermarrying" with a "Mulatto Woman." The woman was Anne, the sister of Daniel Pearl. While British colonial societies identified the brother and sister of mixed heritage more closely with their African or Native American lineage—according to the racial rule of hypodescent—this did not stop their European spouses from choosing them as partners. The decision by Elizabeth Graves and William Marshall and other Europeans to engage in such "shamefull Matches" with people of mixed descent threatened their liberty. At the same time, for some people of color, unions with "white" partners could provide people such as the Pearl siblings with greater social opportunities.[1]

Elizabeth and Daniel Pearl, Anne and William Marshall, and other interracial couples fought for their freedom to live together in the British colonies. If they were respected or had connections in the community, they might find a way to avoid severe prosecution. Many lived undisturbed until an angry neighbor or someone with malicious intent turned the couple in to authorities, which may have been the case with the Pearls and the Marshalls. William was arrested, went to jail, and faced seven years of servitude for choosing to wed the Mulatto Anne, but he did not serve the time. Fortunately, he was a planter who could afford a lawyer, who filed a writ of habeas corpus to get him out of jail. William's attorney escalated his case up to the provincial court in Annapolis, where Maryland's highest magistrates presided over his brother-in-law's case as well. Despite initial hardships, it appears that both couples were eventually successful in their efforts. The attorney general dismissed the case against the Pearls and likely granted the Marshalls a similar decision. These two marriages within one mixed-heritage family represent the experience of many couples who resisted persecution and fought to remain free in the English colonies.[2]

This chapter focuses on the intimate relationships of those identified as Mulatto in the British colonies of the late seventeenth and eighteenth centuries. Mixed-heritage people strategically chose sexual partners and found ways to maneuver around anti-intermixture laws to reach freedom for themselves and their children. Most people of blended ancestry united with other people of African, Native American, or mixed lineage with whom they shared cultural and social connections. Other people of mixed descent fought against social stigma and colonial authority to couple with Europeans, despite the negative repercussions of entering into relationships deemed illegal or characterized as socially dishonorable. While local acceptance of interracial sex and relationships played an important role in these decisions, the choice of a sexual partner (if choice was possible) was personal and situational. A person's gender, race, class, religion, and freedom status all worked together to influence the terms of any given intimate encounter. These and other social factors continually intersected in people's everyday lives and shaped amorous relationships and sexual interactions involving people of blended heritage.[3]

Various anti-intermixture racial ideologies existed throughout English colonial America, though the strongest sentiments emanated from Chesapeake legislators beginning in the second half of the seventeenth century. Authorities restricted relationships between "whites" and "Negroes" based on religious and racial grounds. As these couples' mixed-heritage children came of age and began engaging in intimate unions with other Europeans, colonial lawmakers in Virginia and Maryland expanded matrimonial restrictions to these children and by the end of the century targeted Europeans who openly married people of mixed ancestry. Chesapeake legal systems became a foundational example of how to penalize and stigmatize free people of blended heritage, and several colonies replicated pieces of Virginia's and Maryland's legal codes. However, only officials in North Carolina followed through with systematic prohibitions against marriages between "Mulattoes" and "white" colonists and punished those who engaged in sex and marriage. Patriarchy dominated sexual connections, for elite European men conducted themselves with little impunity, while courts often indicted poor European and mixed women for intermixture violations in Virginia, Maryland, and North Carolina.[4]

Provincial authorities geographically located to the north and south of Virginia, Maryland, and North Carolina implemented less legislation against people of mixed heritage, especially in terms of regulating their sexual behavior. Even so, in areas where fewer prohibitions against intermixture existed—New England, New York, New Jersey, Pennsylvania, Delaware, South Carolina, and the Caribbean—interracial couples had to endure other forms of legal pressures, racial prejudice, and harassment. This often placed additional stresses on these relationships. Virginia, Maryland, and North Carolina were the most oppressive social climates for people of mixed heritage in the British Empire, while regions to the north and the south of these areas displayed more relaxed forms of hypodescent and generally allowed Mulattoes to mix with Europeans. South Carolina and the Atlantic islands cultivated environments that were comparatively more open to intermixture amid large and highly visible populations of color.[5]

The intersections of race, gender, class, and free status explain why certain types of sexual intimacies and relationships were more common than others. Mixed-heritage men such as Daniel Pearl partnered with "white" women, but they were less likely to enter into these relationships than Mulatto women with "white" men. European men regularly engaged in sex with women of African, Indigenous, or mixed lineage—who did not always have a choice to participate in these encounters. While countless sexual liaisons or connections occurred through intimidation or rape, these cases were rarely recorded. Most of the relationships in this chapter involve some type of volition, based on records that appear most frequently. Still, even encounters that included consent do not rule out forms of coercion, force, or manipulation, which was typical of male interactions with women in the colonial period. Intersectional power influenced all intimate connections, but women of color were not simply passive actors. Some mixed-heritage women shaped their exchanges with European men, broke the patriarchy, and flipped their traditional roles as reproducers of enslaved children to producers of free ones.[6]

Most women of mixed descent gave birth in slavery, and like their African and Indigenous counterparts, they brought enslaved children into the world, but mixed women also had the potential to give birth to free "white" children, which made them particularly dangerous to colonial labor and racial systems. Whether in bondage or free, women of blended ancestry could provide a pathway to whiteness as well as freedom for their children by European men, which is another reason colonial authorities considered such relationships illicit. Many elite European colonists attempted to draw a line between "white" and "Negro" in order to keep all people of African descent in bondage, but mixture and mixed-heritage people continually blurred the lines of race and freedom. Even though social and legal understandings of racial boundaries were found in most English colonies by the early eighteenth century, these lines were always porous, shifting, and contested throughout the British Empire.[7]

Fluid socioracial boundaries in certain regions allowed African, Indigenous, and mixed-heritage women to consort with a wide variety of sexual partners and avoid legal penalties, similar to European men. Nevertheless, most women of color sought African, Indigenous, or mixed-heritage husbands, especially men who could provide emotional and economic security and might perhaps climb the social ladder. Although free people of color and Europeans occasionally bucked social norms and intermarried, exogamy — marrying outside one's group — was rare for "Negro" and "Mulatto" slaves. Most free women and men of blended ancestry married other "Negroes," "Mulattoes," "Mustees," or "Indians" and remained close to enslaved communities and family. Mixed free-slave couples that married also worked to locate routes to independence where the free spouse assisted other family members in gaining liberty.

Hypodescent ideology ranked Mulattoes among others with African and Indigenous ancestral roots, and this social position influenced their decisions to largely partner with other people of color. Nonetheless, numerous mixed-heritage women sexually engaged with European men. At times, mixed women invited these relationships, in part because they realized their unique position among women of color: they were able to pass down whiteness to their children by "white" men. While their social mobility was limited in the British colonies, women of blended ancestry found ways to resist and manipulate European patriarchal authority so they could operate more freely and protect their offspring. The children of mixed heritage who resulted from these interracial sexual encounters grew into adulthood looking to achieve what their mothers often could not: liberty, marriage, and stable families.[8]

## MULATTO WOMEN AND MIXED RELATIONSHIPS IN THE EARLY COLONIAL PERIOD

When mixed-heritage people in colonial bondage, along with the poor and plebeian in freedom, could exercise autonomy, they strategically chose from an array of partners: African, European, Indigenous, or those of mixed descent. Like typical relationships of the time, people sought partners who were resourceful and successful according to societal norms. Individuals attempted to find someone who could provide companionship, protection, financial security, and stability in their lives. Certain relationships were born out of physical attraction, friendship, and love, which cemented bonds that might last a lifetime. Partnerships resulted from a combination of mutual affection and finding someone who could help with the material and emotional trials of everyday life. Whether unions resulted from emotion, devotion, or pragmatic coupling, people of mixed ancestry engaged in diverse relationships with partners from all backgrounds.[9]

Since the mid-seventeenth century, Christian ministers legitimated marriages between free Englishmen and enslaved mixed-heritage women. In July 1656, the "Molletto" Elizabeth Key and the Englishman William Greensted were "joyned in the Holy Estate of Matrimony" in Virginia. As discussed in chapter 1, William served as Elizabeth's lawyer and helped secure freedom for her and her children. Around the same time in Bermuda, a Mulatto woman named Thomasina partnered with Englishmen twice. Sometime before 1656, she married George Morris, and after he went to sea and abandoned her for five years, the court permitted her to wed Thomas Johnson. Bermuda authorities also allowed a European mariner named John Davis to marry Penelope Strange, a "molatto" slave woman, in 1660. Penelope was one of many "molatto women" enslaved in Bermuda, and officials recorded the marriage to clarify the contractual terms between her husband and owners. Several unions between European men and women of mixed ancestry appear around this period in Bermuda. Others surely went undocumented in the English colonies, though they took place with some regularity. Sometimes mixed women gained advantages by marrying European men: both Penelope Davis and Elizabeth Key eventually secured freedom through their husbands.[10]

In the seventeenth century, colonial authorities did not always describe unions between Europeans and mixed-heritage people of partial African or Indigenous descent as "intermarrying" because they recognized mixed people's proximity to racial whiteness. English officials appeared less worried about the marriage of Penelope and John Davis and more concerned with the legalities surrounding the enslaved bride and her children by a freeman. John initiated court proceedings to address this issue, and Bermuda authorities allowed him to "use any means" to procure his wife's independence. Until he was able to manumit Penelope, officials gave John permission to rent his wife from her owners for forty shillings a year. He could also protect their future children from being born into bondage by purchasing and exchanging "a negro child in lieu of" each one that Penelope gave birth to while still in slavery.[11]

When a free person married a slave, the couple often went to great lengths to obtain their family's liberty. By 1663, Penelope Davis had given birth to "a little Molatto girl called Joanna," whom Bermuda administrators indentured until the age of twenty-one. Born to a Mulatto mother and an English father, Joanna may have been of three-fourths European descent and was able to elevate her position after her term of servitude. Officials issued an apprenticeship for Joanna in the same manner as for other English servants. The indenture obligated her master to raise the girl "in a Christian way" and provide her with two pairs of clothing at the end of her contract: "One for Sabbath daie, and the other for working dayes" of the week. Perhaps officials hoped she might become a good wife for an Englishman, following the example of her mother.[12]

While mixed-heritage people entered into sexual relationships and marriage with Europeans, lawmakers in 1660s Virginia, Maryland, and Bermuda attempted to penalize mixture between Europeans and those of African or mixed descent. Bermuda was the first English colony to identify people of mixed ancestry by name in 1663, when legislators attempted to banish or bind any "free borne subjects" who would "Mary with, of have any carnall Copulation with any Negroes, Molattoes or Musteses." However, this law was quickly defunct. Regular intermixture in the mid-Atlantic colony shows that the island's cultural atmosphere resembled the Caribbean's, with a twist of New England, both of which took little punitive action against racial mixture itself. Puritan magistrates in Bermuda were more concerned with extramarital sex and bastardy than interracial mixture. Bermuda officials continued to let Mulatto women marry European men "to prevent their living in sin." Meanwhile, legislators in Virginia and Maryland began setting stringent penalties on interracial relationships and exogamy. Regardless of whether a province formalized anti-intermixture laws or not, by the late seventeenth century many English colonists cultivated racial attitudes that encouraged contempt for "whites" who might invite a "Negro" into their home to socialize, serve an "Indian" a meal at their table, or accept a "Mulatto" into their bed.[13]

Stories like those of Elizabeth Key, Penelope Davis, and others show how European husbands might free their Mulatto wives and their mixed children, and although freedom, gifts, and personal favors were not always motivating factors for entering into such relationships, many women of color found ways to use their intimate connections with European men to acquire these things. Nevertheless, mixed-heritage women in slavery knew that sexual encounters with European men did not guarantee freedom or wealth and often brought new dangers such as physical, emotional, and sexual abuse. Many watched their mothers and other women languish in bondage with the dream that a relationship might lead to emancipation. These women sought a bridge to freedom, and even the smallest chance of reaching that goal led some to attempt formalizing relationships with benevolent freemen from various backgrounds. For most, manumission never came, but the hope that it might be possible explains why some enslaved women returned European men's sexual advances or even pursued them.[14]

For some women of color, a free lover's or fiancé's premature death cut short the promise of marriage, leaving the woman and any children trapped in slavery. The story of Catherine Scott, a "molatoe Woman," presents such a case in Lancaster County, Virginia. Likely born in the 1660s or 1670s, Catherine inherited bondage from a slave mother and later gave birth to a son named Daniel, who followed her into legal bondage. Sometime after Daniel's birth, John Beaching bartered for Catherine and her son's freedom by agreeing to tan

1,000 animal pelts for their master, a widow named Elizabeth Spencer. This was hefty compensation for a pair of slaves, but John—who appears to have been a free man of European descent—was skilled in tanning leather hides and had an incentive to complete the job. John had developed a special relationship with Catherine, and Daniel may have been his son. Even if John was not the father, Catherine had plans for her and her son "to be both Christened" in church. She then planned to marry John and become Mrs. Catherine Beaching. Her religious fervor and pursuit of virtuous femininity were displays that separated Catherine from the negative stereotypes that colonial society associated with unwed African slave mothers. The slave system did not allow women to preserve their chastity, and Virginia law no longer acknowledged slave women as marriageable partners. Marriage would bestow upon Catherine a respectability that she could not achieve as a slave.[15]

Unfortunately, tragedy struck before Catherine and John's wedding could take place. Catherine and her son had moved in with John after he paid off their purchase price, but he became ill and Catherine could not nurse him back to health. He died before formally manumitting Catherine and Daniel. Elizabeth Spencer may have intended to free the family according to her agreement with John, but after she married a man named William Man in the mid-1690s, William saw an opportunity to capitalize on keeping Catherine and Daniel in bondage.[16]

Catherine was devastated when she found out that William Man refused to acknowledge her family's freedom. Like other resilient mothers, she could have chosen to flee, perhaps along the Rappahannock River into the Virginian interior or across the Chesapeake Bay into Maryland. Even with geographical knowledge of the area, these routes would have been hard and risky to navigate, especially with a young child in tow. Moving to a new community was also difficult without adequate savings and social connections.[17]

Catherine figured her best chance at emancipation was to take her master to court. In 1698, she gained legal representation to address the Lancaster County court and petitioned the justices to review her case against William Man. William's and Catherine's lawyers debated whether or not John Beaching had fulfilled the original contract with Elizabeth Spencer. William's attorney argued that the contract "was never Completed," so Catherine was not "made A free woman." Catherine's attorney objected and maintained that the exchange took place, insisting that freedom should have been fulfilled after she had moved into John's custody. Catherine's legal counsel further contended that John always intended to free her and Daniel.[18]

There were at least three men who had witnessed the signing of the contract, or bill of sale, and all attested to the original agreement and the transfer of Catherine and Daniel to John. However, the contract could not be presented as evidence; supposedly the piece of paper had "accidentaly burnt" in a house fire. Although it was impossible to produce the contract, the witnesses testified to the "best of their memories" the details of the arrangement. These men substantiated the claim to liberty, and a twelve-man jury of local residents decided in Catherine's favor, declaring her and Daniel free persons. By law, Catherine and John would have faced legal penalties if they had married in Virginia, but they had been prepared to go through with the commitment. Men in the community testified on their behalf, attesting to their relationship.[19]

Catherine Scott's story shows both the challenges and possibilities that women of mixed descent faced when seeking to gain autonomy through a relationship to a European man. This made her path to freedom different from that of most slaves and other people of mixed heritage who escaped from colonial bondage. Her emancipation came through her relationship to a freeman and support from other free European men; her lawyer, witnesses, and members of the jury all facilitated her manumission. In one way, these men honored John Beaching's right as a freeman to emancipate the woman he planned to marry. After her fiancé's death, Catherine showed how a determined enslaved woman fought to escape bondage despite the fact that her initial plan fell apart. Catherine combated negative assumptions about enslaved women and legislation that routinely associated women of mixed ancestry with illicit sex and illegitimacy. Instead, she styled herself as a Christian wife and mother. Despite her background and labor status, the county court stated that Catherine "conceives herselfe to be a freewoman." By defining herself as free, Catherine sought to pass that legacy down to her progeny.[20]

Family ties also reflected and influenced personal identity, and the choice of a life partner was another way that people fashioned themselves and shaped racial perceptions. Catherine Scott and other mixed-heritage people were well aware that they could elevate their position through relationships with Europeans, which could lead to increased social benefits. This boded well for mixed women and their children, including future generations who were born free. Other partnerships could lead to a decline in freedom status, as seen in the cases of European women who had children by men of color (see chapters 1–2). People's partner choices were heavily based on gender. "White" women were less likely to marry Mulatto men because African, Indigenous, or mixed-heritage husbands might lower their social status. On the other hand, women of mixed ancestry commonly elevated their status through short- and long-term relationships with European men. Court documentation regarding such couples appears more often in jurisdictions under heavier prohibitions (Virginia, Maryland, and North Carolina) than in places that generally tolerated mixture (South Carolina and islands throughout the Atlantic). These court cases should not skew our understanding of the prevalence of interracial relationships, but rather they show how frequently officials prosecuted these types of unions.[21]

Whether in the Chesapeake or the Caribbean, lower-class colonists more readily accepted Europeans who married people identified as Mulatto, but elite men rarely formalized their relationships with African, Native American, and mixed-heritage women. Wealthy planter Cary Helyar had an ongoing affair with an unnamed woman of mixed African and European ancestry in early Jamaica. Even though they had two children by the early 1670s, they never married, which was normal in such relationships. The unnamed woman may have aspired to one day become Cary's wife, since her European father and "Negro" mother had allegedly lived in Barbados for several years as a married couple. However, Cary never legitimated their affair, probably due to the hostility that marriage to a slave would attract from the Jamaican elite. Allegedly, Cary ended the relationship when he married a European woman, though he planned to give his mixed-heritage mistress an annuity of thirty-two pounds sterling, provided that she "never trouble him" again. The woman took the financial support and agreed to not seek further compensation for her children from the church parish. Not long after his wedding, Cary died and the ex-mistress sued his estate to secure her promised financial support. Though she lost the case, Cary's brother, William Helyar, made arrangements to support her family. Race, class, and gender hierarchies skewed the power relationships against such concubines, yet many mixed women still found ways to gain security for themselves and their children.[22]

By the early eighteenth century, Jamaica had the highest mixed-heritage population in the British Caribbean, and European men throughout the islands, from large planters to common laborers, regularly fathered children by women of color. Intimate interracial connections were prevalent in the Caribbean and might be characterized on a spectrum that included forcible rape, coercion, and consent. Interactions were further complicated by elements of reciprocity in short- and long-term relationships. When children resulted, European fathers sometimes financially took care of the mothers and their offspring of blended ancestry. For example, wealthy fathers sent a number of their mixed children to be educated in Britain, where less racial animus existed than in the colonies. Physical distance from the provincial racial climate, coupled with wealth and marginal whiteness, shielded these people of mixed descent from the social and legal discrimination they encountered while living in slave societies on the islands.[23]

In the eighteenth century, wealthy free people of color who remained in Jamaica regularly petitioned the general assembly to overcome the legal disadvantages set up to handicap their socioeconomic progress. Officials granted several hundred special privilege bills that allowed an elite cadre of mixed-

*The Barbadoes Mulatto Girl*. The girl, or young woman, appears to be pregnant. She is juxtaposed with two African women.
(Agostino Brunias, 1779, Yale Center for British Art, New Haven, Connecticut)

heritage individuals to access legal rights, placing them nearly on par with other British colonists. This was unheard of in the English colonies of North America. In some ways, these concessions further promoted intermixture with Europeans. At the same time, the House of Assembly of Jamaica targeted lower-class and middling families of blended ancestry with laws that prevented upward social mobility, which was similar to what was being done in colonial legislatures everywhere.[24]

Overall, colonial governments across the British colonies tolerated intimate connections between European men and women of color, but some officials abhorred these relationships and the children they produced. In the early eighteenth century, inhabitants of Antigua, Nevis, Montserrat, and St. Kitts (St. Christopher) were displeased with Daniel Parke, the governor of these Leeward Islands, for his overzealous administration of the provinces and the perceived misuse of authority. The colonists' grievances included the fact that Daniel had called out several planters who held enslaved concubines and had a number of children by these women. In 1710, Daniel wrote the Earl of Dartmouth directly in England, proclaiming that his peers had produced a "slaveish sooty race" of mixed-heritage offspring. "Good God," Daniel decried of his fellow Englishmen, "a people who have not the very forme of godlynesse." He continued that these men "live in profess'd adultrys and owne a mungrill race, the liveing wittnesses of their unnaturall and monstrous lusts." Daniel lambasted these men because they did not uphold the idea of Christian sexual virtue and owned their offspring of blended ancestry. Calling the children a "mungrill race" mirrored the language of Maryland assemblymen in previous decades. Daniel was also not afraid to name names: leading British families like the "Codringtons as well as Griggs and Russells, and others of a low degree" all had Mulatto children. In the Leeward Islands, Jamaica, Barbados, South Carolina, and other British slave societies, contemporaries knew that these relationships were commonplace among European men from all classes.[25]

European men in the Caribbean consorted with African and mixed-heritage paramours more openly than in the Chesapeake, and Daniel Parke's strong dissent against these planters illustrates the cultural differences among colonial regions. "This is not the crime of a few, nor the meanest of their party, nor of the youngest of them," wrote Daniel from Antigua. Part of his frustration with Anglo-Caribbean concubinage stemmed from his cultural upbringing: he was not originally from the islands but had been born and raised in Virginia. He had sat on the General Assembly and governor's council in the 1680s and 1690s, a time when Virginia magistrates debated and passed legislation opposing "abominable mixture." After spending time in Europe, Daniel relocated to Antigua in 1706. From the Chesapeake to the Caribbean he brought a repugnance of ethnoracial mixture along with elite notions of strict racial hypodescent.[26]

By the early eighteenth century, European colonists in multiple English provinces frowned upon racial mixture, or at least the formal recognition or open flaunting of such behavior. These sentiments heavily depended on regional and class differences. Colonial elites were concerned with maintaining high social status, a sentiment linked to polished public personas and ideas of regal bloodlines. Even as aristocrats increasingly disparaged racial mixture, some still engaged in it away from public view. In the Leeward Islands, the Englishmen who had sex with women of color rebuffed Daniel and rejected his leadership for several reasons, including his staunch position on interracial comingling in the Caribbean.

Governor Daniel Parke survived assassination attempts in 1708 and 1709 but stubbornly refused official orders to leave Antigua—a misstep that ultimately cost him his life. In December 1710, inhabitants of St. John's, the capital city, completed their "designe to assassinate" the governor. While Daniel's views regarding intermixture were not the main cause of his downfall, revealing names of men who held slave concubines and fathered mixed-heritage children did not win the governor many friends. As such, he did not have allies who might have stopped the mob that tortured and beat him to death.[27]

### THE MULATTO ESCAPE HATCH AND "COHABITING W[I]TH A MOLLATO" IN THE CHESAPEAKE

While racial hypodescent ideology was most prominent in the Chesapeake, British officials throughout the empire portrayed interracial mixture as immoral and dangerous to colonial societies with well-structured racial hierarchies. People of mixed heritage, and the Europeans who mixed with them, muddied a clear-cut socioracial order that suited upper-class efforts to keep people of African or Native American descent in bondage. Colonial fears around intermixture also echoed European anxieties about devolving from civility into savagery through sustained contact with African and Indigenous peoples in the Americas. These factors help explain why colonial lawmakers made it difficult for Mulattoes to access the benefits that came with marriage and lawful inheritance, especially from European kin. Legislators sought to preserve legitimate ties to whiteness and exclude mixed-heritage people from the economic, legal, and psychological privileges that came with a "white" identity.[28]

Colonial racial boundaries proved permeable in the British provinces, especially as people of blended ancestry continued to couple with Europeans over multiple generations. This type of intermixture led to a variation of what one historian refers to as the "mulatto escape hatch" out of blackness, where a society considers people of mixed ancestry to be "neither black nor white." The escape hatch existed in the British colonies, yet this metaphor only applied to families who could navigate a transition to racial whiteness over successive generations of mixture with Europeans. This type of multigenerational mixture allowed certain families in the English colonies to achieve racial whiteness, as in the French and Latin American colonies. One British traveler to the Caribbean, William Douglass, wrote that European colonists there knew they could "wash the Blackemore white, by generating with the Successive Shades of their own Issue, Children, Grand Children, &[et]c." He continued that "the Progeny at Length become *blonde*, or of a pale White." Colonists suggested that "wash[ing] the Blackemore white" took longer than whitening an "Indian" through multigenerational mixture. Virginia planter-legislator William Byrd II mused that "if a Moor may be washt white in 3 Generations, Surely an Indian might have been blancht in two." Prolonged intermixture with Europeans over the years provided families with a path to move from "Negro" or "Indian" to "pale White." Thus they could overcome racial hypodescent.[29]

There are notable examples in which people of blended ancestry opened the escape hatch by choosing European partners in the Tidewater Chesapeake, where the philosophy of hypodescent was strongest. Near Jamestown, Virginia, John Bunch and Sarah Slayden asked the minister of Blisland Parish to perform their wedding ceremony in the early eighteenth century. However, the reverend sought to avoid violating the "Law to prevent Negroes & White Persons intermarrying" and therefore "refused on pretence of the said Bunch's being a Mulatto." Certainly, the couple was disappointed when the minister informed them that they could not legally wed, but they continued to fight for their right to legitimize their union. In the summer of 1705, they petitioned the provincial council, requesting that they be allowed to marry because John was not a "Negro"; rather, he identified as a "Mulatto" man. After reviewing the evidence, Attorney General Stevens Thomson concluded in September that the act prohibiting "Negroes & White Persons intermarrying" should be "restrictive no further then the very letter" of the law and determined the couple's union "not to be construed beyond" those words. In short, John could marry as he pleased because he was not a "Negro" under the law.[30]

The attorney general's legal opinion showcases how officials irregularly followed provincial mandates and the extent to which colonists misunderstood or overlooked standing legislation within the colony. At the time, no Virginia statute punished ministers for performing these marriages, though one did exist in Maryland and officials may have informally followed it throughout the Chesapeake. Although Virginia law did not penalize those who performed interracial marriage ceremonies, it did punish "negroes, mulattoes, and Indians" who married any "English or other white man or woman." Stevens either ignored this statute or was simply unaware that Virginia magistrates had altered its law in 1691 to punish Europeans who married Mulattoes. Technically, authorities could have legally banished the "white" Sarah Slayden from the colony after she wed her "Mulatto" fiancé. However, there is little evidence that courts followed through with this threat, nor did they have the capacity to do so.[31]

John Bunch and Sarah Slayden's engagement shows that diverse understandings existed among the ruling Chesapeake elite when it came to racial boundaries, terminology, intermixture, and hypodescent. Stevens admitted that he was not familiar with all the racial labels "given to ye issue [children] of such mixtures" and went on to say that he believed the term "Mulatto" could only be "appropriated to the Child of a Negro man begotten upon a white woman." He further hesitated to say whether the offspring "begotten upon a white woman by a Mulatto man can properly be called a Mulatto." Rather, Stevens said he was told that the child of a "Mulatto" and a "white Person" would fall under the category of "Mustee." In other colonies this word denoted mixed-heritage people with some Native American ancestry. Evidently, there was confusion over mixed categories, as meanings of racial terms varied over time and space.[32]

Stevens Thomson not only ruled that John Bunch could not legally be designated a "Negro," but he also declared that the couple's children should not be considered "Mulatto." This presents further evidence that some colonists in the Chesapeake considered a person of one-fourth African descent and three-fourths European descent to be nearly "white" (or a "Mustee"). This was not simply a permissive application of hypodescent. The attorney general's decision fell into the realm of hyperdescent—in which people of mixed ancestry are classified by their socially superior lineage. John and Sarah's children could legally pass through the escape hatch into racial whiteness after two generations of mixture with Europeans.[33]

The legal loophole that Virginia's attorney general nearly created for Mulattoes to slip by bans on intermarriage with Europeans was short-lived. The executive council ordered Stevens "to argue the reasons of his opinion" in front of the governor and General Court, who struck the decision down just weeks later. While writing "An act concerning Slaves and Servants," colonial officials potentially realized that Stevens's ruling had the potential to cause disaster for European planters. Under Virginia's comprehensive slave and servant code, passed in October 1705, the general assembly consolidated and revised previous anti-intermixture statutes and strengthened penalties for "white men and women intermarrying with negroes or mulattos, as by their unlawful coition [sex] with them." This revision of previous anti-intermixture laws instructed the county courts to imprison Europeans who married any "negro or mulatto man or woman, bond or free . . . during the space of six months, without bail." Couples also had to pay a fine of ten pounds sterling, which went to the local parish. In addition, officials administered a fine of 10,000 pounds of tobacco for Christian ministers or anyone else who performed such marriages. Half of this fee went to the province and the other half to the "informer" of the crime. Officials recognized past difficulties with enforcing anti-intermixture legislation and also realized the importance of offering monetary incentives to colonists who turned in their neighbors for violations. This was especially important in rural areas where colonial infrastructure was less developed.[34]

Virginia authorities also went a step further in 1705 by legally defining for the first time in English colonial history who should be considered a Mulatto.

To clear up "all manner of doubts" that could arise over who should be "accounted a mulatto," legislators set a high standard: one great-grandparent of African descent (one-eighth "Negro") or one parent of Native American ancestry (one-half "Indian"). Members of Virginia's General Court surely had in mind the attorney general's recent briefing on John Bunch's intermediate racial classification when they revised and expanded Virginia's legal regulations. Now John and Sarah's children and their children's children would be considered Mulattoes under law, even though most people in colonial society probably would not have recognized them as such.[35]

When legislators made ethnoracial mixture and intermarriage illegal, they hindered the widespread acceptance of sex, love, and marriage across perceived racial boundaries and pushed couples like John Bunch and Sarah Slayden into hiding or forced them to end their relationships. In the summer of 1711, someone turned in William Powell "for Cohabiting w[i]th a Mollato wench" in Norfolk, Virginia. In August, William came to the county court to answer questions about the nature of this living arrangement. William was of European descent, and the unnamed "Mollato" woman—who lived with him as "his hired Servant"—raised suspicions that they had more than a working relationship. Court justices doubted the explanation that the woman merely provided domestic services, yet they threw out the case in October, after William reported that the "Molatto" woman was "gone from him." The court in Norfolk was still somewhat dubious about the end of their joint living arrangement and ordered that William "Doe not Cohabite with the Said wench for the future." Virginia had instituted sufficient mechanisms to police intermixture by granting colonists the power to turn in their neighbors for interracial cohabitation.[36]

William Powell's female companion remained nameless, but the court's racial and gendered use of the terms "Molatto" and "wench" to describe her reveals how colonists routinely denigrated women of African, Indigenous, and mixed lineage. Presumably, the free "Molatto" woman engaged in a sexual relationship with William outside of marriage and outside of the law. We might assume that the relationship was consensual since she was a free woman, though William also employed her, so he had economic control over her livelihood. It was somewhat common for men to force or coerce their female housekeepers into bed. Even if there were genuine feelings between the two, William and his "Molatto" servant could not formalize their arrangement without great hardship. The law made it difficult for these couples to pursue public relationships and drove them into secret and illegitimate liaisons. Virginia legislation figuratively made these mixed-heritage women "wenches" when it legally classified their relationships as illicit.[37]

Interracial couples in the Tidewater Chesapeake kept their relationships hidden to avoid persecution, yet hundreds of recorded pregnancies and newborn children reveal the existence of regular sexual intimacies. These numbers rose as the colonial population expanded throughout the century. In 1710, Virginia authorities brought one mixed-heritage servant up on charges of bastardy in Surry County, across the river from Jamestown. On January 3, the "Malattoe named Mary" arrived at court and identified the father of her child as Stephen Vanhon, a man of European descent. The magistrates ordered Stephen to appear in court and fined Mary "according to Law." Mary's master posted a security bond, which saved her from the whipping post yet indebted her to a longer period of service. Stephen returned to court six months later with two friends who posted a huge bond of 20,000 pounds of tobacco on his behalf. This sizable sum of money went to the Southwark Church parish to pay "any Charge in keeping & maintaining [the] bastard Child." Although Mary's master legally had a right to her offspring's service, the justices did not record binding the child to a thirty-one-year indenture or any contract.[38]

Stephen Vanhon's actions, including the enormous bond, show that he took responsibility for his mixed-heritage offspring by securing his child's freedom. If he did not care for Mary or her child, Stephen would have had little reason to indebt himself to others in order to pay such a large fee—a sum that would take at least several years, if not over a decade, for the average worker to pay off. His likely delivery of their infant child out of bondage suggests a sense of obligation and a caring relationship. Although it is unknown if Stephen married Mary, it is possible that he promised to care for her and their child and honored other commitments made to the "Malattoe" woman.[39]

Unwed mothers fought an uphill battle when facing colonial Chesapeake legislation, yet they maintained a modicum of power because they could name the father in bastardy cases. Authorities appear to have compelled Mary to name Stephen Vanhon as the father of her child in Virginia, and other mixed-heritage women did the same in Maryland. "A certain Mulato Woman Servant ... commonly called Mulato Bess" answered to similar bastardy charges in 1711. When Baltimore County court officials approached Bess, they "demanded of her who was the Father." Bess "made Oath on the Holy Evangelist that a certain William Bond had carnal knowledge of her Body & that he was the True Father of the s[ai]d Child." The court ordered that William, "when convicted," or Bess, "when Free," pay Bess's master "Six hundred pounds of Tobacco in consideration of the Trouble and Disgrace" brought upon her master's house. The "Trouble" of paying for the living expenses of an unmarried servant mother with a newborn child was probably more of a concern than the "Disgrace" it brought upon a master. Servants and slaves who acted of their own accord could reflect poorly on a master, who might appear incapable of managing the household. Still, servant women commonly had children out of wedlock while indentured and masters gained additional service from these bondswomen.[40]

Bess's forthrightness in naming William Bond as the father of her child did not excuse her from the whip. Unlike Stephen Vanhon, William did not step up to pay a fee that would protect Bess or their child. Bess's master did not pay his servant's fine either, which also could have saved her from corporal punishment. Because the poor woman could not pay to absolve her crime, authorities took her to the public pillory where "her Hands thereto [were] fast Tied, Her Body [was] Stript from the Wa[i]st upwards," and she "receive[d] fifteen Lashes on her Bare back well laid on." This punishment was typical for any woman convicted of bastardy at the time. However, race and gender were inextricably linked to "Mulato" Bess's penalty, for she was beaten while the European William Bond simply had to pay a fine.[41]

As the mixed-heritage population increased over time, Maryland also continued to pass laws that prohibited racial exogamy from taking place and followed Virginia by adding Mulattoes to these regulations. In 1715, the Maryland General Assembly mandated that the "Ministers, Pastors and Magistrates" who married "any Negro whatsoever, or Mulatto Slave, with any White Person" could be fined 5,000 pounds of tobacco. This penalty for performing interracial wedding ceremonies was half the fee that was charged in Virginia and half of what had been previously assigned, though it remained a large sum nonetheless. Two years later, Maryland authorities formally restricted "Mulattoes" from "intermarrying with any White Person" by assigning seven years of servitude to the offending "White Woman" or "White Man." As noted in the opening of this chapter, Prince George's County courts tried William Marshall and Elizabeth Graves under this law for marrying the mixed-heritage Pearl siblings.[42]

While Maryland legislators often regarded people of color the same way as in Virginia, they periodically distinguished between "Negroes" and "Mulattoes" or recognized minor legal differences between free Mulattoes and those who were enslaved. Most of the time, the general assembly treated "Mulattoes born of White Women" like other women of color, but it also took unique legislative steps to distance this racial and gendered group from others. In 1717, officials increased the sentences for "Negroes or Mulattoes" who intermarried with "any White Person" by assigning them to slavery, but there was one exception: "Mulattoes born of White Women" only received seven years of servitude, the same as offending "whites." Whether or not this law was ever administered accordingly, Maryland's legislators revealed at least some hesitancy to assign free Mulatto women the same position as other people of color.[43]

A little over a decade later, in 1728, Maryland's assembly labeled "Free Mulatto Women" the same as "White Women" in bastardy law, seeking to punish them equally for the religious crime. Legislators pointed out that there was "no Provision made for the Punishment of Free Mulatto Women having Bastard Children by Negroes and other Slaves" and claimed that "such Copulations are as unnatural and inordinate as between White Women and Negro Men, or other Slaves." While it appears that the men on the council opposed the notion of hypodescent for "Free Mulatto Women" and leaned toward hyperdescent — aligning these mixed women more closely with their free European ancestry — authorities were really more concerned that these free women of blended heritage were slipping through bastardy laws aimed at "White Women." The statute declared "that all such Free Mulatto Women, having Bastard Children . . . shall be subject to the same Penalties that White Women and their Issue are, for having Mulatto Bastards." Here, planter-legislators did few favors for the hundreds of free, mostly servant, mixed women who were now penalized for having children with men of color out of wedlock. Additionally, "Free Mulatto Women" were also sometimes punished when partnering with "white" men. These haphazard statutes show how several generations of colonial officials worked to create and regulate a fixed soci000cial position for women of mixed descent.[44]

### MULATTO INTERMARRIAGE RESTRICTIONS AND DEFINITIONS OF PEOPLE OF "MIXED BLOOD"

While some English magistrates restricted and stigmatized Europeans and people of mixed lineage who intermarried, they rarely concerned themselves with Mulattoes who wed other people of color, which were more common marriages. Most people of blended ancestry chose other African, Indigenous, and mixed-heritage spouses who shared similar backgrounds, but these unions went beyond simply selecting someone whose skin color resembled their own. A number of factors surrounding one's soci000cial position guided the choice of an intimate partner, including ancestry, religion, occupation, and free or bound status. While living in St. George's, Bermuda, the Mulatto Anthony McKenney worked his way out of servitude and eventually purchased his enslaved wife, Hannah Manena — the daughter of an African woman, Priscilla, and her European master, John Elwick. The Mulatto couple eventually moved to New Providence, in the Bahamas, where they owned land, raised their children, attended church as a family, and possibly helped fend off pirate attacks. Records list their apparent descendants as free Mulattoes, and they associated with other free people of color in the eighteenth-century Bahamas.[45]

Like Hannah and Anthony McKenney, many Mulatto couples worked toward the goal of pulling a partner out of bondage. In Virginia the free Mulatto Elizabeth Young purchased her husband, Abram Newton, an enslaved Mulatto man. The two lived together for some time, when Elizabeth died in November 1745. Within weeks after losing his partner, Abram petitioned Virginia's executive council to "grant or confirm to him his freedom." Elizabeth had technically owned her husband, but she wrote a note granting Abram his liberty before her death. On June 13, 1746, the council "Ordered That the said Abram be manumitted and set free according to the Will of the said Elizabeth and the Prayer of the Petitioner." People of color often chose partners from similar ancestral backgrounds because they shared a common sense of struggle. Free, servant, and enslaved Mulattoes faced many of the same challenges in the Chesapeake. One can imagine that Elizabeth and Abram comforted each other in difficult times and knew their commitment was not dependent on freedom status.[46]

Slavery might have influenced, but did not always determine, marriage choices, and people of blended ancestry also united with others across the spectrum of skin color. One "free Mulatto," Peg Toney, married an enslaved "Negro Fellow, about 25 Years of Age, of a yellowish Complexion" in Prince George County, Virginia. While English colonial laws did not formally recognize slave marriages, "Mulatto" Peg and her unnamed "Negro" husband created a family. They had a baby boy who was free after his mother's status, but the father's slavery restricted the family's independence. People of African, Indigenous, and mixed descent fought to avoid fragmented families and found ways to free husbands, wives, and children in efforts to attain stability. Since Peg could not secure her partner's freedom through purchase, the family decided to run away together. Peg essentially stole her husband so they could settle with their child in a place where they could make autonomous decisions about their family's future.[47]

In the Chesapeake, Mulattoes found it easier to marry other people of color, but north of the Chesapeake, colonial lawmakers were not as concerned with free Mulattoes who married Europeans and they passed little legislation against these types of unions. Primarily, this was because mixed-heritage peoples made up a smaller percentage of the population in the English colonies stretching from Pennsylvania to New England. One legal exception came in 1705, when Massachusetts passed an act to curtail sex and marriage between any English man, woman, or person "of any other Christian nation" with "any Negro, or Molatto" man or woman. Authorities seem to have fashioned the ordinance after Virginia codes, yet they chose not to punish mixed children with mandatory servitude. Still, these unions continued, and in later decades officials admitted that the law had not produced the desired outcome because it did not annul marriages that had already taken place. Authorities in Massachusetts passed the strongest anti-intermixture mandate in the northern English provinces, however, like several stand-alone laws found in other English colonies, courts did not prosecute couples with regularity, and future lawmakers never reissued similar acts in the colonial period.[48]

In the 1720s, Delaware and Pennsylvania replicated some of Virginia's and Maryland's anti-intermixture statutes when lawmakers in the colonies bordering the Chesapeake attempted to limit "Negro" and "white" persons from having sex or intermarrying. While governing assemblies in Delaware and Pennsylvania copied certain aspects Virginia and Maryland legislation, they never reissued these legal codes and did not follow them to the same degree. Neither Delaware nor Pennsylvania prevented Mulattoes from marrying Europeans by law. Delaware came closest to punishing the sexual liaisons of "white men" who sired a child by any "Negro or Mulatto woman" with a possible twenty-one lashes and a fine of twenty pounds sterling. Also, both Delaware and Pennsylvania legislators stated that the mixed-heritage offspring of unwed "white" women and "Negro" men would serve the same thirty-one years of servitude that local officials ordinarily assigned in the Chesapeake. While interracial marriages took place in provinces with relatively small slave populations, these unions were not frequent enough to draw sustained attention from lawmakers. In the northern colonies, where social stigma, not the law, deterred most exogamy, people of blended ancestry largely retained the freedom to marry whom they wanted.[49]

South of the Chesapeake, neither of the Carolinas officially restricted ethnoracial intermixture until 1715, when North Carolina lawmakers followed the examples set by Virginia and Maryland. Situated between Virginia and South Carolina, the colony of North Carolina mirrored the Chesapeake in terms of legislating strict hypodescent and harsh treatment of mixed-heritage peoples. Scores of migrants from the Chesapeake moved into the colony and some brought segregationist views with them. A decade after Virginia's anti-intermarriage laws passed in 1705, North Carolina magistrates issued an act stating that "no White man or woman shall intermarry with any Negro, Mulatto, or Indyan Man or Waoman." The fifty-pound penalty did not include extra terms of service per se, but the steep sum would have indebted servants and other low-income people, whom courts could force into labor contracts.[50]

North Carolina administrators found it difficult to formally regulate interracial unions. When the colony's first statute passed in 1715, these relationships had gone unchecked for more than fifty years. Some European colonists were troubled by the willingness of their peers to flout laws prohibiting intermixture. Like in the Chesapeake, the North Carolina General Assembly recorded in 1723, "Complaints have been made by divers Freeholders and Inhabitants of this Government, of great Numbers of Free Negroes, Mulattoes, and other Persons of mixt Blood, that have lately removed themselves into this Government [territory], and that several of them have intermarried with the white Inhabitants of this Province." Many free Africans and mixed-heritage people moved to North Carolina to escape the limitations placed on free people of color in Virginia. Meanwhile, freeholders, or free landowners, made up largely of European planters, had a vested interest in keeping people of mixed descent in slavery or extended servitude. Other European colonists did not want to compete with industrious free people of African or Indigenous ancestry. This is why colonial authorities took actions to persecute people of mixed heritage, who made up a solid portion of free people of color.⁵¹

In the 1720s, legislators in North Carolina kept pace with those in Virginia by passing a series of racial codes in line with other strict hypodescent policies, which aimed to stem further intermixture and oppress existing blended families. In 1723, Virginia and North Carolina both continued to reduce the rights of "Free Negroes, Mulattoes, and other Persons of mixt Blood." Virginia led the way among British colonies and increased legal restrictions the year after alleged plots of slave rebellion, where colonists also implicated free Mulattoes as coconspirators. The assembly passed acts against "free Negros, Mulattos, and Indians" in several areas, which included limits on voting, owning guns, serving in militias, meeting with slaves, and testifying in court. Colonies everywhere passed similar restrictions directed at free people of color throughout the eighteenth century, especially in the wake of suspected or actual slave revolts. Virginia officials also punished the children of "Mulatto" and "Indian" servant mothers held under thirty-one-year indentures with the same extended period in bondage. North Carolina and Maryland did the same, surpassing other colonies by applying hypodescent to multiple generations.⁵²

Legislators passed laws in Virginia (1723), North Carolina (1723), and Maryland (1725) that subjected free "Mulattoes," "Negroes," and "Indians" to heavier taxes, which burdened families of color and dissuaded racial exogamy. North Carolina lawmakers considered "all free Negroes, Mulattoes, and other Persons of that kind, being mixed Blood," to be tithables. All free men and women twelve years and older were taxed the same as what masters paid on all their slaves of the same age, whereas only European men over the age of sixteen were similarly taxed. This statute also included "any White Person or Person whatsoever, Male or Female," who would marry "with any Negro, Mulatto, Mustee, or other Persons of mixed blood." While this did not explicitly outlaw interracial marriage, additional taxes assessed on free people of color dissuaded Europeans from partnering with free Africans, Native Americans, and people of mixed lineage and forced many of these families out of the colonies.⁵³

As in the Chesapeake, magistrates in North Carolina made repeated legislative efforts to restrict mixture, and in these laws they also laid out a legal definition for who was a "Person of Mixed Blood." In 1741, the North Carolina General Assembly mirrored Virginia's anti-intermixture act in its own law to prevent "abominable Mixture and spurious issue." Lawmakers strengthened preexisting statutes by levying heavy fines against couples, clergy, and officials responsible for "intermarrying . . . any white Man or Woman . . . with an Indian, Negro, Mustee, or Mulatto Man or Woman, or any Person of Mixed Blood, to the Third Generation." When the North Carolina General Assembly designated those of one-eighth or more African or Native American lineage to be a "Person of Mixed Blood," they drew a racial dividing line similar to that in Virginia. Several years later, in 1749, North Carolina authorities extended their "Mixed Blood" designation to the Fourth Generation, which pushed hypodescent further than in any other British province during the colonial period.[54]

Were North Carolina officials naïve to believe that they could accurately detect the racial makeup of mixed-heritage people after three or four generations of admixture? Certainly, it was impossible to administer a law that extended tax liabilities to "all Negroes, Mulattoes, Mustees," and any other "Persons of Mixt Blood to the Fourth Generation" or of one-sixteenth African lineage. Virginia did not hold fast to its legal definition of Mulattoes having one-half Indigenous or one-eighth African ancestry. The general assembly had passed this rule to restrict office holding in 1705, and Jamaica passed a similar limit in 1733 to prohibit the right to vote. There, after "Three Degrees removed in a lineal Descent from the Negroe Ancestor," a person could participate in elections, and "no one shall be deemed a Mulatto after the Third Generation" of admixture with Europeans. At that point, Jamaica's legislature determined that mixed-heritage peoples "shall have all the Privileges and Immunities of his Majesty's white Subjects of this Island, provided they are brought up in the Christian Religion." These racial parameters were more aspirational than realistic and gave authorities broad power to determine the race and legal limitations for mixed people who petitioned the courts. Only North Carolina explicitly referred to blood fractions in regard to marriage law, but colonial magistrates were keen to restrict intermarriage for another reason: to hinder legal inheritances.[55]

Although the Caribbean had more relaxed social customs regarding people of mixed descent and their marriage with Europeans, Jamaica again defined blood quantum in 1761 in order to limit inheritances to children of blended ancestry. Legislators moved to prohibit European men from leaving enormous wealth to illegitimate mixed-heritage children, setting the cap at £2,000 for offspring born outside of "lawful wedlock." While some council members dissented to these limitations, Jamaica's assembly decided that the "offspring of a negro," once he or she reached the "fourth degree" of intermixture with Europeans, would have "the same rights and privileges with English subjects born of white parents." This "fourth degree" left the previous law of 1733 unchanged. One Englishman recorded that this boundary included all "descendants of the Negroe blood . . . who are above three steps removed in the lineal digression from the Negro." Like in Virginia, and originally in North Carolina, the "three steps," or three generations, included those of one-half, one-fourth, and one-eighth African ancestry. Once someone reached the "fourth degree," or one-sixteenth African descent with European mixture, he or she would become legally "white."[56]

In all British provinces, people of blended ancestry could cross over into whiteness under the right circumstances, and mixed-heritage women held a key to that process through childbearing. Hundreds of free men and women of mixed ancestry filed legal suits for the same rights as other British subjects in eighteenth-century Jamaica. Sarah Morris was one of these women. Purportedly of one-fourth African and three-fourths European descent, Sarah petitioned the assembly for "the privileges and immunities of a white woman" in 1763. These privileges would also belong to her four-year-old child, Charlotte, the "reputed daughter" of wealthy Scottish merchant and planter Robert Stirling, with whom Sarah had an intimate relationship. Women such as Sarah mixed with European men over multiple generations, acquiring freedom, affluence, and whiteness. Sarah owned "houses, lands, and slaves, to the value of £4,000 and upwards." The court awarded her and Charlotte "the same rights and privileges of English subjects born of white parents," though restricted their ability to provide court testimony against "whites" and limited substantial gifts and inheritances according to Jamaica's law passed a couple years earlier. Still, even these limitations could be overcome, as Sarah later petitioned and was granted the right to leave her daughter, Charlotte, estate holdings in excess of £2,000. Mixed women of color usually gave birth to slaves, but in exceptional cases they provided an escape hatch into racial whiteness.[57]

While English magistrates from Jamaica, North Carolina, and Virginia all stated who should be considered a Mulatto by lineal descent, the "black"-"white" racial divide was always porous. Colonial authorities could not draw a firm racial line between "white" and "Negro" that correlated squarely with free and bound labor, so they sought to legally restrict mixed peoples' rights to legitimacy and the inheritance of British wealth. Many European colonists were unaware of these written codes or ignored them, and some still chose to recognize their children or married intimate partners of "mixed blood" even if their loved ones were not considered "white."[58]

While certain ministers were unwilling to marry interracial couples, there were many Christian clergymen who believed in granting marriage rites to those who identified with the faith. On March 2, 1726, Rev. John Blacknall of Edenton, North Carolina, "did joyn together in the holy estate of Matrimony ... Thomas Spencer a White man and a Malatto Woman named Martha Paul." Reverend Blacknall carried out the wedding ceremony "according to the form of the Church of England" in Chowan County, though the couple lived farther east in the Currituck district on the Atlantic coast. They may have traveled to find someone who could marry them, perhaps after having trouble finding a local minister or justice of the peace. After the wedding, someone reported

Reverend Blacknall to authorities. While provincial lawmakers found it difficult to explicitly supersede the ecclesiastical right for Europeans to marry people of mixed ancestry, they could punish those who performed the ceremonies.[59]

As in the Chesapeake, North Carolina courts brought charges against officials who conducted marriages between people of mixed heritage and Europeans. Whether Reverend Blacknall was found guilty or paid the fifty-pound fine for Thomas Spencer and Martha Paul's marriage is unclear, but it appears he cooperated with the provincial magistrates. After the justices summoned Thomas to appear before them to answer for the crime of marrying the "Malatto" woman Martha, he refused to appear and never sent a response concerning his case. More than likely, the couple simply wanted colonial officials to leave them alone.[60]

As members of the Protestant clergy decided whether they would follow God's law or colonial law, interracial couples had to choose if they would willfully defy intermarriage statutes or risk bastardy and fornication charges. In Westmoreland County, Virginia, the court dropped a fornication case against Richard Allen, a man of European descent, who was living with a "Mulato woman" named Ann, after he presented evidence that they had married in Maryland. Perhaps the couple traveled from Virginia across the Potomac River into Maryland to secretly perform the ceremony and later hid their marriage to avoid prosecution. Though it was a gamble to defy legal codes, marrying in a clandestine location and keeping vows secret upon returning home was a tactical method that may have allowed the couple to circumvent detection.[61]

Colonial governments in Virginia, Maryland, and North Carolina regularly pursued servitude, and sometimes slavery, for Mulattoes involved in intimate relationships, on account of either race mixing or violating religious sanctity. In June of 1735, the court in Queen Anne's County, Maryland, brought Bridget Guy, a "white woman," and Joseph Guy, a "mullatto man," up on charges of "intermarrying contrary to the Act of Assembly." County officials convicted Bridget and Joseph for violating intermixture law and assigned the couple to be sold as servants to the highest bidder. While the court record does not detail the length of time they served, Thomas Hynson Wright purchased Bridget and Joseph Guy "for the Sum of eighteen pounds ten Shillings." This arrangement allowed planters to profit from persecuting people of mixed heritage and their European partners. In the same court session, the very next case concerned Elizabeth Reed, a free "mullatto Woman" who was accused of "fornication with a Negro," who appeared to be an enslaved man. Like Joseph and Bridget Guy, Elizabeth was found guilty, and "the Court sold [her] to Mr. Thomas Wilkinson for the Sum of twelve pounds seventeen Shillings" for an unspecified period of time. The court punished the "mullatto" Elizabeth Reed more for having sex as an unmarried woman ("fornication") and less for the crime of intermixture with a "Negro."[62]

The outcome for Elizabeth Reed, as well as for Bridget and Joseph Guy, demonstrates how authorities policed interracial intimacies but also how gender and race directed how people of mixed heritage might choose intimate partners. The court's decision to prosecute Mulattoes who engaged in sexual relationships with people from different racial and gender backgrounds—one a "white" woman, the other a "Negro" man—shows the limitations that free people of mixed descent faced in the Chesapeake. Judges would not place Joseph in servitude if his wife, Bridget, were not "white." If Elizabeth had been a slave instead of free, officials would not have tried her for the crime of sex with another enslaved man. If her sexual partner were a "white" man instead of a "Negro," there would have been a greater chance that he could protect her through social connections or by paying her fines. Generally, mixed-heritage women could benefit from choosing free European partners, while mixed men doing the same were more likely to face persecution.[63]

Legal freedoms did not always emanate from Christian marriage, but mixed people in bondage who married free people of color or Europeans could potentially increase access to liberty through a free spouse. On the other hand, intermarriage could also carry families further into bondage. The frequency with which courts prosecuted mixed couples varied across counties and provinces, but fears of fines, bondage, beatings, and public shame prevented many people from openly forming or formalizing interracial relationships. This resulted in thousands of mixed-heritage "bastard" children being born as the product of "fornication," something that authorities ostensibly claimed they wanted to avoid. In Virginia, Maryland, North Carolina, and other English provinces, colonists maintained the authority to harass, destabilize, and break up families of blended ancestry, but these people continued to defy the socio-racial order.[64]

## "MULATTO MISTRESSES" AND "MARRIAGE TO A MULATTO" IN SLAVE SOCIETIES

Through the mid-eighteenth century, legislators in Virginia, Maryland, and North Carolina continued passing discriminatory statutes that reflected strong hypodescent ideology, targeting "Mulattoes" along with those identified as "Indian" or "Negro." Although colonists publicly scorned racial intermixture, they were not threatened by all relationships the same. In Virginia, Peter Fontaine lamented in a letter to his brother how "the country swarms with mulatto bastards." He believed European men such as himself should not have "smutted our blood" by mixing "with negro women." Peter further postulated that "instead of this abominable practice which hath polluted the blood of many amongst us, we had taken Indian wives in the first place, it would have made them some compensation for their lands." William Byrd II and other planters also thought marriage between Englishmen and Indigenous women would assist the colonial agenda of opening up North American territories to European conquest while assimilating Native American "Heathens." William pointed to the success of the French in Canada who would "intermarry with a Native."[65]

Both William Byrd II and Peter Fontaine explained how multigenerational intermarriage and mixture between "whites" and "Negroes," as opposed to "whites" and "Indians," would take longer to clear "polluted" African blood and produce "white" people. Peter loosely cited Virginia law, which allowed Mulattoes to "intermarry with the white people" if they were "three generations removed from the black father or mother" by mixture with other Europeans. He also noted that people of one-eighth African ancestry and seven-eighths European descent married other Europeans "every day" in Virginia. These unions are hidden in plain sight in historical records, as colonial officials often identified people of non-European backgrounds in documents but did not list the race of mixed people who were socially accepted as "white."[66]

People of blended heritage had greater leeway to consort with Europeans outside of the Chesapeake at the geographical ends of British colonial America: the northern colonies and the southern plantation slave societies. The Caribbean and South Carolina exhibited greater mixture than the northern provinces and a number of colonists there fundamentally differed in their social and legal approach to exogamous relationships. Even though some assemblymen had concerns about racial mixing, they did not follow lawmakers in the Chesapeake by routinely enacting penalties against intermixture and mixed-heritage people. Demographics shaped the cultural landscape and created a unique social atmosphere in South Carolina and the Caribbean. Swiss traveler Samuel Dyssli described Charlestown and the surrounding areas as a place that looked "more like a negro country than like a country settled by white people." Africans formed a majority of the South Carolina population, similar to the Caribbean colonies, and comprised as many as eight or nine out of ten inhabitants on some plantations.[67]

South Carolina's demographics spurred the diffusion of African and European planter culture found in the Caribbean, which had an effect on notions concerning ethnoracial mixture and people of mixed heritage. European planters, overseers, and other workers commonly had sexual connections and relationships with African and Indigenous women and fathered numerous children of blended ancestry. "The whites mix with the blacks and the blacks with the whites, and if a white man has a child by a black woman, nothing is done to him on account of it," wrote Samuel from Charlestown in 1737. Furthermore, he stated, "It also occurs that the English marry . . . black women, often also Indian women." Even though some colonists in the region found this mixture disagreeable, provincial officials still recognized these marriages.[68]

Like in South Carolina, European men in the Caribbean were often found "cohabiting with Negresses and Mulattas, free or slaves." This was according to Edward Long, a Jamaican-born English planter-politician, who also added, "not one in twenty can be persuaded, that there is either sin; or shame in cohabiting with his slave." Edward wrote scathingly of these colonists and their mixed-heritage offspring, stating that these men "usher into the world a tarnished train of beings." The general acceptance of intermixture in the Caribbean and South Carolina disgusted Englishmen such as Edward, who felt that "white" men dishonored themselves by cohabiting with women of color. At the same time, by passing few restrictions against racial mixture, these societies favored the sexual freedoms of European men.[69]

While European men routinely forced female slaves and free women of color into sexual encounters, some women realized they could improve their economic condition through concubinage or prostitution and exercised some autonomy through these exchanges. Edward Long blasted wealthy European men whom he saw "lavishing their fortune with unbounded liberality upon a common prostitute." Mixed women who agreed to sex with European men increased their chances for material gains and greater freedoms. Edward described the women of color, who sometimes offered men their bodies, as making a conscious decision to profit from their sexuality, though others may have been coerced into even these situations. These "illicit connexions," as Edward called them, were characterized by patriarchal manipulation, control, and violence. Enslaved women might obtain favors through sexual arrangements, but the chance for manumission was always slim. These women weighed the sacrifices, and many held on to the hope of liberty, if not for themselves, then possibly for their children. They also realized that multigenerational mixture with European men lightened their offspring's skin and these women understood that racial whiteness could pass on to their children.[70]

However, enslaved mistresses and free women of color often had little recourse when suffering physical, sexual, and emotional abuse while engaging with European men, and they could not easily exit these arrangements. Even women of mixed ancestry who experienced greater freedoms encountered violence, which played a foundational role in plantation societies. Thomas Thistlewood, an English overseer and planter in Jamaica, documented multiple assaults that he and his male counterparts carried out against women of color. He wrote that Francis Ruecastle was in a relationship with a Mulatto woman named Sappho and "beat etc his Wife sadly." Thomas recorded a particular beating in

Mixed-heritage people sometimes held middling positions between Africans and Europeans on Caribbean plantations, where women of color often had complicated interactions and relationships with European men. (Agostino Brunias, ca. 1770–80, Carmen Thyssen-Bornemisza Collection, Thyssen-Bornemisza Museum, Madrid, Spain)

his diary because Sappho died from it. Thomas recounted how another contemporary of his, Henry Weech, in a jealous rage "cut off the lips, [and] upper lip almost close to [the] Nose, off his Mulatto sweetheart." This was after she gave birth to a dark-skinned child that apparently could not have been fathered by a light-skinned European man. Henry bragged about leaving the woman horribly disfigured, saying that "no Negroe should ever kiss those lips he had." Interestingly, Thomas described the women who engaged with these men as "Wife" and "sweetheart," even though they were savagely mistreated. European men may have had intimate feelings for these Mulatto women, but they loved exercising power more. Mixed women risked abuse when partnering with abusive men, but they also weighed the value of having a European man in their lives who could provide protections under Caribbean slavery.[71]

Gender, class, and power were integral to structuring interracial relationships in the Caribbean. Bryan Edwards, another eighteenth-century English planter and assemblyman in Jamaica, reasoned that free Mulatto women did not normally marry "the young men of their own complexion" because men of color were uneducated and "in too low a state of degradation, to think of matrimony." Bryan pitied "the unfortunate circumstances of their birth," guessing that not 5 percent of these men had formal schooling. He understood that their poor "education and condition in life" left men of mixed ancestry in "a state of degradation," even as he looked past his role in upholding the systems that contributed to this phenomenon. Most men of color were trapped in slavery, and those who were free faced a multitude of social and legal obstacles when seeking economic independence and marriageable partners. Through hard work or inheritance, some mixed-heritage men achieved social respect and prosperity, but they had to overcome the same prejudices expressed by colonists such as Bryan. Few Mulatto men achieved a status high enough to openly engage with European women in the Caribbean. In juxtaposition, mixed-heritage women often had greater social mobility than their male counterparts because they had access to European men who might financially provide for them and their children.[72]

While intermarriage was rare between Europeans and people of mixed ancestry, these unions occurred more often among men and women in the lower social orders, who were less disgraced by these relationships than the upper classes. Bryan Edwards wrote that women of color "are universally maintained by White men of all ranks and conditions, as kept mistresses. The fact is too notorious to be concealed or controverted." Elite European men rarely married these women, however, and instead selected European brides. Bryan admitted that "no White man of decent appearance, unless urged by the temptation of a considerable fortune [through inherited wealth], will condescend to give his hand in marriage to a Mulatto! The very idea is shocking." Even in his denial of these marriages, Bryan admits that European men did sometimes marry women of blended ancestry who had large estates. He also hints that exogamy occurred more often between mixed-heritage women and working-class European men, who were less affected by social stigma than the wealthy.[73]

While mistreatment was far more likely than marriage, the Mulatto concubine wielded a modicum of power when she chose a sexual partner in the British colonies, and occasionally this allowed her to upset the social order. Some African and mixed-heritage women received gifts from their European paramours. Edward Long believed this reversed natural gender and racial roles: "white" men became "the abject, passive slave" and put up with these women's "insults, thefts, and infidelities" in such relationships. What Edward viewed as male weakness was evidence that reciprocity and love could possibly exist between European men and women of color, despite the typically uneven balance of power in these relationships.[74]

### FREE "MULATTOES OR MESTIZOS" IN GEORGIA AND SOUTH CAROLINA

"White" men and women of color generally had greater sexual freedom in colonial society, especially in South Carolina and the Caribbean, and the province of Georgia mirrored these colonies, though it followed into slavery much more cautiously. When the founding British trustees of Georgia established the province in 1733, they sought to create a society without slavery that encouraged poor European immigrants to work industriously on small agricultural landholdings. For nearly twenty years, the trustees banned slavery outright to attract European labor and avoid the issues that came with holding Africans and Native Americans in bondage. Furthermore, South Carolinians viewed Georgia as a buffer zone between them and their Spanish adversaries in Florida, to which hundreds of slaves ran away to seek refuge.[75]

In the British colonial periphery, some mixed-heritage women challenged cultural norms around gender and race and displayed self-sufficiency in partnerships with European men that made some colonists uncomfortable. Around the early 1730s, a female "Mulatto Servant (or Slave)" traveled with Captain Davis, one of the most successful merchants in Savannah, Georgia. Davis had a lucrative business shipping goods to the Caribbean, San Agustín (St. Augustine), and other Atlantic outposts. An English writer revealed that the woman "in Reality was his mistress" and described her as having "an exceeding[ly] fine Shape," adding that aside from her "swarthy" complexion, the mixed-heritage woman was comparable in beauty with other European women. By some appearances, the unnamed woman was Davis's concubine, but he valued this woman for more than her beauty alone. After a tropical illness left Davis without use of his arms and legs, the woman took care of his everyday needs. She helped feed Davis, washed his clothes, dressed him, and carried out his merchant enterprise. She conducted trade deals, balanced his accountbooks, and over time "obtained good Knowledge of his Business." Eventually, Davis allowed "almost every Thing to pass through her Hands, having such Confidence in her, that she had the Custody of all his Cash." In all, Davis "found her very faithful, and of great Service to him" and cherished this woman not only as an intimate or sexual companion but also for her dependability and sharp intellect.[76]

While some European men granted certain privileges to their mixed-heritage partners, notions of hypodescent allowed people with lighter skin to subjugate those only a few shades darker than themselves. People in Savannah knew not only that Davis lived with his "Mulatto Servant" but that he trusted the bondswoman and gave her responsibility over his personal and professional affairs. One observer noted that "all Persons who had any Business with Captain Davis were expected not to treat her with Contempt," and therefore "it may easily be supposed the Life of such Slavery was not a heavy Burden upon her." Even though she may have enjoyed a quasi freedom, the unnamed woman was still a slave and was not always respected. Her debased position became clear when an employee of Davis named Pope insulted the woman in 1739. Pope had used "some Words she did not like," and after she raised her voice in response, he struck her "across the Face with her own Fan." The fight instigated a string of confrontations between Davis and Pope. Would Pope have shown more restraint before striking Davis's mistress if she were his legitimate European wife? As a mixed-heritage servant or slave, she did not carry the same honor that "white" women had in freedom. While Davis treated his female confidante with esteem, others may not have done the same because of her race, gender, and bound status.[77]

This Mulatto woman was loyal to her European partner, yet we must inquire into the reasons for that devotion. Conceivably, she could have easily taken his money, hopped on a boat, and left Savannah to become a free woman. Why did she remain in bondage under Davis? It appears she committed herself to him, although she possibly cared more about keeping a secure position in colonial society. Even an ailing European man could provide financial and legal protections for a woman of mixed heritage bound in the colonies. She may have loved the captain, but if Davis's actions were likewise benevolent then could he have freed her? Maybe he did or promised to do so in the future, which resulted in her obedience. Was this woman a leech that "conspires to bleed" her paramours, as Edward Long commented about other women of color in similar situations, or was she something more to Davis? Edward claimed such a woman knew how to persuade "the man she detests to believe she is most violently smitten with the beauty of his person; in short, over head and ears in love with him." In the end, only Davis's "Mulatto Servant" knew for sure whether her feelings were true or if hers was merely a plot of seduction.[78]

If the unnamed Mulatto woman was truly devoted to Davis, other women of color feigned affection for European men in return for material gains. Edward Long recalled one instance where a wealthy male friend of his passed away and the man's mistress of color showed "outrageous sorrow; beating her head; stamping with her feet; [with] tears pouring down in torrents." As she emphatically lamented the loss of her lover, someone discovered that she had also gone through his desk, "rummaged his pockets . . . and concealed his watch, rings, and money, in the feather-bed upon which the poor wretch had just breathed his last." Edward believed this woman's "honest affection" was simply a ruse used "to dupe the fool." This could have been the case, although perhaps the woman feared that after years of service, her lover might exclude her from his will or that others would withhold promised financial securities. If the couple had mixed-heritage children together, she may have worried that Jamaica's Mulatto inheritance law would rob her offspring of their father's estate. "Negresses and Mulattas" (and their children) involved in these informal partnerships with European men often clung to what they could when the man died or the relationship ended. Rummaging through the belongings of a lover shortly after his death might ensure economic survival for these blended families.[79]

In Georgia, Europeans also took into consideration racial intermixture when deciding to keep African slaves out of the colony. Rev. John Bolzius was one early leader who advocated for only European labor in the province based on the idea of maintaining racial purity. In the 1730s, he was a part of a group of Germanic-speaking Salzburgers who founded the town of Ebenezer on the Savannah River. Reverend Bolzius regularly corresponded with the Rev. George Whitefield—who became one of the most famous preachers and Protestant religious advocates of the eighteenth century. Reverend Whitefield originally came from Britain to pastor Georgia's capital of Savannah, and he later toured the colonies, delivering fiery sermons that attracted thousands and led to a great "awakening" in the spirit of his listeners. In a 1745 letter to Reverend Whitefield, Reverend Bolzius discussed the issue of slavery and weighed in against the introduction of slaves into Georgia. "I am sure," Reverend Bolzius argued, "if the Trustees allow'd to one thousand White Settlers so many Negroes, in a few Years you would meet in the Streets, So as in Carolina, with many Malattoes, & many Negroe children, which in process of time will fill the Colony." Reverend Bolzius warned that if officials gave in to planters' demands to legalize slavery in Georgia, it would bring the same intermixture as in neighboring South Carolina. He noted that some authorities "have made good Laws & Restrictions in favour of the White people, but how many are [there] who pay regard & Obedience to them?" He also understood that people from different racial backgrounds intermixed despite prohibitive laws or common racial antagonisms. Still, South Carolina planters lobbied to legalize slavery in Georgia and drowned out the arguments of those such as Reverend Bolzius. Reverend Whitefield also eventually endorsed slavery and later relied on African slave labor.[80]

The impetus for keeping African slavery out of early Georgia did not stem from abolitionist philosophy but instead originated from "white" supremacist ideology and European fears of becoming a "Negro country" like South Carolina. Protests by proslavery interest groups eventually triumphed around the middle of the century. While some enslaved Africans were already in the colony, the legal "Introduction of Black Slaves or Negroes" came from lawmakers on August 8, 1750. In the same act, Georgia's assembly also punished interracial fornication and outlawed "Intermarriages between the white People and the Negroes or Blacks," which overruled the authority of the church and proclaimed these "unlawful Marriages . . . absolutely null and void." Ironically, while Georgia was the only British province to forbid "black"-"white" intermarriage, officials did not prevent Mulattoes, Mustees, or other people of blended ancestry from mixing with Europeans and later called for mixed peoples to help settle the burgeoning colony.[81]

Free people of mixed heritage had been living in Georgia for decades before the assembly passed legislation that recruited these groups to settle in the colony. In the spring of 1765, provincial magistrates discussed their concern that "Persons born of free Parents being Mulattoes or Mestizos . . . have been discouraged to come into this Province." Unlike other British colonies whose administrators used legal measures to expel free people of color, Georgia's assembly took the opposite approach and reached out to these people of mixed descent. On March 25, legislators passed an act that welcomed "all Persons male and Female of what Nation or Colour soever being born of free parents." Mixed-heritage people had to "give good Testimony" of their loyalty to the king and promise "their Obedience to the Laws" in order to become naturalized British subjects. Then "they, their Wives, and Children may have, Use and enjoy, all the Rights, Priviledges, Powers and Immunities whatsoever which any Person born of British parents within this Province may, can, might, could or of Right ought to have." The only caveat was that they could not vote or become elected members of the general assembly. Despite these stipulations, the invitation to become a member of Georgia's society was one of the strongest formal agreements that a British colonial government offered to people of color, and it specifically extended the policy with mixed-heritage peoples who would create families in mind.[82]

With scant records from colonial Georgia, it is difficult to know how many

"Mulattoes or Mestizos" actually took advantage of the legislature's offer, but there were at least some couples that came to Georgia with the desire to achieve a better life. Sometime around or before 1742, William Davis and Ann Davis (née Hailey) moved to Georgia, and while the couple was of color, they were always reputed to be "Free People." Ann Davis's roots went back to Virginia, the home of her mother, Mary Hailey, and probable father, William Hayly, a man listed as a "Mullatta" in York County. It appears that Virginia laws, which targeted free people of color with harsh treatment, pushed Ann and her husband to seek a new place to call home. On the borders of the British colonial realm, the Davis family acquired land at Carr's Field, located near Turtle River, less than 100 miles north of San Agustín, Florida.[83]

This mixed-heritage family appears to have integrated well into the fledgling colonial society in rural Georgia, in part because people living on the edges of the empire cared less about race than survival. For four years, William Davis served the British Crown in Capt. Mark Carr's company of marines, a regiment commanded by Georgia's first governor and founder, James Oglethorpe. William and his wife Ann had multiple children and depended on their neighbors, just as others relied on them. Elizabeth Gilbert, a midwife of European descent, delivered William Davis Jr., Ann's eldest son. Colonial records later described William Jr. as a "Mulattoe young man" who "behaved himself well." In early Georgia, free people of color found acceptance within colonial society. They cleared forests, planted crops, served in the military, and earned respect among their European peers. On the outskirts of the British Empire, mixed-heritage families could thrive along with other colonists.[84]

Migrating to more secluded colonial locations and intermarrying with Europeans over multiple generations helped some mixed-heritage families rise out of racial subjugation. Another prominent example comes from the Gibsons—a blended family whose "colored" descendants openly intermixed with Europeans since the seventeenth century. By around 1720, some of the Gibsons had left the Tidewater counties along the James River in Virginia and moved to North Carolina. One was Gideon Gibson, a "free colored" man who had some African or Native American ancestry. Gideon settled on the Roanoke River, which fed into the Albemarle Sound, and eventually acquired hundreds of acres of land in Bertie County and Chowan County. He married a European woman, Mary Brown, and together they had several children: Gideon Jr., Tom, Agnes, William, and possibly others. With the growth of legislative discrimination in North Carolina, the Gibsons likely came under the same type of scrutiny that people of color encountered in Virginia.[85]

Racial hostilities probably forced the interracial family to seek refuge away from settled colonists and pushed them further into Indigenous territories. In 1730, the family sold their land on the Roanoke River and traveled farther south.

Around a year after resettling, someone reported to South Carolina's assembly that some "free colored men with their white wives" were living out west in the colony. Although there was no law in South Carolina that prohibited exogamy, the report of "colored men" living with "white wives" worried some in the assembly who were concerned about open social transgressions of sex and racial boundaries.[86]

South Carolina's governor, Robert Johnson, met with Gideon Gibson to inquire about the family settling in the interior of the province. After this meeting, the governor reported to his colleagues that Gideon had been "in good Repute" before he departed Virginia and noted that his "transactions there have been very regular." Gideon previously bought, sold, and paid taxes on lands he owned and likely shared records of these dealings with the governor. He also explained his purpose for relocating to the province, relaying that he was a carpenter and had settled in the colony "for the support of his Family." Not only had he made a solid living for himself, but Gideon also "had seven Negroes of his own," which established him as a planter who supported slavery. Gideon and other free men of color who proved they were committed to upholding the slave system in South Carolina rose in the ranks by profiting from bound labor.[87]

Over several generations the Gibsons intermarried with European women, which helped them climb the racial ladder toward whiteness. Governor Robert Johnson took into consideration Gideon's "good behavior" along with his wife "being a white woman" and noted that there were "several White women Capable of working and being Serviceable in the Country" among the Gibson party. These women ensured that future generations would have European lineage and produce "white" children. Robert defended the Gibson family before other colonial magistrates, determining "that they are not Negroes nor Slaves but Free people." This phrase captured Gideon and his family's racial ambiguity and their middling colonial position: neither "Negro" slaves nor free "whites" but free people of blended ancestry on their way to whiteness. While Gideon was not considered "white," it is clear that he firmly associated with his European ancestry and free status. Many free people of color who coupled with "whites" already shared European ancestry and cultural affinity with their partners. This is why authorities accepted Gideon and his family. The Gibsons were committed to supporting the colonial project in South Carolina and multigenerational mixture with "white" women would help maintain racial hierarchy despite their ethnically blended ancestry.[88]

British authorities in South Carolina, the Caribbean, and provinces on the fringes of empire allowed greater intermixture and at times accepted mixed-heritage people as nearly equal participants, even if not equal subjects under the Crown. Colonies in these regions developed more fluid racial orders than in Tidewater Virginia, Maryland, and North Carolina—places where planter-legislators punished free Mulattoes and their partners for intermarriage, intimate relationships, and casual sex. Areas further removed from colonial centers were vulnerable to attack by the Spanish, the French, and Native Americans. Provinces with large enslaved populations were also susceptible to domestic insurrection by slaves of African, Indigenous, and mixed descent. This is why colonial officials in Spanish, French, and some British colonies were more willing to make concessions to free people of color and treat them as a buffer caste in between "Negro" and "white." This is also why British colonists living in societies with slave majorities in the Caribbean and South Carolina could not risk marginalizing mixed-heritage people who shared European lineage and worked to expand British settler colonialism. Indeed, authorities did not want to alienate blended families such as the Davises in Georgia or the Gibsons in South Carolina.[89]

Free people of mixed ancestry had greater freedom to intermarry with whom they chose and raise families where they were useful to the British Empire. And despite discriminatory laws and everyday prejudices, Mulattoes and other "mixed bloods" found ways to exercise forms of independence that were not always available to those of full African or Indigenous lineage. While legally handicapped in many ways, people of mixed heritage were also able to obtain greater freedoms compared to most "Negroes," and some could escape bondage over several generations of further intermixture with "whites" or other free "Mulattoes." Both social and legal benefits helped swell the ranks of Mulattoes among all free people of color.

# 6

## The Advantages and Disadvantages of Blended Ancestry

In the late 1750s, as competing Native American and European empires clashed amid the Seven Years' War, a "Mulatto Boy" named Sam was born in Frederick Town, Maryland. As an adolescent, he watched the political rift growing between Britain and its colonists in North America. Sam witnessed those tensions boil over during the U.S. Revolution as colonists demanded their liberty from the British Crown. Young Sam desired a similar freedom from his master, John Bland, and he put together a plan to obtain it. The teenager of mixed ancestry resembled other British boys, with "gray Eyes, brown Hair," and "a very light Complexion." Sam knew that his physical features would allow him "to pass for a free Boy." Light skin alone would not automatically deliver freedom, but Sam had other tools to help him get there. While growing up, he had traveled with master John and carefully studied the Chesapeake's geography. Sam also learned to be resourceful and developed an independent demeanor and other skills. According to his owner, Sam had "a smooth artful Tongue, [and was] a great Villain, but a very good Barber." Although his master portrayed some of Sam's attributes as negative, a marketable trade and the ability to speak fluidly, while bending the truth, helped many servants and slaves run away. Perhaps Sam's most useful trait was his confidence and willingness to take risks. Coupling these skills with relatively light skin and European features made his goal of successful escape all the more likely.[1]

Like other people of color, Sam believed he inherently deserved freedom, and his story shows how slaves and servants of mixed ethnoracial ancestry could create opportunities for themselves even from a subjugated position in the British colonies. This chapter focuses on both the advantages and disadvantages that "mixed people" experienced in the British provinces, with an examination of how Mulatto privilege influenced the growing numbers of free people of color. Compared to those of full European descent, mixed-heritage people faced daily forms of racial prejudice that negatively impacted their lives across the colonies. The overwhelming majority were born into bondage and remained there throughout their lives. However, people of "mixed blood," particularly those who were able to lay claim to European lineage, also received clear benefits when compared to other Africans and Native Americans. On rural plantations and in urban centers, colonists commonly awarded preferential treatment to people of mixed backgrounds. These allowances reveal the flexibility within hypodescent ideology, in which society associated those of mixed ancestry with their African or Native American heritage yet, at times, elevated their social standing because of a lineal connection to European ancestors.[2]

Geographic setting and social climate also shaped individual circumstances, for if Sam had been born in colonial Spanish, French, or Indigenous territories, he would have had enhanced access to rights and possibly even freedom. Compared to those in the British Empire, free Mulattoes under the Catholic Spanish or French had a greater likelihood of upward social mobility. Even though people of color met discrimination in all European colonies, slaves in Protestant British provinces were often correct to assume their treatment might improve under Catholic regimes that offered more relaxed socioracial orders and hosted large free mixed populations. While enslaved and free people of mixed descent might have encountered positive treatment depending on their situation in the British Empire, they did not wait idly for better lives. Instead, many chose to escape bondage and sometimes joined other malcontents in the fight for their liberty.[3]

The majority of mixed people having some African or Native American ancestry remained in some sort of bondage in the eighteenth-century British colonies, which prompted many to risk the perils associated with escape for a chance to live among foreign powers or in another English province. British colonists in Virginia, Maryland, and North Carolina most often withheld freedom from mixed-heritage people, including those born free to European mothers. Indeed, colonial planters in these three provinces repeatedly manipulated the boundary between freedom and slavery in favor of the latter. Despite legal restrictions on manumission and attempts to prevent intermixture within the British dominion, the number of free people of color grew throughout the century, and demographic growth was largest in the Chesapeake and the Caribbean islands.[4]

Although the number of mixed-heritage people in the British colonies is impossible to pinpoint, statistics and qualitative records show that they constituted a clear majority among free populations of color. Data suggests that the number of people identified as Mulatto in the Chesapeake reached over 10,000—around 3 percent of the population—after the mid-eighteenth century. These estimates are consistent with Maryland census records that distinctly counted "Mulattoes" as well as "blacks" and "whites" in 1755. By this time, figures and other records reveal that colonists understood that the majority of free people of color were also people of mixed ancestry. Mulattoes and their families gained freedom through various methods over the years: usually from free birth to "white" women and free women of color or through emancipation by a benevolent master and/or father. Further manumission came through legislative changes in the second half of the century, when these blended families moved certain colonial authorities to formally denounce thirty-one-year indentures for freeborn Mulattoes. While some mixed people received shorter indentures, most remained in captivity. Others attempted to negotiate their freedom through the courts, a route that was less accessible to newly imported "saltwater" African slaves. Mixed-heritage people who had the greatest access to the courts and sometimes attained liberty appear frequently in the records, but this should not mask the fact that most of them remained enslaved and their stories usually mirrored those of their darker-skinned kin.[5]

European masters were more likely to grant special concessions to their enslaved men, women, and children of blended ancestry, but bound "Mulattoes" experienced the same types of suffering that "Negro" slaves met while under the yoke of bondage, and sometimes worse. Colonists used violence and the threat of violence to maintain hundreds of thousands of Africans, along with smaller numbers of Indigenous and mixed-heritage people, in captivity. Despite this oppression, "Negroes," "Indians," "Mulattoes," "Mustees," and others of "mixed blood" routinely challenged the authority of their masters, overseers, and others who upheld the institution of slavery. People of mixed descent confronted harsh punishments with the same severity as other slaves, and Europeans often brutally tortured those who made the fateful decision to run away. These efforts to escape bondage and penalties for absconding illustrate the back-and-forth negotiation of power between slave and master.[6]

Enslaved Africans, Native Americans, and people of mixed backgrounds shared in the fight to achieve greater autonomy, and people of blended ancestry held several advantages over their African and Indigenous counterparts when running away from their masters. During escape, European phenotypes aided slaves of mixed heritage by allowing them to craft free identities. This did not mean that only those with light skin, straight hair, and other European features could racially pass into freedom as "white"—or that they desired to do so. While a small number of slaves used their light or "white" skin to facilitate a pathway to independence, free-status passing occurred more often than racial passing in the British colonies.[7]

Status passing took place when enslaved people of mixed ethnoracial descent relied on a combination of clothing, physical appearance, cultural performance, work skills, and other abilities to portray themselves as free persons and colonists accepted them as such. Europeans usually assumed "Negroes" were slaves, and even though "Mulattoes" did not have a fixed social position and most were in perpetual bondage, colonists often knew and accepted the fact that many were free. Statistics influenced racial perceptions of mixed-heritage peoples, and most free people of color were Mulattoes—80 percent in some places. Presumptions about race and status allowed enslaved peoples of mixed lineage to perform as free persons and encourage society to view them as such. Racially ambiguous bodies and the ability to shape colonial perceptions of free status gave Mulattoes an advantage over other enslaved peoples when attempting to flee captivity. Slaves with Indigenous ancestry held a similar edge over Africans when running away. Mustees—people of Native American descent mixed with some African or European lineage—carried attributes that assisted their journey toward freedom as well. People of mixed heritage skillfully used their in-between status to exploit the inherent complexities of racial caste systems, and many were able to gain benefits in the British colonies. This type of resistance is why the social construction of mixed-race people in the colonial era was fluid and multifaceted, which allowed certain people of "mixed blood" the ability to straddle attachments to bondage and liberty.[8]

## WARS OF EMPIRE AND FREEDOM OUTSIDE THE BRITISH EMPIRE

In the eighteenth century, ethnoracial mixture was pervasive in Spanish Latin America, in Portuguese-controlled Brazil, throughout the Caribbean, and in North America—where the Spanish, French, and British vied for control over Indigenous territories. Conflicting empires in the Atlantic world caused social upheaval in the Americas, which provided opportunities for those in slavery and servitude to escape bondage. While anti-"Negro" and anti-"Indian" racism was prevalent in all European colonies, enslaved people of color in the British provinces ran away to places where views surrounding race were more nuanced and flexible. Sometimes this meant leaving British-controlled regions on the Atlantic Coast for a nearby colony or Indigenous territories in the "backcountry" to the west. At other times runaways from the British colonies sought refuge with another European power. French and Spanish provinces in North America had sizeable free populations of color, and the possibility of social mobility attracted people of mixed lineage, among others, to these areas.[9]

Like the English, the French also held multiple views on intermixture, which typically occurred with Indigenous peoples in North America. Some early eighteenth-century French colonists feared that marriages between the French and Native Americans would "mix good blood with bad." They claimed these *sang-mêlés* ("mixed-bloods") had tainted "whiteness and purity of blood." Still, French missionaries and magistrates encouraged their men to marry Indigenous women so they could "form only one people and one blood." These authorities touted intermarriage as a solution to the negative effects of concubinage and fornication with "Indian" women. Marriage could also smooth the way for Catholic conversion efforts and facilitate trade. Overall, trade alliances and sexual relationships between peoples from two sides of the Atlantic were frequent in Canada, and the French referred to mixed Franco-Indigenous people as *métis*.[10]

Unlike the British, the Catholic empires of France and Spain were compelled to tolerate ethnoracial mixture and mixed-heritage people, in part because these Europeans and Native Americans had become interdependent. In North America, the British, Dutch, French, and Spanish fought over Indigenous territories and access to trade in beaver, deer, and other animal furs. While Europeans desired valuable animal pelts, various Indigenous peoples sought metal tools and weapons (especially guns) to hunt game and build strength against other groups who had already acquired these items. Europeans routinely courted Native American allies and often relied on Indigenous involvement to help defeat their enemies. Interactions between Europeans and Native Americans led to sexual intimacies. While these connections were common, they were also heavily gendered, as mostly "white" men participated in interracial relationships with "Indian" women. English authorities looked down on the Catholic empires and the open acknowledgment of intermixture in French and Spanish colonial societies. Many of these mixed Indigenous-European people—known as Métis, Mustees, or Mestizos—lived on the outskirts of the British colonies, or within them. They too considered the pros and cons of aligning themselves with various European empires.[11]

Compared to the English, French and Spanish colonial societies may have appeared more inviting to people of color because the Catholic regimes were willing to live alongside Native Americans and integrate with different cultures and peoples. This imperial approach aided French trade with Native Americans, a colonial priority that superseded taking direct control over huge tracts of land—actions associated with English settler colonialism. The French often won Native American allies to their side during European conflicts because of their respect for Indigenous ways of life and the tendency to intermix. This mixture led to Métis who rose to prominence as cultural brokers because they could navigate between French and Indigenous worlds. In English colonies, Mulattoes and Mustees generally experienced greater restrictions, though they too could move more easily among various communities. While French colonies did not have racially egalitarian societies, they and their Native American allies sometimes drew people of color from the British colonies.[12]

In North America, some people in slavery and servitude in the British colonies hoped that joining the French or Native American groups would allow them to obtain increased social mobility. James Wenyam was "a Molatto Man ... of middle Stature" with a noticeable red beard, who in 1746 planned to run away from his master in Kent County, Delaware. Before he absconded, James attempted to recruit a fellow bondsman, "a Negro Man, whom he wanted to go with him." He assured the African man that "he had often been in the back Woods with his Master," so he knew the land well enough to make it successfully into western Indigenous territories. James suggested that the two men leave Delaware, then venture out of the British colonies and "go to the French and Indians, and fight for them." As the British were currently battling French and Indigenous forces during King George's War, this seemed like a good idea, at least to James. While his confidant turned down the offer to escape, James determined that leaving the British colonies would provide a better alternative to his current situation and ran away to the West to start a new life.[13]

The French and their Indigenous allies took in people from a wide variety of ancestral backgrounds, and during the Seven Years' War—the greatest Anglo-Franco-Indigenous conflict in North America until the U.S. Revolution—British colonists feared their slaves would run off to join their French adversaries. In 1755, a mixed slave named Toby escaped with an English indentured servant named James Francis in Kent County, Maryland. Their British master believed they headed west, toward the French enemy. He described Toby as "neither a very bright or very dark Mulatto," who had carpentry and cooper skills and understood most work around the plantation. Toby's owner lamented that "whilst we have the French such near Neighbors, we shall not have the least Security in that kind of Property." He was correct. Holding people in chattel bondage was difficult in the British colonies, especially when other Europeans might welcome defectors. Africans and people of mixed heritage under British slavery had more to gain by uniting with the French and Native Americans—who were threatened by British immigrants moving west over the Appalachian Mountains into their territories.[14]

The social instability produced by war created opportunities for discontented bondsmen and bondswomen in the British colonies to escape into French and Native American communities. If runaways like Toby and James made it to French outposts, they might aid their masters' rival with information, labor, and military strength. This was another reason British colonists considered slaves and free people of color enemies within their own territory.

Fears of domestic insurrection ran high during wartime, and when "white" anxieties of revolt were heightened, colonial officials suspected mixed-heritage people of siding with Africans and Native Americans. During the Seven Years' War, the governors of Pennsylvania, Virginia, Maryland, and North Carolina met in 1757 to discuss stationing troops in South Carolina and Georgia to protect the more vulnerable southern colonies. British authorities believed the French would carry out an attack by sea from Saint-Domingue or over land from the Alabama Fort, near Mobile, with the help of the Creeks. Provincial officials were also keenly aware that external threats could spark internal insurrection among their slaves. Two years later, South Carolina colonists believed they had uncovered evidence of such a conspiracy, and courts tried a freeman of mixed heritage, Philip John, finding him guilty of "seditious and treasonable Practices" for encouraging their slaves to rebel. Reportedly, Philip had said, "The white People shou'd be all underground, that the Sword shou'd go thro' the Land, and it should shine with their blood, that there should be no more white King's Governors or great men, but the negro's should live happily & have Laws of their own." Authorities whipped and branded Philip "for endeavouring to stir up Sedition among the Negroes," but it appears that he was released afterward.[15]

Despite being a freeman, Philip John was not satisfied with the hierarchy of colonial society and may have fought for equality with the help of others who lived under subjugation. An African slave, Caesar, was also named in planning the rebellion, and Philip may have worked with him to deliver messages to other "Negroes" and "Indians." The *South-Carolina Gazette* reported that Philip had often said "that the *Indians* were to be concerned in the extirpation of the white People from the Face of this Earth." These reports exacerbated British fears at a time when Cherokees were attacking British colonists in the "backcountry" and French privateers were taking their ships off South Carolina's coast. Colonists probably embellished rumors of internal conspiracies, but people of color were aware that these external enemies of the British might be good allies. Caesar and Philip allegedly constructed a plan to revolt with the help of John Pendarvis, a wealthy Mulatto, who perhaps offered £700 to purchase arms that would fund the "insurrection of the Negroes against the white people." Caesar, John, and other coconspirators escaped death, but officials recaptured Philip and hanged him. Uprisings by enslaved "Negroes," free "Mulattoes," the French, and nearby "Indians" struck terror into the hearts of British colonists yet offered hope to people of color who sought to improve their condition.[16]

Like the French, the Spanish in Florida attracted a number of rebellious slaves from British plantations, mainly from the South Carolina and Georgia Lowcountry. In Florida, a number of African, Indigenous, and mixed-heritage peoples lived in and near San Agustín (St. Augustine). South Carolina officials complained that many of the Catholic colony's Florida inhabitants were "*Mulatto's* of savage Dispositions." The British decried the rampant mixture in

Spanish Florida — and throughout Latin America — especially since the Spanish Crown welcomed slave runaways and paid free people of color to organize in militias to protect the province from the neighboring British. Jack was a "mulatto man slave" in South Carolina who, like others, had heard of San Agustín's promise and ran away during the Seven Years' War. His owner believed Jack had passed as free and "inlisted himself in one of the provincial scouts of rangers." Whether or not he fought for the English or a Spanish regiment is unknown, but he knew he could move through Georgia "on his way to the *Spaniards*" and liberty in Florida. Rumors of Jack's activities kept his master searching for the runaway over two years after his escape. By then, Jack might have learned Spanish and taken up their offer of freedom.[17]

Slaves in South Carolina and Georgia knew their masters' Catholic enemies welcomed those defecting from the British colonies. While the Spanish also discriminated against those of African and Indigenous ancestry, colonial communication networks circulated stories that San Agustín offered refuge to slaves. While getting to Spanish Florida involved tremendous risk, manumission and protection from reenslavement appealed to Africans under British bondage. In the early 1760s, brothers Peter and Joe were "dark mulatto slaves" in South Carolina who weighed their options and decided to leave their owner for Florida. The slaves were valuable carpenters, sawyers, tanners, and shoemakers, which is why their master offered a large £150 reward after they ran away together to the "back settlements." The brothers were "remarkably" intelligent, and it was assumed they would head for San Agustín to join up with the Spanish.[18]

If the two made it to San Agustín, they may have been some of the last slaves that the Spanish government formally welcomed into the fold. The 1763 Treaty of Paris, which formally ended the Seven Years' War, left the prewar boundaries of European empires essentially the same in Europe, but the agreement significantly expanded Britain's claims over Native American lands. Spain ceded Florida to Britain, so there would no longer be official sanctuary in San Agustín for slaves who ran away from their British masters. The more significant change was that France agreed to give up its colonial pursuits in North America to its British rival. Though many French remained, France's official departure from most of North America left many Indigenous peoples without a nearby European ally, and enslaved people had one less option for escape. Britain claimed all Indigenous lands east of the Mississippi River, and Spain received the right to claim territory to the west of the river. France gave up most of its land claims in North America because it was willing to sacrifice the fur trade and its partnerships with Indigenous peoples in order to retain several Caribbean islands, including Saint-Domingue, which by this time had surpassed Barbados as the number-one sugar-producing colony in the world. The island also had an extremely large mixed-heritage population.[19]

A man of color in the Caribbean directs two women along with a child. While their ancestral backgrounds are not listed, the people in this picture appear to be of African, Indigenous, and mixed descent. (Agostino Brunias, ca. 1780, Yale Center for British Art, New Haven, Connecticut)

Saint-Domingue and Barbados were two of the most important colonies in the history of sugar production, and like many Caribbean islands, they were characterized by a mix of African, European, and Indigenous cultures and peoples. By the mid-eighteenth century, the British, Dutch, French, and Spanish ran lucrative plantation economies in the Caribbean. Jamaica, Cuba, Puerto Rico, and Hispaniola (containing the colonies of Saint-Domingue and Santo Domingo) had the largest populations of mixed ancestry among the islands. Each colony had unique demographics, which included a middling class of free

*Advantages and Disadvantages of Blended Ancestry* : 207

people of color who were socially and racially positioned between free "whites" and enslaved "Negroes," "Indians," and other people of mixed backgrounds. The Spanish-controlled Santo Domingo (later the Dominican Republic) contained a significant mixed population of African, Indigenous, and Spanish peoples. Fueled by large African importation and the sugar industry, Saint-Domingue (later Haiti) had a predominantly African population, which included free people of color who commonly descended from French masters and their African slaves. As in other Catholic slave societies, many French master-fathers freed their mixed children, referred to as *mulâtres* (Mulattoes) or *gens de couleur* (people of color). In 1700 there were nearly 500 free *gens de couleur* in Saint-Domingue, and the number climbed to almost 2,500 by 1730. Most *gens de couleur* were of mixed lineage like other free people of color throughout colonial America.[20]

Relaxed sentiments toward intermixture in Saint-Domingue did not mean that all French colonists accepted the practice, just as some Englishmen were willing to accept the elevation of mixed-heritage people in Caribbean societies. French laws outlined in the first 1685 *Code Noir* allowed racial exogamy, but the 1724 code forbid such marriages in Louisiana, and in 1731 French officials in Europe directed Saint-Domingue colonists to prevent the intermarriage of *blancs* ("whites") with *négresses* and *mulâtresses* because "it was a stain upon the whites" ("c'est une tache pour les blancs"). Even though the practice was stigmatized, French men in Saint-Domingue and elsewhere continued to mix with, and sometimes marry, women of color. European men did the same in other Caribbean colonies. In Jamaica, planter Edward Long considered free Mulattoes a "middle class" between "white and black" and wrote that "they ought to hold some degree of distinction." He even laid out a systematic plan that would produce "a regular establishment of three ranks of men" in a racial hierarchy where "the Whites would hold the highest place." Despite these "white" supremacist beliefs, Edward said, "I can foresee no mischief that can arise from the enfranchisement of every Mulatto child."[21]

## MULATTOES BY THE NUMBERS AND BECOMING FREE PEOPLE OF COLOR

Certainly, people of blended ancestry were innumerable in Spanish and Portuguese Latin America, which contained hundreds of thousands of *mulatos* and *mestizos/mestiços* and the largest amount of ethnoracial mixture in the continental Americas by the eighteenth century. While colonial head counts are also difficult to come by in the Caribbean, the Spanish islands of Cuba, Puerto Rico, and Santo Domingo and French Saint-Domingue had the largest numbers. Saint-Domingue had a significant tally of free people of color, largely the result of French planters mixing with women of color and freeing their mixed-heritage children. On the eve of the French Revolution and Haitian Revolution, estimates of *gens de couleur* were around 28,000–30,000 (roughly 5 percent of the population). While this figure approached the 40,000 French "whites" on the island, over 450,000 slaves dwarfed both free populations. Again, not all free people of color were of mixed ancestry, but when considering that the majority of those in Saint-Domingue were *mulâtres libres* or *sang-mêlés*, it is clear that the colony had one of the leading free mixed-heritage populations in the Caribbean next to the Spanish islands. Even as free populations of color grew in the British Caribbean over the century, their numbers were much smaller than on the major French and Spanish islands. Still, hypodescent operated across all European colonies, because free people of color could only rise to attain the same socioracial position as "whites" after several generations of intermixture with other Europeans.[22]

By the mid-eighteenth century, demographics show that Virginia, Maryland, and Jamaica had the largest populations of so-called Mulattoes in the British Americas, especially among free people of color. Barbados, South Carolina, and North Carolina followed, with significant numbers of people identified as Mulatto, though archival evidence and census data is lacking to provide reasonable estimates. Despite legislative efforts to prevent intermixture, figures show that there were more Mulattoes in the Chesapeake than in any other British colonial region. In 1755 Maryland tax officials took an extremely accurate colonial census that included "whites," "blacks," and "Mulattoes," both free and enslaved. That year, Maryland counted 3,592 total Mulattoes, including 2,132 slaves and 1,460 free people. This made up 2.3 percent of the overall population and 7.8 percent of the population of color. While these percentages are relatively low, one number stands out: Mulattoes comprised 80.4 percent of all free people of color in Maryland, leaving no doubt that mixed-heritage people made up the vast majority of free people of color. This was also true in Virginia, which had similar demographics to its sister colony in the Chesapeake.[23]

Of all the colonies in British America, Virginia had the largest population and total number of people labeled as Mulatto in the eighteenth century, followed by Jamaica and Maryland. While demographically similar to Maryland, Virginia had more racial intermixture over a longer time span. Around 1755, estimates of Mulattoes in Virginia numbered roughly 6,000 in slavery and 4,000 among free people of color, and it became the first British colony to reach 10,000 Mulattoes. Jamaica had an overwhelming African majority, similar to Saint-Domingue and other Caribbean islands; nine out of ten inhabitants were enslaved. While Jamaica had much more uneven ratios in terms of race than the colonial Chesapeake, patterns of emancipation still favored people of mixed ancestry. Based on census averages, the colony had about 3,000 free people of

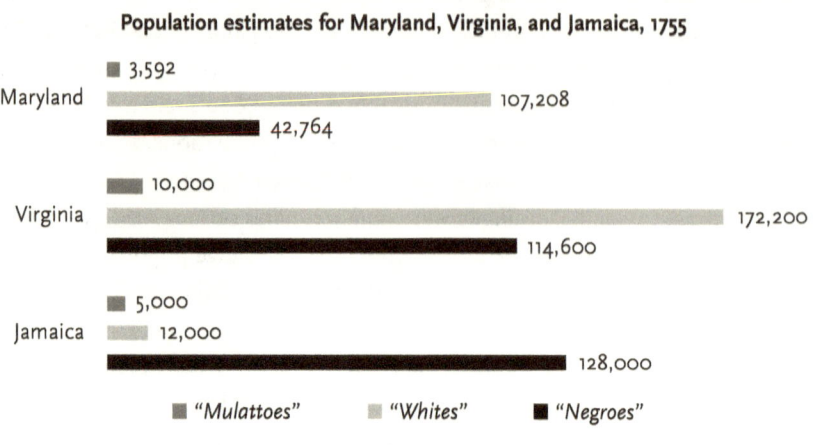

**Population estimates for Maryland, Virginia, and Jamaica, 1755**

Maryland: ■ 3,592; ▬ 107,208; ▬ 42,764

Virginia: ■ 10,000; ▬ 172,200; ▬ 114,600

Jamaica: ■ 5,000; ▬ 12,000; ▬ 128,000

■ "Mulattoes"   ▬ "Whites"   ▬ "Negroes"

*Sources*: "Account of the Number of Souls," 261; Livesay, *Children of Uncertain Fortune*, 24; Newman, *Dark Inheritance*, 17; Heuman, *Between Black and White*, 7; Long, *The History of Jamaica*, 337.

*Note*: Officials in each county tallied individual head counts for Maryland's population in the census of 1755. This census provides the most accurate statistics, while estimates for Virginia's and Jamaica's populations are based on other census materials and corresponding data. Figures do not count all people of mixed heritage but only those whom colonists would have referred to as Mulatto. A 1762–3 Jamaica census counts free people of color at 3,408, which is how I came to the 1755 estimate of 3,000 free people of color, with about 2,000 being free "Mulattoes" and 1,000 free "Negroes" (and 3,000 enslaved "Mulattoes," for 5,000 total). These approximate figures are based on statistical analysis of historical data and comparisons with Mulatto populations in the Chesapeake. Though we may have come to slightly different numbers in places, I am indebted to the work of Daniel Livesay and Brooke Newman.

color in 1755, with at least two-thirds of that population being "Mulatto" while the other third would have been "Negro" or "Indian." Statistical analysis points to around 5,000 Mulattoes total on the Jamaican island, half the number of those in Virginia. These are conservative calculations based on mixed-heritage people making up a small portion of the overall population in the Chesapeake and Caribbean: roughly 3 percent at the time. These estimates confirm that there were thousands of Mulattoes and other mixed people living throughout the British colonies by the middle of the century.[24]

Even though the majority of free people of color were of blended ancestry, most people of mixed heritage remained in slavery. In Maryland, six out of every ten Mulattoes (59.4 percent) were enslaved, while four out of ten (40.6 percent) were free. This 60/40 percent free-to-enslaved ratio appears accurate in Jamaica as well, but the number of enslaved "Mulattoes" was proportionally even smaller, dwarfed by huge "Negro" slave majorities. Mulattoes made up

Population estimates and percentages for Maryland, Virginia, and Jamaica, 1755

| | Total | "Whites" | Slaves | FPC | Free "Negroes" | Enslaved "Negroes" | Total "Negroes" | Free "Mulattoes" | Enslaved "Mulattoes" | Total "Mulattoes" |
|---|---|---|---|---|---|---|---|---|---|---|
| MARYLAND | 153,564 | 107,208 | 44,539 | 1,817 | 357 | 42,407 | 42,764 | 1,460 | 2,132 | 3,592 |
| % population of color | — | — | 96.1% | 3.9% | 0.8% | 91.5% | 92.3% | 3.2% | 4.6% | 7.8% |
| % of total population | 100% | 69.8% | 29.0% | 1.2% | 0.2% | 27.6% | 27.9% | 1.0% | 1.4% | 2.3% |
| VIRGINIA | 296,800 | 172,200 | 119,600 | 5,000 | 1,000 | 113,600 | 114,600 | 4,000 | 6,000 | 10,000 |
| % population of color | — | — | 96.0% | 4.0% | 0.8% | 91.2% | 92.0% | 3.2% | 4.8% | 8.0% |
| % of total population | 100% | 58.0% | 40.3% | 1.7% | 0.3% | 38.3% | 38.6% | 1.4% | 2.0% | 3.4% |
| JAMAICA | 145,000 | 12,000 | 130,000 | 3,000 | 1,000 | 127,000 | 128,000 | 2,000 | 3,000 | 5,000 |
| % population of color | — | — | 97.7% | 2.3% | 0.75% | 95.5% | 96.2% | 1.5% | 2.3% | 3.8% |
| % of total population | 100% | 8.3% | 89.7% | 2.1% | 0.69% | 87.6% | 88.3% | 1.4% | 2.1% | 3.5% |

*Sources:* "Account of the Number of Souls," 261; Berlin, *Slaves without Masters*, 49; Susan B. Carter et al., *Historical Statistics*, 13–14, 33–34, 52–53; Livesay, *Children of Uncertain Fortune*, 24; Newman, *Dark Inheritance*, 17.

*Note:* Maryland population statistics are most accurate for 1755 because each county tallied its individuals. However, Ira Berlin notes that free people of color, when officially numerated, were undercounted because many "doubtless avoided census marshals."

nearly 5 percent of the total enslaved population in Maryland, a fraction that likely holds true for Virginia and correlates with other projections. Mulattoes in the Chesapeake accounted for about one in every twenty slaves and four out of five free people of color. Although overall totals in the Chesapeake and British North America surpassed those in Jamaica, mixed people also tallied significant numbers on the island colonies of Barbados, Bermuda, Antigua, and other Leeward Islands.[25]

While specific quantitative data is sparse for people of mixed ancestry in the British colonies, several factors support statistics that show that Mulattoes made up solid majorities among free people of color. First, since the seventeenth century, children of mixed heritage were customarily and legally free when born to free women. This was responsible for their relatively high numbers in the Chesapeake, where free European women mixed with men of African or Indigenous descent. Virginia and Maryland had closer "black" and "white" racial parity than most other island societies, which produced the conditions for a large Mulatto population, especially in the Tidewater counties. Second, European men regularly fathered children by women of color across the colonies. Slave masters emancipated women and children of mixed ancestry at disproportionately high rates throughout the colonial period in every province—the Caribbean and South Carolina perhaps had the highest rates. Third, blended families that stemmed from those freed through a European matriarch's womb or a patriarch's benevolence continued to reproduce free children through multigenerational mixture, thus adding to the population born in liberty. Finally, British colonial governments restricted slave manumission into the eighteenth century, which made it more difficult for "saltwater" and creole Africans to easily enter the ranks of free society. The legal constriction of emancipation sustained the natural increase among existing free populations of color that were predominantly of mixed African, European, and Indigenous backgrounds. Hence, mixed-heritage populations made up the colonial foundations for free communities of color that appeared in subsequent generations.[26]

Compared to the average African in slavery, people of blended ancestry with ties to European descent had greater possibilities to escape bondage through either European maternal or paternal lineage. A good share of free people of color in the Chesapeake attained freedom through a European foremother, yet colonial law under *partus sequitur ventrem* relegated the majority of mixed people, born to women of color, to a lifetime of bondage through their mother's womb. These offspring were the product of European masters, overseers, laborers, and male visitors to plantations who routinely engaged in sex with enslaved women. There were no laws that punished those who raped female slaves, and masters benefited from the fecundity of their bondswomen, regardless of how they became pregnant. African, Indigenous, and mixed-heritage men also had sexual liaisons and engaged in consensual relationships with enslaved women whom they did not own. These men of color were not always financially able to free these women or their enslaved offspring, nor were many plebian European men who might have wanted to do the same. Most European master-fathers did not legally free their enslaved children, but having a free father from any background improved the chances of manumission for slaves of mixed descent, giving them an advantage over other enslaved African and Indigenous peoples.[27]

European master-fathers occasionally chose to free their children of blended ancestry and sometimes provided monetary gifts and inheritances in provinces with slave majorities: South Carolina, Jamaica, Barbados, and other Atlantic islands. Information is scarce on European fathers who freed their mixed-heritage children, because they rarely acknowledged their paternity in emancipation records. However, documents in South Carolina show that one in every three legal manumissions identified a Mulatto or Mustee recipient, and four out of ten were children. While some free people of color freed family members or slaves they held, European masters appear responsible for the majority of these acts. In 1735, the South Carolina planter Joseph Pendarvis "set at liberty" his "Negro Woman" Parthena and several of her children. Less than a year later, when he wrote his will, Joseph revealed that he "lived with" Parthena. Joseph left Parthena and her seven children his estate, which included a 1,000-acre plantation at Green's Savannah along with horses, cattle, and slaves. James, Brand, William, John, Mary, Thomas, and Elizabeth took Joseph's last name and were purported to be his children by Parthena. Some went on to expand their father's wealth through slaveholding, married Europeans, and had families who were recorded as free "whites."[28]

In the British Caribbean, the practice of fathering and freeing children by slaves was prevalent, even if it occurred less than in the French and Spanish colonies. Wealthy planter Sir William Codrington admitted his paternity in his will and left huge inheritances from the proceeds of his Barbados plantations to William and John, "two *Mulatto* boys ... by a *negro* woman." Sir William also claimed a third son, Thomas, by "another negro" woman and left him an annuity and £500 when the boy turned twenty-one. Some British men held slaves as concubines or kept a small harem of enslaved women for sexual gratification. Whether sex was forced, coerced, consensual, or a combination is not always easy to determine, nor is it apparent if guilt or affection motivated men to leave inheritances to their mixed progeny. Nonetheless, some of these children grew up with great financial dispensations and a fair amount of privilege.[29]

In slave societies, emancipation of mixed-heritage children accounted for a significant portion of all slave manumissions, and although the lack of documentation often obscures family connections, men of diverse class statuses and

| South Carolina slave manumissions by race, age, and sex, 1721–1776 | | | Number | Percentage |
|---|---|---|---|---|
| | Race | "Negro" | 124 | 66.0 |
| | | "Mulatto" | 55 | 29.3 |
| | | "Mustee" | 7 | 3.7 |
| | | "Indian" | 2 | 1.1 |
| Source: Miscellaneous Records, Books H, EE, FF, GG, HH, II, KK, LL, MM, NN, OO, PP, RR, SS, TT, UU, VV, WW, XX, ZZ, and BBB, South Carolina Department of Archives and History, Columbia. | Age | Adults | 137 | 58.1 |
| | | Children | 99 | 41.9 |
| | Sex | Female | 123 | 55.2 |
| | | Male | 100 | 44.8 |

Note: From 1721 through 1776, colonial officials recorded at least 240 legal slave manumissions in Charlestown, South Carolina. Only records that identify race, age, or sex have been counted in this data. While this is not an exhaustive account of people released at local levels, Mulattoes and Mustees make up a significant portion of those freed (approximately one-third). However, these figures also show that there was no wide-scale legal emancipation of mixed-heritage people in the colonial period.

racial backgrounds gave in different ways to their mixed offspring. Fathers from all backgrounds sometimes provided for these enslaved children and occasionally gave them money or material gifts. Even if they were not freed, some children benefited from knowing their fathers in other ways. Parents pushed to have their sons brought up in a vocation learning a trade and had their daughters taught suitable crafts and common domestic skills.[30]

Some men of wealth in the Caribbean sent their mixed offspring to Britain hoping that they would be shielded from colonial racism and that they would find "white" spouses. These fathers promoted formal education and the genteel culture of high British society, which their sons and daughters took up as they left provincial life behind. Jamaican planter Edward Long satirized the wealthy Englishmen who believed their "tawney" mixed-heritage children could "cultivate and improve . . . valuable talents" through a British education. "To accomplish this end," Edward noted that "no expence nor pains are spared; the indulgent father, big with expectation of the future *éclat* [brilliance] of his hopeful progeny," was willing to pay for schooling in Westminster, Eton, or Chelsea. Mixed children who traveled across the Atlantic may have felt ambivalent about their sociracial position, especially if they returned to the Americas. This is why many who had grown up accustomed to refined English culture never returned to the Caribbean and married "white" men and women, sometimes at their father's explicit request. Free families of color who slipped into elite British social circles had typically gone through multiple generations of intermixture and were often held to be "white," though it was difficult to shake the dishonorable connection to slavery through their ancestors.[31]

People of blended ancestry who remained in Europe and married into the upper echelons of British society were the exceptions, as most were not affluent and labored along with the African masses in slavery. This association with bondage is why Englishmen complained about African-descended people who remained in London and the "mother country." Edward Long and others decried the "mulatto progeny" born to British women and African men in the metropole. In 1772, Edward worried that "in the course of a few generations more, the English blood will become so contaminated with this mixture." Edward also reflected anxieties about class as well as race. He was less concerned with mixture among the lowest tiers of society but feared the Mulatto "alloy may spread so extensively, as even to reach the middle, and then the higher orders of the people, till the whole nation resembles the *Portuguese* and *Moriscos* in complexion of skin and baseness of mind." This Anglo-supremacist thinking conveyed a form of racial hypodescent that incorporated nascent ideas of degeneracy and biological racism.[32]

Other elite Englishmen reiterated hypodescent ideologies, including those who lived in colonies where mixture was usually more accepted. South Carolinian Henry Laurens lamented the growing number of "Mulatties in London" while visiting there. Another Caribbean politician and planter, Samuel Estwick, sought to curb African importation into Barbados, as to "preserve the race of Britons from stain and contamination." Although most free people of color had European lineage, these notions connected blood purity to subjecthood and determined that the taint of "mixed blood" disqualified free Mulattoes from the full protection of rights under British authority. Even though their population was relatively small by the mid-eighteenth century, free people of color were highly visible in the British Empire. While a connection to European kinship allowed some Mulattoes mobility across the Atlantic world, British fears of the taint of African and Indigenous heritage led to restrictions that kept mixed people's freedoms thin.[33]

## SITUATIONAL ADVANTAGES: FREEING MULATTO SERVANTS AND PUNISHING MULATTO SLAVES

Whether a person of mixed descent was advantaged or disadvantaged by his or her ancestry was largely situational and based on a number of factors, with parentage being paramount. Free maternity granted legal access to liberty in all British provinces, but by the 1720s officials primarily in Virginia, Maryland, and North Carolina routinely circumvented this freedom by forcing mixed-heritage children born to free mothers into thirty-one years of servitude. Planters considered these thirty-one-year indentures fair and legally binding, whether or not they obtained contracts. When masters customarily bound free mixed children without approval by provincial courts or other officials, and held these people beyond what the laws allowed, this indenture system transformed into de facto slavery. Colonists in these provinces falsely indentured and enslaved thousands of mixed people in this manner during the eighteenth century.[34]

The life experience of numerous free mixed-heritage youth in Virginia, Maryland, and North Carolina reflected a system of slavery more than servitude, another signifier of the strong hypodescent legislation that permeated these areas. In 1738, North Carolina authorities ordered Abraham Blackall and Henry Baker to return a "mullatter boy" who the two men "pretended to be bound" in servitude. Abraham and Henry were the former parish churchwardens at St. Paul's Parish, which was not coincidental. Churchwardens were supposed to serve the community but often acted in favor of their own financial interests when establishing unlawful indentures for illegitimate children. In this case, the sitting churchwardens called on Abraham and Henry to either return the "mullatter boy" or pay forty pounds sterling to the parish. The impending fine might motivate the men to return the boy safely, but simply paying the fine would not relieve the anguish caused to the boy's family and friends, especially if he were sold far away and could never return home.[35]

At any time, profiteers might rip free people of color away from their families and sell them into extended bondage, and children were often the most vulnerable targets. Typically, young people could be physically subdued into captivity more easily than adults. Children were also more likely to be unaware of laws that could protect them and might not know where to turn for help if they were kidnapped. These were significant drawbacks for free children of color.[36]

People of mixed heritage and their families complained about the practice of enslaving free children of color and fought to hold offenders accountable for illegally assigning those of African, Native American, and mixed descent to extended labor contracts. In 1733, the members of North Carolina's House Committee of Propositions and Grievances reported that they "had several complaints laid before them" about various "free People, Negroes & Molattoes" who were indentured "contrary to the consent of the Parties bound out." These unlawful actions were "well known" and systematic, and county officials were among those implicated. The committee indicted eight justices of the peace from the "Bertie Precinct" and other parts of North Carolina. The report recommended that the accused stand before the general assembly for "the practice of binding out Free Negroes and Molattoes" and moved to take action "so that speedy Justice may be done and that the Parties injured may have relief." While provincial authorities recognized these widespread abuses, it was difficult to put a stop to "such an illegal practice" when local officials were orchestrating the contracts or colonists simply operated without formal indentures.[37]

Colonial magistrates intended for masters to provide servants with food, clothing, and valuable labor skills under apprenticeships, but for freeborn Mulattoes this was another area that frequently put them at a disadvantage. The basic structure of apprentice indentures was similar for Europeans, but guardians regularly signed on to fewer responsibilities for mixed-heritage children and held them to longer terms. In 1736, North Carolina authorities bound out the Mulatto girl Delaney Bright, who became an orphan at two years old after her mother died. Delaney's contract stated that her master had to provide "Meat Drink Lodging and Apperelle fitting for Mallattoe's." This language implied that her master was not obligated to provide for the young girl in the same manner as for European children. Under indentures for people of mixed descent, authorities also sometimes replaced the term "apprentice" with "servant" in the language of the contract, which released the master from the obligation to teach literacy or a trade, a common responsibility that came with indentures for European adolescents. Agreements for "Negro," "Indian," and "Mulatto," children were less reciprocal and more beneficial for the master, who also might sell the child for longer periods of time or indefinitely. In this manner, countless free children of blended ancestry fell into slavery.[38]

The practice of selling free people of mixed heritage as servants or slaves became so pervasive in some colonies that legislatures eventually addressed the complaints of mixed people and their families. After decades of doing little to stop the illegal sale of these children, some colonial magistrates took steps to inhibit the practice by allowing Mulattoes the right to sue their masters in court and adjusted the length of the thirty-one-year indenture terms. In 1760 Delaware magistrates granted people of mixed ancestry who were "entitled to their freedom" the right to bring cases of unlawful enslavement to court. Two years later, North Carolina's assembly reduced the thirty-one-year sentences given to Mulatto and Mustee children to twenty-one years, which fell in line with those for European children. The justices also aimed to reform unfair indenture obligations by mandating that masters provide such mixed children with "Diet, Clothes, Lodging, [and] Accommodations fit and necessary; and shall teach or cause him or her to be taught, to read and Write." These were legislative wins for blended families, but these measures were not totally equalizing. European girls were released from indenture after eighteen years, while "every such Female Child being a Mulatto or Mustee" would serve until twenty-one. Many colonists also continued to mistreat mixed-heritage children in servitude and still held them for longer periods of time than the laws permitted. Nevertheless, these legislative moves marked a significant shift in efforts to combat those who attempted to hold free Mulattoes in lifelong bondage.[39]

Evidence suggests that strict racial hypodescent began to ease after the Seven Years' War in the Chesapeake as well. After repeated complaints from mixed people and their family members, Virginia followed North Carolina and rejected its nearly seventy-five-year policy of extending thirty-plus-year indentures to Mulattoes. As in other colonies, the Virginia General Assembly recognized that "ill disposed persons have ... been guilty of selling and disposing of mulattoes and others as slaves, who by the laws of this colony are subject to a service only of thirty one years." For decades, officials received complaints that cited numerous abuses against people of mixed descent, but they did little to stop the custom. Virginia's legislators finally took decisive action in 1765 with "An Act to prevent the practice of selling persons as slaves that are not so." If anyone sold "any such mulatto, or other servant" past thirty-one years, that person would face a penalty of fifty pounds sterling, and if the offender could not pay, then he or she would have to serve out the rest of the servant's indenture term. Perhaps most important, the assembly also declared that any mixed-heritage "bastard child by a negro or mulatto" would serve a normal indenture period of eighteen years for girls and twenty-one years for boys.[40]

Colonial authorities knew that decreasing the thirty-one-year-term indentures would impede the systematic practice of enslaving free Mulattoes. Three decades provided too much time for corrupt masters to change the terms of an indenture agreement and sell someone into other provinces. Plus, with no legal requirement to record these contracts, it was all but impossible to keep masters from enslaving these children. After thirty years, there were fewer people who could serve as a witness and give adequate proof of an original indenture. Parents often moved or passed away and were not always able to advocate for freeing their bound children. Magistrates recognized it would be useful to shorten the terms of service for mixed children to help ensure they served the same terms as European colonists. The Virginia justices also cited the "unreasonable severity" of the thirty-one-year terms of service and overturned several laws that had been passed and renewed in 1691, 1705, 1723, and 1753. The reformative 1765 law had a liberalizing effect for free mixed-heritage people, placing many on equal legal footing with their European counterparts. This was a huge victory for free families of color, and in the following years they pushed further to attack unfair colonial policies.[41]

Free "Mulattoes" and "Negroes" experienced victories in the fight for legal protections at the same time that Virginia's highest government officials were debating colonists' rights under British monarchy. Future patriot Richard Henry Lee arranged the equalizing Mulatto indenture law, which authorities debated and approved around the same time that they put forward the Virginia Resolves denouncing the Stamp Act. Free people of color strategically attached other petitions for equality to the revolutionary rhetoric of the Founding Fathers in the years leading up to the U.S. Revolution. "A *Petition* of the People called Mulattoes and free Negroes" repeatedly came before Virginia's House of Burgesses in 1769 arguing that—since European women were not tithable—the extra taxes placed on their "Wives and Daughters" over age sixteen placed undue economic stress on their families. Since the seventeenth century free people of color had protested and refused to pay these burdensome taxes, but after this petition the general assembly agreed that taxing "free negro, mulatto, and Indian women" the same as men was "derogatory of the rights of free-born subjects." At the time, Virginia's assemblymen were concurrently combating British Parliament's Townshend Acts, so repealing discriminatory taxes on these families of color was surely not lost on them. The historical milieu allowed free people of color an opportunity to tap into the atmosphere of colonial resistance against oppressive monarchy. Furthermore, gains made by free people of color to reduce taxes and protect their families against slavery helped loosen racial hypodescent.[42]

Even though Virginia and North Carolina legislators ended the discriminatory thirty-one-year indentures, the law did not operate ex post facto and dissolve the contracts of Mulattoes currently bound out as servants. When Virginia's ruling passed in 1765, Samuel "Sam" Howell was a "young Mulatto man" around twenty-three years old. Sam may have been fighting for his freedom since the age of twenty-one and had already lost a lawsuit against his master in the Cumberland County court, where he "was adjudged to serve his full time." Chances are that Sam heard talk about the revised indenture law for Mulattoes, which inspired him to leave his master "to apply to some lawyer at *Williamsburg* to try to get his freedom." A decision by the provincial court in Virginia's capital would overrule the judgment made at the county level. Sam was invested in understanding the legalities regarding his bound condition and spoke with multiple lawyers about his case. After traveling to Williamsburg, he was able to discuss his case with the attorney general, who told Sam that "he could not get free until his time was out."[43]

Sam's case would determine not only his fate but also that of his younger brother Simon Howell, who was similarly bound. By the spring of 1766, Sam had left his master and was absconded for over six months. Despite being told he would have to serve at least seven more years, he secured legal counsel and took his case to the General Court. Unfortunately for the Howell brothers, the court justices ruled against Sam's independent status. After exhausting all formal paths to freedom, Sam and Simon Howell decided they would not wait to fulfill their service and ran away from their master to "pass for free."[44]

Sam Howell had always considered himself "a free man," and mixed-heritage people took their liberty when they could not legally secure it. For example, Nanny, described as a "tall mulatto wench," ran away at least twice in the years after Virginia reformed its indenture laws for Mulattoes. Like the Howell brothers, Nanny first attempted to go through the courts. In 1768 she "obtained a pass from one of the justices" of Albemarle County, which she used "to seek out witnesses to support her claim" of independence. Maybe she ran into trouble locating witnesses who could name her free maternal ancestors, or perhaps Nanny did not have any and it was always her plan to use the pass as a ruse to aid her escape. Regardless, when Nanny realized she would not be able to obtain legal freedom, she ran away from her master "to pass for a free woman." While the law no longer applied notions of hypodescent to certain newborn "mulatto bastards," the status of older mixed people already in bonds remained the same.[45]

Many mixed people struggled to make a case for freedom in court, and when their legal options were exhausted, they had to escape or submit to bondage. Around the age of twenty-one, the "Mulatto Man Slave" Aaron Griffin, took his master, Henry Randolph, to the Virginia court "for his Freedom." The court decided the case in October 1770, and even though the justices recognized that "many of his Colour got their Freedom" by law, they ruled that Aaron would not be one of them. Aaron decided that escape was his only way out, so he plotted and left his owner in June. This attempt was not his first, for his master had previously punished Aaron with brands on each cheek, marking him as a runaway. Six months after this escape, Aaron had not returned and thus became an outlawed slave who could be punished with death. His master's son, John Randolph, offered five pounds currency for the slave and doubled the price for anyone who took the life of the obstinate Mulatto. "Whoever brings me his Head shall have TEN POUNDS Reward," John wrote. Though this may sound severe by today's standards, slave owners often used brutal beatings, body mutilation such as branding, or decapitation as a deterrent to other slaves, who might then think twice about attempting an escape.[46]

While colonial laws made freedom accessible to Mulatto servants of free birth, harsh punishments inflicted on slaves show that masters did not treat runaways of mixed ancestry any differently than slaves of full African lineage. For example, slave owners commonly branded their slaves to outwardly label known runaways. The practice took place with servants as well, but unlike Europeans, who might be punished in this manner for running away, masters customarily branded African, Indigenous, and mixed-heritage people to identify them as property. In 1737 South Carolina, Francis Goddard described his escaped slave Sarah as a "Mustee Wench," noting marks on her body. Francis was responsible for the hot iron that marked his initials, "FG," into the flesh of Sarah's right shoulder and right cheek. Slave masters routinely treated "Mulattoes" and "Mustees" just as harshly as "Negroes," showing little Mulatto advantage over those of full African descent.[47]

While European masters used branding to mark or discipline their slaves, the most widespread form of punishment was the whip. Masters readily utilized this form of behavior "correction" on slaves and servants they considered disobedient. Slave owners did not always carry out the whippings themselves but recruited overseers, other slaves, or law enforcement officers to lacerate the bodies of enslaved men, women, and children. One Charlestown master ordered that whoever captured Ruth, a runaway "Mustee young Wench," should deliver "50 good Lashes" upon the woman before returning the fugitive. The punishment did not break Ruth's spirit, however, or prevent her from running away again some years later. In Caroline County, Virginia, another master threatened a "small Mulatto Man" named Peter with the whip. Peter was "well known by the Gentlemen in the Country" as a horse keeper, and he always walked around with a large wad "of tobacco in his Mouth." After Peter ran away with an older "tawney Negro man" named Will, their master requested that any constable who captured the runaways "give them 20 Lashes" each, the same penalty as for others of African or Indigenous ancestry.[48]

There were undoubtedly instances where mixed-heritage slaves experienced beatings and other punishments in connection to their master-fathers or on account of their European lineage. The wives of slave owners had little power to stop their husbands from siring children in the slave quarters and met these mixed offspring and their mothers with scorn and vitriol. These men also sometimes sold their mixed progeny to placate their wives, hide their shame, and skirt paternal responsibilities, which also separated these children from family members. These hardships fortified the resiliency of Mulattoes, whom masters often described as stubborn. Like other people of color, those of mixed ancestry regularly broke the unspoken rules of socioracial deference. Simon Harman, "a mulatto man slave... about 28 years old," stood an inch or two over five and a half feet, and his nose was "very thin and high." His appearance may have resembled that of a "white" father who had sold him away, and it afforded him the opportunity "to pass as a free man." Simon also had "many scars on his back, occasioned by whipping."[49]

After Simon ran away from his owner in western Virginia, he may have attempted to reunite with family and friends in Accomack County on the Eastern Shore. It appears he never made it that far, as authorities seized Simon and brought him to the jail in Norfolk. Simon remained relentless even after capture. He refused to give his name to the jailor and maintained that he was a freeman. Officers said that even though he perfectly matched the runaway description in the newspaper, Simon would "not confess that he belongs to any one." Perhaps this was true in Simon's mind, yet after his identity was discovered, this recalcitrance likely earned him another fresh set of stripes upon his back.[50]

Even though slaves went through physical and psychological trauma for exercising their autonomy, they found ways to enjoy life, and even small freedoms might sustain their spirit. Telling stories, sharing jokes, smoking or chewing tobacco, playing games, eating, drinking, gambling, dancing, singing, or playing music together were all everyday undertakings. A man named Tom shared in these activities with others while living in Prince George County, Virginia. He was another mixed-heritage slave who was severely reprimanded for repeated escape attempts. Tom's master said the slave had "bushy Hair" and a tendency "to grin when he speaks, or is spoken to." Tom maintained a positive spirit despite severe circumstances. However, one wonders if he was able to smile after his master had him "shackled, Handcuffed, and [had] an Iron Collar [put] about his Neck, with Prongs, and [added] to some of them Links." Self-confident and unrelenting, the crafty "Mulattoe Man slave" figured out a way to remove the torturous device so he could escape again. Another "Mulatto Man" in Virginia named John escaped from a similar iron device with the help of a friend. John's master assumed that some "evil-disposed person" had removed the "iron Collar about his Neck" to help the slave run off. Masters had these metal contraptions with noisy chain links placed on slaves as a form of punishment and control. John's owner was convinced that the slave "could not have travelled" far while wearing such a device because he would easily be captured traveling out in the open, and it was difficult to maneuver when moving through thick trees and the tangled brush of dense forests. Iron shackles, chains, and collars were just some of the tools that colonial slave owners used to regulate slave behavior, regardless of skin color.[51]

Masters used metal shackles, leather whips, and branding irons on slaves from various backgrounds, and bodily dismemberment was another tool they applied to defiant slaves. In 1774, James Fairle of Warwick County, Virginia, issued this form of punishment, which the English had used for centuries, for his slave Abner. James explained that his "Mulatto Fellow" was "quarrelsome when in Liquor, to which he [Abner] is much addicted." It was either Abner's drunken backtalk or his penchant for absconding for short periods of time that impelled his master to have "both of his ears cropped." Maybe Abner felt his European lineage entitled him to speak freely, which came easier while intoxicated, yet he was punished nonetheless.[52]

Other masters became so enraged with slaves that they simply offered rewards for having their bondsmen and bondswomen executed. Moses, a "mulatto fellow," ran away from his owner near Jamestown so that he could be with his wife, who had also run away from her master. After more than a year on the run, authorities declared Moses an outlaw and offered a twenty-pound reward to anyone who would "produce the head of the said fellow, severed from his body." In February 1757, Mary Ellis offered a similar reward in Charlestown, South Carolina, for the return of a thirty-year-old Mustee woman named Catherina. "Whoever takes the said wench dead or alive, and delivers her to me, shall have a reward of 10 pounds," read the advertisement. Having mixed ancestry benefited some but could not save others from punishments that few Europeans would receive under English law.[53]

Sometime later, Catherina decided to return to her master or was captured alive, though her defiance continued to frustrate her owner, Mary Ellis. On Friday, October 13, the year after her escape, Catherina ran away yet again. This time Mary offered forty shillings for Catherina's return and fifty pounds "for her Head." Fifty pounds was a substantial sum, and the amount implies that Mary took Catherina's repeated disappearances personally. Captivity, freedom, and autonomy were also deeply personal issues for runaways. Catherina had little concern for her master's loss and was willing to risk losing her head, or other severe punishment, for the chance to experience liberty.[54]

### PASSING FOR "FREE MULATTOES"

Despite confronting harsh treatment under British colonial slavery, Mulattoes often maintained advantages over other Africans and Native Americans when running away to effectively become their own masters. People of mixed heritage had a higher chance of gaining better prospects than the average African slave had of gaining legal freedom, and "free Mulattoes" typically had job skills that allowed them to enjoy greater wealth, health, and an array of other benefits over "free Negroes." Oftentimes, free people of mixed descent enjoyed more autonomous lives than darker-skinned people of color. This kind of light-skinned racial privilege was born in the colonial period, yet it was always situational and based on an individual's particular set of social circumstances. For instance, when running away, mixed-heritage slaves might pass as free and some also racially passed for "white." If they could acquire suitable clothing and maintain confidence in their cultural performance as a free person of color, they could occupy a racial middle ground in between "black" and "white," where colonists assumed they were free people.[55]

Mixed-heritage people's physical appearance combined with diverse cultural and professional skills allowed them to move more easily out of bondage into the ranks of free society. Runaway slaves with a marketable trade might succeed in their attempts to escape from their masters, gain employment, and start new lives in other counties or colonies. Servants and slaves completed all types of work on colonial plantations and within their masters' households, from agricultural to domestic and artisan labor. People of African, Native American, and mixed descent cared for their masters' children, tended to their owners' family members when sick, and performed all sorts of housework. They sewed, mended, and washed clothes and linens. They piloted boats over water and drove animals that pulled carriages and wagons over roads and plows through fields. In addition to crop agriculture, they fed and cared for livestock, butchered animals and hunted game, and prepared and cooked meals. Carpenters chopped wood, constructed buildings, fences, and furniture, and produced anything and everything used in the colonial world. Varying levels of competence were required for all jobs, but masters valued adeptness in artisan trades over the tasks performed by field laborers.[56]

While jobs where not fixed by ancestry, "Mulattoes" and "Negroes" born in the Americas were often trained as artisans, while most newly imported Africans worked as field hands. Slaves from West Africa came to the Americas with knowledge in agricultural practices, which included proficiency in animal husbandry and an array of techniques in crop production. African, Native American, and mixed-heritage laborers passed down methods used to sow, weed, and harvest plants that increased crop yields. And masters sought slaves with this knowledge. For example, Lowcountry planters coveted slaves familiar with rice planting, irrigation, cultivation, and processing. Those who had special expertise were considered the most valuable on plantations. Carpenters, blacksmiths, coopers, millwrights, ship builders, pilots, mechanics, and other artisans fetched the highest prices. Masters allowed some enslaved artisans to exercise semiautonomy by hiring themselves out. These slaves had to report back to their owners and hand over wages they collected, though sometimes they retained a portion of their earnings. Over time, some were able to save up enough money to buy freedom for themselves or family members. When these slaves could not secure liberty, some chose to run away from their masters and craftsmen sought employment in their professions. These trades helped many people of mixed ancestry attain not only physical independence but also financial stability for their families and descendants.[57]

Many people of blended ancestry survived as free by using skills they had learned while in bondage to attain economic security through their work. In Charlestown, South Carolina, one master described three of his runaways: a "Mulatto" named Betty and two "Negro" women named Flora and Lady. The 1761 advertisement only mentioned that Betty had a marketable talent, noting that the Mulatto with "short *Indian* hair is well known in *Charles-Town*, where perhaps she may hire herself out at needle-work." While Flora and Lady may have been knowledgeable in household or field labor, Betty was "an exceeding[ly] good seamstress," which her master knew would help her make a living as a free woman. Skilled Mulattoes regularly appeared in runaway newspaper ads next to other creole Africans who were born or grew up in the Americas. These craft trades were typical of advantages experienced by many Mulattoes.[58]

Hierarchy existed among slaves, and one of the reasons Mulattoes and other "country born" African slaves were near the top of that social order was because they were creoles. Creoles could be of any background, spoke English or other European languages, and had grown accustomed to colonial life or adapted to European culture in the Americas. Eighteenth-century growth in the North American slave population resulted largely from more balanced sex ratios and in the second half of the century, "country born" slaves of African or mixed ancestry outnumbered "saltwater" slaves in the Chesapeake. These creole slaves had advantages over newly arrived African-born "saltwater" slaves, including when running away. All types of slaves fled their masters, but creoles had more cultural capital to work with during escape because they could operate independently in colonial European societies. Many Mulattoes had even greater advantages.[59]

A combination of cultural knowledge, work skills, and physical traits made movement far easier for slaves of mixed heritage who decided to run away. Peter Deadfoot of Stafford County, Virginia, is a great example of how a slave of mixed descent could acquire several skilled trades. The "Mulatto slave" was a butcher, carter, plowman, sawyer, and waterman (pilot). According to his master, he could also break oxen, had some understanding of shoemaking, and was "one of the best scythemen, either with or without a cradle, in *America*"— meaning that while wielding a scythe he could cut down wheat and other grains or tall grasses with great speed and agility. Indeed, his owner said that Peter was "so ingenious a fellow that he can turn his hand to any thing." The highly talented bondsman would have had little problem passing for a freeman, "as such a fellow would readily get employment." Peter also knew his worth and showed "a great share of pride," though he also remained humble and was "very obliging." Labor expertise granted this "Mulatto slave" tangible advantages over most other bondsmen.[60]

Marketable trades allowed men such as Peter Deadfoot to successfully run away and remain free, especially when their professions remained useful to European colonists. Slaves with such abilities were sometimes able to save up money for legal manumission, but owners were also reluctant to let go of profitable workers. Peter was either unwilling or unable to engage in self-purchase, so in April 1768 he escaped while hired out as a sawyer and was still unaccounted for six months later. People of color, slave and free, "Negroes" and "Mulattoes," used their intellect, confidence, and other means to pursue lives in which they could survive independently.[61]

Since such a large percentage of the free population of color in the British colonies was of mixed ancestry, those who lived in bondage found that they might blend in with other free Mulattoes. On January 7, 1764, a "mulattoe fellow" named John ran away in rural South Carolina. His master directly stated that John would try "to pass himself for a free mulattoe." John was a repeat escapee and went to great lengths to secure his freedom. He perhaps carefully chose a Saturday night to flee because slaves typically had Sundays off from work. If John were not found missing right away, he would have a head start after he left the plantation and ventured across "Indian-Land" just north of the Savannah River. The bondsman had likely traveled across long distances before. Many knew him as "Virginia John," and it is plausible that he originated from the colony. He also had an "R" branded into his forehead, indicating that a previous master had sold him as a runaway. John may have defaced the brand or covered the scar with "an old gold laced hat." John's master said that his slave also created pseudonyms and changed names "as it suits him" and went by John Dennis or John Poppeay. Whatever tactics he used, John was determined to live as a freeman and knew that meant creatively passing himself off as a "free mulattoe."[62]

Slaves tried to pass as Mulattoes who were born free, even if their masters did not racially identify them as such. Ben and Jack were described as "two Negroe men" with a "yellow" or "yellowish complexion" who obtained false papers "by which they pass for free mulattoes." They left New Jersey in June 1769 and made their way to Philadelphia, where their masters believed the two would attempt to get on board a ship and secure their getaway by sea. While they may have had European or Native American ancestry further back in their lineage, their masters did not label them as *true* Mulattoes. In the same month, another "Negroe man," Moses Grimes, "passed for a Mulattoe" when he ran away from his master in Pennsylvania. His owner described Moses as "very yellow" and implied that he took the identity of a Mulatto so that he could more easily "pass for a free man."[63]

People with Indigenous lineage also decided to flee their masters after they found out that Native American heritage would not legally free them. This was the case for Jim, or James, Cheshire, a man of mixed African and Indigenous ancestry who lived in Cumberland County, Virginia. In October of 1772, Jim went "to the General Court to seek for his Freedom" and argued that he had "a Right to his Freedom" because "His Father was an *Indian*." Apparently, however, he was not aware how legal bondage passed down through the family line. Even though Jim took his father's surname and had "long black Hair resembling an *Indian's*," this did not convince the General Court to change existing legislation. Jim inherited bondage through the maternal line, as his mother was an African slave. After finding out that he was enslaved despite his "Indian" ancestry, the twenty-seven-year-old man ran away from his master.[64]

Enslaved people of Native American heritage often used their intelligence, cultural tools, and physical appearance to take on a free "Indian" identity when escaping from slavery. Jack Brown was a "half Indian fellow" who was "pretty light" and had run away from more than one master in Virginia. Authorities said Jack spoke "plain and bold" and would "endeavour to pass for a free man." They knew that he had passed himself off as free before, since he once lived independently for three years "under that character." After capture, he vexed authorities with subsequent attempts to abscond. Slaves of Native American ancestry had advantages over other African slaves because they could rely on Indigenous knowledge, free relatives, or communities who might conceal, protect, and guide them to safety. In addition to his Indigenous and probable European heritage, "light" skin and confidence allowed Jack to craft a free persona while on the run.[65]

Masters often knew a slave's parents or other kinfolk when they described them as "yellow" or light-skinned "Negroes" who attempted to "pass for free mulattoes" or "Indians." While some colonists forgot, figuratively erased, or created the lineage of slaves based on their own racial perceptions, most owners attempted to communicate descriptions as accurately as possible to increase their chances of returning runaways. Lineage, race, and bound or free status were connected in the wider European colonial mind. This is why eighteenth-century colonists most often associated slaves with "Negro" ancestry and why they connected free people of color with the mixed heritage of "Mulattoes." In these terms, the application of hypodescent was always much stricter in slavery than it was in freedom.[66]

### PERFORMING FREEDOM AND RACIAL PASSING

On the eve of the U.S. Revolution, regular ethnoracial mixture had been occurring for over 150 years in English colonial America. The racially ambiguous bodies of free and enslaved people of color displayed the extent of multigenerational mixture. People of blended ancestry produced a fissure in societies where status was often racially coded, especially within labor systems. Many servants and slaves of mixed heritage adeptly accessed a racial gap between monoracial categories when running away. Colonial authorities combated this by designing institutions that would keep people in bondage and recapture escapees. Planters used patrols to police the roads, and sheriffs jailed runaways, administered punishment, and returned escaped "Negroes," "Indians," and "Mulattoes" to their owners. Masters also used print media to describe runaways' bodies, clothing, skills, personalities, and the lengths they would go to reach freedom. Colonists often called the skin color of mixed people "bright," "light," "yellowish," or having a "yellow complexion," which often resulted from European mixture with African or Indigenous peoples. Those who appeared racially "white" had the best chance of passing as free, but racial passing was only one of many tactics that helped mixed-heritage people perform freedom.[67]

When Mulatto slaves approached whiteness in their physical appearance, masters could modify a runaway's body to mark his or her race and tie the runaway back to bondage. Edward Rutland of Northampton County, Virginia, wrote that his slave Annas was "a very white Mulatto wench" with "straight hair." Annas was nineteen years old when she made an unsuccessful attempt to leave her master in 1767. She remained defiant after capture and ran away from Edward again two years later. This time her master described her as a "mustee slave woman"—revealing that she may have been of European and Native American ancestry. Her light skin allowed Annas to move through colonial society as a free Mulatto or Mustee or possibly even as a "white" woman. This is why Edward had an "E" branded on her right cheek and an "R" burned on the left. Her master's initials emblazoned upon her flesh were meant to mark her as an unfree woman, but Edward noted that the enslaved Annas's skin was so light that the brand "cannot be discerned except [when] near to her." For slaves branded on the face, having light or "very white" skin might aid their runaway attempt in multiple ways.[68]

Performing freedom was more difficult for slaves who bore the signs of their owners on their bodies, which is exactly why masters marked them in this manner. Samuel Sherwin used a hot iron to place the letters "S on one cheek, and R on the other" of his "mulatto fellow" Peter in Amelia County, Virginia. Men and women went to enormous lengths to remove such marks. Peter attempted "to take them out, or deface them" by either cutting or further burning himself. Just five days after Peter's master branded him for running away, the unrelenting slave fled again. Like many resistant runaways, he attempted to change clothes and obtain work aboard a ship, as he had done in the past. These stories illustrate how slave and master both competed to outsmart one another by pulling off the more cunning maneuver.[69]

The most successful runaways had to be able to perform as free men or women in order to avoid the appearance of being a slave, which required the intellectual acuity to tell convincing stories. Escapees were often said to have had a "smooth tongue" for storytelling, which is how they interacted with other colonists without raising suspicions of their enslaved past. This is how many remained free for long periods of time and avoided capture when interacting with other colonists. In 1762, the "Mulatto Woman" Violet was around twenty-five years old when she ran away from her master in New Jersey. She spent several years on the run and evaded capture on multiple occasions. Violet was so "Cunning and Artful" that after she was recaptured in 1764, she escaped again from a jail in Frederick Town, Maryland. After this getaway, she disappeared, though after several years it was discovered that she settled down in Frederick County as a free woman. Her motivations for remaining free were clear: she had three children and possibly a long-term relationship with the father. "Any person who may take her up must secure her strictly," her owner warned in 1771, "or she will certainly escape again." Violet was "remarkably" clever enough to avoid captivity for nearly a decade or more.[70]

Slaves of all backgrounds used deception to achieve small freedoms or independence, yet mixed-heritage peoples had the largest array of tools to aid their escape. Billy, or Will, a "light coloured Mulatto Man," displayed a wide skill set when he ran away in Prince George County, Virginia. His master described Will as a good-looking twenty-year-old who had a knack for "gaining the good Graces of almost every Body who will listen to his bewitching and deceitful Tongue, which seldom or ever speaks the Truth." As a means of survival, slaves regularly bent or twisted the truth to deceive their masters, overseers, colonial officials, and everyday colonists. Despite the harsh words concerning Will's character, his master made no complaint about the bondsman's usefulness: "From his Ingenuity, he is capable of doing almost any Sort of Business." Will could easily gain employment as a freeman, since he had years of experience as a miller, stonemason, and iron founder. Indeed, Will was likely employed casting iron when he ran away from the Neabsco Furnace on March 16, 1774. His expertise and intellectual capacity allowed him to remain free for at least six months, but Will also had something that most other Africans did not have: "light coloured" skin.[71]

By the mid-eighteenth century, many slaves and servants of mixed European and African or Native American lineage had relatively light skin tones, and masters described abilities as well as skin color when explaining what made it easy for people to pass as free persons. In Virginia, Ben was a twenty-five-year-old "Mulatto Servant Man of a middle Stature," who had "a remarkable thick Beard" and stuttered when he spoke. In the spring of 1771, Ben's master figured that the bondsman would leave the colony and end up "passing for a free Person, which he may easily do from his Colour and Artfulness." As a person of blended ancestry, Ben could use his light skin while skillfully performing freedom to enhance his prospects of a successful escape. However, his stutter and other factors hurt his chances.[72]

While many people of blended ancestry did domestic and artisan work, most were involved in agricultural field labor; lighter skin did not remove mixed-heritage people from the physically demanding jobs required by masters on plantations. Ben ran away with clothes "commonly given to Field Negroes," indicating that he was a field hand, the occupation held by most Mulatto and Mustee slaves and servants. Ben probably tried to quickly get rid of clothing that associated him with bondage, and changed his dress—one of the first things that most servants and slaves sought to do either before or immediately after running away. By the 1770s, many field hands in the Chesapeake were familiar with cultivating wheat, corn, and crops other than tobacco. Around this time, tobacco planters were moving away from the former agricultural staple in response to falling prices, stagnating production, and rising debt on many Chesapeake plantations. With intimate knowledge of how to grow a variety of

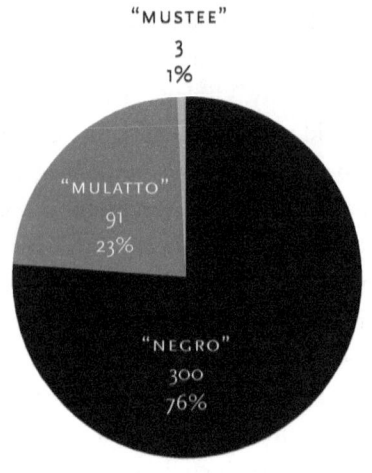

Racial descriptions of runaways of color in the *Maryland Gazette* and *Maryland Journal and Baltimore Advertiser*, 1745–1775

Source: Windley, *Runaway Slave Advertisements*, 2:1–114, 191–93.

Note: Two "Mulatto" slaves who are described as appearing "Indian" are placed in the "Mustee" category.

crops, servants like Ben envisioned that they might one day cultivate and harvest their own fields.[73]

Ben's master was certain that the servant's "Colour and Artfulness" helped him in "passing for a free person," a benefit that coincided with what Chesapeake numbers show: mixed-heritage people with European ancestry and lighter skin were more likely to run away than Africans with darker skin tones. While there were far more runaway advertisements describing "Negroes" with dark complexions, figures show that almost one in four runaways in Maryland from 1745 to 1775 were described as Mulatto, even though they made up a much lower percentage of the overall slave population (around 5 percent). Disproportionately high rates of mixed-heritage runaways are likewise seen in Virginia.[74]

Those in bondage in the Chesapeake and elsewhere in colonial America knew that Mulattoes had an easier path to independence because light-skinned privilege might grant them the presumption of freedom. After the "Negro Woman" Sarah escaped in Virginia, her owner called her "very artful" and added, "Though not a Mulatto, [she] may attempt to pass for a free Woman." Colonists frequently associated free people of color with being "Mulatto" and conversely associated "Negroes" with slavery. Dark skin did not stop African slaves from running away in large numbers. However, those of mixed descent knew their lighter skin gave them an edge to successfully flee bondage, because colonists were less likely to question the movement of people they assumed had liberty. Masters thought their slaves were pulling off a ruse by passing as free, but many mixed slaves of European ancestry believed that freedom was their birthright.[75]

Aside from skin color, geographical location and job placement on a rural plantation or within an urban household also influenced mixed people's lives in bondage and their decision to attempt an escape. The aforementioned Ben left his master in the countryside, where most worked as field hands, while others in urban areas were more likely to occupy domestic roles. One house slave of mixed descent, Christmas, personally waited on James Mercer, who came from an elite Virginia family. Christmas was familiar with life in the city and lived with the Mercer family in the town of Fredericksburg. Since James's infancy, Christmas was raised to wait on his young master, and they grew up together. Instead of doing field labor, Christmas helped dress James, attended to his bedside when he was sick, and even shaved him as an adult. Serving in a wealthy family meant that the waiting man dressed "extremely well," usually nicer than most Europeans. Christmas was called a "genteel Fellow" whose manners were "very pleasant." Nevertheless, Christmas bristled under his owner's commands and grew tired of serving James, which is why he chose to run away in the early 1770s.[76]

Christmas had become accustomed to a high-status lifestyle through his training in the house of a wealthy Virginia family, but the mixed-heritage man could never rise beyond his station as a slave. James Mercer, however, rose in elite Virginia society and eventually sat in the Virginia House of Burgesses. Brought up in the surroundings of a home that contained colonial luxuries, some house slaves understood and even identified with refined European culture. Ironically, Christmas's knowledge of the colonial world, his training, and his adeptness in upper-class European customs aided his chance to succeed as a freeman when he decided to leave his master. Christmas also had other assets that would help him move over into free society.[77]

By the mid-eighteenth century, certain slaves of African or Native American descent had also descended from multiple lines of European ancestry, which meant they often had fair skin, straight hair, and facial features that allowed them to appear racially "white." In terms of physical characteristics, some people of blended heritage were indistinguishable from those of full European lineage. Christmas's runaway description said that he is "well featured" (i.e., has a European phenotype) and his "Complexion is rather light" since his father was a "light Mulatto." When he looked in the mirror, Christmas may have wondered what separated him from his owner, who was perhaps only a shade or two lighter than him. Although bondage hindered Christmas, he was born with the advantage of near whiteness. Besides "light" skin, he had a number of other attributes that would help him reach his goal, including determination and mental aptitude. James said that Christmas "is very fluent of Speech, speaks with great Propriety, and is so artful that he can invent a plausible Tale at a Moment's Warning." According to his master, it would be easy for the runaway to "pass unmolested ... as a Freeman." Christmas intended to do just that.[78]

It was not easy for slaves who worked in the master's house, where they were always within reach of their owners and continually reminded of their social inferiority. Such slaves lived within constant earshot of verbal insults and many suffered regular physical violence. Women not only engaged in domestic labor but also dealt with sexual harassment and other abuses by masters, family members, and visitors. House slaves knew the lavish lifestyles enjoyed by their European owners came at the expense of those separated by the veil of African or Indigenous heritage. Granted, domestics had access to material luxuries that field hands or artisan bondsmen might rarely encounter. However, house slaves lived under the master's close watch and had to deal with disrespect and intimate assaults that epitomized enslaved men and women's lack of autonomy. Christmas knew that a gentleman's slave was still a slave, as his darker ancestry overshadowed his European lineage.[79]

In the spring of 1772, Christmas had had enough of serving the Mercer family, so he plotted secretly, packed his belongings, and one day left Fredericksburg. Even though his master knew that freedom would "be most desirable" to Christmas, James Mercer still had trouble understanding why his bondsman had recently "grown wanton in Licentiousness" and committed "several gross Acts of ill Behaviour" the week before escaping. Perhaps some isolated incident or a series of events had upset Christmas, but it is plausible that the insults he had endured built up over time. James never considered that his slave might have the same hopes and desires as he did.[80]

Although it is unknown what became of Christmas, he had about as many attributes as any other person likely to achieve success in freedom. Written literacy was perhaps one of the most important skills that assisted him, and other slaves, in any attempt at liberty. Christmas could read and probably write, tools that were extremely dangerous when wielded by slaves. European colonists could question people of color about their free status at any time, and colonial officials could jail people of color as suspected runaways if they did not have a travel pass or written proof of freedom. Literate slaves could produce these documents at will. Another "Mulatto Servant Man," John Dancer, was born around the middle of the century and was literate as an adult in King and Queen County, Virginia. "He writes intelligibly," said his master, who suspected that John would make use of this capability "to pass for a Freeman." Since a forged pass was all one needed to travel freely, the ability to read and write may have been even more useful for safe passage than whiteness.[81]

Bondsmen such as Christmas and John, and other slaves who had the capacity to spin a story about their freedom through letters, engaged in a practice that many European colonists took part in during the 1770s: declaring their independence. John's runaway advertisement appeared in the *Virginia Gazette* in February and March of 1775, just weeks before the first shots were fired between colonial militias and British regular troops at Lexington and Concord in Massachusetts. Tensions mounted in several colonies by the end of the year as talk of revolution spread. In November, the royal-appointed governor of Virginia, Lord Dunmore, issued a proclamation that offered freedom to servants and slaves who would join "His Majesty's Troops" against the colonial "rebels." Around 1,000 bondsmen of color answered the call and fled their masters to fight for their own liberty, striking fear into the hearts of colonists and turning many loyalists to the patriot cause. Out of the 1,000 or so slaves who defected to British troops, there were certainly some of blended heritage who used the opportunity to emancipate themselves. Perhaps Yellow Peter was one of them, who appeared "in Governor Dunmore's regiment with a musket on his back and a sword by his side."[82]

Those who did not readily fit into monoracial categories or might be taken for "white" benefited from their physical appearance while laboring on plantations, serving in households, suing in courtrooms, and stealing themselves from their masters. Mixed-heritage people's lives were comparable to those of full African descent, but British colonists sometimes showed better treatment to Mulattoes, which resulted in material gains, higher rates of freedom, and other advantages in colonial societies. Whether intentional or inadvertent, this favoritism resulted in most free people of color in the British Empire being of mixed ancestry by the mid-eighteenth century. Still, most people from mixed ethnoracial backgrounds were enslaved or held in other forms of bondage. They and their families used common presumptions of who was free to push the limits of hypodescent, and they sometimes succeeded in raising their social status.

However, despite the advantages that came with blended heritage, hypodescent ideology prevented most people of "mixed blood" from achieving equality with "whites" in the British colonies. Some mixed people exercised rights at local levels that resembled those of their European neighbors, but the majority did not and instead languished under slavery in the same turmoil as any other African or Indigenous slave. Mulattoes and other mixed people never achieved complete social, political, or economic equality. Only those who could cross over to the "white" side of the racial divide through multigenerational mixture could experience the sustained and permanent privileges that came with whiteness. In short, European lineage allowed social mobility for some people of blended ancestry, but unless colonists perceived them as "white," they remained generally dishonored in British provincial communities, and the same would follow in the burgeoning United States.[83]

# CONCLUSION

In June of 1774, two Mulattoes, Sall and her husband, Cornelius, escaped from bondage in Yorktown, Virginia. Their struggle for personal independence mirrored the goals of many colonists in the 1770s who sought to remove themselves from the monarchical powers of the British Crown and Parliament. Cornelius and Sall traveled over 100 miles north to reach Fredericksburg, where planters "considered [them] as free People" and hired the couple to work cultivating crops over the summer. They planned to save up enough money following the harvest "to proceed back upon the Frontiers of Virginia," where they could farm their own piece of land and live happily undisturbed. Unfortunately, the dream was interrupted when someone in Fredericksburg suspected Cornelius of being a runaway and authorities captured him. Constables took him to the York County jail, but before his master retrieved him from the jailhouse, Cornelius once again broke free and desperately tried to reunite with his wife. Was Sall captured too? Did she follow Cornelius back to Yorktown, or did they plan to rendezvous elsewhere? Or was Sall left with no choice but to move on without her husband? The sources do not tell.[1]

We do know that during the same summer months that Cornelius and Sall sought their liberty, the men who later became known as the Founding Fathers of the United States were making preparations for the first Continental Congress. They would meet in the fall of 1774 in Philadelphia to address what they considered oppressive government under the British monarchy and parliament, and over the following years they would wage a successful war to free themselves from British control and form a new nation. As some of the future Founding Fathers flipped through the pages of the *Virginia Gazette* that summer, they may have skimmed or passed over the details of Cornelius and Sall. Virginia gentlemen were familiar with the descriptions of the Mulatto slaves and servants regularly featured in these ads. They were also well aware that some of their own bondsmen and bondswomen also had mixed lineage. Some of the colonial leaders even advertised in the newspaper for the return of their runaway Mulattoes. Although these men knew that some slaves, like themselves, had European ancestors, this class of planter-legislators did not believe that their slaves deserved the same freedom from tyranny.[2]

RUN away from the subscriber, in *Amelia* county, in *August* last, a Mulatto man named *Sam*, about 35 years old, 5 feet 7 or 8 inches high, very well made, and is branded on each cheek with the letters IR, which form a sort of a scar. Whoever takes up and secures the said slave so that I get him again, or delivers him to me, or to Mr. *Henry Randolph*, in *Chesterfield*, shall have THREE POUNDS reward.

3          JOHN RANDOLPH.

---

RUN away from the subscriber, in *Hanover* county, a Mulatto man slave named *Charles*, 22 years old, about 5 feet nine inches high, slim made, of a light complexion, has straight hair, and has been used to work at the carpenter's business: He took with him a middle sized black mare, neither docked or branded, but a little galled in the shoulders by carting: He has a blue fearnought coat, and a green plains coat with metal buttons, and is supposed to be gone towards *North Carolina*. Whoever apprehends the said slave, and brings him to me, shall have FORTY SHILLINGS reward, besides what the law allows, and if taken out of the colony FIVE POUNDS.

3          JOHN SNELSON.

---

RUN away from the subscriber, the 10th of *June* last, a tall slim Mulatto man named *John Allen*, by trade a shoemaker; he is under articles of agreement for two years. Whoever will apprehend him, and deliver him to me, at *Norfolk*, shall receive Twenty Shillings reward.

JOHN MUIRHEAD.

---

CHARLES CITY county, *Oct.* 15, 1769.

RUN away from the subscriber, on the 23d of last month, a Mulatto boy named *William Hood*, about 16 years old, he is remarkably smart and sensible, and as he has been two voyages to sea, will probably endeavour to get on board of some vessel. He has several scars on his head, and his fore teeth are very broad; had on a shirt and trowsers, and a felt hat bound with ferrit. All masters of vessels, and others, are hereby forewarned from harbouring or entertaining him, and whoever will apprehend and secure him, so that I may get him again, shall have FORTY SHILLINGS, on applying to    tf.    HENRY MINSON.

Mulatto runaways in the *Virginia Gazette* (2nd ed.), December 7, 1769. (Colonial Williamsburg Foundation, Williamsburg, Virginia)

Hypodescent ideology represented a cognitive dissonance in the minds of British colonists, who viewed "Mulattoes" of mixed African and European heritage as more "Negro" than "white," yet many colonists also accepted that there was middle ground between these two races. Clearly, Europeans associated mixed people with their African or Native American ancestry and viewed them as people of color, but this framework of racial hypodescent was flexible, for people of mixed African and European or Indigenous and European lineage were able to occupy spaces above other "Negroes" or "Indians." In practice, colonists in the Anglo-Caribbean islands and North America recognized that people of "mixed blood" had multiple backgrounds and granted privileges to some people of blended ancestry. Although mixed-heritage people always complicated the so-called color line, the idea of a line, or even of static monoracial categories, was untenable because all racial categories are socially created.[3]

During the Revolutionary era, EuroAmericans brought colonial racial beliefs into the U.S. republic, as hypodescent ideology was rearticulated in the early national period. The historical trajectory of American racial formation has always been elastic, strengthening when restrictions impeded people's lives and loosening when possibilities opened up to allow improved social mobility. Whether freedoms were expanding or contracting, individuals continually renegotiated their socioracial position over time and place. In some instances, mixed people could move relatively easily into whiteness, yet in other locations or social settings, colonists commonly treated people of mixed ancestry as any other "Negro" or "Indian." The colonial Chesapeake was an incubator for the more stringent version of hypodescent philosophy that later came to dominate in the United States. While there were ebbs and flows in this history, and a longer story that leads to the one-drop rule, this book has shown how English colonists first established the framework of hypodescent in the British provinces over the century and a half before there was a United States of America.[4]

The actions of European planter-legislators, people of mixed heritage, and their blended families are integral to understanding the foundations of mixed-race ideologies in the Anglo-American colonies. As provincial lawmakers acted to prevent intermixture and sought to attach mixed children to bound labor, the people themselves fought back to maintain their autonomy. Mixed-heritage people exposed inconsistencies inherent within colonial socioracial orders, which is why Mulattoes and other mixed people were so dangerous in the eyes of the elite. Although most mixed people encountered greater hardships than "whites," struggles by people of "mixed blood" and their families led to increased freedoms and other privileges over "Negroes." People of mixed lineage and their kinfolk repeatedly fought authorities for their freedom and negotiated other forms of self-determination, and their efforts helped force the racial order to remain somewhat fluid throughout the colonial period. This resistance prevented colonists from extending hypodescent to its absolute extreme, the one-drop rule, where a person of discernable or traceable African ancestry was socially and legally considered "black."

Cornelius and Sall's journey in the mid-1770s illustrates both the obstacles and (near) successes of mixed-heritage people among all people of African and Native American lineage as they fought to gain and maintain freedom in the British colonies. Before the U.S. Revolution, the majority of free people of color in these provinces were also of mixed ancestry, which influenced the colonial perception of free Mulattoes like Cornelius and Sall. This aided the couple's escape because they could pass for "free People" more easily than average African slaves. Still, most people of blended heritage remained in bondage, and running away did not automatically secure their liberty. Cornelius and Sall's story also highlights one freedom struggle at the end of the colonial period in North America as well as part of the great U.S. paradox: that the colonial masters who outwardly called for liberty when declaring independence from British monarchy also held roughly 20 percent of the population in slavery.[5]

*Blurring the Lines of Race and Freedom* helps us understand how people first came to think about the idea of racial mixture in English colonial North America and the Atlantic islands by investigating how European colonists in these provinces conceptualized notions of race and ethnoracial intermixture, and how people of mixed heritage and their families responded to these ideas. During the seventeenth and eighteenth centuries, the English colonies in the Americas contained vast diversity, including a multitude of Indigenous American groups, a wide variety of European immigrants, and people of various ethnic backgrounds from the African continent. Wealthy elites, legislators, and middling planters established institutions that led to the formation of racial groups, and everyday colonists also supported systems that deemed particular groups eligible for servitude and slavery. The English identified "Negroes," "Indians," "Mulattoes," "Mustees," and other people of "mixed blood" as inferior and subordinated them under European "whites" within the colonial racial hierarchy. These sentiments were not simply taught or passed down from one generation to the next, but colonists continually reified racial ideologies through everyday practices, language, legislation, courts, labor systems, and other institutions.[6]

Governing officials made strategic choices and carefully orchestrated legal statutes to protect and increase their financial investments in bound plantation labor, which fueled lucrative production of crops such as sugar, tobacco, and rice. Anti-intermixture laws were no exception and appear aspirational in their attempts to prevent all mixture, especially in places where interracial liaisons were somewhat common between "white," "Negro," "Indian," and "Mulatto" women and men. In the face of extended bondage, lower-class European women continued to sexually engage with men of color, giving birth to children of blended heritage. Punishments inhibited, though never totally extinguished, the birth of Mulatto children born to "white" women, but they did create a significant amount of cheap labor for planters in Virginia, Maryland, and North Carolina. It is no coincidence that planter-legislators ratified the heaviest restrictions against interracial mixture and people of mixed ancestry in the English colonies with some of the largest numbers of Mulattoes.

It is often stated that Europeans did not normally enslave their own, but that was only as long as they were perceived to be "white." Aside from one statute in Maryland that made slaves of European women who "doe intermarry with Negro Slaves," the English did in fact enslave thousands of people with European lineage: those Mulattoes and mixed people whose ancestral ties could also be traced to an African or Indigenous slave mother. Many English believed that "Negro" and "Indian" blood corrupted and figuratively erased the "white" makeup of mixed-heritage people, lowered them on the racial ladder, and made them eligible for bondage. Colonial slave law mandated slavery heritable through the maternal line, which meant mixed children born to enslaved "Negro," "Indian," and "Mulatto" women by "white" men would be slaves. English colonists justified prolonged servitude and slavery for people of mixed ancestry based on notions of hypodescent. However, after multiple generations of mixture with Europeans, these families could be figuratively redeemed and their racial status could become "white" once again.[7]

English notions of race, racial mixture, and mixed-heritage peoples had origins connected to early Iberian seafaring and interactions with African peoples, Christian religious views, and the Moorish occupation of the Iberian Peninsula; these ideas were then brought to the colonial Americas. Many Europeans viewed intermixture through the lens of blood purity (*limpieza de sangre*) and linked soci…racial status to labor roles in the American colonies, where freedom and bondage intersected with race, class, and gender. English colonists had learned from the Spanish and Portuguese, who brought protoracial beliefs to the Americas in the fifteenth and sixteenth centuries, but Anglo-Americans took these ideas to new heights with the creation of the concept of "abominable mixture and spurious issue." This phrase, from Virginia's 1691 landmark legislation, and the ideology behind it pushed forward negative ideas of racial intermixture and portrayed mixed-heritage people as deplorable, though as the preceding pages have shown, it took much more than this one law to institute notions of hypodescent.[8]

While the English borrowed ideas from the Spanish and other Europeans, their racial ideologies evolved under a brand of Protestant settler colonialism that attempted to contain or control intermixture with non-Europeans, especially in North America. Compared to their Catholic counterparts, the English largely came to oppose ethnoracial mixture with Native Americans, and even fewer accepted the open acknowledgment of sexual intimacies with Africans. By the eighteenth century, certain Protestant provinces and Catholic colonies had diverged along different paths, though in the same direction, concerning mixture in their respective empires. Neither English, French, nor Spanish elites openly approved of mixed-heritage people occupying the highest ranks of society, though Catholic empires more readily accepted intermixture and allowed people of blended ancestry considerable upward social mobility.

I argue for a more dynamic interpretation of racial hypodescent in the colonial period, in which all European societies relegated children of mixed heritage closer to the position of their socially inferior parentage, though to varying degrees. A hypodescent framework that is flexible allows us to explain how British colonists subjugated Mulattoes and other people of "mixed blood," yet mixed people still had greater advantages to rise above their African or Indigenous parentage. Planter-legislators in Virginia and Maryland began to develop a stricter form of hypodescent in the Tidewater counties during the latter half of the seventeenth century, which coincided with a demographic shift toward African slave labor in the English provinces. In the early eighteenth century, colonial officials in North Carolina followed those in the Chesapeake, and general assemblies in all three colonies repeatedly passed harsh laws aimed at keeping non-"white" African, Indigenous, and mixed-heritage peoples from mixing with "white" Europeans.

While Virginia, Maryland, and North Carolina passed the strongest policies against racial mixture and mixed people during the colonial period, the institution of these decrees was never absolute. These three colonial governments were persistent in their pursuit of legal restrictions and extended bondage for mixed-heritage people, but county courts inconsistently enforced these regulations. It took officials in these three colonies repeated efforts to disseminate laws that targeted families of blended ancestry. Remote areas were often slow to enact standards passed in provincial capitals, and the farther people lived from major colonial centers, the harder it was for officials to institute legal statutes that regulated people's lives.[9]

Relying on legislative trial and error, Virginia, Maryland, and North Carolina lawmakers passed ordinances that persecuted ethnoracial mixture and people of mixed ancestry, while British officials in other provinces generally developed more relaxed boundaries. Far less African slavery existed in New England, New York, New Jersey, Pennsylvania, and Delaware than in the Chesapeake, the Carolinas, and the Caribbean. In the northern colonies, people of color never reached a critical mass that caused widespread colonial fears of interracial mixture. While those who mixed still faced social stigma and some anti-intermixture statutes appeared in the northern provinces, magistrates lightly enforced these laws and did not create repetitive legislation. In the Caribbean and South Carolina, Africans made up a majority of the population, and intermixture was prevalent, largely unregulated, and somewhat accepted. Overall, the geographical northern and southern ends of the British Americas adopted more relaxed forms of hypodescent, yet provincial legislatures still kept free "Negroes," "Indians," "Mulattoes," and other "mixed bloods" in check by placing limitations on their rights as British subjects.[10]

There were British colonial officials everywhere who found interracial mixture distasteful, but there were some who decided or were forced to extend rights to free people of mixed heritage, especially in places with the highest slave populations. Again, regulations moderated privileges for free people of blended ancestry, but provincial magistrates could not justify keeping them from enjoying at least some of the rights associated with European lineage that were guaranteed to free British subjects. While this allowed socioracial mobility for some, a "mulatto escape hatch" that could lead to whiteness was closed to the majority of mixed-heritage people in the British colonies. Only a small number of free Mulattoes who had obtained wealth and mixed over successive generations with Europeans might become "white."[11]

Native Americans also intermixed with Africans and Europeans, and colonists applied the word Mulatto to people who had some Indigenous lineage as well. In certain areas, English colonists referred to people of partial Native American descent as Mustees. So-called Mustees made up a significant portion of the blended population in South Carolina, where many were born out of the convergence of the transatlantic African slave trade and the Native American slave trade. English colonists put tens of thousands of slaves up for sale in Charlestown, and these populations mixed together on rice and indigo plantations in the surrounding Lowcountry.[12]

For most mixed people throughout the British colonies, the racial label of "Mulatto" became a symbol that represented illicit sexual behavior and illegitimacy, which shaped colonial views of them as a degenerate group. The fashioning of mixed-heritage people as a deplorable half caste in the colonial period, at times expressed an early form of hybrid degeneracy—the belief that mixed offspring are somehow innately weaker than either parent. Since colonial times, the English blasted their Catholic adversaries for frequent intermixture with African and Indigenous peoples using this rationale. Writing from Antigua while serving as governor of the Leeward Islands, Sir Nathaniel Johnson reported that "the Spanish of the West Indies, for however brave their ancestors may have been, have degenerated into a dastardly and mongrel herd of mulattos, mustees and other spurious mixtures, and are now certainly become the very scum of mankind." This 1689 statement is one of the earliest articulations of hybrid degeneracy. Sir Nathaniel's views are a rendition of those expressed by later racial scientists in the late nineteenth and early twentieth century, who believed that human hybridity resulted from interracial mixture and threatened to end the alleged progress of European civilization. English colonists articulated similar notions about "Negro" and "Indian" blood corrupting whiteness. However, some colonists also conveyed the view that European blood would predominate after successive generations of intermixture with Europeans and could eventually clear a family of "Negro" or "Indian" blood.[13]

But what did people of mixed heritage think about themselves? This question is not important solely for the sake of bringing marginalized people to the center of the story, but by doing so, we are able to view more of the historical picture and bring it into better focus. People of mixed ancestry were well aware of their lowly position in colonial society and believed that they and their children deserved better than slavery, servitude, and subjugation. Mixed people in bondage often relied on their European lineage in their quest for freedom, namely by recognizing their Christian faith, kinship connections, or racial whiteness. Despite laws that said otherwise, Mulattoes believed that European heritage and Christian baptism entitled them to the same free status as other British subjects. They yearned for literacy and education so they might deepen their understanding of biblical teachings and improve their social position by reaping the benefits of their own labor. Free people of blended ancestry wanted to raise their families with dignity, sought inclusion among their peers, and hoped to achieve financial stability and prosperity in English colonial societies.[14]

Fluid hypodescent in the colonial period allowed a number of mixed-heritage people access to a modicum of "white" privilege associated with their European ancestry, but this did not mean they could all pass for "white" or that they sought to personally identify as such. Runaway advertisements for "white" or "light coloured" Mulattoes imply a nascent form of the one-drop rule, because masters always described their mixed bondsmen and bondswomen as people of color, even when they gave physical descriptions that were indistinguishable from those of Europeans. Still, most mixed people would attempt to "pass as free" and might identify with more than one ethnoracial background. In practice, mixed individuals and their families moved between racial categories at different points in their lives or over generations. This is why people of mixed descent highlighted their European ancestry when they petitioned colonial courts for freedom and downplayed African or Indigenous origins. They also understood that race was malleable and shaped by perception.

Despite making overtures to whiteness when in front of authorities, most mixed people grew up and identified with others of African, Native American, and blended heritage. They most often cultivated relationships with people of color, with whom they had common cultures and a shared sense of struggle against colonial oppressions. Most selected intimate partners of African or Indigenous lineage and fought alongside their family members for greater autonomy. Sometimes they partnered with Europeans who might help improve their opportunities in colonial society. Others sought out Native American communities, where they might locate independence, acceptance, and protection from bondage.

Mixed-heritage people applied several tactics to seek freedom and used a combination of survival strategies based on their individual circumstances to maneuver through the colonial world. A smaller number of mixed people sought to use their light skin to join Europeans as equals and sometimes chose to avoid close associations with "Negroes" and "Indians" in order to distance themselves from negative stereotypes associated with people of color. While some people of blended ancestry definitely thought of themselves as superior to other people of color, there is far more evidence of allegiance with Africans and Native Americans than of animosities. Many were willing to stand in solidarity with those of African or Indigenous descent. These alliances appear not only in court records but also in actions. People of mixed ancestry frequently ran away to communities of color and areas outside the reach of the English colonies for refuge, relying on the knowledge of their ancestors and elders to guide them to safety. This mixed-heritage freedom struggle was part of a wider resistance by people of African, Indigenous, and poor European descent to hold on to their traditions, escape bondage, and reconstitute their families.

---

European colonists in English America worried about ethnoracial mixture, because people of blended heritage blurred racial lines and made it difficult for planters and professionals to maintain all mixed people in a position of bondage. Most wealthy planter-legislators across the colonies stigmatized open racial intermixture and marginalized mixed offspring under the framework of hypodescent because it was in their best economic interest to hold people of blended ancestry in bondage for as long as possible. The majority of mixed-heritage people in the English colonies were in some form of servitude or slavery, and those who were born free presented provincial magistrates with a legal conundrum. The liminal position of Mulattoes and other mixed people in the socioracial order confused a clear-cut "black" and "white" binary that directly corresponded with slavery and freedom. However, this "black"-"white" racial binary had always been a false dichotomy, created and supported in the minds of colonists who benefited from reaffirming racial categories and upholding racial systems.

Even as negative perceptions of Mulattoes, Mustees, and "Persons of Mixt

Blood" became ingrained in Anglo-American societies during the colonial era, some people held positive views of mixed-heritage peoples. There were a number of Europeans who felt that "Mulattoes" should have greater rights than "Negroes" or "Indians," although perhaps not the same as "whites." In the mid-eighteenth century, Englishman Edmund Burke wondered if colonists should "find out some medium between liberty and absolute slavery, in which we might place all mulattoes after a certain limited servitude . . . ?" In social practice and in law, this "medium" between freedom and slavery existed for certain people of mixed descent. Across the British Atlantic world, people of mixed ancestry held varying positions within the socioracial hierarchy, and whether slave or free, they all sought greater independence. How they gained and maintained liberty or displayed personal autonomy, even if limited, is a major theme that has run throughout this book. People of blended heritage and their families worked to provide their descendants with the tools needed to seek further freedoms, even if the constraints produced by colonialism undermined true self-determination.[15]

People who occupied intermediate positions between monoracial categories in English colonial societies frustrated the planter class, many of whom wanted to keep all people of color in perpetual bondage. British planters, merchants, professionals, and legislators organized to keep the lines of race and freedom from becoming blurred, yet people of mixed backgrounds contested and complicated colonial efforts to enforce strict racial codes. There was no linear or straight path leading from weak to stronger racial hypodescent over the colonial period, because mixed-heritage people and their families continually fought for freedom and forced English authorities to renegotiate legal terms regarding bondage after the mid-eighteenth century. During the U.S. Revolutionary era of the 1760s through the 1780s, people of color used the rhetoric of liberty to pursue increased freedoms in the burgeoning nation. People of blended heritage in the U.S. national era continued to experience benefits and drawbacks in both law and custom when compared to African Americans and EuroAmericans.

Without drawing further conclusions about later centuries based on this colonial study, it is clear that racial hypodescent strengthened in the United States from the nineteenth to the twentieth century. During the U.S. Civil War, EuroAmericans coined and propagated the term "miscegenation" to denote the mixing of the races. Authorities worked further to contain people with complex and fluid identities within strict monoracial boundaries, as the one-drop rule came to represent the most extreme form of hypodescent. Although not all states adhered to these racial standards, ideas around race purity were at the foundation of Jim Crow segregation in the U.S. South. After the legislative end of U.S. segregation by the 1960s and the case of *Loving v. Virginia* (1967) found anti-miscegenation laws unconstitutional, so-called interracial couples and their children flourished in the final decades of the twentieth century and into the twenty-first.[16]

Even though the one-drop rule did not exist in the colonial period as it did later in the United States, its ideological origins are found in the racial hypodescent ideology of the seventeenth- and eighteenth-century English colonies. In some ways, renewed ethnoracial mixture in the United States over the past several decades reflects much earlier intermingling in the English colonies over 300 years ago, when European colonists decided to restrict people's lives through penalty and ostracism. Legal prohibitions targeting racial intermixture have now been lifted for over fifty years, and while there have been renewed cries against "race mixing," most people in the United States today are moving toward greater celebrations of diversity and the multiplicity that makes up many of our ancestries.[17]

As in the colonial period, mixed-heritage identities have and will continue to be mercurial, disputed, and political. As many of us continue to remove the figurative shackles of colonialism and grapple with personal identity in light of complex histories, people of diverse ethnic and racial backgrounds are also reclaiming multiple lineages. U.S. President Barack Obama's acknowledgment of his mixed ancestry, DNA tests (though controversial), and the ability to "mark one or more" racial boxes on federal censuses since 2000 are just a few things that have challenged people in the United States to reconsider monoracial categories. As more people in the twenty-first century become aware that race is, and always has been, a social fiction, we must also remember that the idea of racial mixture is equally fallacious.[18]

# NOTES

### ABBREVIATIONS

| | |
|---|---|
| AOM | *Archives of Maryland* |
| ARPMA | *The Acts and Resolves, Public and Private, of the Province of Massachusetts Bay* |
| CRNC | *The Colonial Records of North Carolina* |
| CRSGA | *The Colonial Records of the State of Georgia* |
| EJCCV | *Executive Journals of the Council of Colonial Virginia* |
| LSDE | *Laws of the State of Delaware* |
| LVA | Library of Virginia, Richmond |
| MG | *Maryland Gazette* |
| MSA | Maryland State Archives, Annapolis |
| PAGAM | *Proceedings and Acts of the General Assembly of Maryland* |
| PG | *Pennsylvania Gazette* |
| SALSC | *The Statutes at Large of South Carolina* |
| SALVA | *The Statutes at Large: Being a Collection of All the Laws of Virginia, from the First Session of the Legislature in the Year 1619* |
| SCDAH | South Carolina Department of Archives and History, Columbia |
| SCG | *South-Carolina Gazette* |
| SCGCJ | *South-Carolina Gazette and Country Journal* |
| SRNC | *The State Records of North Carolina* |
| VG | *Virginia Gazette* (1st ed.) |
| VG2 | *Virginia Gazette* (2nd ed.) |

### INTRODUCTION

1. William Hand Browne, ed., *AOM*, vol. 13, *PAGAM, April 1684–June 1692* (Baltimore: Maryland Historical Society, 1894), 292–95, 302–3.

2. Browne, 13:292–95.

3. Browne, 13:292–95, 302–3.

4. Browne, 13:292–95, 302–3, 390, 456–57.

5. Browne, 13:292–95, 302–3, 390, 456–57.

6. Browne, 13:294, 302, 457.

7. Englishman Granville Sharp uses the phrase "mixed people or Mulattoes" to discuss people of mixed African and European parentage in 1769. Granville Sharp, *A Representation of the Injustice and Dangerous Tendency of Tolerating Slavery* (London: printed for Benjamin White and Robert Horsfield, 1769), 109.

8. I draw from what Ariela Gross identifies as the "legal construction of race." Ariela Gross, "Beyond Black and White: Cultural Approaches to Race and Slavery," *Columbia Law Review* 101, no. 3 (2001): 643–45; James Horn, *Adapting to a New World: English Society in the Seventeenth-Century Chesapeake* (Chapel Hill: University of North Carolina Press, 1994), 2.

9. I use the term "ethnoracial" instead of simply "ethnic" or "racial," as there are several cultural assumptions attached to a person's regional ancestry, group origin, or ethnic identity that are often inextricably linked with ideas of race. Rogers Brubaker, "Ethnicity without Groups," *European Journal of Sociology* 43, no. 2 (2002): 163–89; David A. Hollinger, *Postethnic America: Beyond Multiculturalism*, 10th anniversary ed. (New York: Basic Books, 2006), 227–28. I use "Indigenous" throughout the book to refer to the peoples who first established themselves in the Western Hemisphere tens of thousands of years before European immigration. James Merrell, "Coming to Terms with Early America," *William and Mary Quarterly* 69, no. 3 (2012): 535–40; J. H. Elliott, *Empires of the Atlantic World: Britain and Spain in America, 1492–1830* (New Haven, Conn.: Yale University Press, 2006), 29.

10. Joel Williamson, *New People: Miscegenation and Mulattoes in the United States* (New York: Free Press, 1980), xi–xiv; Sidney Kaplan, "The Miscegenation Issue in the Election of 1864," *Journal of Negro History* 34, no. 3 (1949): 274–343; Philip D. Morgan, *Slave Counterpoint: Black Culture in the Eighteenth-Century Chesapeake and Lowcountry* (Chapel Hill: University of North Carolina Press, 1998), xvii; Kathleen M. Brown, *Good Wives, Nasty Wenches, and Anxious Patriarchs: Gender, Race, and Power in Colonial Virginia* (Chapel Hill: University of North Carolina Press, 1996), 107–36, 187–244. For other discussions of racial mixture in Virginia, see Winthrop D. Jordan, *White over Black: American Attitudes toward the Negro, 1550–1812* (Chapel Hill: University of North Carolina Press, 1968); Joshua D. Rothman, *Notorious in the Neighborhood: Sex and Families across the Color Line, 1787–1861* (Chapel Hill: University of North Carolina Press, 2003); and Annette Gordon-Reed, *The Hemingses of Monticello: An American Family* (New York: W. W. Norton, 2008). For similar studies of ethnoracial mixture in colonial North America, see Martha Hodes, ed., *Sex, Love, Race: Crossing Boundaries in North American History* (New York: New York University Press, 1999); Kirsten Fischer, *Suspect Relations: Sex, Race, and Resistance in Colonial North Carolina* (Ithaca, N.Y.: Cornell University Press, 2002); and Jennifer M. Spear, *Race, Sex, and Social Order in Early New Orleans* (Baltimore: John Hopkins University Press, 2009). For other general histories of racial mixture and mixed-heritage peoples in early North America, see Martha Hodes, *White Women, Black Men: Illicit Sex in the Nineteenth-Century South* (New Haven, Conn.: Yale University Press, 1997); Gary B. Nash, *Forbidden Love: The Hidden History of Mixed-Race America*, 2nd ed. (Los Angeles: University of California Regents, National Center for History in the Schools, 2010); Daniel J. Sharfstein, *The Invisible Line: Three American Families and the Secret Journey from Black to White* (New York: Penguin, 2011); and Greg Carter, *The United States of the United Races: A Utopian History of Racial Mixing* (New York: New York University Press, 2013).

11. Daniel Livesay, *Children of Uncertain Fortune: Mixed-Race Jamaicans in Britain and the Atlantic Family, 1733–1833* (Chapel Hill: University of North Carolina Press, 2018); Brooke N. Newman, *A Dark Inheritance: Blood, Race, and Sex in Colonial Jamaica* (New Haven, Conn.: Yale University Press, 2018).

12. A. Leon Higginbotham Jr. and Barbara K. Kopytoff, "Racial Purity and Interracial

Sex in the Law of Colonial and Antebellum Virginia," *Georgetown Law Journal* 77, no. 6 (1989): 1967–2029.

13. Daniel J. Sharfstein, "Crossing the Color Line: Racial Migration and the One-Drop Rule, 1600–1860," *Minnesota Law Review* 91, no. 3 (2007): 592–656; Winthrop D. Jordan, "Historical Origins of the One-Drop Racial Rule in the United States," ed. Paul Spickard, *Journal of Critical Mixed Race Studies* 1, no. 1 (2014): 98–132.

14. Anthropologist Marvin Harris coined the term "hypodescent" and applied the concept to the Latin American context. Marvin Harris, *Patterns of Race in the Americas* (New York: Walker, 1964), 56; David A. Hollinger, "Amalgamation and Hypodescent: The Question of Ethnoracial Mixture in the History of the United States," *American Historical Review* 108, no. 5 (2003): 1363–90.

15. There has been growing scholarship on hypodescent and the one-drop rule, starting with F. James Davis, *Who Is Black? One Nation's Definition* (University Park: Pennsylvania State University Press, 1991). Other informative sociological works explore first-generation and multigenerational intermixture and the hardening of the one-drop rule. G. Reginald Daniel, *More Than Black? Multiracial Identity and the New Racial Order* (Philadelphia: Temple University Press, 2002); Scott Leon Washington, "Hypodescent: A History of the Crystallization of the One-Drop Rule in the United States, 1880–1940," PhD diss., Princeton University, 2011.

16. For important scholarship on racial mixture and social identity in colonial Latin America, see Magnus Mörner, *Race Mixture in the History of Latin America* (Boston: Little, Brown, 1967); Joanne Rappaport, *The Disappearing Mestizo: Configuring Difference in the Colonial New Kingdom of Granada* (Durham, N.C.: Duke University Press, 2014); and Ann Twinam, *Purchasing Whiteness: Pardos, Mulattos, and the Quest for Social Mobility in the Spanish Indies* (Stanford, Calif.: Stanford University Press, 2015).

17. Ronald Takaki, *A Different Mirror: A History of Multicultural America* (Boston: Little, Brown, 1993), 21–23; Annette Kolodny, *In Search of First Contact: The Vikings of Vinland, the Peoples of the Dawnland, and the Anglo-American Anxiety of Discovery* (Durham, N.C.: Duke University Press, 2012), 4–18, 64–69.

18. Jack D. Forbes, *Africans and Native Americans: The Language of Race and the Evolution of Red-Black Peoples* (Urbana-Champaign: University of Illinois Press, 1993), 100–101, 139; Jean E. Feerick, *Strangers in Blood: Relocating Race in the Renaissance* (Toronto: University of Toronto Press, 2010), 4–13; Newman, *Dark Inheritance*, 6–7, 77.

19. Patrick J. Carroll, *Blacks in Colonial Veracruz: Race, Ethnicity, and Regional Development* (Austin: University of Texas Press, 1991), 79–80, 84–90; Peter H. Wood, *Strange New Land: African in Colonial America* (New York: Oxford University Press, 2003), 1–12. Many terms accompanied *mestiza/o* and *mulata/o* before these two became the most popular for defining people of mixed ancestry in Latin America. As early as 1569, Iberian and Latin dictionaries equated hybridity with the words *mestiza/o* and *mulata/o*. *Mestizo* came from the Latin *mixticius*, used as far back as the thirteenth century to define someone of "mixed blood," or a person having parents from two different groups of people (e.g., one Jewish and one Egyptian parent). Mid-sixteenth-century Portuguese dictionaries defined people using phrases such as *o homem mulato* ("the *mulato* man"). While most people labeled as *mulata/o* were of mixed ancestry, not all had one African and one European parent. Some people used *mulata/o* to describe skin tone, much like the term *loro*, which the Spanish commonly applied to a variety of people with a dark, dusky, or brown complexion. Over time both the Spanish and Portuguese used *pardo* and *mulato*

more exclusively for people of mixed lineage who had brown skin. The same took place with the Spanish *mestizo* and Portuguese *mestiço* and *mamaluco*. All of these words came to denote someone of known mixed heritage in the Iberian languages. For a deeper look at the lexicon, see Forbes, *Africans and Native Americans*, 100–125. For the thirteenth-century use of *mestizo* as a biblical reference for children of Egyptian and Jewish parentage, see Alfonso X, *General estoria: Primera parte*, ed. Antonio García Solalinde (Madrid: Centro de Estudios Históricos, 1930), 579.

20. The word *mulato* originating from *mulo* (mule) is possible yet contested, since the first explicit connection appears in Spanish dictionaries in the early seventeenth century. By then, *mulato* had already been applied to humans for around 100 years. Forbes, *Africans and Native Americans*, 125–48.

21. Jordan, *White over Black*, 61; James H. Sweet, "The Iberian Roots of American Racist Thought," *William and Mary Quarterly* 54, no. 1 (1997): 143–66.

22. Elliott, *Empires of the Atlantic World*, 153–55.

23. John Francis Maxwell, *Slavery and the Catholic Church: The History of Catholic Teaching concerning the Moral Legitimacy of the Institution of Slavery* (Chichester, UK: Barry Rose, 1975), 68–74; Elliott, *Empires of the Atlantic World*, 97–99; Andrés Reséndez, *The Other Slavery: The Uncovered Story of Indian Enslavement in America* (New York: Houghton Mifflin Harcourt, 2016), 46–47; Katharine Gerbner, *Christian Slavery: Conversion and Race in the Protestant Atlantic World* (Philadelphia: University of Pennsylvania Press, 2018), 16–21.

24. Spear, *Race, Sex, and Social Order*, 59–68; Twinam, *Purchasing Whiteness*, 92–95.

25. See Elliott, *Empires of the Atlantic World*; and Perry Miller, "Errand into the Wilderness," *William and Mary Quarterly* 10, no. 1 (1953): 3–32.

26. Spear, *Race, Sex, and Social Order*, 59–68.

27. Christopher Tomlins, *Freedom Bound: Law, Labor, and Civil Identity in Colonizing English America, 1580–1865* (New York: Cambridge University Press, 2010), 54–61; David D. Smits, "'Abominable Mixture': Toward the Repudiation of Anglo-Indian Intermarriage in Seventeenth-Century Virginia," *Virginia Magazine of History and Biography* 95, no. 2 (1987): 157–92; Ann Marie Plane, *Colonial Intimacies: Indian Marriage in Early New England* (Ithaca, N.Y.: Cornell University Press, 2000), 132–33, 146–47; Richard Godbeer, *Sexual Revolution in Early America* (Baltimore: Johns Hopkins University Press, 2002), 154–89.

28. Ilona Katzew, *Casta Painting: Images of Race in Eighteenth-Century Mexico* (New Haven, Conn.: Yale University Press, 2004), 39–42.

29. Katzew, 1–4, 48–51, 201–4; Nash, *Forbidden Love*, 45–62.

30. Edward Long, *The History of Jamaica, or, General Survey of the Antient and Modern State of the Island: With Reflections on Its Situation Settlements, Inhabitants, Climate, Products, Commerce, Laws, and Government*, Vol. II (London: T. Lowndes, 1774), 327.

31. Gary B. Nash, "The Hidden History of Mestizo America," *Journal of American History* 82, no. 3 (1995): 941–64.

32. Williamson, *New People*, 14; Peter H. Wood, *Black Majority: Negroes in Colonial South Carolina from 1670 through the Stono Rebellion* (New York: W. W. Norton, 1975), 98–99, 131–32.

33. *PG*, Jan. 24, 1749, Oct. 12, 1752.

34. Michael Omi and Howard Winant, *Racial Formation in the United States*, 3rd ed. (New York: Routledge, 2015), 112; Jordan, *White over Black*, 95.

35. Omi and Winant, *Racial Formation in the United States*, 105–32.

36. *PG*, Sept. 4, 1760; *VG2*, Nov. 11, 1773. There were several versions of the colonial *Virginia Gazette*, and three different editions are identified in the notes and bibliography for this book. See "Virginia Gazettes," The Colonial Williamsburg Foundation, http://research.history.org/DigitalLibrary/va-gazettes/VGAllIssues.cfm.

37. *VG*, Mar. 1, Sept. 22, 1738; *SCG*, Mar. 21, 1761; *PG*, May 15, 1755.

38. *SCG*, Apr. 12, 1773; *PG*, Oct. 23, 1760; *PG*, May 24, 1750.

39. *VG*, Apr. 11, 1766; *PG*, Sept. 13, 1764. Peter Carroll of Baltimore County, Maryland, said his "Mulatto Slave named Mike . . . much resembles an Indian in Colour." *MG*, July 15, 1762; *VG*, June 7, 1770. For an excellent study of the colonial descriptions of complexion, see Sharon Block, *Colonial Complexions: Race and Bodies in Eighteenth-Century America* (Philadelphia: University of Pennsylvania Press, 2018).

40. *SCG*, July 28, 1759; *SCGCJ*, Feb. 8, 1774.

41. Runaway ads are filled with descriptions of slaves from Africa who are listed as "yellow." In South Carolina, Primus was an "Eboe Negro Man" and had "a very yellow complexion," according to his master. *SCG*, July 5, 1735.

42. Omi and Winant, *Racial Formation in the United States*, 108–9.

43. Robert Wald Sussman, *The Myth of Race: The Troubling Persistence of an Unscientific Idea* (Cambridge, Mass.: Harvard University Press, 2014), 1; Nash, *Forbidden Love*, v–vi, 15–17; Eduardo Bonilla-Silva, "The Essential Social Fact of Race," *American Sociological Review* 64, no. 6 (1999): 899; Omi and Winant, *Racial Formation in the United States*, 110–12.

44. Bonilla-Silva, "Essential Social Fact," 902–3.

45. Bonilla-Silva, 902–3.

CHAPTER 1

1. Dates throughout have been adjusted to coincide with the Gregorian calendar. Patent Record, 1645–57, liber ABH, fol. 65, Land Office, MSA; Andrew White, "A Briefe Relation of the Voyage unto Maryland," in *Narratives of Early Maryland, 1633–1684*, ed. Clayton Colman Hall (New York: Charles Scribner's Sons, 1910), 70–74; N. C. Brooks, ed., *A Relation of the Colony of the Lord Baron of Baltimore, in Maryland, near Virginia: A Narrative of the First Voyage to Maryland by the Rev. Father Andrew White, and Sundry Reports* (Baltimore: Maryland Historical Society, 1847), 19–20; William Hand Browne, ed., *AOM*, vol. 3, *Proceedings and Acts of the Council of Maryland, 1636–1637* (Baltimore: Maryland Historical Society, 1885), 259.

2. William Hand Browne, ed., *AOM*, vol. 4, *Judicial and Testamentary Business of the Provincial Court, 1637–1650* (Baltimore: Maryland Historical Society, 1887), 138; David S. Bogen, "Mathias de Sousa: Maryland's First Colonist of African Descent," *Maryland Historical Magazine* 96, no. 1 (2001): 69–71; Lois Green Carr, Philip D. Morgan, and Jean Burrell Russo, eds., *Colonial Chesapeake Society* (Chapel Hill: University of North Carolina Press, 1988), 74–76.

3. Edmund S. Morgan, *American Slavery, American Freedom: The Ordeal of Colonial Virginia* (New York: W. W. Norton, 1975), 297–307; William Waller Hening, ed., *SALVA* (Richmond, Va.: Samuel Pleasants Jr., 1810), 2:170; William Hand Browne, ed., *AOM*, vol. 1, *PAGAM, January 1637/8–September 1664* (Baltimore: Maryland Historical Society, 1883), 533–34; John B. Whittington, "The Origin and Nature of African Slavery in Seventeenth Century Maryland," *Maryland Historical Magazine* 73, no. 3 (1978): 236–45.

4. Kathleen M. Brown, *Good Wives, Nasty Wenches, and Anxious Patriarchs: Gender, Race, and Power in Colonial Virginia* (Chapel Hill: University of North Carolina Press, 1996),

196–98; Jennifer L. Morgan, *Laboring Women: Reproduction and Gender in New World Slavery* (Philadelphia: University of Pennsylvania Press, 2004), 71–73; William Waller Hening, ed., *SALVA* (New York: Thomas Desilver, 1823), 3:86–88.

5. Granville Sharp, *A Representation of the Injustice and Dangerous Tendency of Tolerating Slavery* (London: printed for Benjamin White and Robert Horsfield, 1769), 109; Marvin Harris, *Patterns of Race in the Americas* (New York: Walker, 1964), 56.

6. Benjamin Keen, ed., *The Life of the Admiral Christopher Columbus by His Son Ferdinand* (New Brunswick, N.J.: Rutgers University Press, 1959), 119–20.

7. Douglas T. Peck, "Lucas Vásquez de Ayllón's Doomed Colony of San Miguel de Gualdape," *Georgia Historical Quarterly* 85, no. 2 (2001): 183–98; Richard Hakluyt, ed., *The Principal Navigations, Voyages, Traffiques and Discoveries of the English Nation* (Glasgow, UK: James MacLehose and Sons, 1904), 8:423–38; Andrés Reséndez, *A Land So Strange: The Epic Journey of Cabeza de Vaca* (New York: Basic Books, 2009), 7, 183, 225–26; Kathleen A. Deagan, "Mestizaje in Colonial St. Augustine," *Ethnohistory* 20, no. 1 (1973): 55–65.

8. Helen C. Rountree, *Pocahontas's People: The Powhatan Indians of Virginia through Four Centuries* (Norman: University of Oklahoma Press, 1990), 20–24; Lee Miller, *A Kingdom Strange: The Brief and Tragic History of the Lost Colony of Roanoke* (New York: Basic Books, 2010), 207–19, 223–38.

9. Brown, *Good Wives, Nasty Wenches*, 54; George Chapman, Ben Jonson, and John Marston, *Eastward Ho!*, ed. R. W. Van Fossen (Manchester, UK: Manchester University Press, 1999), 138.

10. Rountree, *Pocahontas's People*, 29–31; Frederic W. Gleach, *Powhatan's World and Colonial Virginia: A Conflict of Cultures* (Lincoln: University of Nebraska Press, 2000), 25–26; Camilla Townsend, *Pocahontas and the Powhatan Dilemma* (New York: Hill and Wang, 2004), 47–50, 154.

11. Marcia Zug, "Lonely Colonist Seeks Wife: The Forgotten History of America's First Mail Order Brides," *Duke Journal of Gender Law and Policy* 20, no. 1 (2012): 89–90; Alfred Cave, *Lethal Encounters: Englishmen and Indians in Colonial Virginia* (Lincoln: University of Nebraska Press, 2013), 75.

12. David D. Smits, "'Abominable Mixture': Toward the Repudiation of Anglo-Indian Intermarriage in Seventeenth-Century Virginia," *Virginia Magazine of History and Biography* 95, no. 2 (1987): 157–92. Rebecca Goetz notes that intimate Anglo-Indigenous relationships occurred before the 1622 Powhatan attack on Jamestown. After the massacre, Virginia colonists largely set themselves apart from Native Americans based on religious grounds. Rebecca Anne Goetz, *The Baptism of Early Virginia: How Christianity Created Race* (Baltimore: Johns Hopkins University Press, 2012), 57–60, 65–67; Townsend, *Pocahontas and the Powhatan Dilemma*, 13–14.

13. Townsend, *Pocahontas and the Powhatan Dilemma*, 153–54; Richard Godbeer, *Sexual Revolution in Early America* (Baltimore: Johns Hopkins University Press, 2002), 161–63; Ra[l]phe Hamor, *A True Discourse of the Present Estate of Virginia, and the Success of the Affaires There till the 18 of June 1614* (London, 1615), 61–68.

14. "Letter from John Rolfe to Sir Thos. Dale," *Virginia Magazine of History and Biography* 22, no. 1 (1914): 150–57; Townsend, *Pocahontas and the Powhatan Dilemma*, 115–17; Brown, *Good Wives, Nasty Wenches*, 63–64.

15. John Smith, *The Generall Historie of Virginia, New-England, and the Summer Iles* (London: I. D. and I. H. for Michael Sparkes, 1624), 123; Allan Kulikoff, *Tobacco and Slaves: The Development of Southern Cultures in the Chesapeake, 1680–1800* (Chapel Hill: University

of North Carolina Press, 1986), 28–29; Christopher Tomlins, *Freedom Bound: Law, Labor, and Civil Identity in Colonizing English America, 1580–1865* (New York: Cambridge University Press, 2010), 37.

16. John Hammond, "Leah and Rachell, or the Two Fruitful Sisters of Virginia and Mary-Land," in Clayton Colman Hall, *Narratives of Early Maryland*, 279–308; Lois Green Carr, Russell R. Menard, and Lorena S. Walsh, *Robert Cole's World: Agriculture and Society in Early Maryland* (Chapel Hill: University of North Carolina Press, 1991), 12–17.

17. "The Ancestors and Descendants of John Rolfe with Notices of Some Connected Families," pt. 1, *Virginia Magazine of History and Biography* 21, no. 2 (1913): 208–11; Townsend, *Pocahontas and the Powhatan Dilemma*, 124–25, 130–31, 143, 153–54, 174–75, 191n12; Goetz, *Baptism of Early Virginia*, 52–55.

18. "Ancestors and Descendants of John Rolfe," pt. 1, 208–11; Jane Carson, "The Will of John Rolfe," *Virginia Magazine of History and Biography* 58, no. 1 (1950): 58–65; Townsend, *Pocahontas and the Powhatan Dilemma*, 174–75.

19. Townsend, *Pocahontas and the Powhatan Dilemma*, 174–75.

20. Records in Bass family Bible recorded under "Booke of John Basse Norfolk County Virga. Ao. Di. 1675," in Albert D. Bell, *Bass Families of the South: A Collection of Historical and Genealogical Source Materials from Public and Private Records* (Rocky Mount, N.C.: Albert D. Bell, 1961), 11–16; Rountree, *Pocahontas's People*, 108–9; Paul Heinegg, *Free African Americans of North Carolina, Virginia, and South Carolina, from the Colonial Period to About 1820*, 5th ed. (Baltimore: Clearfield, 2005), 1:111–12.

21. Goetz, *Baptism of Early Virginia*, 69–71; Samuel Kercheval, *History of the Valley of Virginia*, 3rd ed. (Woodstock, Va.: W. N. Grabill, 1902), xv–xvi; Bruce E. Steiner, "The Catholic Brents of Colonial Virginia: An Instance of Practical Toleration," *Virginia Magazine of History and Biography* 70, no. 4 (1962): 393, 398–99.

22. Kercheval, *History of the Valley of Virginia*, xv–xvi; H. R. McIlwaine, ed., *Journals of the House of Burgesses of Virginia, 1659/60–1693* (Richmond: Virginia State Library, 1914), 14, 16, 69; Steiner, "Catholic Brents of Colonial Virginia," 398–99; Goetz, *Baptism of Early Virginia*, 69–71.

23. Joanne Rappaport, *The Disappearing Mestizo: Configuring Difference in the Colonial New Kingdom of Granada* (Durham, N.C.: Duke University Press, 2014), 38–42, 44–49; Ann Twinam, *Purchasing Whiteness: Pardos, Mulattos, and the Quest for Social Mobility in the Spanish Indies* (Standford, Calif.: Stanford University Press, 2015), 89–90, 100–101; Jean E. Feerick, *Strangers in Blood: Relocating Race in the Renaissance* (Toronto, ON: University of Toronto Press, 2010), 7–9, 28–29.

24. James Horn, *Adapting to a New World: English Society in the Seventeenth-Century Chesapeake* (Chapel Hill: University of North Carolina Press, 1994), 131–33.

25. Engel Sluiter, "New Light on the '20. and Odd Negroes' Arriving in Virginia, August 1619," *William and Mary Quarterly* 54, no. 2 (1997): 395–98; John Thornton, "The African Experience of the '20. and Odd Negroes' Arriving in Virginia in 1619," *William and Mary Quarterly* 55, no. 3 (1998): 421–34; Linda M. Heywood and John K. Thornton, *Central Africans, Atlantic Creoles, and the Foundation of the Americas, 1585–1660* (New York: Cambridge University Press, 2007), 5–8.

26. William Waller Hening, ed., *SALVA* (New York: R. and W. and G. Bartow, 1823), 1:146, 552; Warren M. Billings, ed., *The Old Dominion in the Seventeenth Century: A Documentary History of Virginia, 1606–1689* (Chapel Hill: University of North Carolina Press, 1975), 165–66; Winthrop D. Jordan, *White over Black: American Attitudes toward the Negro, 1550–1812* (Chapel Hill: University of North Carolina Press, 1968), 78–79.

27. Ira Berlin, *Many Thousands Gone: The First Two Centuries of Slavery in North America* (Cambridge, Mass.: Belknap Press of Harvard University Press, 1998), 29, 39–43; Patent Record, fols. 19–20, 37, Land Office, MSA; General Assembly Upper House Proceedings, 1637–58, liber MC, fol. 178, MSA; Patent Record, 1645–57, liber ABH, fol. 65, Land Office, MSA; Bogen, "Mathias de Sousa," 70–72; Clayton Colman Hall, *Narratives of Early Maryland*, 25–45.

28. Richard Jobson, *The Golden Trade or a Dicovery of the River Gambra, and the Golden Trade of the Aethiopians*, ed. Charles G. Kingsley (Teignmouth, UK: E. E. Speight and R. H. Walpole, 1623), 35–36; Clayton Colman Hall, *Narratives of Early Maryland*, 25–45.

29. Patent Record, fols. 19–20, 37, Land Office, MSA; General Assembly Upper House Proceedings, 1637–58, liber MC, fol. 178, MSA; Patent Record, 1645–57, liber ABH, fol. 65, Land Office, MSA; Bogen, "Mathias de Sousa," 78–80; William E. Nelson, *The Common Law in Colonial America*, vol. 1, *The Chesapeake and New England, 1607–1660* (New York: Oxford University Press, 2008), 46. The first Maryland law for servitude in 1639 limited servants over eighteen years old to four years of service. Browne, *AOM*, 1:41, 80. Another Mulatto man, possibly named Francisco, may have entered the Chesapeake sometime between 1634 and 1635, but aside from a small notation, there is no extant information about him. Browne, *AOM*, 3:258; Bogen, "Mathias de Sousa," 71–72.

30. Jordan, *White over Black*, 61; Simon P. Newman, *A New World of Labor: The Development of Plantation Slavery in the British Atlantic* (Philadelphia: University of Pennsylvania Press, 2013), 57–59, 91–92.

31. Patent Record, fols. 19–20, 37, Land Office, MSA; Northumberland County Record Books, 1652–58, fols. 66–67, LVA; Richard S. Dunn, *Sugar and Slaves: The Rise of the Planter Class in the English West Indies, 1624–1713* (Chapel Hill: University of North Carolina Press, 1972), 252–56; J. H. Lefroy, *Memorials of the Discovery and Early Settlement of the Bermudas or Somers Islands* (London: Longmans, Green, 1879), 2:52, 197; Virginia Bernhard, *Slaves and Slaveholders in Bermuda, 1616–1782* (Columbia: University of Missouri Press, 1999), 51–55; Goetz, *Baptism of Early Virginia*, 73–74; James C. Brandow, ed., *Genealogies of Barbados Families: From Caribbeana and the Journal of the Barbados Museum and Historical Society* (Baltimore: Clearfield, 1997), 381.

32. Dunn, *Sugar and Slaves*, 252–55; Edmund S. Morgan, *American Slavery, American Freedom*, 327–28; T. H. Breen and Stephen Innes, *"Myne Owne Ground": Race and Freedom on Virginia's Eastern Shore, 1640–1676* (New York: Oxford University Press, 1980), 5–6.

33. Berlin, *Many Thousands Gone*, 95–97, 109–10; Dunn, *Sugar and Slaves*, 87, 155, 254–55, 312; Hilary McD. Beckles, *Natural Rebels: A Social History of Enslaved Black Women in Barbados* (New Brunswick, N.J.: Rutgers University Press, 1989), 134; John J. McCusker and Russell R. Menard, *The Economy of British America, 1607–1789* (Chapel Hill: University of North Carolina Press, 1991), 153; Tomlins, *Freedom Bound*, 37, 41.

34. Dunn, *Sugar and Slaves*, 87, 155, 312; Susan B. Carter, Scott Sigmund Gartner, Michael R. Haines, Alan L. Olmstead, Richard Sutch, and Galvan Wright, eds., *Historical Statistics of the United States*, "Colonial Statistics," tables Eg13–14, Eg33–34, Eg52–53, Eg60–63.

35. George M. Fredrickson, "Toward a Social Interpretation of the Development of American Racism," in *Key Issues in the Afro-American Experience*, ed. Nathan I. Huggins, Martin Kilson, Daniel M. Fox, and John Morton Blum (New York: Harcourt Brace Jovanovich, 1971), 240–54; Michael Omi and Howard Winant, *Racial Formation in the United States*, 3rd ed. (New York: Routledge, 2015), 112–15.

36. Northumberland County Record Books, 1652–58, fols. 66–67, LVA; Northumberland County Order Book, 1652–65, fol. 40, LVA; Billings, *Old Dominion*, 165–69; Warren M. Billings, "The Cases of Fernando and Elizabeth Key: A Note on the Status of Blacks in Seventeenth-Century Virginia," *William and Mary Quarterly* 30, no. 3 (1973): 467–74; Taunya Lovell Banks, "Dangerous Woman: Elizabeth Key's Freedom Suit—Subjecthood and Racialized Identity in Seventeenth Century Colonial Virginia," *Akron Law Review* 41, no. 3 (2008): 799–837.

37. Kulikoff, *Tobacco and Slaves*, 169–73; Tomlins, *Freedom Bound*, 241–43, 275–76; "Mottrom—Wright—Spencer—Ariss—Buckner," *William and Mary Quarterly* 17, no. 1 (1908): 53–54; Northumberland County Order Book, 1652–65, fol. 40, LVA; Northumberland County Record Books, 1652–58, fols. 66–67, LVA; Billings, *Old Dominion*, 165–69; "Bernard Family," *William and Mary Quarterly* 5, no. 3 (1897): 186–87; Lyon Gardiner Tyler, ed., *Encyclopedia of Virginia Biography* (New York, 1915), 1:112; Banks, "Dangerous Woman," 820–23.

38. Northumberland County Record Books, 1652–58, fol. 85, LVA; Billings, *Old Dominion*, 165–69; Banks, "Dangerous Woman," 809–12, 824–30.

39. William Greensted's surname and that of his family members is spelled variously throughout colonial documentation. Northumberland County Record Books, 1652–58, fol. 85; 1652–65, fols. 46, 49; and 1658–66, fol. 28, all in LVA; Billings, *Old Dominion*, 165–69.

40. Northumberland County Order Book, 1652–65, fol. 49, LVA; Billings, *Old Dominion*, 165–69. On the transition of the meaning of the word "wench" to denote exclusively African women, see Brown, *Good Wives, Nasty Wenches*, 7–9, 368–70.

41. Winthrop Jordan writes that the English had "an ethnocentric tendency to find blackness repulsive" but admits, "Perhaps it would be more accurate to say that settlers in Virginia (and Maryland after settlement in 1634) made their decisions concerning Negroes while relatively virginal, relatively free from external influences and from firm preconceptions." Jordan, *White over Black*, 9, 72; Anthony S. Parent Jr., *Foul Means: The Formation of a Slave Society in Virginia, 1660–1740* (Chapel Hill: University of North Carolina Press, 2003), 118–19; Edward B. Rugemer, "The Development of Mastery and Race in the Comprehensive Slave Codes of the Greater Caribbean during the Seventeenth Century," *William and Mary Quarterly* 70, no. 3 (2013): 429–58; Ariela Gross, "Beyond Black and White: Cultural Approaches to Race and Slavery," *Columbia Law Review* 101, no. 3 (2001): 643–45.

42. Hening, *SALVA*, 2:170; Tomlins, *Freedom Bound*, 455–57; Thomas D. Morris, *Southern Slavery and the Law, 1619–1860* (Chapel Hill: University of North Carolina Press, 1996), 43–49; Jennifer L. Morgan, *Laboring Women*, 43–49. Warren Billings suggests that legislators combed through English common law and, after finding nothing that applied to Mulattoes, they settled on the concept of *partus sequitur ventrem* (the offspring follows the womb) found in civil law. Billings, "Cases of Fernando and Elizabeth Key," 473.

43. Browne, *AOM*, 1:526–27, 533–34; Whittington, "Origin and Nature," 238–39; Martha Hodes, *White Women, Black Men: Illicit Sex in the Nineteenth-Century South* (New Haven, Conn.: Yale University Press, 1997), 28–31.

44. Browne, *AOM*, 1:533–34; Hening, *SALVA*, 2:170.

45. Browne, *AOM*, 1:533–34; Edmund S. Morgan, *American Slavery, American Freedom*, 336; Brown, *Good Wives, Nasty Wenches*, 82–84, 410–11n43.

46. In 1644, Antigua had the earliest law "against Carnall Coppulations between Christian and Heathen," implying that Europeans were Christian while African and

Indigenous peoples were heathen. Dunn, *Sugar and Slaves*, 228, 252–56; Goetz, *Baptism of Early Virginia*, 73–82; David Barry Gaspar, *Bondmen and Rebels: A Study of Master-Slave Relations in Antigua*, 2nd ed. (Durham, N.C.: Duke University Press, 1993), 167; Lefroy, *Memorials of the Discovery*, 2:190–91; Bernhard, *Slaves and Slaveholders in Bermuda*, 91–93; York County Deeds, Orders, Wills 6, 1677–84, 498, LVA.

47. Godbeer, *Sexual Revolution*, 163, 193–94, 202–3.

48. Browne, *AOM*, 1:526–27, 533–34.

49. Browne, 1:526–27, 533–34; Hening, *SALVA*, 2:170, 3:86–88; Bernhard, *Slaves and Slaveholders in Bermuda*, 50–56, 92.

50. "The Bland Manuscript," in U.S. Library of Congress, *The Thomas Jefferson Papers*, ser. 8, *Virginia Records, 1606–1737*, vol. 6, *Charters of the Virginia Company of London, Laws, Abstracts of Rolls in the Offices of State, 1606–92*, 232. Many scholars have incorrectly cited the years regarding Manuel's bondage by citing "The Randolph Manuscript: Virginia Seventeenth Century Records," pt. 2, *Virginia Magazine of History and Biography* 17, no. 3 (July 1909): 232; and Helen Tunnicliff Catterall, ed., *Judicial Cases concerning American Slavery and the Negro*, vol. 1, *Cases from the Courts of England, Virginia, West Virginia, and Kentucky* (Washington, D.C.: Carnegie Institution of Washington, 1926), 58–59. Catterall's publication is a transcribed copy of the Randolph Manuscript and incorrectly places Manuel's original freedom suit at 1644, while the Bland Manuscript correctly shows that his case for freedom was presented to the court in 1664. Therefore, Manuel served only one more year as a servant, not twenty-one additional years, as others have mistakenly suggested. The Randolph Manuscript is an eighteenth-century copy of the Bland, and therefore the Bland Manuscript is closer to the original, more accurate source. "The Randolph Manuscript: Virginia Seventeenth Century Records," pt. 1, *Virginia Magazine of History and Biography* 15, no. 4 (April 1908): 390; Hening, *SALVA*, 2:113–14; Parent, *Foul Means*, 112–13; Goetz, *Baptism of Early Virginia*, 86–90, 102–5.

51. "Bland Manuscript," 232; Goetz, *Baptism of Early Virginia*, 86–90, 102–5; Hening, *SALVA*, 2:260.

52. Nelson, *Common Law in Colonial America*, 1:4; William M. Wiecek, "The Statutory Law of Slavery and Race in the Thirteen Mainland Colonies of British America," *William and Mary Quarterly* 34, no. 2 (1977): 258–80.

53. Edmund S. Morgan, *American Slavery, American Freedom*, 327–37, 344–46; Hening, *SALVA*, 2:296, 299–300, 490–91; William Hand Browne, ed., *AOM*, vol. 5, *Proceedings of the Council of Maryland, 1667–1687/8* (Baltimore: Maryland Historical Society, 1887), 267–68; William Hand Browne, ed., *AOM*, vol. 7, *PAGAM, October 1678–November 1683* (Baltimore: Maryland Historical Society, 1889), 76.

54. Jordan, *White over Black*, 165–67; Feerick, *Strangers in Blood*, 111–12, 158–60, 163.

55. "Extracts from the County Records [Middlesex]," *Virginia Magazine of History and Biography* 8, no. 2 (1900), 187.

56. "Extracts from the County Records," 187; Berlin, *Many Thousands Gone*, 26–39, 39–43.

57. "Extracts from the County Records," 187.

58. Thomas Meeres, 67–70, and Mr. Henry and Frances Morgan, 592–95, both in liber/vol. 1, 1674–1703; Edward Roe, 177–78; John Anderson, 252; and Neel Clarke, 276–80, all in liber/vol. 2, 1676; Robert Dun, 48–50, vol. 4, 1677–78; Thomas Stagg, 13–17, and Baker Brooke, 480–96, both in vol. 6, 1679; Benjamin Rozer, 98–101, 107, and William Calvert, 206–16, both in vol. 7c, 1682; James Downs, 193–97, and Robert Ridgely, 295–300, both in

vol. 8, 1683–86; John White, 185–87; Mary Truman, 205–6; John Kirke, 338–40, 382; and Henry Staples, 513–15, all in vol. 9, 1686–88; and John Baker, 111–13, vol. 10, 1688–92, all in Maryland Prerogative Court (Inventories and Accounts), ser. 1674–1718, MSA. Accomack County Deeds, Wills, Etc., 1682–97, 91a, 93a–95, 96a, LVA; Joseph Douglas Deal, *Race and Class in Colonial Virginia: Indians, Englishmen, and Africans on the Eastern Shore during the Seventeenth Century* (New York: Garland, 1993), 103–4.

59. Lancaster County Wills, 1674–89, 91, LVA.

60. Provincial Court Judgements, vol. D.D., no. 17, and vol. 61, pt. 1, 1770–71, 233–44, MSA; Browne, *AOM*, 7:203–5; Hodes, *White Women, Black Men*, 19–38.

61. Browne, *AOM*, 7:203–5; Charles County Inventories, 1677–1717, 258–61, MSA.

62. Atwood S. Barwick, ed., *AOM*, vol. 87, *Somerset County Court, Judicial Record, 1671–1675*, pt. 1 (Lakeville, Conn.: MSA, 1999), 155; Hening, *SALVA*, 1:252–53, 438–39, 441–42.

63. Barwick, *AOM*, 87:155.

64. Accomack County Orders, 1703–9, 91a, LVA; Deal, *Race and Class*, 357–59.

65. Accomack County Orders, 1703–9, 91a, LVA; Deal, *Race and Class*, 357–59.

66. Northampton County Deeds, Wills, Etc. 4, 1654–55, folders 54, 60–61, LVA; Deal, *Race and Class*, 357–59; Heinegg, *Free African Americans of North Carolina*, 2:786–87; Peter H. Wood, *Strange New Land: African in Colonial America* (New York: Oxford University Press, 2003), 23–24.

67. Accomack County Orders, 1690–97, 6, 124, 134, 135, 142a, 221, 243, LVA; Deal, *Race and Class*, 359–60.

68. Accomack County Orders, 1690–97, 6, 124, 134, 135, 142a, 221, LVA; Deal, *Race and Class*, 359–62; Heinegg, *Free African Americans of North Carolina*, 2:786–87.

69. Courts freed William Catillah in 1695 at twenty-four. York County Deeds, Orders, Wills 7, 1684–87, 61, LVA; York County Deeds, Orders, Wills 10, 1694–97, 137, 153, LVA. In 1644, New England officials also assigned a boy named Jacob to a thirty-year indenture. Jacob's mother was a Pequot captive and his father an English servant. Margaret Ellen Newell, *Brethren by Nature: New England Indians, Colonists, and the Origins of American Slavery* (Ithaca, N.Y.: Cornell University Press, 2015), 127.

70. Hening, *SALVA*, 3:250–52.

71. Some speculate that Thomas Rolfe married Englishwoman Jane Poythress, though the evidence is unsubtantiated. William B. Hall, "The Poythress Family: A Study of Francis, Francis, Francis, and Francis," *William and Mary Quarterly* 14, no. 1 (1934), 78–79; "Ancestors and Descendants of John Rolfe," pt. 1, 208–11; "The Ancestors and Descendants of John Rolfe with Notices of Some Connected Families," pts. 2 and 3, *Virginia Magazine of History and Biography* 22, no. 1 (1914): 103–7; 22, no. 2 (1914): 215–17; "Nansemond Indian Ancestry of Some Bass Families," in Bell, *Bass Families of the South*, 11–16.

72. Allyson Hobbs, *A Chosen Exile: A History of Racial Passing in American Life* (Cambridge, Mass.: Harvard University Press, 2014), 28–45.

73. Northumberland County Record Books, 1658–66, fols. 44, 62, and 1666–72, fol. 20; and Northumberland County Order Books, 1666–78, fols. 107, 109, and 1678–98, fols. 37, 337, all in LVA. Taunya Lovell Banks notes that a John Grinstead and his family were all listed as "white" in Northumberland County's 1830 U.S. census. If they were descendants of Elizabeth Key and William Greensted, they had attained this racial status much earlier, in the seventeenth century. Banks, "Dangerous Woman," 836–37.

74. Hening, *SALVA*, 3:86–88, 250–52; William Hand Browne, ed., *AOM*, vol. 13, *PAGAM, April 1684–June 1692* (Baltimore: Maryland Historical Society, 1894), 546–49.

## CHAPTER 2

1. Norfolk County Deed Book 5, 1686–95, pt. 2 (Orders), 190, LVA. Later records identify Mary Sparrow and her children as "Molato." Norfolk County Deed Book 9, 1710–17, 69, 77, LVA.

2. Norfolk County Deed Book 5, 1686–95, pt. 2 (Orders), 190, LVA.

3. William Waller Hening, ed., *SALVA* (New York: Thomas Desilver, 1823), 3:86–88.

4. Hening, 3:86–88. Colonial life expectancy and mortality rates are not easy to determine, though on average, servants and slaves probably lived shorter lives than free people. Daniel Blake Smith, "Mortality and Family in the Colonial Chesapeake," *Journal of Interdisciplinary History* 8, no. 3 (1978): 403–18; James M. Gallman, "Mortality among White Males, Colonial North Carolina," *Social Science History* 4, no. 3 (1980): 295–316.

5. I am indebted to historian Kathleen Brown's research in this chapter and through much of my work. She writes, "Fornication between white women and black men threatened not only to compromise the utility of female servants ... but to blur racial distinctions and increase the free black population." Kathleen M. Brown, *Good Wives, Nasty Wenches, and Anxious Patriarchs: Gender, Race, and Power in Colonial Virginia* (Chapel Hill: University of North Carolina Press, 1996), 187, 251–52.

6. Allan Kulikoff, *Tobacco and Slaves: The Development of Southern Cultures in the Chesapeake, 1680–1800* (Chapel Hill: University of North Carolina Press, 1986), 12–13; Debra Meyers and Melanie Perreault, eds., *Colonial Chesapeake: New Perspectives* (Lanham, Md.: Lexington Books, 2006), 81–102.

7. Kulikoff, *Tobacco and Slaves*, 8–10; Alejandro Portes, "Social Capital: Its Origins and Applications in Modern Sociology," *Annual Review of Sociology* 24 (1998): 1–24; Kathleen M. Brown, *Good Wives, Nasty Wenches*, 247–52.

8. Kulikoff, *Tobacco and Slaves*, 28–44; Frederic W. Gleach, *Powhatan's World and Colonial Virginia: A Conflict of Cultures* (Lincoln: University of Nebraska Press, 2000), 22–26; Christopher Tomlins, *Freedom Bound: Law, Labor, and Civil Identity in Colonizing English America, 1580–1865* (New York: Cambridge University Press, 2010), 57–61.

9. James Horn, *Adapting to a New World: English Society in the Seventeenth-Century Chesapeake* (Chapel Hill: University of North Carolina Press, 1994), 149–60; Lois Green Carr, Russell R. Menard, and Lorena S. Walsh, *Robert Cole's World: Agriculture and Society in Early Maryland* (Chapel Hill: University of North Carolina Press, 1991), 26–31; Kulikoff, *Tobacco and Slaves*, 35–39.

10. Horn, *Adapting to a New World*, 147–48; Kulikoff, *Tobacco and Slaves*, 12–13.

11. William Hand Browne, ed., *AOM*, vol. 1, *PAGAM, January 1637/8–September 1664* (Baltimore: Maryland Historical Society, 1883), 533–34; William Hand Browne, ed., *AOM*, vol. 7, *PAGAM, October 1678–November 1683* (Baltimore: Maryland Historical Society, 1889), 203–5; Kathleen M. Brown, *Good Wives, Nasty Wenches*, 188–201; Daniel Livesay, *Children of Uncertain Fortune: Mixed-Race Jamaicans in Britain and the Atlantic Family, 1733–1833* (Chapel Hill: University of North Carolina Press, 2018), 52–58. Georgia did annul "intermarriages between the white People and the Negroes or Blacks" in 1750, though it is not clear how widely this law was enforced (see chapter 5). Allen D. Candler, ed., *CRSGA* (Atlanta: Franklin, 1904), 1:59–60.

12. Kermit Hall and Pater Karsten, *The Magic Mirror: Law in American History* (New York: Oxford University Press, 1989), 37–39.

13. Warren M. Billings, "The Law of Servants and Slaves in Seventeenth-Century Virginia," *Virginia Magazine of History and Biography* 99, no. 1 (1991): 45–62; Kathleen M.

Brown, *Good Wives, Nasty Wenches*, 196–201; Anthony S. Parent Jr., *Foul Means: The Formation of a Slave Society in Virginia, 1660–1740* (Chapel Hill: University of North Carolina Press, 2003), 105–7. W. E. B. Du Bois says that "white" laborers "were compensated in part by a sort of public and physcological wage." W. E. B. Du Bois, *Black Reconstruction in America* (1935; repr., Cleveland, Ohio: Meridian, 1964), 700–701.

14. Westmoreland County Orders, 1690–98, 40–41, LVA.

15. Westmoreland County Orders, 1690–98, 40–41, LVA; William Waller Hening, ed., *SALVA* (New York: R. and W. and G. Bartow, 1823), 1:441–43; Hening, *SALVA*, 3:86–88. In late 1703, the Westmoreland County court "ordered that two Mulatto serv[an]ts" be transferred to Patrick Spence Jr., who inherited them from his father by the same name. While the children are not named, they were likely two of the Tate children. Westmoreland County Orders, 1698–1705, 210a, LVA.

16. Hening, *SALVA*, 3:86–88; Kathleen M. Brown, *Good Wives, Nasty Wenches*, 197–207, 210. A similar anti-intermixture law in Bermuda also appeared difficult to enforce. J. H. Lefroy, *Memorials of the Discovery and Early Settlement of the Bermudas or Somers Islands* (London: Longmans, Green, 1879), 2:190.

17. William Hand Browne, ed., *AOM*, vol. 13, *PAGAM, April 1684–June 1692* (Baltimore: Maryland Historical Society, 1894), 546–49.

18. Hening, *SALVA*, 3:86–88; Browne, *AOM*, 13:546–49; Rebecca Anne Goetz, "Rethinking the 'Unthinking Decision': Old Questions and New Problems in the History of Slavery and Race in the Colonial South," *Journal of Southern History* 75, no. 3 (2009): 599–613.

19. Hening, *SALVA*, 3:86–88; Browne, *AOM*, 13:546–49.

20. Lancaster County Order Book 5, 1702–13, 127, LVA. The law also stipulated that a woman having an illegitimate child by "any negro or mulatto" man had to pay the fifteen pounds of silver within one month of the child's birth. Hening, *SALVA*, 3:86–88. The month following Catherine McCollins's case in September 1705, the Virginia General Assembly drew up legislation that went even further to punish mixed-heritage children and their families. Rebecca Anne Goetz, *The Baptism of Early Virginia: How Christianity Created Race* (Baltimore: Johns Hopkins University Press, 2012), 82–85.

21. Hening, *SALVA*, 3:86–88; Browne, *AOM*, 1:533–34, 7:203–5, 13:546–48. I have not located any cases of Mulattoes in seventeenth-century Maryland who were bound to thirty-year indentures according to the 1664 act, which the assembly overturned in 1681. The first thirty-one-year-term indentures in Maryland appear in the early eighteenth century.

22. Charles County Court and Land Records, 1690–92, 337, and 1693–94, 9, both in MSA.

23. Browne, *AOM*, 13:165, 306–7, 351, 566–67; Harry Wright Newman, *Charles County Gentry: A Genealogical History of Six Emigrants—Thomas Dent, John Dent, Richard Edelen, John Hanson, George Newman, Humphrey Warren* (Baltimore: Genealogical Publishing, 1971), 9–12.

24. Browne, *AOM*, 1:533–34, 7:203–5, 13:304–8, 546–48.

25. Browne, 7:203–5, 13:304–8.

26. This is an early application of "mungrell" to human couplings, though the term "mongrell" appears in an English-Latin dictionary under "Hybrida" in 1538 ("Hybrides" is also defined as "halfe wylde"). "Mongril" appears again when *mulato* makes its first appearance in an English dictionary in 1656: "*Mulato* (Span.) the son of a woman Blackmore, and a man of another Nation, or *é contra*; one that is of a mongril complexion."

English dictionaries consistently associated hybridity ("hybrida") with "mongrel" from the sixteenth through eighteenth centuries. Thomas Eliot, *The Dictionary of Syr Thomas Eliot Knyght* (London, 1538); Thomas Blount, *Glossographia Anglicana Nova: Or, A Dictionary* (London: Tho. Newcomb, 1656); Edward Phillips, *The New World of English Words: Or, A General Dictionary* (London: E. Tyler, 1658); Edward Phillips, *The New World of English Words: Or, Universal English Dictionary*, ed. J. K. Philobibl, 7th ed. (London: printed for J. Phillips at the King's-Arms in S. Paul's-Church-Yard, 1720). The Maryland General Assembly minutes regarding William Dent and Daniel Clark's recommendations are worth noting in full: "As to the word Slavery they [William Dent and Daniel Clark] do not use it in the Act, but Oblige all white Women that shall Marry to Negroe Men to be Servants during the Life of the Man whom they Marry although it may hap[pi]ly Amount to Slavery in Effect, yet is it not the same in Terminis, and may possibly prove otherwise, so that the Law of England is not Repugned." Browne, *AOM*, 13:306-7.

27. Browne, *AOM*, 13:306-7; Hening, *SALVA*, 3:86-88.

28. When Maryland's assemblymen legally discouraged "white Women" from partnering with "Negroe Men" they engineered one of the main building blocks for "white" supremacist ideology. Browne, *AOM*, 13:304-7, 546-49.

29. Browne, 13:305-7, 546-49.

30. The final 1692 Maryland statute declared, "Any freeborn English or white woman that shall ... intermarry with or permit herself to be begotten with child by any Negro or other Slave" would be subject to an extra seven years of servitude. Any "free Negro" husband would "forfeit his freedome and become a Servant ... during his natural life." Browne, 13:308, 547; William Waller Hening, ed., *SALVA* (Richmond: Samuel Pleasants Jr., 1810), 2:170; Hening, *SALVA*, 3:86-88; Philip J. Schwartz, *Slave Laws in Virginia* (Athens: University of Georgia Press, 1996), 1-12.

31. Hening, *SALVA*, 3:86-88; Browne, *AOM*, 13:546-49; Abbott Emerson Smith, *Colonists in Bondage: White Servitude and Convict Labor in America, 1607-1776* (Chapel Hill: University of North Carolina Press, 1947), 232.

32. Hall and Karsten, *Magic Mirror*, 12-14, 24-26.

33. Charles County Court and Land Records, 1690-92, 337, and 1693-94, 9, both in MSA.

34. Charles County Court and Land Records, 1693-94, 9, 52-53, MSA.

35. Charles County Court and Land Records, 1693-94, 242; and Charles County Court Record, 1696-98, 373, and 1699-1701, 176, all in MSA.

36. Charles County Court Record, 1699-1701, 176, and 1701-04, 327, both in MSA.

37. The grand jury called upon a witness named Thomas Stone, presumably to testify against Mary Fountain, but he did not appear. A Captain Hoskins "and severall other Gent[le]men" testified in court "that he [Stone] was absent on lawfull" reasons, which the court found to be a reasonable excuse. It is not clear what effect this may have had on the court carrying out Mary's punishment. Charles County Court and Land Records, 1693-94, 242, and 1696-98, 373; and Charles County Court Record, 1699-1701, 176, and 1701-4, 327, all in MSA.

38. Lancaster County Order Book 4, 1696-1702, 172, LVA; Kathleen M. Brown, *Good Wives, Nasty Wenches*, 201.

39. Lancaster County Order Book 4, 1696-1702, 172, LVA; Hening, *SALVA*, 3:86-88.

40. Lancaster County Order Book 5, 1702-13, 32, LVA; Daniel Blake Smith, "Mortality and Family," 411-14.

41. Mulatto bastardy statistics come from extant documents found in Paul Heinegg's

genealogical research on free African Americans. These are not exhaustive, as many county and provincial papers succumbed to the climate, negligence, and the burning of courthouse repositories during the U.S. Revolution and Civil War. Paul Heinegg, *Free African Americans of North Carolina, Virginia, and South Carolina, from the Colonial Period to About 1820*, 5th ed., 2 vols. (Baltimore: Clearfield, 2005); Paul Heinegg, *Free African Americans of Maryland and Delaware: From the Colonial Period to 1810* (Baltimore: Clearfield, 2000); Research Notes no. 30, Lost Records Localities: Counties and Cities with Missing Records, LVA.

42. Lois Green Carr, Philip D. Morgan, and Jean Burrell Russo, eds., *Colonial Chesapeake Society* (Chapel Hill: University of North Carolina Press, 1988), 171–73; Kathleen M. Brown, *Good Wives, Nasty Wenches*, 194–205.

43. Elizabeth City Council Orders, 1692–99, 19, 38, 69, 70, 72, 78, LVA.

44. Elizabeth City Council Orders, 1692–99, 78, LVA.

45. Later documents identify Ann Wall's children as John and Thomas Swann. Elizabeth City Council Orders, 1692–99, 78, LVA; Norfolk County Deed Book (Orders), 1710–17, 46, 48, 56, 62, 71, 74, LVA.

46. Prince George's County Court Record, 1699–1705, 321a, MSA.

47. Prince George's County Court Record, 1699–1705, 321a, MSA.

48. H. R. McIlwaine, ed., *Journals of the House of Burgesses of Virginia, 1695–1696, 1696–1697, 1698, 1699, 1700–1702* (Richmond: Library of Virginia, 1913), 148; H. R. McIlwaine, ed., *Journals of the House of Burgesses of Virginia, 1702/3–1705, 1705–1706, 1710–1712* (Richmond: Virginia State Library, 1912), 56.

49. Philip Alexander Bruce, *Economic History of Virginia in the Seventeenth Century: An Inquiry into the Material Condition of the People, Based upon Original and Contemporaneous Records* (New York: Macmillan, 1896), 2:111–12; Lorena S. Walsh, *From Calabar to Carter's Grove: The History of a Virginian Slave Community* (Charlottesville: University Press of Virginia, 1997), 34; McIlwaine, *Burgesses of Virginia, 1702/3*, 56; Livesay, *Children of Uncertain Fortune*, 51; Brooke N. Newman, *A Dark Inheritance: Blood, Race, and Sex in Colonial Jamaica* (New Haven, Conn.: Yale University Press, 2018), 6–7.

50. H. R. McIlwaine, ed., *Legislative Journals of the Council of Colonial Virginia* (Richmond: Virginia State Library, 1918), 1:262; Bruce, *Economic History of Virginia*, 2:111–13; Lorena Walsh, "Community Networks in the Early Chesapeake," in Carr, Morgan, and Russo, *Colonial Chesapeake Society*, 200–241.

51. Hening, *SALVA*, 3:250–52.

52. Hening, 3:250–52; Thomas D. Morris, *Southern Slavery and the Law, 1619–1860* (Chapel Hill: University of North Carolina Press, 1996), 22–23.

53. Keneisha M. Green, "Who's Who: Exploring the Discrepancy between the Methods of Defining African Americans and Native Americans," *American Indian Law Review* 31, no. 1 (2006/2007): 93–110. Sharon Block also notes the idea of "white"-washing the color of Africans in the eighteenth century. Sharon Block, *Colonial Complexions: Race and Bodies in Eighteenth-Century America* (Philadelphia: University of Pennsylvania Press, 2018), 30–31.

54. Hening, *SALVA*, 3:250–52; McIlwaine, *Burgesses of Virginia, 1702/3*, 56.

55. Hening, *SALVA*, 3:86–88, 250–52, 452–54; Edward B. Rugemer, "The Development of Mastery and Race in the Comprehensive Slave Codes of the Greater Caribbean during the Seventeenth Century," *William and Mary Quarterly* 70, no. 3 (2013): 429–58.

56. McIlwaine, *Burgesses of Virginia, 1702/3*, 56; Hening, *SALVA*, 3:86–88, 453–54.

57. York County Deeds, Orders, Wills 9, 1691–94, 318, 352, LVA.

58. Thomas F. Brown and Leah C. Sims, "'To Swear Him Free': Ethnic Memory as Social Capital in Eighteenth-Century Freedom Petitions," in Meyers and Perreault, *Colonial Chesapeake*, 81–102; York County Deeds, Orders, Wills 9, 1691–94, 318, 352, LVA.

59. Charles County Court, vol. E, no. 2, 1711–15, 307, MSA.

60. Browne, *AOM*, 1:533–34.

61. Provincial Court Judgements, vol. V.D., no. 1, 1713–16, 150–52, MSA.

62. Richmond County Order Book 2, 1694–99, 263–64, LVA.

63. Hall and Karsten, *Magic Mirror*, 22–23.

64. Westmoreland County Orders, 1698–1705, 169a, 172a, LVA.

65. Tomlins, *Freedom Bound*, 78–82. See William Catillah's case in chapter 1. York County Deeds, Orders, Wills 7, 1684–87, 61, LVA; York County Deeds, Orders, Wills 10, 1694–97, 137, 152–53, LVA.

66. Richmond County Order Book 2, 1694–99, 263–64; and Westmoreland County Orders, 1698–1705, 169a, 172a, and 1705–21, 116, 145a, 217, all in LVA.

67. Prince George's County Court Records, 1710–15, 80, 124, 126, 611, MSA.

68. Elizabeth Taylor's older daughter was Mary Kelly, alias Taylor. In 1711, Mary was bound to William Coxey until the age of sixteen, which suggests she may have been of full European ancestry. Prince George's County Court Records, 1710–15, 80, 124, 126, 611, and 1715–20, 181, 185, both in MSA.

69. Prince George's County Court Records, 1710–15, 80, 124, 126, 611, MSA.

70. Kirsten Fischer, *Suspect Relations: Sex, Race, and Resistance in Colonial North Carolina* (Ithaca, N.Y.: Cornell University Press, 2002), 122–26; Daniel Blake Smith, "Mortality and Family"; Gallman, "Mortality among White Males," 295–316.

71. Kathleen M. Brown, *Good Wives, Nasty Wenches*, 319–24; Parent, *Foul Means*, 197–99.

72. Charles County Court Record, vol. A, no. 2, 1701–4, 251, MSA.

73. Morris, *Southern Slavery and the Law*, 37–43.

74. York County Deeds, Orders, Wills 6, 1677–84, 498, LVA; York County Deeds, Orders, Wills 12, 1702–6, 67, LVA; Kathleen M. Brown, *Good Wives, Nasty Wenches*, 131, 205.

75. York County Deeds, Orders, Wills 12, 1702–6, 67, 180–81, 188, LVA; Fischer, *Suspect Relations*, 122–29.

76. York County Deeds, Orders, Wills 12, 1702–6, 67, 180–81, 188, LVA.

77. York County Deeds, Orders, Wills 12, 1702–6, 67, 180–81, 188, LVA.

78. York County Deeds, Orders, Wills 12, 1702–6, 67, 180–81, 188, LVA.

79. William Catillah and other "Molotto" servants went to the same York County court that Mary Banks indentured her daughters under, so the magistrates had experience with these cases. York County Deeds, Orders, Wills 9, 1691–94, LVA. The Banks sisters were split by indentures that assigned Hannah and Elizabeth Banks to Peter and Martin Goodwin, respectively, though the family may have still lived together. York County Deeds, Orders, Wills 12, 1702–6, 67, 180–81, 188, LVA; Hening, *SALVA*, 3:86–88; Lancaster County Order Book 5, 1702–13, 127, LVA.

80. Tomlins, *Freedom Bound*, 35–42.

CHAPTER 3

1. Mehitable and James Gilbertson's infant daughter appears as Anne in the historical records, though her father calls her by the nickname Nansy in his will. Secretary of State, Misc. Records, 1719–21, 57–59, SCDAH; Record of Wills, 1671–1724, 1:49–50, SCDAH; Anne King Gregorie, ed., *Records of the Court of Chancery of South Carolina, 1671–1779*

(Washington, D.C.: American Historical Association, 1950), 278–80; E. Horace Fitchett, "The Traditions of the Free Negro in Charleston, South Carolina," *Journal of Negro History* 25, no. 2 (1940): 139–40.

2. Secretary of State, Misc. Records, 1719–21, 57–59, SCDAH; Record of Wills, 1671–1724, 1:49–50, SCDAH; Peter H. Wood, *Black Majority: Negroes in Colonial South Carolina from 1670 through the Stono Rebellion* (New York: W. W. Norton, 1975), 98–101.

3. Secretary of State, Misc. Records, 1719–21, 57–59, SCDAH; Record of Wills, 1671–1724, 1:49–50, SCDAH; Gregorie, *Records of the Court*, 278–80.

4. Secretary of State, Misc. Records, 1719–21, 57–59, SCDAH; Record of Wills, 1671–1724, 1:49–50, SCDAH; Gregorie, *Records of the Court*, 278–80.

5. Marvin Harris, *Patterns of Race in the Americas* (New York: Walker, 1964), 56.

6. Jack D. Forbes, *Africans and Native Americans: The Language of Race and the Evolution of Red-Black Peoples* (Urbana-Champaign: University of Illinois Press, 1993), 88, 221–28.

7. Margaret Ellen Newell, *Brethren by Nature: New England Indians, Colonists, and the Origins of American Slavery* (Ithaca, N.Y.: Cornell University Press, 2015), 222, 227, 232–35.

8. Wood, *Black Majority*, 142–45; Noeleen McIlvenna, *A Very Mutinous People: The Struggle for North Carolina, 1660–1713* (Chapel Hill: University of North Carolina Press, 2009), 15–24, 127.

9. Hypodescent ideology operated differently among various European colonial powers. Harris, *Patterns of Race*, 56.

10. Richard Godbeer, *Sexual Revolution in Early America* (Baltimore: Johns Hopkins University Press, 2002), 154–89; Daniel R. Mandell, "The Sage of Sarah Muckamugg: Indian and African American Intermarriage in Colonial New England," in *Sex, Love, Race: Crossing Boundaries in North American History*, ed. Martha Hodes (New York: New York University Press, 1999), 72–90.

11. Christopher Tomlins, *Freedom Bound: Law, Labor, and Civil Identity in Colonizing English America, 1580–1865* (New York: Cambridge University Press, 2010), 54–56; Wendy Warren, *New England Bound: Slavery and Colonization in Early America* (New York: Liveright, 2016), 21–24, 50.

12. Warren, *New England Bound*, 89–96; Newell, *Brethren by Nature*, 53–59. The Massachusetts Body of Liberties, established in 1641, did not specify heritable slavery: "There shall never be any bond slaverie, villinage or Captivitie amongst us unles it be lawfull Captives taken in just warres, and such strangers as willingly selle themselves or are sold to us. And these shall have all the liberties and Christian usages which the law of god established in Israell concerning such persons doeth morally require." *Collections of the Massachusetts Historical Society*, ser. 3 (Boston: Charles C. Little and James Brown, 1843), 8:231; Helen Tunnicliff Catterall, ed., *Judicial Cases concerning American Slavery and the Negro*, vol. 4, *Cases from the Courts of New England, the Middle States, and the District of Columbia* (Washington, D.C.: Carnegie Institution of Washington, 1936), 470–71.

13. George Francis Dow, ed., *Records and Files of the Quarterly Courts of Essex County, Massachusetts* (Salem, Mass.: Essex Institute, 1911), 196, 287, 323; Warren, *New England Bound*, 161–75; Nathaniel B. Shurtleff, ed., *Records of the Colony of New Plymouth in New England: Court Orders*, vol. 6, *1678–1691* (Boston: William White, 1856), 177; Jared Ross Hardesty, *Unfreedom: Slavery and Dependence in Eighteenth-Century Boston* (New York: New York University Press, 2018), 97–99.

14. *The Charters and General Laws of the Colony and Province of Massachusetts Bay* (Boston: T. B. Wait, 1814), 745–47; John Codman Hurd, *The Law of Freedom and Bondage in the United States* (Boston: Little, Brown, 1858), 1:254–77.

15. Catterall, *Judicial Cases concerning American Slavery*, 4:419; Newell, *Brethren by Nature*, 1–3, 15–16.

16. Anthony Stevens-Acevedo, Tom Weterings, and Leonor Alvarez Francés, *Juan Rodriguez and the Beginnings of New York City* (New York: CUNY Dominican Studies Institute, 2013); Graham Russell Hodges, *Root and Branch: African Americans in New York and New Jersey, 1613–1863* (Chapel Hill: University of North Carolina Press, 1999), 6–7.

17. Jacob Steendam references the widespread European belief that God had cursed Ham (Cham) in the Bible with racial blackness, while his brother Japhet apparently went unscathed and maintained his whiteness. Winthrop D. Jordan, *White over Black: American Attitudes toward the Negro, 1550–1812* (Chapel Hill: University of North Carolina Press, 1968), 17–20, 83–84. When people of mixed heritage shared the "blood" of Europeans, they rose to prominence and occupied a "hybrid position" on the African continent. Pernille Ipsen, *Daughters of the Trade: Atlantic Slavers and Interracial Marriage on the Gold Coast* (Philadelphia: University of Pennsylvania Press, 2015), 54–83.

18. In New Netherland some Africans experienced a type of "half freedom" in which they worked for the Dutch West India Company for part of the year and paid an annual tax to live independently. Not everyone had this arrangement, and Dutch masters still abused their slaves, as families were bought, sold, and separated from one another. A. Leon Higginbotham Jr., *In the Matter of Color: Race and the American Legal Process; The Colonial Period* (New York: Oxford University Press, 1978), 103–9; Leo Hershkowitz, "The Troublesome Turk: An Illustration of Judicial Process in New Amsterdam," *New York History* 46, no. 4 (1965): 299–310; Berthold Fernow, ed., *The Records of New Amsterdam from 1653 to 1674 Anno Domini* (New York: Knickerbocker, 1897), 204; William H. Williams, *Slavery and Freedom in Delaware, 1639–1865* (Wilmington, Del.: Rowman and Littlefield, 1999), 1–10.

19. Lorenzo Johnston Greene, *The Negro in Colonial New England* (New York: Atheneum, 1968), 200–202; Catherine Adams and Elizabeth H. Pleck, *Love of Freedom: Black Women in Colonial and Revolutionary New England* (New York: Oxford University Press, 2010), 112–13, 131–32; Edward Armstrong, ed., *The Record of the Court at Upland, in Pennsylvania, 1676 to 1681* (Philadelphia: Joseph M. Mitchell, 1959), 51–52.

20. *Minutes of the Provincial Council of Pennsylvania*, vol. 2, *Containing the Proceedings of Council from December 18, 1700, to May 16, 1717* (Harrisburg, Pa.: Theophilus Finn, 1838), 112–13, 121; Katharine Gerbner, *Christian Slavery: Conversion and Race in the Protestant Atlantic World* (Philadelphia: University of Pennsylvania Press, 2018), 22–30.

21. Gary B. Nash and Jean R. Soderlund, *Freedom by Degrees: Emancipation in Pennsylvania and Its Aftermath* (New York: Oxford University Press, 1991), 41–73; Samuel Sewall, *The Selling of Joseph: A Memorial* (Boston: Bartholomew Green and John Allen, 1700), 2; Mark A. Peterson, "The Selling of Joseph: Bostonians, Antislavery, and the Protestant International, 1689–1733," *Massachusetts Historical Review* 4 (2002): iv, 1–22.

22. Samuel Sewall could also hardly imagine that African men "might make Husbands for our Daughters." Sewall, *Selling of Joseph*, 1–2; Peterson, "Selling of Joseph"; *ARPMA*, vol. 1, *1692–1714* (Boston: Wright and Potter, 1869), 578.

23. Ira Berlin, *Many Thousands Gone: The First Two Centuries of Slavery in North America* (Cambridge, Mass.: Belknap Press of Harvard University Press, 1998), 177–82, 187–88; Hodges, *Root and Branch*, 10–12, 34–53; Henry B. Hoff, "The de Vries Family of Tappan, New York: A Study in Assimilation," *American Genealogist* 72 (1997): 345–52; Hurd, *Law of Freedom and Bondage*, 1:277–85; Samuel Nevill, ed., *The Acts of the General Assembly of the Province of New-Jersey* (Philadelphia: William Bradford, 1752), 23; Samuel Allinson, ed.,

*Acts of the General Assembly of the Province of New-Jersey* (Burlington, N.J.: Isaac Collins, 1776), 5; *Acts of Assembly, Passed in the Province of New-York, from 1691, to 1718* (London: John Baskett, 1719), 142; A. Judd Northrup, *Slavery in New York, a Historical Sketch* (Albany: University of the State of New York, 1900), 278–79.

24. Daniel Horsmanden, *A Journal of the Proceedings in the Detection of the Conspiracy Formed by Some White People, in Conjunction with Negro and Other Slaves, for Burning the City of New-York in America, and Murdering the Inhabitants* (New York: James Parker, 1744), 2–3; Jill Lepore, *New York Burning: Liberty, Slavery, and Conspiracy in Eighteenth-Century Manhattan* (New York: Vintage Books, 2006), 36–39, 85–90, 119–20.

25. Timothy Mather Cooley, *Sketches of the Life and Character of the Rev. Lemuel Haynes* (New York: Harper and Brothers, 1837), 28–32; Richard D. Brown, "'Not Only Extreme Poverty, but the Worst Kind of Orphanage': Lemuel Haynes and the Boundaries of Racial Tolerance on the Yankee Frontier, 1770–1820," *New England Quarterly* 61, no. 4 (1988): 502–5.

26. Berlin, *Many Thousands Gone*, 179–82; Gary B. Nash, *Forging Freedom: The Formation of Philadelphia's Black Community, 1720–1840* (Cambridge, Mass.: Harvard University Press, 1988), 27–37; PG, Feb. 19, 1756, Mar. 31, 1757; *New-York Gazette*, Nov. 13, 1732.

27. W. W. Griest, ed., *Pennsylvania Archives*, ser. 4, vol. 2, *Papers of the Governors, 1747–1759* (Harrisburg: State of Pennsylvania, 1900), 64–67; ARPMA, 1:535–36; Hurd, *Law of Freedom and Bondage*, 1:266; *A Report of the Record Commissioners of the City of Boston*, vol. 8, *Containing the Boston Records from 1700 to 1728* (Boston: Rockwell and Churchill, 1883), 167–70; *A Report of the Record Commissioners of the City of Boston*, vol. 12, *Containing the Boston Records from 1729 to 1742* (Boston: Rockwell and Churchill, 1885), 139.

28. *American Weekly Mercury*, Oct. 24, 1734; Ann Marie Plane, *Colonial Intimacies: Indian Marriage in Early New England* (Ithaca, N.Y.: Cornell University Press, 2000), 122–23, 132–33, 146–47.

29. Helen C. Rountree, *Pocahontas's People: The Powhatan Indians of Virginia through Four Centuries* (Norman: University of Oklahoma Press, 1990), 20–24; Lee Miller, *A Kingdom Strange: The Brief and Tragic History of the Lost Colony of Roanoke* (New York: Basic Books, 2010), 207–19, 223–38.

30. McIlvenna, *Very Mutinous People*, 3, 21; Godbeer, *Sexual Revolution*, 154–89.

31. McIlvenna, *Very Mutinous People*, 3–5, 21.

32. Alexander S. Salley Jr., ed., *Narratives of Early Carolina, 1650–1708* (New York: Charles Scribner's Sons, 1911), 66–67; Wood, *Black Majority*, 16–20.

33. Alan Gallay, *The Indian Slave Trade: The Rise of the English Empire in the American South, 1670–1717* (New Haven, Conn.: Yale University Press, 2002), 47–48; McIlvenna, *Very Mutinous People*, 3–5.

34. The original 1663 charter set the northern point at 36° north latitude, in the middle of the Albemarle Sound, but the line was moved 30 minutes north to the current Virginia–North Carolina border in 1665. McIlvenna, *Very Mutinous People*, 3–5, 20–21, 24–25, 34–35, 56, 84, 93; William L. Saunders, ed., CRNC, vol. 1, *1662–1712* (Raleigh, N.C.: P. M. Hale, 1886), 366, 770; Godbeer, *Sexual Revolution*, 190–224. Ira Berlin pulls from Peter H. Wood when describing "sawbuck equality," in which slaves worked side by side with their masters. Ira Berlin, "Time, Space, and the Evolution of Afro-American Society on British Mainland North America," *American Historical Review* 85, no. 1 (1980): 55; Berlin, *Many Thousands Gone*, 66.

35. Colin G. Calloway, ed., *The World Turned Upside Down: Indian Voices from Early America* (Boston: Bedford/St. Martin's, 1994), 20–22, 38–39.

36. J. Leitch Wright Jr., *The Only Land They Knew: The Tragic Story of American Indians in the Old South* (New York: Free Press, 1981), 31–38, 69–70; Gallay, *Indian Slave Trade*, 8, 29, 186. See also Alan Gallay, ed., *Indian Slavery in Colonial America* (Lincoln: University of Nebraska Press, 2009).

37. Gallay, *Indian Slave Trade*, 44–52, 94–97, 103–4.

38. Gallay, 294–300.

39. Colonists accused Native American slaves of many "conspiracies, outrages, barbarities, murders, burglaries, thefts, and other notorious crimes" against their European masters in New England. *Act and Laws, Passed by the General Court or Assembly of His Majesties Province of New-Hampshire in New-England* (Boston: B. Green, 1726), 49; McIlvenna, *Very Mutinous People*, 98–100; Gallay, *Indian Slave Trade*, 48–50; Kirsten Fischer, *Suspect Relations: Sex, Race, and Resistance in Colonial North Carolina* (Ithaca, N.Y.: Cornell University Press, 2002), 79–82. For other examples of "Indian" slaves in early South Carolina, see Christopher Smith, 134, and Richard Prize, 165, both in Will Book, 1687–1710; Holland Axtell, 17, Will Book, 1692–93; and Thomas Dalton, 10, Thomas Permian, 16, Paul Torquett, 19, Anthony Cordes, 26, Richard Harris, 28, George Frost, 30, Hugh Cockran, 42, and George Evans, 60, all in Charleston County Will Book, 1711–18, all in SCDAH.

40. Records of the Register of the Province, 1675–96, 18, SCDAH; Records of the Secretary of the Province, 1675–95, 21, SCDAH.

41. Records of the Register of the Province, 1675–96, 18, SCDAH; Records of the Secretary of the Province, 1675–95, 21, SCDAH.

42. Wood, *Black Majority*, 27–34; Peter H. Wood, *Strange New Land: African in Colonial America* (New York: Oxford University Press, 2003), 26–27.

43. Records of the Register of the Province, 1675–96, 99, SCDAH; Forbes, *Africans and Native Americans*, 128–29.

44. Will Book, 1687–1710, 165, SCDAH.

45. Will Book, 1687–1710, 165, SCDAH; John Lawson, *A New Voyage to Carolina: Containing the Exact Description and Natural History of That County; Together with the Present State Thereof* (London, 1709), 184–85.

46. Walter Clark, ed., *SRNC*, vol. 25, *Laws 1789–1790 and Supplement Omitted Laws, 1669–1783* (Goldsboro, N.C.: Nash Brothers, 1906), 170–72.

47. David La Vere, *The Tuscarora War: Indians, Settlers, and the Fight for the Carolina Colonies* (Chapel Hill: University of North Carolina Press, 2013), 21–30, 69; Gallay, *Indian Slave Trade*, 262–68.

48. Gallay, *Indian Slave Trade*, 262–68, 273, 285; Eric E. Bowne, *The Westo Indians: Slave Traders of the Early Colonial South* (Tuscaloosa: University of Alabama Press, 2005), 18–19.

49. Gallay, *Indian Slave Trade*, 294–99; David J. McCord, ed., *SALSC*, vol. 7, *Containing the Acts Relating to Charleston, Courts, Slaves, and Rivers* (Columbia, S.C.: A. S. Johnston, 1840), 352.

50. Woodes Rogers, *A Cruising Voyage round the World: First to the South-Seas, Thence to the East-Indies, and Homewards by the Cape of Good Hope* (London: A. Bell and B. Lintot, 1712), 203, 278–79. In the illustration, the description of Betty as "mestizo" on January 10, 1761, was changed to "mustee" on February 21 and 28, 1761. SCG, Dec. 30, 1760, Jan. 10, Feb. 21, 28, 1761. See also an ad for a runaway slave named Cato, whose description was also changed from "mestizo" to "mustee" in SCG, Mar. 24, June 23, 1757.

51. H. R. McIlwaine, ed., *EJCCV*, vol. 3, *May 1, 1705–October 23, 1721* (Richmond: Virginia State Library, 1928), 28, 30–31; *Colonial Laws of New York from the Year 1664 to the*

*Revolution* (Albany, N.Y.: James B. Lyon, 1896), 1:597–98; Hugh Jones, *The Present State of Virginia* (London: J. Clarke, 1724), 36–38; Richard L. Morton, "The Reverend Hugh Jones: Lord Baltimore's Mathematician," *William and Mary Quarterly* 7, no. 1 (1950): 112–13.

52. Accomack County Orders, 1703–9, 75, LVA; Northampton County Orders, 1732–42, 26, 35, LVA; Jean M. Mihalyka, ed., *Loose Papers and Sundry Court Cases*, vol. 1, *1628–1731, Northampton County, Virginia* (Eastville, Va.: Hickory House, 1997), 239; Jean M. Mihalyka, ed., *Loose Papers and Sundry Court Cases*, vol. 2, *1732–1744/5, Northampton County, Virginia* (Eastville, Va.: Hickory House, 2000), 11.

53. William L. McDowell, ed., *Journals of the Commissioners of the Indian Trade, September 20, 1710–August 29, 1718* (Columbia: South Carolina Archives Department, 1955), 198–99.

54. While European slave traders preferred African men, and men early outnumbered women in the Lowcountry, the transatlantic slave trade consisted of a majority of African women and children. Jennifer L. Morgan, *Laboring Women: Reproduction and Gender in New World Slavery* (Philadelphia: University of Pennsylvania Press, 2004), 50–51; David Eltis, *The Rise of African Slavery in the Americas* (New York: Cambridge University Press, 2000), 94–101; John Norris, *Profitable Advice for Rich and Poor: In a Dialogue, or Discourse between James Freeman, a Carolina Planter, and Simon Question, a West-Country Farmer; Containing a Description, or True Relation of South Carolina, an English Plantation, or Colony, in America* (London: J. How, 1712), 88–89.

55. Gallay, *Indian Slave Trade*, 200–201; Norris, *Profitable Advice for Rich and Poor*, 92–95; Judith A. Carney, *Black Rice: The African Origins of Rice Cultivation in the Americas* (Cambridge, Mass.: Harvard University Press, 2001), 71.

56. Carney, *Black Rice*, 78–86; Gallay, *Indian Slave Trade*, 90, 294–99; Norris, *Profitable Advice for Rich and Poor*, 92–95; Wood, *Black Majority*, 55–62.

57. Robert Daniell, May 1, 1718, 75, Charleston County Will Book, 1711–18, SCDAH.

58. Gallay, *Indian Slave Trade*, 327–38.

59. Gallay, 334–35; William L. Ramsey, *The Yamasee War: A Study of Culture, Economy, and Conflict in the Colonial South* (Lincoln: University of Nebraska Press, 2008), 121–23; D. Andrew Johnson, "Displacing Captives in Colonial South Carolina: Native American Enslavement and the Rise of the Colonial State after the Yamasee War," *Journal of Early American History* 7, no. 2 (2017): 115–40.

60. Original bill of sale, Aug. 8, 1721, 3, Misc. Records, vol. GG, 1746–49, SCDAH.

61. *SCG*, Oct. 20, 1739.

62. *SCG*, Oct. 20, 1739.

63. For other "Mustee Negroes" in South Carolina, see *SCG*, June 1, 1734, Jan. 8, Mar. 7, 1741, Nov. 28, 1761, Nov. 13, 1762, Aug. 10, 24, 1765; and *SCGCJ*, Mar. 4, 1766; *SCG*, Oct. 28, 1732, July 21, 1733, May 31, 1735, Apr. 13, 1738.

64. Like many slave owners, Paul's master, Blake Leay White, promised that Paul "shall be forgiven" if the bondsman decided to "come home of his own accord." *SCGCJ*, July 31, 1770.

65. *SCG*, June 9, 1733.

66. *SCG*, June 9, 1733.

67. Thomas Cooper, ed., *SALSC*, vol. 3, *Containing the Acts from 1716, Exclusive, to 1752, Inclusive* (Columbia, S.C.: A. S. Johnston, 1838), 69–84; Gallay, *Indian Slave Trade*, 69, 76–77.

68. Cooper, *SALSC*, 3:69–84; Norris, *Profitable Advice for Rich and Poor*, 94–95.

69. Early manumission among charter generations of slaves may have been why some

free people of color claimed in later centuries that their ancestors had never been enslaved. Indeed, some could trace their lineage back to European or Native American ancestors who were always free or to Africans who traveled over the Atlantic in bondage yet earned freedom after a period of time in the early English colonies. These men and women perhaps never accepted the title of slave. Fitchett, "Traditions of the Free Negro," 139–42; Joel Williamson, *New People: Miscegenation and Mulattoes in the United States* (New York: Free Press, 1980), 14–17.

70. Edward B. Rugemer, "The Development of Mastery and Race in the Comprehensive Slave Codes of the Greater Caribbean during the Seventeenth Century," *William and Mary Quarterly* 70, no. 3 (2013): 429–58.

71. James Horn, *Adapting to a New World: English Society in the Seventeenth-Century Chesapeake* (Chapel Hill: University of North Carolina Press, 1994), 137; William Waller Hening, ed., *SALVA* (New York: Thomas Desilver, 1823), 3:452–53; William Hand Browne, ed., *AOM*, vol. 30, *PAGAM, April 1715–August 1716* (Baltimore: Maryland Historical Society, 1910), 289–90; Walter Clark, ed., *SRNC*, vol. 23, *Laws 1715–1776* (Goldsboro, N.C.: Nash Brothers, 1904), 65; *LSDE* (New Castle, Del.: printed by Samuel and John Adams, 1797), 1:108–9; *The Statutes at Large of Pennsylvania*, vol. 4, *1724–1744* (Philadelphia: Clarence M. Busch, 1897), 62–63; Hurd, *Law of Freedom and Bondage*, 1:286–93.

72. Robert J. Cain, ed., *CRNC*, vol. 7, *Records of the Executive Council, 1664–1734* (Raleigh: North Carolina Department of Cultural Resources, 1984), 40.

73. William S. Price Jr., ed., *CRNC*, vol. 5, *North Carolina Higher-Court Records, 1709–1723* (Raleigh: North Carolina Department of Cultural Resources, 1977), 114–15; Clark, *SRNC*, 23:5, 64–65; Hening, *SALVA*, 3:452–53.

74. Price, *CRNC*, 5:114–15.

75. Price, 5:114–15.

76. Price, 5:114–15; Clayton Colman Hall, ed., *AOM*, vol. 33, *PAGAM, May 1717–April 1720* (Baltimore: Lord Baltimore Press, 1913), 111; Hening, *SALVA*, 3:453–54.

77. Hening, *SALVA*, 3:250–52; William Waller Hening, ed., *SALVA* (Richmond: Franklin Press–W. W. Gray, 1820), 4:133–34; Hall, *AOM*, 33:111. Virginia and other provinces allowed testimony from "Negroes, Mulattos, or Indians, bond or free," under certain circumstances—usually in cases of other slaves committing capital offenses. Hening, *SALVA*, 4:127–28, 326–27; William Waller Hening, ed., *SALVA* (Richmond: Franklin Press–W. W. Gray, 1819), 5:244–45.

78. Clark, *SRNC*, 23:106–7; Hening, *SALVA*, 4:133–34; Clayton Colman Hall, ed., *AOM*, vol. 35, *PAGAM, October 1724–July 1726* (Baltimore: Maryland Historical Society, 1915), 427; Paul Heinegg, *Free African Americans of North Carolina, Virginia, and South Carolina, from the Colonial Period to About 1820*, 5th ed. (Baltimore: Clearfield, 2005), 1:553.

79. South Carolina addressed ethnoracial intermixture in a 1717 bastardy statute, which mirrored several stipulations issued in Maryland just two years earlier. Cooper, *SALSC*, 3:14–21.

80. William L. Saunders, ed., *CRNC*, vol. 2, *1713 to 1728* (Raleigh, N.C.: P. M. Hale, 1886), 214–15; Thomas Cooper, ed., *SALSC*, vol. 2, *Containing the Acts from 1682 to 1716, Inclusive* (Columbia, S.C.: A. S. Johnston, 1837), 688–89; Hening, *SALVA*, 3:250–52, 4:133–34; Jordan, *White over Black*, 176.

81. South Carolina legislators may not have punished mixed-heritage children with European ancestry as severely as those in the Chesapeake because authorities were wary of placing stipulations on European men, who sometimes freed their mixed-heritage children. Wood, *Black Majority*, 98–101.

82. Hening, *SALVA*, 3:250–52, 452–54; Browne, *AOM*, 30:283–90; Clark, *SRNC*, 23: 62–66.

CHAPTER 4

1. Thomas N. Ingersoll, "'Releese Us out of This Cruell Bondegg': An Appeal from Virginia in 1723," *William and Mary Quarterly* 51, no. 4 (1994): 777–82.

2. Ingersoll, 777–82.

3. Ingersoll, 777–82; British Public Record Office, C.O. 5/1324, Virginia Colonial Records Project, LVA; William Waller Hening, ed., *SALVA* (Richmond: Franklin Press–W. W. Gray, 1820), 4:126–34; Herbert Aptheker, *American Negro Slave Revolts*, 4th ed. (New York: International Publishers, 1963), 176–78; Thomas D. Morris, *Southern Slavery and the Law, 1619–1860* (Chapel Hill: University of North Carolina Press, 1996), 267; William C. Rucker, *River Flows On: Black Resistance, Culture, and Identity Formation in Early America* (Baton Rouge: Louisiana State University Press, 2008), 130–32; "Queries Respecting the Slavery and Emancipation of Negroes in Massachusetts, Proposed by the Hon. Judge Tucker of Virginia, and Answered by the Rev. Dr. Beknap," in *Collections of the Massachusetts Historical Society*, ser. 1 (Boston, 1795), 4:191–211.

4. Their letter says "that there is in this Land of verJennia a Sort of people that is Calld molatters," almost as if to say this is what other people called them. They do not say that they *were* "molatters," suggesting they did not identify themselves by the term. Ingersoll, "'Releese Us,'" 781.

5. Walter Clark, ed., *SRNC*, vol. 23, *Laws 1715–1776* (Goldsboro, N.C.: Nash Brothers, 1904), 106, 345, 526. For people described as "half Indian," see *PG*, Apr. 28, 1737 (Moses Williams); *SCG*, Apr. 12, 1773 (Frank); *VG2*, Mar. 10, 1774 (Jack Brown); Johann Martin Bolzius, "Reliable Answer to Some Submitted Questions Concerning the Land Carolina," *William and Mary Quarterly* 14, no. 2 (1957): 235; Granville Sharp, *A Representation of the Injustice and Dangerous Tendency of Tolerating Slavery* (London: printed for Benjamin White and Robert Horsfield, 1769), 109; Brooke N. Newman, *A Dark Inheritance: Blood, Race, and Sex in Colonial Jamaica* (New Haven, Conn.: Yale University Press, 2018), 75–80; and James H. Merrell, "'The Cast of His Countenance': Reading Andrew Montour," in Ronald Hoffman, Mechel Sobel, and Fredrika J. Teute, eds., *Through a Glass Darkly: Reflections on Personal Identity in Early America* (Chapel Hill: University of North Carolina Press, 1997), 13–39.

6. Honor Sachs, "'Freedom by a Judgement': The Legal History of an Afro-Indian Family," *Law and History Review* 30, no. 1 (2012): 173–203.

7. Sharon Block, *Colonial Complexions: Race and Bodies in Eighteenth-Century America* (Philadelphia: University of Pennsylvania Press, 2018).

8. Ariela Gross, *What Blood Won't Tell: A History of Race on Trial in America* (Cambridge, Mass.: Harvard University Press, 2008), 1–3.

9. Joel Williamson, *New People: Miscegenation and Mulattoes in the United States* (New York: Free Press, 1980), 15–17; Daniel Livesay, *Children of Uncertain Fortune: Mixed-Race Jamaicans in Britain and the Atlantic Family, 1733–1833* (Chapel Hill: University of North Carolina Press, 2018), 9–11; Newman, *Dark Inheritance*, 15–18.

10. Philip D. Morgan, *Slave Counterpoint: Black Culture in the Eighteenth-Century Chesapeake and Lowcountry* (Chapel Hill: University of North Carolina Press, 1998), 608–9; William Hall, ed., *LSDE, to the Year of Our Lord, One Thousand Eight Hundred and Twenty Nine Inclusive*, rev. ed. (Wilmington, Del.: R. Porter and Son, 1829), 406.

11. Anne Arundel County Court Judgements, vol. V.D., no. 1, 1714–16, 244–46, MSA.

12. Anne Arundel County Court Judgements, vol. V.D., no. 1, 1714–16, 93, 178, 244–46, MSA; Thomas F. Brown and Leah C. Sims, "'To Swear Him Free': Ethnic Memory as Social Capital in Eighteenth-Century Freedom Petitions," in *Colonial Chesapeake: New Perspectives*, ed. Debra Meyers and Melanie Perreault (Lanham, Md.: Lexington Books, 2006), 81–83.

13. Anne Arundel County Court Judgements, vol. V.D., no. 1, 1714–16, 93, 178, 244–46, MSA.

14. It is possible that Mary Davis could not travel the distance to Anne Arundel County to give her testimony in person because another master held her as a servant or slave. Anne Arundel County Court Judgements, vol. V.D., no. 1, 1714–16, 93, 178, 244–46, MSA; Thomas F. Brown and Sims, "'To Swear Him Free,'" 81–82, 89–92.

15. Thomas F. Brown and Sims, "'To Swear Him Free,'" 81–82, 89–92. Henry Wharton was Rose's godfather, the same man who sought to keep the Mulatto Lewis Mingo enslaved for life in chapter 2. Anne Arundel County Court Judgements, vol. V.D., no. 1, 1714–16, 93, 178, 244–46, MSA.

16. Ira Berlin, *Many Thousands Gone: The First Two Centuries of Slavery in North America* (Cambridge, Mass.: Belknap Press of Harvard University Press, 1998), 45; Katharine Gerbner, *Christian Slavery: Conversion and Race in the Protestant Atlantic World* (Philadelphia: University of Pennsylvania Press, 2018), 22–25, 74–75; Anne Arundel County Court Judgements, vol. V.D., no. 1, 1714–16, 93, 178, 244–46, MSA.

17. Rebecca Anne Goetz, *The Baptism of Early Virginia: How Christianity Created Race* (Baltimore: Johns Hopkins University Press, 2012), 8–10; William Hand Browne, ed., *AOM*, vol. 1, *PAGAM, January 1637/8–September 1664* (Baltimore: Maryland Historical Society, 1883), 533–34; William Hand Browne, ed., *AOM*, vol. 7, *PAGAM, October 1678–November 1683* (Baltimore: Maryland Historical Society, 1889), 203–5. Justices could have also decided that Rose Davis deserved twenty-one years of service under the 1692 law that mandated this term for mixed-heritage children born "within such marriage." William Hand Browne, ed., *AOM*, vol. 13, *PAGAM, April 1684–June 1692* (Baltimore: Maryland Historical Society, 1894), 546–49.

18. Anne Arundel County Court Judgements, vol. V.D., no. 1, 1714–16, 93, 178, 244–46, MSA; Thomas F. Brown and Sims, "'To Swear Him Free,'" 81–82, 89–92; Maura Jane Farrelly, *Papist Patriots: The Making of an American Catholic Identity* (New York: Oxford University Press, 2012), 26–27.

19. Ingersoll, "'Releese Us,'" 777–82.

20. Ingersoll, 781–82.

21. Ingersoll, 781–82; William Waller Hening, ed., *SALVA* (New York: Thomas Desilver, 1823), 3:87, 453; Hening, *SALVA*, 4:133; Kathleen M. Brown, *Good Wives, Nasty Wenches, and Anxious Patriarchs: Gender, Race, and Power in Colonial Virginia* (Chapel Hill: University of North Carolina Press, 1996), 230–33, 295–96; Kirsten Fischer, *Suspect Relations: Sex, Race, and Resistance in Colonial North Carolina* (Ithaca, N.Y.: Cornell University Press, 2002), 124–29.

22. Hening, *SALVA*, 3:87, 453, 4:133; Margaret Ellen Newell, *Brethren by Nature: New England Indians, Colonists, and the Origins of American Slavery* (Ithaca, N.Y.: Cornell University Press, 2015), 14–15; Kathleen M. Brown, *Good Wives, Nasty Wenches*, 230–33, 295–96; Fischer, *Suspect Relations*, 124–29.

23. Existing records show over 800 mixed-heritage servants in Virginia, over 200 in Maryland, and at least 250 in North Carolina. A special thanks goes to Danielle Ford for

her painstaking collection and enumeration of these sources. Paul Heinegg, *Free African Americans of North Carolina, Virginia, and South Carolina, from the Colonial Period to About 1820*, 5th ed., 2 vols. (Baltimore: Clearfield, 2005); Paul Heinegg, *Free African Americans of Maryland and Delaware: From the Colonial Period to 1810* (Baltimore: Clearfield, 2000).

24. Ingersoll, "'Releese Us,'" 777–82.

25. Ingersoll, 781–82; Patricia U. Bonomi, *Under the Cope of Heaven: Religion, Society, and Politics in Colonial America*, updated ed. (New York: Oxford University Press, 2003), 119–22.

26. Ingersoll, "'Releese Us,'" 781–82.

27. Ingersoll, 781–82.

28. Gerbner, *Christian Slavery*, 74–79; Jared Ross Hardesty, *Unfreedom: Slavery and Dependence in Eighteenth-Century Boston* (New York: New York University Press, 2018), 97; Gary B. Nash, *Forging Freedom: The Formation of Philadelphia's Black Community, 1720–1840* (Cambridge, Mass.: Harvard University Press, 1988), 35–36; Frank J. Klingberg, *An Appraisal of the Negro in Colonial South Carolina* (Washington, D.C.: Associated Publishers, 1941), 84–86.

29. Klingberg, *Appraisal of the Negro*, 84–86; Albert J. Raboteau, *Slave Religion: The "Invisible Institution" in the Antebellum South*, updated ed. (New York: Oxford University Press, 2004), 114–19.

30. *PG*, May 30, 1765; *Virginia Gazette* (3rd ed.), Sept. 8, 15, 22, 1775; Raboteau, *Slave Religion*, 264–65; Michael A. Gomez, *Exchanging Our Country Marks: The Transformation of African Identities in the Colonial and Antebellum South* (Chapel Hill: University of North Carolina Press, 1998), 39–40, 240.

31. Ingersoll, "'Releese Us,'" 782; *Virginia Gazette* (3rd ed.), Sept. 8, 1775; Ira Berlin, *Slaves without Masters: The Free Negro in the Antebellum South* (New York: New Press, 1974), 49–50; Morgan, *Slave Counterpoint*, 485, 555–58.

32. Mechel Sobel, *The World They Made Together: Black and White Values in Eighteenth-Century Virginia* (Princeton, N.J.: Princeton University Press, 1987), 3–11; Morgan, *Slave Counterpoint*; Raboteau, *Slave Religion*, 12–13, 30, 42.

33. Heinegg, *Free African Americans of North Carolina*, 2:1220–23; Lois Green Carr, Philip D. Morgan, and Jean Burrell Russo, eds., *Colonial Chesapeake Society* (Chapel Hill: University of North Carolina Press, 1988), 299–303; Joseph Douglas Deal, *Race and Class in Colonial Virginia: Indians, Englishmen, and Africans on the Eastern Shore during the Seventeenth Century* (New York: Garland, 1993), 399–405.

34. Deal, *Race and Class*, 399–405.

35. Heinegg, *Free African Americans of North Carolina*, 2:1221–22; Carr, Morgan, and Russo, *Colonial Chesapeake Society*, 299–303.

36. Heinegg, *Free African Americans of North Carolina*, 2:1221–23; Carr, Morgan, and Russo, *Colonial Chesapeake Society*, 302–3.

37. Heinegg, *Free African Americans of North Carolina*, 2:1221–22.

38. Hening, *SALVA*, 4:133–34; William L. Saunders, ed., *CRNC*, vol. 2, *1713 to 1728* (Raleigh, N.C.: P. M. Hale, 1886), 2:213–15; Thomas Cooper, ed., *SALSC*, vol. 3, *Containing the Acts from 1716, Exclusive, to 1752, Inclusive* (Columbia, S.C.: A. S. Johnston, 1838), 136; Newman, *Dark Inheritance*, 75–80.

39. Hening, *SALVA*, 4:133–34; British Public Record Office, C.O. 5/1323, 5/1366, 5/1324, Virginia Colonial Records Project, LVA; Emory G. Evans, "A Question of Complexion: Documents Concerning the Negro and the Franchise in Eighteenth-Century Virginia," *Virginia Magazine of History and Biography* 71, no. 4 (1963): 411–15.

40. British Public Record Office, C.O. 5/1324, Virginia Colonial Records Project, LVA; Evans, "Question of Complexion," 411–15; Newman, *Dark Inheritance*, 28–32.

41. British Public Record Office, C.O. 5/1323, 5/1366, 5/1324, Virginia Colonial Records Project, LVA; Evans, "Question of Complexion," 411–15.

42. British Public Record Office, C.O. 5/1324, Virginia Colonial Records Project, LVA.

43. British Public Record Office, C.O. 5/1324, Virginia Colonial Records Project, LVA; "Queries Respecting the Slavery and Emancipation," 208–9.

44. British Public Record Office, C.O. 5/1324, Virginia Colonial Records Project, LVA.

45. Alice Walker defines colorism as the "prejudicial or preferential treatment of same-race people based solely on their color." Alice Walker, *In Search of Our Mothers' Gardens: Womanist Prose* (New York: Harcourt, 1983), 290–91; Trina Jones, "Shades of Brown: The Law of Skin Color," *Duke Law Journal* 49, no. 6 (2000): 1487–557.

46. British Public Record Office, C.O. 5/1324, Virginia Colonial Records Project, LVA; Edward Long, *The History of Jamaica, or, General Survey of the Antient and Modern State of the Island: With Reflections on Its Situation Settlements, Inhabitants, Climate, Products, Commerce, Laws, and Government*, vol. II (London: T. Lowndes, 1774), 320, 328–30.

47. Long, *History of Jamaica*, 328–30; George Theodore Wilkinson, *An Authentic History of the Cato-Street Conspiracy* (London: Thomas Kelly, 1820), 320; Livesay, *Children of Uncertain Fortune*, 362–65; Heather Miyano Kopelson, *Faithful Bodies: Performing Religion and Race in the Puritan Atlantic* (New York: New York University Press, 2014), 203–4. In Harriet Jacobs's nineteenth-century narrative, she despises "a free colored man, who tried to pass himself off for white." He had hunted Harriet after she escaped from her master, and he "was always ready to do any mean work for the sake of currying favor with white people." Other evidence of the time points to colorism between "black" and "Mulatto" slaves. Harriet Jacobs, *Incidents in the Life of a Slave Girl*, ed. Jean Fagan Yellin, enlarged ed. (Cambridge, Mass.: Harvard University Press, 1987; first published 1861 for the author [Boston]), 119–20; Herbert G. Gutman, *The Black Family in Slavery and Freedom, 1750–1925* (New York: Pantheon Books, 1976), 550–51n28.

48. *PG*, Sept. 7, 1733; *SCG*, Mar. 22, 1735. Historian J. A. Leo Lemay attributes Blackamore's editorial to Benjamin Franklin. While I agree with Lemay's assertion, I have chosen to cite Blackamore as the author throughout. J. A. Leo Lemay, *The Canon of Benjamin Franklin 1722–1776: New Attributions and Reconsiderations* (Newark: University of Delaware Press, 1986), 78–79; Benjamin Franklin, *Benjamin Franklin: Silence Dogood, the Busy-Body, and Early Writings*, ed. J. A. Leo Lemay (New York: Library of America, 2009), 218–20; William Pencak, "Benjamin Franklin, Trickster," *Trickster's Way* 3, no. 1 (2004), art. 2, pp. 3–4.

49. *PG*, Sept. 7, 1733; *SCG*, Mar. 22, 1735.

50. *PG*, Sept. 7, 1733; *SCG*, Mar. 22, 1735.

51. In the nineteenth century, a "mulatto woman" named Sally asked her master, Fanny Kemble, that she be promoted "to some less laborious kind of work" and through her request stated "that hoeing in the field was so hard to her on 'account of her colour.'" Fanny, who also carried abolitionist sentiments, came to realize that "the faintest admixture of white blood in their black veins appears at once, by common consent of their own race, to raise them in the scale of humanity." Frances Anne Kemble, *Journal of a Residence on a Georgian Plantation in 1838–1839* (New York: Harper and Brothers, 1863), 193–94; *PG*, Sept. 7, 1733; *SCG*, Mar. 22, 1735; Howard Bodenhorn, *The Color Factor: The Economics of African-American Well-Being in the Nineteenth-Century South* (New York: Oxford University Press, 2015), 68–69.

52. In the antebellum era, one slaveholder wrote of Mulattoes: "Tho Distinct from Us, They will not associate with the Negro, either in Church or else where." William Dusinberre, *Them Dark Days: Slavery in the American Rice Swamps* (Athens: University of Georgia Press, 1996), 114–15; PG, Sept. 7, 1733; SCG, Mar. 22, 1735. Ira Berlin writes, "Thus did the color divisions that supported slavery became suffused throughout the black community: what whites did to browns, browns would do to blacks." Berlin, *Many Thousands Gone*, 323–24.

53. PG, Sept. 7, 1733; SCG, Mar. 22, 1735; Susan B. Carter, Scott Sigmund Gartner, Michael R. Haines, Alan L. Olmstead, Richard Sutch, and Galvan Wright, eds., *Historical Statistics of the United States*, millennial ed., online ver. (New York: Cambridge University Press, 2006), "Colonial Statistics," tables Eg63–64.

54. PG, Sept. 7, 1733; SCG, Mar. 22, 1735; Newman, *Dark Inheritance*, 75–80.

55. Robert L. Harris Jr., "Charleston's Free Afro-American Elite: The Brown Fellowship Society and the Humane Brotherhood," *South Carolina Historical Magazine* 82, no. 4 (October 1981): 289–310.

56. PG, Sept. 7, 1733; SCG, Mar. 22, 1735.

57. SCG, Mar. 22, 1735; British Public Record Office, C.O. 5/1324, Virginia Colonial Records Project, LVA.

58. John A. Lent, "Oldest Existing Commonwealth Caribbean Newspapers," *Caribbean Quarterly* 22, no. 4 (1976): 90–106; Roderick Cave, "Early Printing and the Book Trade in the West Indies," *Library Quarterly: Information, Community, Policy* 48, no. 2 (1978): 163–92; Morgan, *Slave Counterpoint*, 524–30.

59. SCG, May 25, 1734, Aug. 8, 1743; Morgan, *Slave Counterpoint*, 525–30.

60. VG, Feb. 5, 1767; PG, June 8, 1749; Robert Olwell, "Becoming Free: Manumission and the Genesis of a Free Black Community in South Carolina, 1740–90," *Slavery and Abolition* 17, no. 1 (1996): 7.

61. VG, Sept. 10, 1772; PG, Apr. 26, 1744; Morgan, *Slave Counterpoint*, 524–30.

62. VG, July 14, 1774; Morgan, *Slave Counterpoint*, 540–48.

63. VG, Sept. 8, 1774.

64. SCGCJ, Apr. 30, 1771–Mar. 10, 1772, with multiple ads run for a year.

65. SCG, Nov. 13, 1743, Jan. 2, 1744; Morgan, *Slave Counterpoint*, 539–43.

66. PG, Oct. 1, 1747.

67. PG, Oct. 1, 1747; SCG, Feb. 29, 1748.

68. William L. McDowell, ed., *Documents Relating to Indian Affairs, May 21, 1750–August 7, 1754* (Columbia: South Carolina Archives Department, 1958), 462–64. See June Namias, *White Captives: Gender and Ethnicity on the American Frontier* (Chapel Hill: University of North Carolina Press, 1993); and Colin G. Calloway, ed., *The World Turned Upside Down: Indian Voices from Early America* (Boston: Bedford/St. Martin's, 1994), 71–77.

69. McDowell, *Documents Relating to Indian Affairs*, 190, 462–64; Jack D. Forbes, *Africans and Native Americans: The Language of Race and the Evolution of Red-Black Peoples* (Urbana-Champaign: University of Illinois Press, 1993), 221–25.

70. McDowell, *Documents Relating to Indian Affairs*, 190, 492–94.

71. *New-York Weekly Journal*, Oct. 27, 1740; *New-York Gazette, or, The Weekly Post-Boy*, June 23, 1755; Graham Russell Hodges and Alan Edward Brown, eds., *"Pretends to Be Free": Runaway Slave Advertisements from Colonial and Revolutionary New York and New Jersey* (New York: Garland, 1994), 16–17, 52–53, 74; PG, July 31, 1740.

72. PG, Oct. 2, 1760, Nov. 17, 1768; SCG, Feb. 8, 1748.

73. PG, Apr. 28, 1737, Sept. 26, 1745. Many relationships appear in the records between

Irish and Africans in the colonial period and later in the antebellum United States. Graham Hodges, "'Desirable Companions and Lovers': Irish and African Americans in the Sixth Ward, 1830–1870," in *The New York Irish*, ed. Ronald H. Bayor and Timothy J. Meagher (Baltimore: Johns Hopkins University Press, 1997), 107–24.

74. *PG*, Apr. 28, 1737, Sept. 26, 1745, Aug. 6, 1767; McDowell, *Documents Relating to Indian Affairs*, 68, 251, 271, 377, 410, 474.

75. *SCG*, Oct. 10, 1761, July 24–Oct. 16, 1762.

76. *PG*, June 19, 1776; Ariela Gross, "'Of Portuguese Origin': Litigating Identity and Citizenship among the 'Little Races' in Nineteenth-Century America," *Law and History Review* 25, no. 3 (2007): 467–512.

77. *PG*, Sept. 13, 1764. For more on Iberian Mulattoes in the colonial period, see Pablo E. Pérez-Mallaína, *Spain's Men of the Sea: Daily Life on the Indies Fleets in the Sixteenth Century*, ed. Carla Rahn Phillips (Baltimore: John Hopkins University Press, 1998), 38, 172–74, 213–14.

78. *American Weekly Mercury*, Sept. 26, 1734, Aug. 26, 1736. Winthrop Jordan discusses "passing" as "unnecessary" in places where those of mixed ancestry were "regarded as midway between black and white." With a focus on the nineteenth century, Werner Sollors and Allyson Hobbs both recognize runaway slave notices as the first places where people passed as "free." Winthrop D. Jordan, *White over Black: American Attitudes toward the Negro, 1550–1812* (Chapel Hill: University of North Carolina Press, 1968), 171; Werner Sollors, *Neither Black nor White yet Both: Thematic Explorations of Interracial Literature* (New York: Oxford University Press, 1997), 255; Allyson Hobbs, *A Chosen Exile: A History of Racial Passing in American Life* (Cambridge, Mass.: Harvard University Press, 2014), 29–36.

79. Gerald W. Mullin, *Flight and Rebellion: Slave Resistance in Eighteenth-Century Virginia* (New York: Oxford University Press, 1972), 98; *VG*, Feb. 18–June 3, 1773; *VG2*, Feb. 18–June 3, 1773.

80. *VG*, Feb. 18–June 3, 1773; *VG2*, Feb. 18–June 3, 1773.

81. *MG*, Sept. 2, 1746; *PG*, Sept. 11, 1746.

82. *MG*, Sept. 2, 1746; *PG*, Sept. 11, 1746.

83. *PG*, May 9, 1751.

84. *MG*, Oct. 20, 1763; *PG*, Nov. 10, 1763.

85. People of blended heritage in the colonial period probably did not suffer the same social and psychological dilemmas around racial passing that afflicted those in later centuries in the United States. Hobbs, *Chosen Exile*, 29–35.

86. Many communities neglected to enforce racial codes in the colonial period. See the Gibson and Spencer families in Daniel J. Sharfstein, *The Invisible Line: Three American Families and the Secret Journey from Black to White* (New York: Penguin, 2011).

CHAPTER 5

1. Prince George's County Court Record, AA, 1742–43, 191, MSA; William Hand Browne, ed., *AOM*, vol. 1, *PAGAM, January 1637/8–September 1664* (Baltimore: Maryland Historical Society, 1883), 533–34; Paul Heinegg, *Free African Americans of Maryland and Delaware: From the Colonial Period to 1810* (Baltimore: Clearfield, 2000), 279–80.

2. Prince George's County Court Record, AA, 1742–43, 191, MSA; Prince George's County Court Proceedings, Court Record, CC, 1743–44, 17, MSA; Heinegg, *Free African Americans of Maryland*, 279–80.

3. Kathleen M. Brown, *Good Wives, Nasty Wenches, and Anxious Patriarchs: Gender, Race, and Power in Colonial Virginia* (Chapel Hill: University of North Carolina Press, 1996), 126–28; Howard Bodenhorn, *The Color Factor: The Economics of African-American Well-Being in the Nineteenth-Century South* (New York: Oxford University Press, 2015), 98–122.

4. William Waller Hening, ed., *SALVA* (New York: Thomas Desilver, 1823), 3:86–88, 452–54; William Hand Browne, ed., *AOM*, vol. 13, *PAGAM, April 1684–June 1692* (Baltimore: Maryland Historical Society, 1894), 546–49; William Hand Browne, ed., *AOM*, vol. 30, *PAGAM, April 1715–August 1716* (Baltimore: Maryland Historical Society, 1910), 289–90; Clayton Colman Hall, ed., *AOM*, vol. 33, *PAGAM, May 1717–April 1720* (Baltimore: Lord Baltimore Press, 1913), 111–13; Bernard Christian Steiner, ed., *AOM*, vol. 36, *PAGAM, July 1727–August 1729* (Baltimore: Maryland Historical Society, 1916), 275–76; Walter Clark, ed., *SRNC*, vol. 23, *Laws 1715–1776* (Goldsboro, N.C.: Nash Brothers, 1904), 64–65.

5. William L. Saunders, ed., *CRNC*, vol. 2, *1713 to 1728* (Raleigh, N.C.: P. M. Hale, 1886), 214–15; Thomas Cooper, ed., *SALSC*, vol. 3, *Containing the Acts from 1716, Exclusive, to 1752, Inclusive* (Columbia, S.C.: A. S. Johnston, 1838), 136; William Waller Hening, ed., *SALVA* (Richmond: Franklin Press–W. W. Gray, 1820), 4:133–34; Joel Williamson, *New People: Miscegenation and Mulattoes in the United States* (New York: Free Press, 1980), 14–17; Daniel Livesay, *Children of Uncertain Fortune: Mixed-Race Jamaicans in Britain and the Atlantic Family, 1733–1833* (Chapel Hill: University of North Carolina Press, 2018); Brooke N. Newman, *A Dark Inheritance: Blood, Race, and Sex in Colonial Jamaica* (New Haven, Conn.: Yale University Press, 2018).

6. Sharon Block, *Rape and Sexual Power in Early America* (Chapel Hill: University of North Carolina Press, 2006), 16–18, 63–74; María Raquél Casas, *Married to a Daughter of the Land: Spanish-Mexican Women and Interethnic Marriage in California, 1820–1880* (Reno: University of Nevada Press, 2007), 12–14; Brown, *Good Wives, Nasty Wenches*, 209–11; Jennifer L. Morgan, *Laboring Women: Reproduction and Gender in New World Slavery* (Philadelphia: University of Pennsylvania Press, 2004), 3–7.

7. I am indebted to Jennifer Morgan's research throughout this chapter. Jennifer L. Morgan, *Laboring Women*, 69–106; Philip D. Morgan, *Slave Counterpoint: Black Culture in the Eighteenth-Century Chesapeake and Lowcountry* (Chapel Hill: University of North Carolina Press, 1998), 488–89, 498–99.

8. Newman, *Dark Inheritance*, 20–21.

9. For various research on intermixture and exogamous marriage in colonial North America, see Gary B. Nash, Jennifer M. Spear, Graham Russell Hodges, Daniel R. Mandell, Richard Godbeer, and Peter W. Bardaglio in *Sex, Love, Race: Crossing Boundaries in North American History*, ed. Martha Hodes (New York: New York University Press, 1999).

10. Northumberland County, Record Books 1652–58, fol. 85, LVA; Warren M. Billings, ed., *The Old Dominion in the Seventeenth Century: A Documentary History of Virginia, 1606–1689* (Chapel Hill: University of North Carolina Press, 1975), 165–69; Heather Miyano Kopelson, *Faithful Bodies: Performing Religion and Race in the Puritan Atlantic* (New York: New York University Press, 2014), 227–28; J. H. Lefroy, *Memorials of the Discovery and Early Settlement of the Bermudas or Somers Islands* (London: Longmans, Green, 1879), 2:141.

11. Lefroy, *Memorials of the Discovery*, 2:141.

12. Lefroy, 2:141, 197; Virginia Bernhard, *Slaves and Slaveholders in Bermuda, 1616–1782* (Columbia: University of Missouri Press, 1999), 91–93.

13. Lefroy, *Memorials of the Discovery*, 2:190–91. Bermuda authorities permitted the

marriage of Thomas Wood to the "Mulatto woman" Ann Simons "to prevent their living in sin." Kopelson, *Faithful Bodies*, 226–30; Hening, *SALVA*, 3:86–88; Browne, *AOM*, 13: 546–49.

14. The negotiation of power, sex, and freedom between female slaves and male slave owners is a common feature in the both the colonial period and the early national era, notably with Sally Hemings and Thomas Jefferson. For more on the "treaty" or agreement between Sally and Thomas, see Annette Gordon-Reed, *The Hemingses of Monticello: An American Family* (New York: W. W. Norton, 2008); and Philip D. Morgan, "Interracial Sex in the Chesapeake and the British Atlantic World, c. 1700–1820," in *Sally Hemings and Thomas Jefferson: History, Memory, and Civic Culture*, ed. Jan Ellen Lewis and Peter S. Onuf (Charlottesville: University of Virginia Press, 1999), 62–66, 70–73. For the history of a mixed-heritage slave who combats the predatory sexual advances of her master, see Harriet Jacobs, *Incidents in the Life of a Slave Girl*, ed. Jean Fagan Yellin, enlarged ed. (Cambridge, Mass.: Harvard University Press, 1987; first published 1861 for the author [Boston]).

15. Lancaster County Orders 4, 1696–1702, 42–44, LVA; Deborah Gray White, *Ar'n't I a Woman: Female Slaves in the Plantation South* (New York: W. W. Norton, 1999), 27–46; Jennifer L. Morgan, *Laboring Women*, 3–7, 27, 42–45.

16. Lancaster County Orders 4, 1696–1702, 42–44, LVA.

17. On the importance of the local connections within colonial communities, see Lois Green Carr, Russell R. Menard, and Lorena S. Walsh, *Robert Cole's World: Agriculture and Society in Early Maryland* (Chapel Hill: University of North Carolina Press, 1991), 137–42.

18. Lancaster County Orders 4, 1696–1702, 42–44, LVA.

19. Though the Lancaster County court ordered that "Catherin[e] Scott & her Child are free And doe accordingly discharge her from y s[ai]d [William] Man," William appealed the decision to the General Court of Virginia. Lancaster County Orders 4, 1696–1702, 42–44, LVA.

20. Brown, *Good Wives, Nasty Wenches*, 238.

21. Joshua D. Rothman, *Notorious in the Neighborhood: Sex and Families across the Color Line, 1787–1861* (Chapel Hill: University of North Carolina Press, 2003), 4–11; Livesay, *Children of Uncertain Fortune*, 45–46, 103–4.

22. J. Harry Bennett, "Cary Helyar, Merchant and Planter of Seventeenth-Century Jamaica," *William and Mary Quarterly* 21, no. 1 (1964): 75; Richard S. Dunn, *Sugar and Slaves: The Rise of the Planter Class in the English West Indies, 1624–1713* (Chapel Hill: University of North Carolina Press, 1972), 212–21, 252–53.

23. Livesay, *Children of Uncertain Fortune*, 10–18.

24. Edward Long wrote that "Freed Blacks and Mulattoes ... hold a limited freedom" in Jamaica. Edward Long, *The History of Jamaica, or, General Survey of the Antient and Modern State of the Island: With Reflections on Its Situation Settlements, Inhabitants, Climate, Products, Commerce, Laws, and Government, Vol. II* (London: T. Lowndes, 1774), 320–22; Livesay, *Children of Uncertain Fortune*, 10–18, 40–52; Newman, *Dark Inheritance*, 121–28.

25. Dunn, *Sugar and Slaves*, 135–36, 143–46. Governor Daniel Parke also declared that "Mr. Perrie and old Col. Williams, as well as young Mr. Warner," kept intimate company with enslaved women. Governor Parke to the Earl of Dartmouth, Sept. 9, 1710 (fol. 391), in *Calendar of State Papers Colonial, America and West Indies*, vol. 25, 1710–1711, ed. Cecil Headlam (London: His Majesty's Stationery Office, 1924), 185–214.

26. Governor Parke to the Earl of Dartmouth, Sept. 9, 1710 (fol. 391), in Headlam, *Calendar of State Papers*, 25:185–214; Alan Burns, *History of the British West Indies* (London:

Allen and Unwin, 1954), 417–18; Helen Hill Miller, *Colonel Parke of Virginia: "The Greatest Hector in the Town"* (Chapel Hill, N.C.: Algonquin Books, 1989), xv, 8–9; Hening, *SALVA*, 3:86–88.

27. Dunn, *Sugar and Slaves*, 143–46; Miller, *Colonel Parke of Virginia*, 179–204.

28. Jill Lepore, *The Name of War: King Philip's War and the Origins of American Identity* (New York: Vintage Books, 1999), xiv–xv; Katy L. Chiles, *Transformable Race: Surprising Metamorphoses in the Literature of Early America* (New York: Oxford University Press, 2014), 1–3; Sharon Block, *Colonial Complexions: Race and Bodies in Eighteenth-Century America* (Philadelphia: University of Pennsylvania Press, 2018), 22–23; Livesay, *Children of Uncertain Fortune*, 103–4; Newman, *Dark Inheritance*, 75–84.

29. Carl Degler coined the "mulatto escape hatch" metaphor to refer to mixed-heritage people in Brazil who accessed the middle of a three-tier racial caste system, which stood in contradistinction to the binary racial system found in the United States. Carl N. Degler, *Neither Black nor White: Race Relations in Brazil and the United States* (London: Macmillan, 1971), 107, 223–25, 228–29; Block, *Colonial Complexions*, 30–31; William Douglass, *A Summary, Historical and Political, of the First Planting, Progressive Improvements, and Present State of the British Settlements in North-America* (Boston: Rogers and Fowle, 1749), 1:158; John Spencer Bassett, ed., *The Writings of "Colonel William Byrd of Westover in Virginia Esqr."* (New York: Doubleday, Page, 1901), 9.

30. H. R. McIlwaine, ed., *EJCCV*, vol. 3, *May 1, 1705–October 23, 1721* (Richmond: Virginia State Library, 1928), 28, 30–31.

31. Browne, *AOM*, 13:304–8; McIlwaine, *EJCCV*, 3:28, 30–31; Hening, *SALVA*, 3:86–88; Kopelson, *Faithful Bodies*, 251–52.

32. McIlwaine, *EJCCV*, 3:30–31; Jack D. Forbes, *Africans and Native Americans: The Language of Race and the Evolution of Red-Black Peoples* (Urbana-Champaign: University of Illinois Press, 1993), 221–23.

33. McIlwaine, *EJCCV*, 3:30–31.

34. McIlwaine, 3:30–31; Peter W. Bardaglio, "'Shamefull Matches': The Regulation of Interracial Sex and Marriage in the South before 1900," in Hodes, *Sex, Love, Race*, 112–16; H. R. McIlwaine, ed., *Journals of the House of Burgesses of Virginia, 1702/3–1705, 1705–1706, 1710–1712* (Richmond: Virginia State Library, 1912), 56; Hening, *SALVA*, 3:86–88, 252, 452–54; Clayton Colman Hall, *AOM*, 33:112.

35. Hening, *SALVA*, 3:250–52; 452–54.

36. Norfolk County Deed Book 9, 1710–17, 16, 17, 20, LVA (pages located in "Orders," appearing after "Deeds").

37. Norfolk County Deed Book 9, 1710–17, 16, 17, 20, LVA; Brown, *Good Wives, Nasty Wenches*, 7–9; Block, *Rape and Sexual Power*, 66.

38. Surry County, Orders, 1691–1713, 331, 336, 346, LVA.

39. Surry County, Orders, 1691–1713, 331, 336, 346, LVA. Later in the eighteenth century, Virginia and North Carolina records show several free Mulattoes with the surname Vaughan, who could be descended from Mary and Stephen Vanhon. Paul Heinegg, *Free African Americans of North Carolina, Virginia, and South Carolina, from the Colonial Period to About 1820*, 5th ed. (Baltimore: Clearfield, 2005), 2:1187–88.

40. Baltimore County Proceedings, 1711–13, 247, MSA; Brown, *Good Wives, Nasty Wenches*, 192–201.

41. As in many cases, the Baltimore County court did not record binding out Bess and William Bond's child, though they may have done so later. Baltimore County Proceedings, 1711–13, 247, MSA.

42. Browne, *AOM*, 13:546–49, 30:289; Clayton Colman Hall, *AOM*, 33:111–13; Hening, *SALVA*, 3:454.

43. Clayton Colman Hall, *AOM*, 33:111–13; Steiner, *AOM*, 36:275–76.

44. Steiner, *AOM*, 36: 275–76; Browne, *AOM*, 30:289–90; Clayton Colman Hall, *AOM*, 33:111–13.

45. Kopelson, *Faithful Bodies*, 204–12.

46. Herbert Gutman notes the prevalence of mixture in the marriage records of newly freed slaves after the Civil War, and Howard Bodenhorn has statistically shown a correlation in skin color among married people of color in the antebellum era. Herbert G. Gutman, *The Black Family in Slavery and Freedom, 1750–1925* (New York: Pantheon Books, 1976), 18–19; Bodenhorn, *Color Factor*, 98–122; William L. Hall, ed., *EJCCV*, vol. 5, *November 1, 1739–May 7, 1754* (Richmond: Virginia State Library, 1945), 195–96, 214–15.

47. *VG*, Jan. 28, 1775; Philip D. Morgan, *Slave Counterpoint*, 538–40.

48. *ARPMA*, vol. 1, *1692–1714* (Boston: Wright and Potter, 1869), 578; Hening, *SALVA*, 3:86–88; Lorenzo Johnston Greene, *The Negro in Colonial New England* (New York: Atheneum, 1968), 206–10.

49. Delaware authorities cut off both ears of "any Negro or Mulatto" slave who attempted to rape a "white woman." *LSDE* (New Castle, Del.: printed by Samuel and John Adams, 1797), 1:104–6, 108–9, 380; William H. Williams, *Slavery and Freedom in Delaware, 1639–1865* (Wilmington, Del.: Rowman and Littlefield, 1999), 112–113; *The Statutes at Large of Pennsylvania*, vol. 4, *1724–1744* (Philadelphia: Clarence M. Busch, 1897), 59–64. In 1723, Bermuda authorities sought to punish "white women" who had children "by any Negroe or other slave," though the penalties for "fornication" and "bastardy" were similar for other couples. Kopelson, *Faithful Bodies*, 249–50, 264–69.

50. Clark, *SRNC*, 23:64–65.

51. Noeleen McIlvenna, *A Very Mutinous People: The Struggle for North Carolina, 1660–1713* (Chapel Hill: University of North Carolina Press, 2009), 89–90, 133–34; Clark, *SRNC*, 23:106.

52. Hening, *SALVA*, 4:119–20, 127, 129, 131, 133–34; Livesay, *Children of Uncertain Fortune*, 31; Clark, *SRNC*, 23:106; Steiner, *AOM*, 36:275–76.

53. Virginia and Maryland set the tithable age for free women of color at sixteen years. Hening, *SALVA*, 4:133–34; Clark, *SRNC*, 23:72, 106; Clayton Colman Hall, ed., *AOM*, vol. 35, *PAGAM, October 1724–July 1726* (Baltimore: Maryland Historical Society, 1915), 427; Brown, *Good Wives, Nasty Wenches*, 120–28. Despite laws against it, ethnoracial mixture continued in North Carolina in the following centuries. Warren E. Milteer Jr., "The Strategies of Forbidden Love: Family across Racial Boundaries in Nineteenth-Century North Carolina," *Journal of Social History* 47, no. 3 (2014): 612–26.

54. Clark, *SRNC*, 23:160, 345.

55. Clark, 23:106, 160, 202–4; William Waller Hening, ed., *SALVA* (Richmond: Samuel Pleasants Jr., 1810), 2:252; *Acts of Assembly, Passed in the Island of Jamaica: From the Year 1681 to the Year 1768, Inclusive* (St. Jago de la Vega, Jamaica: Lowry and Sherlock, 1769), 1:179–81. In the early eighteenth century, Barbados lawmakers attempted to prohibit voting and court testimony by anyone "whose original Extract shall be proved to have been from a Negro." However, this appears more aspirational and less indicative of popular sentiment in the islands, as certain free Mulattoes were able to vote on other Caribbean islands. Winthrop D. Jordan, *White over Black: American Attitudes toward the Negro, 1550–1812* (Chapel Hill: University of North Carolina Press, 1968), 176–77.

56. Clark, *SRNC*, 23:106; Hening, *SALVA*, 3:250–51; Jordan, *White over Black*, 168; John

Henry Howard, ed., *The Laws of the British Colonies, in the West Indies and Other Parts of America, concerning Real and Personal Property and Manumission of Slaves* (London: William Henry Bond, 1827), 1:58–60; Long, *History of Jamaica*, 320–21.

57. Jennifer L. Morgan, *Laboring Women*, 69–106; Livesay, *Children of Uncertain Fortune*, 40; Newman, *Dark Inheritance*, 120–28; Alan L. Karras, *Sojourners in the Sun: Scottish Migrants in Jamaica and the Chesapeake, 1740–1800* (Ithaca, N.Y.: Cornell University Press, 1992), 71–72.

58. See the Gibson and Spencer families in Daniel J. Sharfstein, *The Invisible Line: Three American Families and the Secret Journey from Black to White* (New York: Penguin, 2011).

59. Ira Berlin, *Many Thousands Gone: The First Two Centuries of Slavery in North America* (Cambridge, Mass.: Belknap Press of Harvard University Press, 1998), 60–61; Rebecca Anne Goetz, *The Baptism of Early Virginia: How Christianity Created Race* (Baltimore: Johns Hopkins University Press, 2012), 86–100; Chowan County General Court Misc. Papers, folder "Papers pertaining to marriages," North Carolina State Archives, Raleigh.

60. Surprisingly, the Reverend John Blacknall appears to have turned himself in for marrying Thomas Spencer and Martha Paul. If Reverend Blacknall brought himself to the courts, he may have reduced his penalty, since a portion of fines went to those who reported offenders. He would then only have had to pay half of the fifty-pound fine. Chowan County General Court Misc. Papers, folder "Papers pertaining to marriages," North Carolina State Archives, Raleigh; Robert J. Cain, ed., *CRNC*, vol. 6, *North Carolina Higher-Court Minutes, 1724–1730* (Raleigh, N.C.: Department of Cultural Resources Division of Archives and History, 1981), 141, 143, 183, 327, 328; Saunders, *CRNC*, 2:662, 672, 700, 706–7, 714.

61. Westmoreland County Orders 1731–39, 75a, 296, 302, LVA; Heinegg, *Free African Americans of North Carolina*, 1:42; Brown, *Good Wives, Nasty Wenches*, 81, 92–94, 187–92. Interracial couples secretly traveled to other territories to formalize their relationships and legitimize their children in the nineteenth century. Bernie D. Jones, *Fathers of Conscience: Mixed-Race Inheritance in the Antebellum South* (Athens: University of Georgia Press, 2009), 129.

62. Queen Anne's County Court Judgement Record, 1732–35, 526, MSA. Kirsten Fischer rightly notes that "the political impact of any given transgression hinged more on *who* was breaking the law than on what actually transpired." In some cases, colonial courts were willing to punish free mixed-heritage women who had sex with African slaves. Kirsten Fischer, *Suspect Relations: Sex, Race, and Resistance in Colonial North Carolina* (Ithaca, N.Y.: Cornell University Press, 2002), 122.

63. Queen Anne's County Court Judgement Record, 1732–35, 526, MSA; Brown, *Good Wives, Nasty Wenches*, 237–40; Martha Hodes, *White Women, Black Men: Illicit Sex in the Nineteenth-Century South* (New Haven, Conn.: Yale University Press, 1997), 22–27.

64. Hening, *SALVA*, 4:452–54.

65. Peter Fontaine may have favored mixture with Native Americans because he believed "Indian children" were born "white" and only became darker in the sun after their families smeared them with "bears' grease." Peter Fontaine to Moses Fontaine, Mar. 30, 1757, in Ann Maury, *Memoirs of a Huguenot Family: Translated and Compiled from the Orginal Autobiography of the Rev. James Fontaine* (New York: George P. Putnam, 1853), 348–53; Bassett, "Colonel William Byrd," 8–10; Jordan, *White over Black*, 163; Brown, *Good Wives, Nasty Wenches*, 243.

66. Bassett, "Colonel William Byrd," 9; Maury, *Memoirs of a Huguenot Family*, 348–53.

67. One French traveler to the Chesapeake in 1791 wrote: "Woe to the white man who

would have the most secret love affair with a Negress, or colored woman! He would be scorned, dishonored; every house would be closed to him: he would be detested." The traveler was informed that "the inhabitants of the Carolinas and of Georgia are less scrupulous about these intrigues than are the inhabitants of Virginia, Maryland, and the northern states." Ferdinand-M. Bayard, *Travels of a Frenchman in Maryland and Virginia, with a Description of Philadelphia and Baltimore, in 1791*, ed. Ben C. McCrary (Ann Arbor, Mich.: Edwards Brothers, 1950), 20; Cooper, *SALSC*, 3:14, 19–20; William S. Price Jr., ed., *CRNC*, vol. 5, *North Carolina Higher-Court Records, 1709–1723* (Raleigh: North Carolina Department of Cultural Resources, 1977), 114–15; Clayton Colman Hall, *AOM*, 33:111; Dunn, *Sugar and Slaves*, 252–56; Newman, *Dark Inheritance*, 16–18; Samuel Dyssli to family and friends in Switzerland, Dec. 2, 1737, in *The South Carolina Historical and Genealogical Magazine*, ed. Mabel Louise Webber (Baltimore: Williams and Wilkins, 1922), 23:89–91; Peter H. Wood, *Black Majority: Negroes in Colonial South Carolina from 1670 through the Stono Rebellion* (New York: W. W. Norton, 1975), 234; Hennig Cohen, "Literary Reflections of Slavery from the South Carolina Gazette," *Journal of Negro History* 37, no. 2 (1952): 188–93.

68. William Dusinberre, *Them Dark Days: Slavery in the American Rice Swamps* (Athens: University of Georgia Press, 1996), 111–14; Samuel Dyssli to family and friends in Switzerland, Dec. 2, 1737, in Webber, *South Carolina Historical*, 23:89–91.

69. Long, *History of Jamaica*, 328; Livesay, *Children of Uncertain Fortune*, 62–63.

70. South Carolina magistrates complained about prostitution among women of color in Charlestown: "We present the too common practice of criminal conversation with negro and other slave wenches in this province, as an Enormity and Evil of general Ill-Consequene." *SCG*, Mar. 28, 1743; Long, *History of Jamaica*, 227, 230; Peter H. Wood, *Black Majority*, 233–36. Thomas Thistlewood relates a story in which an enslaved Mandingo woman named Lettice tried "to perswade" his nephew "to ly with her" because she "wanted to have a child for a master." Philip D. Morgan, "Interracial Sex in the Chesapeake," 69–73; Livesay, *Children of Uncertain Fortune*, 62–63.

71. *VG*, Mar. 31, 1774; Trevor Burnard, *Mastery, Tyranny, and Desire: Thomas Thistlewood and His Slaves in the Anglo-Jamaican World* (Chapel Hill: University of North Carolina Press, 2004), 237–38.

72. Bryan Edwards, *The History, Civil and Commercial, of the British Colonies in the West Indies* (London: John Stockdale, 1793), 2:20–22; Livesay, *Children of Uncertain Fortune*, 45–46, 75–77, 103–4.

73. While Bryan Edwards borrowed significant portions of his text on "persons of mixed blood (usually termed *People of Colour*) and Native blacks of free condition" from Edward Long's *History of Jamaica* (1774), the quoted portions used here appear to be his own writing on the subject. Edwards, *History, Civil and Commercial*, 2:20–26.

74. Lisa Ze Winters, *The Mulatta Concubine: Terror, Intimacy, Freedom, and Desire in the Black Atlantic* (Athens: University of Georgia Press, 2016), 1–4; Long, *History of Jamaica*, 327–28.

75. Betty Wood, *Slavery in Colonial Georgia, 1730–1775* (Athens: University of Georgia Press, 1984), 2–9; Noeleen McIlvenna, *The Short Life of Free Georgia: Class and Slavery in the Colonial South* (Chapel Hill: University of North Carolina Press, 2015).

76. Allen D. Candler, ed., *CRSGA*, vol. 4, *Stephens Journal, 1737–1740* (Atlanta: Franklin, 1906), 343–45.

77. Candler, *CRSGA*, 4:343–45.

78. Long, *History of Jamaica*, 331–32; Candler, *CRSGA*, 4:343–45.

79. Long, *History of Jamaica*, 328, 331–32.

80. John Martin Bolzius to Rev. Whitefield, Dec. 24, 1745, in *CRSGA*, vol. 24, *Original Papers, Correspondence, Trustees, General Oglethorpe and Others*, ed. Allen D. Candler and Lucian Lamar Knight (Atlanta: Chas. P. Byrd, 1915), 442; McIlvenna, *Short Life of Free Georgia*, 64–68.

81. Georgia officials also made fornication with a "Negroe or Black" illegal for European men and women and set a ten-pound fine. They did not assign additional servitude for the adults involved in or for the children produced from such relationships. Betty Wood, *Slavery in Colonial Georgia*, 76; Allen D. Candler, ed., *CRSGA* (Atlanta: Franklin, 1904), 1:59–60.

82. Allen D. Candler, ed., *CRSGA*, vol. 18, *Statutes Enacted by the Royal Legislature of Georgia from Its First Session in 1754 to 1768* (Atlanta: Chas. P. Byrd, 1910), 659.

83. Misc. Records, NN, 409–10, SCDAH; Deeds, Orders, Wills 12, 1702–6, 136, LVA; Heinegg, *Free African Americans of North Carolina*, 1:581–82.

84. Misc. Records, NN, 409–10, SCDAH; McIlvenna, *Short Life of Free Georgia*, 3.

85. Jordan, *White over Black*, 171–73; Peter H. Wood, *Black Majority*, 100–101; Williamson, *New People*, 30–32; Sharfstein, *Invisible Line*, 20–26; Heinegg, *Free African Americans of North Carolina*, 1:528–29.

86. Jordan, *White over Black*, 171–73.

87. Jordan, 171–73.

88. Jordan, 171–73.

89. Ira Berlin, *Slaves without Masters: The Free Negro in the Antebellum South* (New York: New Press, 1974), 364–66.

CHAPTER 6

1. *VG*, Nov. 17, 1774–June 3, 1775.

2. Howard Bodenhorn's work focuses on data analysis of free people of color in the U.S. antebellum era. Howard Bodenhorn, *The Color Factor: The Economics of African-American Well-Being in the Nineteenth-Century South* (New York: Oxford University Press, 2015), 1, 33.

3. J. H. Elliott, *Empires of the Atlantic World: Britain and Spain in America, 1492–1830* (New Haven, Conn.: Yale University Press, 2006), 168–73; Jennifer M. Spear, *Race, Sex, and Social Order in Early New Orleans* (Baltimore: John Hopkins University Press, 2009), 11–14.

4. William Waller Hening, ed., *SALVA* (New York: Thomas Desilver, 1823), 3:86–88, 452–54; William Waller Hening, ed., *SALVA* (Richmond: Franklin Press–W. W. Gray, 1820), 4:133; William Hand Browne, ed., *AOM*, vol. 7, *PAGAM, October 1678–November 1683* (Baltimore: Maryland Historical Society, 1889), 203–5; William Hand Browne, ed., *AOM*, vol. 13, *PAGAM, April 1684–June 1692* (Baltimore: Maryland Historical Society, 1894), 546–49; William Hand Browne, ed., *AOM*, vol. 30, *PAGAM, April 1715–August 1716* (Baltimore: Maryland Historical Society, 1910), 289–90; Walter Clark, ed., *SRNC*, vol. 23, *Laws 1715–1776* (Goldsboro, N.C.: Nash Brothers, 1904), 64–65, 160–61.

5. These estimates of Mulatto numbers are somewhat conservative and may have been higher. Ira Berlin notes that free people of color were "substantially underenumerated," because they stayed away from census takers. Ira Berlin, *Slaves without Masters: The Free Negro in the Antebellum South* (New York: New Press, 1974), 49–50; Ira Berlin, *Many Thousands Gone: The First Two Centuries of Slavery in North America* (Cambridge, Mass.: Belknap Press of Harvard University Press, 1998), 36–38, 109–10, 136–37, 156–57.

6. Philip D. Morgan, *Slave Counterpoint: Black Culture in the Eighteenth-Century Chesapeake and Lowcountry* (Chapel Hill: University of North Carolina Press, 1998), 385–98.

7. Winthrop D. Jordan, *White over Black: American Attitudes toward the Negro, 1550–1812* (Chapel Hill: University of North Carolina Press, 1968), 171; Allyson Hobbs, *A Chosen Exile: A History of Racial Passing in American Life* (Cambridge, Mass.: Harvard University Press, 2014), 25–30.

8. Eugene D. Genovese, *Roll, Jordan, Roll: The World the Slaves Made* (New York: Pantheon Books, 1974), 327–28; Jordan, *White over Black*, 167–70, 174–78.

9. Elliott, *Empires of the Atlantic World*, 281–83.

10. Spear, *Race, Sex, and Social Order*, 21–42.

11. Fred Anderson, *Crucible of War: The Seven Years' War and the Fate of Empire in British North America, 1754–1766* (New York: Knopf, 2000), 11–32.

12. Anderson, 11–32; James H. Merrell, "'The Cast of His Countenance': Reading Andrew Montour," in *Through a Glass Darkly: Reflections on Personal Identity in Early America*, ed. Ronald Hoffman, Mechel Sobel, and Fredrika J. Teute (Chapel Hill: University of North Carolina Press, 1997), 13–39.

13. *PG*, July 31, 1746; James Axtell, *The Invasion Within: The Contest of Cultures in Colonial North America* (New York: Oxford University Press, 1985), 287–97.

14. *MG*, Mar. 20, 1755; *PG*, Mar. 25, 1755.

15. Robert Olwell, "Becoming Free: Manumission and the Genesis of a Free Black Community in South Carolina, 1740–90," *Slavery and Abolition* 17, no. 1 (1996): 2; Gerald Horne, *The Counter-Revolution of 1776: Slave Resistance and the Origins of the United States of America* (New York: New York University Press, 2014), 178; Daniel J. Tortura, *Carolina in Crisis: Cherokees, Colonists, and Slaves in the American Southeast, 1756–1763* (Chapel Hill: University of North Carolina Press, 2015), 65–67.

16. Tortura, *Carolina in Crisis*, 65–67.

17. Jane Landers, *Black Society in Spanish Florida* (Urbana: University of Illinois Press, 1999), 37–38; B. R. Carroll, ed., *Historical Collections of South Carolina* (New York: Harper and Brothers, 1836), 2:348–50; *SCG*, Oct. 10, 1761, July 24–Oct. 16, 1762.

18. Alejandra Dubcovsky, *Informed Power: Communication in the Early American South* (Cambridge, Mass.: Harvard University Press, 2016), 1–3, 114–17; *SCG*, Nov. 20, 1762.

19. Anderson, *Crucible of War*, 505–6, 508–10.

20. Bradley G. Bond, ed., *French Colonial Louisiana and the Atlantic World: An Elegy* (Baton Rouge: Louisiana State University Press, 2005), 177–80; Spear, *Race, Sex, and Social Order*, 65; Jennifer L. Palmer, *Intimate Bonds: Family and Slavery in the French Atlantic* (Philadelphia: University of Pennsylvania Press, 2016), 11–12.

21. Paul Leroy-Beaulieu, *De la colonisation chez les peuples modernes* (Paris: Journal de Économistes, 1874), 182; Spear, *Race, Sex, and Social Order*, 61–68; Palmer, *Intimate Bonds*, 11–16; Edward Long, *The History of Jamaica, or, General Survey of the Antient and Modern State of the Island: With Reflections on Its Situation Settlements, Inhabitants, Climate, Products, Commerce, Laws, and Government*, vol. II (London: T. Lowndes, 1774), 332–35.

22. Alexander de Humboldt and Aimé Bonpland, *Personal Narrative of Travels to the Equinoctial Regions of the New Continent* (London: Paternoster Row, 1826), 820–27; Palmer, *Intimate Bonds*, 239n43; William K. Knight, ed., *General History of the Caribbean*, vol. 3, *The Slave Societies of the Caribbean* (London: UNESCO, 1997), 48–50.

23. In Barbados, the numbers for Mulattoes and mixed-heritage people are difficult to determine. The enumeration of free people of color appear dramatically low at 488 (1768)

and 534 (1773) out of a population that hovered around 80,000–110,000 during the second half of the eighteenth century. "An Account of the Number of Souls in the Province of Maryland, in the Year 1755," *Gentleman's Magazine, and Historical Chronicle* 34 (1764): 261; David H. Makinson, *Barbados: A Study of North-America-West-Indian Relations 1739–1789* (London: Mouton, 1964), 15; John J. McCusker and Russell R. Menard, *The Economy of British America, 1607–1789* (Chapel Hill: University of North Carolina Press, 1991), 151–53.

24. Daniel Livesay, *Children of Uncertain Fortune: Mixed-Race Jamaicans in Britain and the Atlantic Family, 1733–1833* (Chapel Hill: University of North Carolina Press, 2018), 24; Brooke N. Newman, *A Dark Inheritance: Blood, Race, and Sex in Colonial Jamaica* (New Haven, Conn.: Yale University Press, 2018), 17; Gad J. Heuman, *Between Black and White: Race, Politics, and the Free Coloreds in Jamaica, 1792–1865* (Westport, Conn.: Greenwood, 1981), 7; Long, *History of Jamaica*, 337; "Account of the Number of Souls," 261.

25. "Account of the Number of Souls," 261; Virginia Bernhard, *Slaves and Slaveholders in Bermuda, 1616–1782* (Columbia: University of Missouri Press, 1999), 97–98, 187; Robert V. Wells, *The Population of the British Colonies in America before 1776: A Survey of Census Data* (Princeton, N.J.: Princeton University Press, 1975), 196, 209, 238.

26. "Account of the Number of Souls," 261; Susan B. Carter, Scott Sigmund Gartner, Michael R. Haines, Alan L. Olmstead, Richard Sutch, and Galvan Wright, eds., *Historical Statistics of the United States*, millennial ed., online ver. (New York: Cambridge University Press, 2006), "Colonial Statistics," tables Eg. 33–34, 52–53; Joel Williamson, *New People: Miscegenation and Mulattoes in the United States* (New York: Free Press, 1980), 14, 25; Peter H. Wood, *Black Majority: Negroes in Colonial South Carolina from 1670 through the Stono Rebellion* (New York: W. W. Norton, 1975), 98–100.

27. Misc. Records, 1721–76, SCDAH; Olwell, "Becoming Free."

28. Some have estimated that mixed-heritage children accounted for approximately one-third of all colonial manumissions in South Carolina. My independent research also confirms this, though we do not always know who is responsible for the emancipatory acts. Wood, *Black Majority*, 100; Berlin, *Slaves without Masters*, 151–52; Misc. Records AB, Mortgages, 1735–36, 90–92, SCDAH; Charleston County, Record of Wills, 1732–37, 3:240–42, SCDAH; Larry Koger, *Black Slaveowners: Free Black Slave Masters in South Carolina, 1790–1860* (Columbia: University of South Carolina Press, 1995), 13–14; Misc. Records, WW, 77–80, SCDAH.

29. Francis Vesey, ed., *Reports of Cases Argued and Determined in the High Court of Chancery, in the Time of Lord Chancellor Hardwicke, from the Year 1746-7, to 1755*, 3rd ed. (Philadelphia: Robert H. Small, 1788), 1:512–17; Trevor Burnard, *Mastery, Tyranny, and Desire: Thomas Thistlewood and His Slaves in the Anglo-Jamaican World* (Chapel Hill: University of North Carolina Press, 2004), 53–54; Livesay, *Children of Uncertain Fortune*, 59–60.

30. Livesay, *Children of Uncertain Fortune*, 101–2.

31. Long, *History of Jamaica*, 328–30; Livesay, *Children of Uncertain Fortune*, 97–112, 152–74.

32. Edward Long, *Candid Reflections upon the Judgement Lately Awarded by the Court of King's Bench, in Westminster-Hall, on What Is Commonly Called the Negroe-Cause, by a Planter* (London: T. Lowndes, 1772), 48–49.

33. George C. Rogers Jr. and David R. Chesnutt, eds., *The Papers of Henry Laurens*, vol. 9, *April 19, 1773–Dec. 12, 1774* (Columbia: University of South Carolina Press, 1981), 316–18; Samuel Estwick, *Considerations on the Negroe Cause Commonly so Called: Addressed to the Right Honourable Lord Mansfield, Lord Chief Justice of the Court of King's Bench, &c.*

(London: J. Dodsley, 1772), 44; Livesay, *Children of Uncertain Fortune*, 27, 63–66, 74–77, 109–10, 125–26; Newman, *Dark Inheritance*, 138–42.

34. William L. Saunders, ed., *CRNC*, vol. 3, *1728–1734* (Raleigh, N.C.: P. M. Hale, 1886), 556–57.

35. Thomas N. Ingersoll, "'Releese Us out of This Cruell Bondegg': An Appeal from Virginia in 1723," *William and Mary Quarterly* 51, no. 4 (1994): 777–82; Kirsten Fischer, *Suspect Relations: Sex, Race, and Resistance in Colonial North Carolina* (Ithaca, N.Y.: Cornell University Press, 2002), 101–3, 122–26; Robert J. Cain, ed., *CRNC*, vol. 10, *The Church of England in North Carolina: Documents, 1699–1741* (Raleigh: North Carolina Department of Cultural Resources, 1999), 489.

36. Kathleen M. Brown, *Good Wives, Nasty Wenches, and Anxious Patriarchs: Gender, Race, and Power in Colonial Virginia* (Chapel Hill: University of North Carolina Press, 1996), 230; Holly Brewer, *By Birth or Consent: Children, Law, and the Anglo-American Revolution in Authority* (Chapel Hill: University of North Carolina Press, 2007), 230–31, 263–64.

37. Saunders, *CRNC*, 3:556–57; Fischer, *Suspect Relations*, 230–31n49.

38. Fischer, *Suspect Relations*, 123–25, 230n45, 231n49; Allan Kulikoff, *Tobacco and Slaves: The Development of Southern Cultures in the Chesapeake, 1680–1800* (Chapel Hill: University of North Carolina Press, 1986), 169–70; Brewer, *By Birth or Consent*, 230–32, 242–46.

39. William H. Williams, *Slavery and Freedom in Delaware, 1639–1865* (Wilmington, Del.: Rowman and Littlefield, 1999), 113; John Codman Hurd, *The Law of Freedom and Bondage in the United States* (Boston: Little, Brown, 1858), 1:292–93. North Carolina's law also directed courts to establish European male orphans under apprenticeships "to some Tradesman, Merchant, Mariner, or other Person approved by the Court" until they turned twenty-one. Courts apprenticed European female children "to some suitable Employment" until eighteen years old. Clark, *SRNC*, 23:65, 160–61, 345, 581.

40. Saunders, *CRNC*, 3:556–57; Fischer, *Suspect Relations*, 230–31n49; William Waller Hening, ed., *SALVA* (Richmond: J. and G. Cochran, 1821), 8:133–35.

41. Hening, *SALVA*, 4:133; William Waller Hening, ed., *SALVA* (Richmond: Franklin Press-W. W. Gray, 1819), 6:357; Hening, *SALVA*, 8:133–35.

42. Turk McCleskey, *The Road to Black Ned's Forge: A Story of Race, Sex, and Trade on the Colonial American Frontier* (Charlottesville: University of Virginia Press, 2014), 165–66. The Virginia Resolves were passed on Thursday, May 30, 1765, and the reduction in time for Mulatto identures was debated in the preceding days and presented Saturday, June 1, 1765. John Pendleton Kennedy, ed., *Journals of the House of Burgesses of Virginia, 1761–1765* (Richmond: Virginia State Library, 1907), 262, 287, 305, 342, 345–46, 359–60, 363; John Pendleton Kennedy, ed., *Journals of the House of Burgesses of Virginia, 1766–1769* (Richmond: Virginia State Library, 1906), 198–99, 203, 246, 267, 275, 295, 304; H. R. McIlwaine, ed., *Legislative Journals of the Council of Colonial Virginia* (Richmond: Virginia State Library, 1919), 3:1397, 1400–1401; Hening, *SALVA*, 8:133–35, 393.

43. *VG*, May 2, 1766, Aug. 16, 1770.

44. *VG*, May 2, 1766, Aug. 16, 1770.

45. *VG*, Sept. 5, 1766, July 28, 1768.

46. *VG*, Dec. 17, 1767, Apr. 21, 1768, Jan. 10, 1771; Thomas D. Morris, *Southern Slavery and the Law, 1619–1860* (Chapel Hill: University of North Carolina Press, 1996), 340–43.

47. *SCG*, Mar. 12, 1737; Sharon Block, *Colonial Complexions: Race and Bodies in Eighteenth-Century America* (Philadelphia: University of Pennsylvania Press, 2018), 133–34. Howard Bodenhorn refers to a general "mulatto advantage," though I am more

comfortable with the phrase "Mulatto privilege," since there were also many disadvantages for people of mixed ancestry. These privileges were situational, often temporary, and varied between individuals. Howard Bodenhorn, "The Mulatto Advantage: The Biological Consequences of Complexion in Rural Antebellum Virginia," *Journal of Interdisciplinary History* 33, no. 1 (2002): 21–46.

48. *SCG*, Feb. 1, 1739, Aug. 4, 1746, May 9, 1745; Block, *Colonial Complexions*, 132–33.

49. Born in the nineteenth century, Frederick Douglass's mother was a "colored, and quite dark" slave and his "father was a white man." He knew of cases where Mulatto slaves "invariably suffer greater hardships, and have more to contend with, than others," especially under the hand of the slave mistress (the master's wife). "The master is frequently compelled to sell this class of his slaves," he wrote. Harriet Jacobs, another slave of mixed ancestry, wrote of her master's sexual harassment and his wife's ill treatment toward her: "I was an object of her jealousy, and, consequently, of her hatred; and I knew I could not expect kindness or confidence from her under the circumstances in which I was placed." Frederick Douglass, *Narrative of the Life of Frederick Douglass, an American Slave* (Boston: Anti-Slavery Office, 1845), 2–5; Harriet Jacobs, *Incidents in the Life of a Slave Girl*, ed. Jean Fagan Yellin, enlarged ed. (Cambridge, Mass.: Harvard University Press, 1987; first published 1861 for the author [Boston]), 53; *VG2*, Oct. 22, 1772.

50. *VG2*, Oct. 22, Nov. 19, 1772.

51. *VG*, May 9, June 20, Oct. 31, 1751, Sept. 2, 1757.

52. *VG*, Mar. 31, 1774.

53. *VG2*, May 30, 1771. A 1672 law made it lawful for anyone "to kill or wound" any "such negroe, mollatto, Indian slave, or servant for life" who was in "resistance." Included in Virginia's 1691 act aimed at preventing "abominable mixture and spurious issue" is a clause for the reimbursement of such slaves from the public levy. William Waller Hening, ed., *SALVA* (Richmond: Samuel Pleasants Jr., 1810), 2:299–300; Hening, *SALVA*, 3:86, 460–61, 4:130–31, 6:110–11; *SCG*, Feb. 3, 1757, Oct. 20, 1758; Block, *Colonial Complexions*, 133.

54. South Carolina authorities also reimbursed masters when slaves were killed while running away or in rebellion. *SCG*, Feb. 3, 1757, Oct. 20, 1758; David J. McCord, ed., *SALSC*, vol. 7, *Containing the Acts Relating to Charleston, Courts, Slaves, and Rivers* (Columbia, S.C.: A. S. Johnston, 1840), 357–58.

55. Bodenhorn, *Color Factor*, 1–4, 33, 68–69, 96–97, 165–66, 186–87.

56. Morgan, *Slave Counterpoint*, 204–54.

57. Wood, *Black Majority*, 35–37, 55–62; Morgan, *Slave Counterpoint*, 204–12.

58. *SCG*, Mar. 21, 1761.

59. Berlin, *Many Thousands Gone*, 47, 126–29.

60. *VG2*, Oct. 27, 1768; Berlin, *Many Thousands Gone*, 134–37, 156–57.

61. *VG2*, Oct. 27, 1768; McCleskey, *Road to Black Ned's Forge*, 3–4, 167–70.

62. *Georgia Gazette*, Feb. 2, 1764; Lathan A. Windley, ed., *Runaway Slave Advertisements: A Documentary History from the 1730s to 1790*, vol. 4, *Georgia* (Westport, Conn.: Greenwood, 1983), 4; *SCG*, July 25, 1768.

63. *PG*, June 29, July 13, 1769; Block, *Colonial Complexions*, 103–4.

64. *VG*, Nov. 26, 1772. See David, a "Mulatto Slave" living in Dinwiddie County, Virginia, who also said he was "of the *Indian* Breed." *VG*, July 15, 22, 29, 1773. Mixed African and Indigenous slaves in Latin America similarly argued that their "Indian" lineage should legally grant them freedom. Joanne Rappaport, *The Disappearing Mestizo: Configuring Difference in the Colonial New Kingdom of Granada* (Durham, N.C.: Duke University Press, 2014), 72–79.

65. *VG2*, Mar. 10, 1774.

66. Block, *Colonial Complexions*, 104–8.

67. John Hope Franklin and Loren Schweninger, *Runaway Slaves: Rebels on the Plantation* (New York: Oxford University Press, 1999), 149–56, 170–81. See Block, *Colonial Complexions*. For race as performance, see Ariela Gross, "Performing Whiteness," in *What Blood Won't Tell: A History of Race on Trial in America* (Cambridge, Mass.: Harvard University Press, 2008), 48–72.

68. Annas's name is spelled differently in various sources. *VG*, Jan. 28, 1768, June 14, 1770; Block, *Colonial Complexions*, 133–34.

69. *VG2*, May 9, 1771.

70. *SCG*, Feb. 15, 1752; *MG*, Apr. 10, 1766; *VG*, May 2, 1766; *PG*, July 4, 1771; Berlin, *Many Thousands Gone*, 128.

71. *VG*, Apr. 14–Sept. 8, 1774; *PG*, Apr. 27, 1774; Berlin, *Many Thousands Gone*, 128.

72. *VG*, May 16, 1771.

73. *VG*, May 16, 1771; Kulikoff, *Tobacco and Slaves*, 118–22, 157–61.

74. Lathan A. Windley, ed., *Runaway Slave Advertisements: A Documentary History from the 1730s to 1790*, vol. 2, *Maryland* (Westport, Conn.: Greenwood, 1983), 1–114, 191–93; Gerald W. Mullin, *Flight and Rebellion: Slave Resistance in Eighteenth-Century Virginia* (New York: Oxford University Press, 1972), 108.

75. *VG*, May 6, 1773; Morgan, *Slave Counterpoint*, 524–30.

76. *VG*, Mar. 19, 1772.

77. *VG*, Mar. 19, 1772; James Mercer Garnett, "James Mercer," *William and Mary Quarterly* 17, no. 2 (1908): 85–99.

78. *VG*, Mar. 19, 1772.

79. *VG*, Mar. 19, 1772; Morgan, *Slave Counterpoint*, 353–58.

80. *VG*, Mar. 19, 1772.

81. *VG*, Feb. 18, 25, Mar. 4, 11, 1775, Sept. 29, 1768. The "mulatto fellow" Daniel Cumbo was another urban slave who left his master, in Charles City, Virginia. He could write or knew someone who could write for him. Daniel escaped with "a forged pass, and passes as a freeman," said his master. *VG2*, Oct. 21, 1773. In Jamaica, "every free Mulatto, Negro, or Indian" who was not a planter owning ten slaves or more was ordered to register for a free certificate and wear a "Badge of a blue Cross" on his or her right shoulder. *Acts of Assembly, Passed in the Island of Jamaica: From the Year 1681 to the Year 1768, Inclusive* (St. Jago de la Vega, Jamaica: Lowry and Sherlock, 1769), 1:116.

82. *VG*, Mar. 11, 1775; Woody Holton, *Forced Founders: Indians, Debtors, Slaves, and the Making of the American Revolution in Virginia* (Chapel Hill: University of North Carolina Press, 1999) 156–61. Howard Bodenhorn finds that approximately 70 percent of free people of color described as "yellow" or "light" were listed as Mulatto in mid-nineteenth-century Virginia censuses. Bodenhorn, *Color Factor*, 6.

83. Orlando Patterson, *Slavery and Social Death: A Comparative Study* (Cambridge, Mass.: Harvard University Press, 1982), 10–12.

CONCLUSION

1. *VG*, June 16, 30, July 28, Aug. 4, 11, 1774; *VG2*, June 30, July 28, Aug. 4, 11, 1774.

2. *VG*, June 16, 30, July 28, Aug. 4, 11, 1774; *VG2*, June 30, July 28, Aug. 4, 11, 1774, Sept. 7, 1769. See Thomas Jefferson's advertisement for the return of "a Mulatto called Sandy" in *VG*, Sept. 21, 1769.

3. Barbara Fields, "Slavery, Race and Ideology in the United States of America," *New Left Review*, no. 181 (1990): 95–118.

4. Fields, 95–118; Jack P. Greene, *Pursuits of Happiness: The Social Development of Early Modern British Colonies and the Formation of American Culture* (Chapel Hill: University of North Carolina Press, 1988), 1–5; Daniel J. Sharfstein, "Crossing the Color Line: Racial Migration and the One-Drop Rule, 1600–1860," *Minnesota Law Review* 91, no. 3 (2007): 592–656.

5. Edmund S. Morgan, *American Slavery, American Freedom: The Ordeal of Colonial Virginia* (New York: W. W. Norton, 1975), 1–6.

6. Barbara Fields, "Slavery, Race and Ideology"; Thomas C. Holt, "Marking: Race, Race-Making, and the Writing of History," *American Historical Review* 100, no. 1 (February 1995): 1–20.

7. William Hand Browne, ed., *AOM*, vol. 1, *PAGAM, January 1637/8–September 1664* (Baltimore: Maryland Historical Society, 1883), 533–34.

8. William Waller Hening, ed., *SALVA* (New York: Thomas Desilver, 1823), 3:86–88.

9. William Waller Hening, ed., *SALVA* (Richmond: Samuel Pleasants Jr., 1810), 2:170; Hening, *SALVA*, 3:86–88; Browne, *AOM*, 1:533–34; William Hand Browne, ed., *AOM*, vol. 7, *PAGAM, October 1678–November 1683* (Baltimore: Maryland Historical Society, 1889), 203–5; William Hand Browne, ed., *AOM*, vol. 13, *PAGAM, April 1684–June 1692* (Baltimore: Maryland Historical Society, 1894), 546–49; Walter Clark, ed., *SRNC*, vol. 23, *Laws 1715–1776* (Goldsboro, N.C.: Nash Brothers, 1904), 64–65.

10. *LSDE* (New Castle, Del.: printed by Samuel and John Adams, 1797), 1:108–9; John Codman Hurd, *The Law of Freedom and Bondage in the United States* (Boston: Little, Brown, 1858), 1:292; *The Statutes at Large of Pennsylvania*, vol. 4, *1724–1744* (Philadelphia: Clarence M. Busch, 1897), 62–63.

11. Carl N. Degler, *Neither Black nor White: Race Relations in Brazil and the United States* (London: Macmillan, 1971), 107, 223–25.

12. Alan Gallay, *The Indian Slave Trade: The Rise of the English Empire in the American South, 1670–1717* (New Haven, Conn.: Yale University Press, 2002), 294–99.

13. Greg Carter, *The United States of the United Races: A Utopian History of Racial Mixing* (New York: New York University Press, 2013), 60, 108–10. Sir Nathaniel Johnson went on to become governor of South Carolina in the early eighteenth century. Sir Nathaniel Johnson to Lords of Trade and Plantations, April 20, 1689 (fol. 83), in *Calendar of State Papers, Colonial Series, America and West Indies*, vol. 13, *1689–1692*, ed. J. W. Fortescue, 25–27 (London: Mackie, 1901); Sharon Block, *Colonial Complexions: Race and Bodies in Eighteenth-Century America* (Philadelphia: University of Pennsylvania Press, 2018), 30–32.

14. Thomas N. Ingersoll, "'Releese Us out of This Cruell Bondegg': An Appeal from Virginia in 1723," *William and Mary Quarterly* 51, no. 4 (1994): 777–82.

15. Edmund Burke, *An Account of the European Settlements in America*, vol. II, 3rd ed. (London: printed for R. and J. Dodsley, 1760), 130–31.

16. Carter, *United States of the United Races*, 156–57.

17. Sharfstein, "Crossing the Color Line," 610–15.

18. Kim M. Williams, *Mark One or More: Civil Rights in Multiracial America* (Ann Arbor: University of Michigan Press, 2006), 2; Carter, *United States of the United Races*, 161–91, 201–16; Karen E. Fields and Barbara J. Fields, *Racecraft: The Soul of Inequality in American Life* (London: Verso, 2012), 1–4.

# BIBLIOGRAPHY

### ARCHIVES

Library of Virginia, Richmond
Maryland State Archives, Annapolis
North Carolina State Archives, Raleigh

South Carolina Department of Archives
and History, Columbia

### NEWSPAPERS

*American Weekly Mercury* (Philadelphia)
*Georgia Gazette*
*Maryland Gazette*
*New-York Gazette*
*New-York Gazette, or, The Weekly Post-Boy*
*New-York Weekly Journal*
*Pennsylvania Gazette*
*South-Carolina Gazette*
*South-Carolina Gazette and Country Journal*

*Virginia Gazette* (1st ed., edited by William Parks et al., 1730–80)
*Virginia Gazette* (2nd ed., edited by William Rind, Clementina Rind, and John Pinkney, 1766–76)
*Virginia Gazette* (3rd ed., edited by Alexander Purdie, John Clarkson, and Augustine Davis, 1775–80)

### PUBLISHED SOURCES

"An Account of the Number of Souls in the Province of Maryland, in the Year 1755." *Gentleman's Magazine, and Historical Chronicle* 34 (1764): 261.

*Act and Laws, Passed by the General Court or Assembly of His Majesties Province of New-Hampshire in New-England.* Boston: B. Green, 1726.

*The Acts and Resolves, Public and Private, of the Province of Massachusetts Bay.* Vol. 1, 1692–1714. Boston: Wright and Potter, 1869.

*Acts of Assembly, Passed in the Island of Jamaica: From the Year 1681 to the Year 1768, Inclusive.* Vol. 1. St. Jago de la Vega, Jamaica: Lowry and Sherlock, 1769.

*Acts of Assembly, Passed in the Province of New-York, from 1691, to 1718.* London: John Baskett, 1719.

Adams, Catherine, and Elizabeth H. Pleck. *Love of Freedom: Black Women in Colonial and Revolutionary New England.* New York: Oxford University Press, 2010.

Alfonso X. *General estoria: Primera parte.* Edited by Antonio García Solalinde. Madrid: Centro de Estudios Históricos, 1930.

Allinson, Samuel, ed. *Acts of the General Assembly of the Province of New-Jersey.* Burlington, N.J.: Isaac Collins, 1776.

"The Ancestors and Descendants of John Rolfe with Notices of Some Connected

Families." Pts. 1–3. *Virginia Magazine of History and Biography* 21, no. 2 (1913): 208–11; 22, no. 1 (1914): 103–7; 22, no. 2 (1914): 215–17.

Anderson, Fred. *Crucible of War: The Seven Years' War and the Fate of Empire in British North America, 1754–1766*. New York: Knopf, 2000.

Aptheker, Herbert. *American Negro Slave Revolts*. 4th ed. New York: International Publishers, 1963.

Armstrong, Edward, ed. *The Record of the Court at Upland, in Pennsylvania, 1676 to 1681*. Philadelphia: Joseph M. Mitchell, 1959.

Axtell, James. *The Invasion Within: The Contest of Cultures in Colonial North America*. New York: Oxford University Press, 1985.

Banks, Taunya Lovell. "Dangerous Woman: Elizabeth Key's Freedom Suit—Subjecthood and Racialized Identity in Seventeenth Century Colonial Virginia." *Akron Law Review* 41, no. 3 (2008): 799–837.

Barwick, Atwood S., ed. *Archives of Maryland*. Vol. 87, *Somerset County Court, Judicial Record, 1671–1675*. Pt. 1. Lakeville, Conn.: Maryland State Archives, 1999.

Bassett, John Spencer, ed. *The Writings of "Colonel William Byrd of Westover in Virginia Esqr."* New York: Doubleday, Page, 1901.

Bayard, Ferdinand-M. *Travels of a Frenchman in Maryland and Virginia, with a Description of Philadelphia and Baltimore, in 1791*. Edited by Ben C. McCrary. Ann Arbor, Mich.: Edwards Brothers, 1950.

Bayor, Ronald H., and Timothy J. Meagher, eds. *The New York Irish*. Baltimore: Johns Hopkins University Press, 1997.

Beckles, Hilary McD. *Natural Rebels: A Social History of Enslaved Black Women in Barbados*. New Brunswick, N.J.: Rutgers University Press, 1989.

Bell, Albert D. *Bass Families of the South: A Collection of Historical and Genealogical Source Materials from Public and Private Records*. Rocky Mount, N.C.: Albert D. Bell, 1961.

Bennett, J. Harry. "Cary Helyar, Merchant and Planter of Seventeenth-Century Jamaica." *William and Mary Quarterly* 21, no. 1 (1964): 53–76.

Berlin, Ira. *Many Thousands Gone: The First Two Centuries of Slavery in North America*. Cambridge, Mass.: Belknap Press of Harvard University Press, 1998.

———. *Slaves without Masters: The Free Negro in the Antebellum South*. New York: New Press, 1974.

———. "Time, Space, and the Evolution of Afro-American Society on British Mainland North America." *American Historical Review* 85, no. 1 (1980): 44–78.

"Bernard Family." *William and Mary Quarterly* 5, no. 3 (1897): 181–87.

Bernhard, Virginia. *Slaves and Slaveholders in Bermuda, 1616–1782*. Columbia: University of Missouri Press, 1999.

Beverly, Robert. *The History of Virginia, in Four Parts*. 4 vols. London: R. Parker, 1705.

Billings, Warren M. "The Cases of Fernando and Elizabeth Key: A Note on the Status of Blacks in Seventeenth-Century Virginia." *William and Mary Quarterly* 30, no. 3 (1973): 467–74.

———. "The Law of Servants and Slaves in Seventeenth-Century Virginia." *Virginia Magazine of History and Biography* 99, no. 1 (1991): 45–62.

———, ed. *The Old Dominion in the Seventeenth Century: A Documentary History of Virginia, 1606–1689*. Chapel Hill: University of North Carolina Press, 1975.

Block, Sharon. *Colonial Complexions: Race and Bodies in Eighteenth-Century America*. Philadelphia: University of Pennsylvania Press, 2018.

———. *Rape and Sexual Power in Early America*. Chapel Hill: University of North Carolina Press, 2006.

Blount, Thomas. *Glossographia Anglicana Nova: Or, A Dictionary*. London: Tho. Newcomb, 1656.

Bodenhorn, Howard. *The Color Factor: The Economics of African-American Well-Being in the Nineteenth-Century South*. New York: Oxford University Press, 2015.

———. "The Mulatto Advantage: The Biological Consequences of Complexion in Rural Antebellum Virginia." *Journal of Interdisciplinary History* 33, no. 1 (2002): 21–46.

Bogen, David S. "Mathias de Sousa: Maryland's First Colonist of African Descent." *Maryland Historical Magazine* 96, no. 1 (2001): 68–85.

Bolzius, Johann Martin. "Reliable Answer to Some Submitted Questions concerning the Land Carolina." *William and Mary Quarterly* 14, no. 2 (1957): 223–61.

Bond, Bradley G., ed. *French Colonial Louisiana and the Atlantic World: An Elegy*. Baton Rouge: Louisiana State University Press, 2005.

Bonilla-Silva, Eduardo. "The Essential Social Fact of Race." *American Sociological Review* 64, no. 6 (1999): 899–906.

Bonomi, Patricia U. *Under the Cope of Heaven: Religion, Society, and Politics in Colonial America*. Updated ed. New York: Oxford University Press, 2003.

Bowne, Eric E. *The Westo Indians: Slave Traders of the Early Colonial South*. Tuscaloosa: University of Alabama Press, 2005.

Brandow, James C., ed. *Genealogies of Barbados Families: From Caribbeana and the Journal of the Barbados Museum and Historical Society*. Baltimore: Clearfield, 1997.

Breen, T. H., and Stephen Innes. *"Myne Owne Ground": Race and Freedom on Virginia's Eastern Shore, 1640–1676*. New York: Oxford University Press, 1980.

Brewer, Holly. *By Birth or Consent: Children, Law, and the Anglo-American Revolution in Authority*. Chapel Hill: University of North Carolina Press, 2007.

Brooks, N. C., ed. *A Relation of the Colony of the Lord Baron of Baltimore, in Maryland, near Virginia: A Narrative of the First Voyage to Maryland by the Rev. Father Andrew White, and Sundry Reports*. Baltimore: Maryland Historical Society, 1847.

Brown, Kathleen M. *Good Wives, Nasty Wenches, and Anxious Patriarchs: Gender, Race, and Power in Colonial Virginia*. Chapel Hill: University of North Carolina Press, 1996.

Brown, Richard D. "'Not Only Extreme Poverty, but the Worst Kind of Orphanage': Lemuel Haynes and the Boundaries of Racial Tolerance on the Yankee Frontier, 1770–1820." *New England Quarterly* 61, no. 4 (1988): 502–18.

Browne, William Hand, ed. *Archives of Maryland*. Vol. 1, *Proceedings and Acts of the General Assembly of Maryland, January 1637/8–September 1664*. Baltimore: Maryland Historical Society, 1883.

———, ed. *Archives of Maryland*. Vol. 3, *Proceedings and Acts of the Council of Maryland, 1636–1637*. Baltimore: Maryland Historical Society, 1885.

———, ed. *Archives of Maryland*. Vol. 4, *Judicial and Testamentary Business of the Provincial Court, 1637–1650*. Baltimore: Maryland Historical Society, 1887.

———, ed. *Archives of Maryland*. Vol. 5, *Proceedings of the Council of Maryland, 1667–1687/8*. Baltimore: Maryland Historical Society, 1887.

———, ed. *Archives of Maryland*. Vol. 7, *Proceedings and Acts of the General Assembly of Maryland, October 1678–November 1683*. Baltimore: Maryland Historical Society, 1889.

———, ed. *Archives of Maryland*. Vol. 13, *Proceedings and Acts of the General Assembly of Maryland, April 1684–June 1692*. Baltimore: Maryland Historical Society, 1894.

———, ed. *Archives of Maryland*. Vol. 30, *Proceedings and Acts of the General Assembly of Maryland, April 1715–August 1716*. Baltimore: Maryland Historical Society, 1910.

Brubaker, Rogers. "Ethnicity without Groups." *European Journal of Sociology* 43, no. 2 (2002): 163–89.

Bruce, Philip Alexander. *Economic History of Virginia in the Seventeenth Century: An Inquiry into the Material Condition of the People, Based upon Original and Contemporaneous Records*. Vol. 2. New York: Macmillan, 1896.

Burke, William, and Edmund Burke. *An Account of the European Settlements in America*. 3rd ed. London: printed for R. and J. Dodsley, 1760.

Burnard, Trevor. *Mastery, Tyranny, and Desire: Thomas Thistlewood and His Slaves in the Anglo-Jamaican World*. Chapel Hill: University of North Carolina Press, 2004.

Burns, Alan. *History of the British West Indies*. London: Allen and Unwin, 1954.

Cain, Robert J., ed. *The Colonial Records of North Carolina*. Vol. 6, *North Carolina Higher-Court Minutes, 1724–1730*. Raleigh, N.C.: Department of Cultural Resources Division of Archives and History, 1981.

———, ed. *The Colonial Records of North Carolina*. Vol. 7, *Records of the Executive Council, 1664–1734*. Raleigh: North Carolina Department of Cultural Resources, 1984.

———, ed. *The Colonial Records of North Carolina*. Vol. 10, *The Church of England in North Carolina: Documents, 1699–1741*. Raleigh: North Carolina Department of Cultural Resources, 1999.

Calloway, Colin G., ed. *The World Turned Upside Down: Indian Voices from Early America*. Boston: Bedford/St. Martin's, 1994.

Candler, Allen D., ed. *The Colonial Records of the State of Georgia*. Vol. 1. Atlanta: Franklin, 1904.

———, ed. *The Colonial Records of the State of Georgia*. Vol. 4, *Stephens Journal, 1737–1740*. Atlanta: Franklin, 1906.

———, ed. *The Colonial Records of the State of Georgia*. Vol. 18, *Statutes Enacted by the Royal Legislature of Georgia from Its First Session in 1754 to 1768*. Atlanta: Chas. P. Byrd, 1910.

Candler, Allen D., and Lucian Lamar Knight, eds. *The Colonial Records of the State of Georgia*. Vol. 24, *Original Papers, Correspondence, Trustees, General Oglethorpe and Others*. Atlanta: Chas. P. Byrd, 1915.

Carney, Judith A. *Black Rice: The African Origins of Rice Cultivation in the Americas*. Cambridge, Mass.: Harvard University Press, 2001.

Carr, Lois Green, Russell R. Menard, and Lorena S. Walsh. *Robert Cole's World: Agriculture and Society in Early Maryland*. Chapel Hill: University of North Carolina Press, 1991.

Carr, Lois Green, Philip D. Morgan, and Jean Burrell Russo, eds. *Colonial Chesapeake Society*. Chapel Hill: University of North Carolina Press, 1988.

Carroll, B. R., ed. *Historical Collections of South Carolina*. Vol. 2. New York: Harper and Brothers, 1836.

Carroll, Patrick J. *Blacks in Colonial Veracruz: Race, Ethnicity, and Regional Development*. Austin: University of Texas Press, 1991.

Carson, Jane. "The Will of John Rolfe." *Virginia Magazine of History and Biography* 58, no. 1 (1950): 58–65.

Carter, Greg. *The United States of the United Races: A Utopian History of Racial Mixing*. New York: New York University Press, 2013.

Carter, Susan B., Scott Sigmund Gartner, Michael R. Haines, Alan L. Olmstead, Richard

Sutch, and Galvan Wright, eds. *Historical Statistics of the United States.* Millennial ed. Online ver. New York: Cambridge University Press, 2006.

Casas, María Raquél. *Married to a Daughter of the Land: Spanish-Mexican Women and Interethnic Marriage in California, 1820–1880.* Reno: University of Nevada Press, 2007.

Catterall, Helen Tunnicliff, ed. *Judicial Cases concerning American Slavery and the Negro.* Vol. 1, *Cases from the Courts of England, Virginia, West Virginia, and Kentucky.* Washington, D.C.: Carnegie Institution of Washington, 1926.

———, ed. *Judicial Cases concerning American Slavery and the Negro.* Vol. 4, *Cases from the Courts of New England, the Middle States, and the District of Columbia.* Washington, D.C.: Carnegie Institution of Washington, 1936.

Cave, Alfred. *Lethal Encounters: Englishmen and Indians in Colonial Virginia.* Lincoln: University of Nebraska Press, 2013.

Cave, Roderick. "Early Printing and the Book Trade in the West Indies." *Library Quarterly: Information, Community, Policy* 48, no. 2 (1978): 163–92.

Chapman, George, Ben Jonson, and John Marston. *Eastward Ho!* Edited by R. W. Van Fossen. Manchester, UK: Manchester University Press, 1999.

*The Charters and General Laws of the Colony and Province of Massachusetts Bay.* Boston: T. B. Wait, 1814.

Chiles, Katy L. *Transformable Race: Surprising Metamorphoses in the Literature of Early America.* New York: Oxford University Press, 2014.

Clark, Walter, ed. *The State Records of North Carolina.* Vol. 23, *Laws 1715–1776.* Goldsboro, N.C.: Nash Brothers, 1904.

———, ed. *The State Records of North Carolina.* Vol. 25, *Laws 1789–1790 and Supplement Omitted Laws, 1669–1783.* Goldsboro, N.C.: Nash Brothers, 1906.

Cohen, Hennig. "Literary Reflections of Slavery from the South Carolina Gazette." *Journal of Negro History* 37, no. 2 (1952): 188–93.

*Collections of the Massachusetts Historical Society.* Ser. 1. Vol. 4. Boston, 1795.

*Collections of the Massachusetts Historical Society.* Ser. 3. Vol. 8. Boston: Charles C. Little and James Brown, 1843. https://catalog.hathitrust.org/Record/008881846.

*Colonial Laws of New York from the Year 1664 to the Revolution.* Vol. 1. Albany, N.Y.: James B. Lyon, 1896.

Cooley, Timothy Mather. *Sketches of the Life and Character of the Rev. Lemuel Haynes.* New York: Harper and Brothers, 1837.

Cooper, Thomas, ed. *The Statutes at Large of South Carolina.* Vol. 2, *Containing the Acts from 1682 to 1716, Inclusive.* Columbia, S.C.: A. S. Johnston, 1837.

———, ed. *The Statutes at Large of South Carolina.* Vol. 3, *Containing the Acts from 1716, Exclusive, to 1752, Inclusive.* Columbia, S.C.: A. S. Johnston, 1838.

Daniel, G. Reginald. *More Than Black? Multiracial Identity and the New Racial Order.* Philadelphia: Temple University Press, 2002.

Davis, F. James. *Who Is Black? One Nation's Definition.* University Park: Pennsylvania State University Press, 1991.

Deagan, Kathleen A. "Mestizaje in Colonial St. Augustine." *Ethnohistory* 20, no. 1 (1973): 55–65.

Deal, Joseph Douglas. *Race and Class in Colonial Virginia: Indians, Englishmen, and Africans on the Eastern Shore during the Seventeenth Century.* New York: Garland, 1993.

Degler, Carl N. *Neither Black nor White: Race Relations in Brazil and the United States.* London: Macmillan, 1971.

Douglass, Frederick. *Narrative of the Life of Frederick Douglass, an American Slave*. Boston: Anti-Slavery Office, 1845.

Douglass, William. *A Summary, Historical and Political, of the First Planting, Progressive Improvements, and Present State of the British Settlements in North-America*. Vol. 1. Boston: Rogers and Fowle, 1749.

Dow, George Francis, ed. *Records and Files of the Quarterly Courts of Essex County, Massachusetts*. Salem, Mass.: Essex Institute, 1911.

Dubcovsky, Alejandra. *Informed Power: Communication in the Early American South*. Cambridge, Mass.: Harvard University Press, 2016.

Du Bois, W. E. B. *Black Reconstruction in America*. 1935. Reprint, Cleveland, Ohio: Meridian, 1964.

Dunn, Richard S. *Sugar and Slaves: The Rise of the Planter Class in the English West Indies, 1624–1713*. Chapel Hill: University of North Carolina Press, 1972.

Dusinberre, William. *Them Dark Days: Slavery in the American Rice Swamps*. Athens: University of Georgia Press, 1996.

Edwards, Bryan. *The History, Civil and Commercial, of the British Colonies in the West Indies*. Vol. 2. London: John Stockdale, 1793.

Eliot, Thomas. *The Dictionary of Syr Thomas Eliot Knyght*. London, 1538.

Elliott, J. H. *Empires of the Atlantic World: Britain and Spain in America, 1492–1830*. New Haven, Conn.: Yale University Press, 2006.

Eltis, David. *The Rise of African Slavery in the Americas*. New York: Cambridge University Press, 2000.

Estwick, Samuel. *Considerations on the Negroe Cause Commonly So Called: Addressed to the Right Honourable Lord Mansfield, Lord Chief Justice of the Court of King's Bench, &c.* London: J. Dodsley, 1772.

Evans, Emory G. "A Question of Complexion: Documents concerning the Negro and the Franchise in Eighteenth-Century Virginia." *Virginia Magazine of History and Biography* 71, no. 4 (1963): 411–15.

"Extracts from the County Records [Middlesex]." *Virginia Magazine of History and Biography* 8, no. 2 (1900): 171–94.

Farrelly, Maura Jane. *Papist Patriots: The Making of an American Catholic Identity*. New York: Oxford University Press, 2012.

Feerick, Jean E. *Strangers in Blood: Relocating Race in the Renaissance*. Toronto, ON: University of Toronto Press, 2010.

Fernow, Berthold, ed. *The Records of New Amsterdam from 1653 to 1674 Anno Domini*. New York: Knickerbocker, 1897.

Fields, Barbara. "Slavery, Race and Ideology in the United States of America." *New Left Review*, no. 181 (1990): 95–118.

Fields, Karen E., and Barbara J. Fields. *Racecraft: The Soul of Inequality in American Life*. London: Verso, 2012.

Fischer, Kirsten. *Suspect Relations: Sex, Race, and Resistance in Colonial North Carolina*. Ithaca, N.Y.: Cornell University Press, 2002.

Fisher, Andrew B., and Matthew O'Hara, eds. *Imperial Subjects: Race and Identity in Colonial Latin America*. Durham, N.C.: Duke University Press, 2009.

Fitchett, E. Horace. "The Traditions of the Free Negro in Charleston, South Carolina." *Journal of Negro History* 25, no. 2 (1940): 139–52.

Forbes, Jack D. *Africans and Native Americans: The Language of Race and the Evolution of Red-Black Peoples*. Urbana-Champaign: University of Illinois Press, 1993.

Fortescue, J. W., ed. *Calendar of State Papers, Colonial Series, America and West Indies.* Vol. 13, *1689–1692*. London: Mackie, 1901.

Franklin, Benjamin. *Benjamin Franklin: Silence Dogood, the Busy-Body, and Early Writings.* Edited by J. A. Leo Lemay. New York: Library of America, 2009.

Franklin, John Hope, and Loren Schweninger. *Runaway Slaves: Rebels on the Plantation.* New York: Oxford University Press, 1999.

Gallay, Alan, ed. *Indian Slavery in Colonial America.* Lincoln: University of Nebraska Press, 2009.

———. *The Indian Slave Trade: The Rise of the English Empire in the American South, 1670–1717.* New Haven, Conn.: Yale University Press, 2002.

Gallman, James M. "Mortality among White Males, Colonial North Carolina." *Social Science History* 4, no. 3 (1980): 295–316.

Garnett, James Mercer. "James Mercer." *William and Mary Quarterly* 17, no. 2 (1908): 85–99.

Gaspar, David Barry. *Bondmen and Rebels: A Study of Master-Slave Relations in Antigua.* 2nd ed. Durham, N.C.: Duke University Press, 1993.

Genovese, Eugene D. *Roll, Jordan, Roll: The World the Slaves Made.* New York: Pantheon Books, 1974.

Gerbner, Katharine. *Christian Slavery: Conversion and Race in the Protestant Atlantic World.* Philadelphia: University of Pennsylvania Press, 2018.

Gleach, Frederic W. *Powhatan's World and Colonial Virginia: A Conflict of Cultures.* Lincoln: University of Nebraska Press, 2000.

Godbeer, Richard. *Sexual Revolution in Early America.* Baltimore: Johns Hopkins University Press, 2002.

Goetz, Rebecca Anne. *The Baptism of Early Virginia: How Christianity Created Race.* Baltimore: Johns Hopkins University Press, 2012.

———. "Rethinking the 'Unthinking Decision': Old Questions and New Problems in the History of Slavery and Race in the Colonial South." *Journal of Southern History* 75, no. 3 (2009): 599–613.

Gomez, Michael A. *Exchanging Our Country Marks: The Transformation of African Identities in the Colonial and Antebellum South.* Chapel Hill: University of North Carolina Press, 1998.

Gordon-Reed, Annette. *The Hemingses of Monticello: An American Family.* New York: W. W. Norton, 2008.

Green, Keneisha M. "Who's Who: Exploring the Discrepancy between the Methods of Defining African Americans and Native Americans." *American Indian Law Review* 31, no. 1 (2006/2007): 93–110.

Greene, Jack P. *Pursuits of Happiness: The Social Development of Early Modern British Colonies and the Formation of American Culture.* Chapel Hill: University of North Carolina Press, 1988.

Greene, Lorenzo Johnston. *The Negro in Colonial New England.* New York: Atheneum, 1968.

Gregorie, Anne King, ed. *Records of the Court of Chancery of South Carolina, 1671–1779.* Washington, D.C.: American Historical Association, 1950.

Griest, W. W., ed. *Pennsylvania Archives.* Ser. 4. Vol. 2, *Papers of the Governors, 1747–1759.* Harrisburg: State of Pennsylvania, 1900.

Gross, Ariela J. "Beyond Black and White: Cultural Approaches to Race and Slavery." *Columbia Law Review* 101, no. 3 (2001): 640–90.

———. "'Of Portuguese Origin': Litigating Identity and Citizenship among the 'Little Races' in Nineteenth-Century America." *Law and History Review* 25, no. 3 (2007): 467–512.

———. *What Blood Won't Tell: A History of Race on Trial in America*. Cambridge, Mass.: Harvard University Press, 2008.

Gutman, Herbert G. *The Black Family in Slavery and Freedom, 1750–1925*. New York: Pantheon Books, 1976.

Hakluyt, Richard, ed. *The Principal Navigations, Voyages, Traffiques and Discoveries of the English Nation*. 12 vols. Glasgow, UK: James MacLehose and Sons, 1904.

Hall, Clayton Colman, ed. *Archives of Maryland*. Vol. 33, *Proceedings and Acts of the General Assembly of Maryland, May 1717–April 1720*. Baltimore: Lord Baltimore Press, 1913.

———, ed. *Archives of Maryland*. Vol. 35, *Proceedings and Acts of the General Assembly of Maryland, October 1724–July 1726*. Baltimore: Maryland Historical Society, 1915.

———, ed. *Narratives of Early Maryland, 1633–1684*. New York: Charles Scribner's Sons, 1910.

Hall, Kermit, and Pater Karsten. *The Magic Mirror: Law in American History*. New York: Oxford University Press, 1989.

Hall, William, ed. *Laws of the State of Delaware, to the Year of Our Lord, One Thousand Eight Hundred and Twenty Nine Inclusive*. Rev. ed. Wilmington, Del.: R. Porter and Son, 1829.

Hall, William B. "The Poythress Family: A Study of Francis, Francis, Francis, and Francis." *William and Mary Quarterly* 14, no. 1 (1934): 77–84.

Hall, William L., ed. *Executive Journals of the Council of Colonial Virginia*. Vol. 5, *November 1, 1739–May 7, 1754*. Richmond: Virginia State Library, 1945.

Hamor, Ra[l]phe. *A True Discourse of the Present Estate of Virginia, and the Success of the Affaires There till the 18 of June 1614*. London, 1615.

Hardesty, Jared Ross. *Unfreedom: Slavery and Dependence in Eighteenth-Century Boston*. New York: New York University Press, 2018.

Harris, Marvin. *Patterns of Race in the Americas*. New York: Walker, 1964.

Harris, Robert L., Jr. "Charleston's Free Afro-American Elite: The Brown Fellowship Society and the Humane Brotherhood." *South Carolina Historical Magazine* 82, no. 4 (October 1981): 289–310.

Headlam, Cecil, ed. *Calendar of State Papers Colonial, America and West Indies*. Vol. 25, 1710–1711. London: His Majesty's Stationery Office, 1924, www.british-history.ac.uk/cal-state-papers/colonial/america-west-indies/vol25/pp185-214.

Heinegg, Paul. *Free African Americans of Maryland and Delaware: From the Colonial Period to 1810*. Baltimore: Clearfield, 2000.

———. *Free African Americans of North Carolina, Virginia, and South Carolina, from the Colonial Period to About 1820*. 5th ed. 2 vols. Baltimore: Clearfield, 2005.

Hening, William Waller, ed. *The Statutes at Large: Being a Collection of All the Laws of Virginia, from the First Session of the Legislature in the Year 1619*. Vol. 1. New York: R. and W. and G. Bartow, 1823.

———, ed. *The Statutes at Large: Being a Collection of All the Laws of Virginia, from the First Session of the Legislature in the Year 1619*. Vol. 2. Richmond, Va.: Samuel Pleasants Jr., 1810.

———, ed. *The Statutes at Large: Being a Collection of All the Laws of Virginia, from the First Session of the Legislature in the Year 1619*. Vol. 3. New York: Thomas Desilver, 1823.

———, ed. *The Statutes at Large: Being a Collection of All the Laws of Virginia, from* the First Session of the Legislature in the Year 1619. Vols. 4–6. Richmond, Va.: Franklin Press–W. W. Gray, 1819–20.

———, ed. *The Statutes at Large: Being a Collection of All the Laws of Virginia, from the First Session of the Legislature in the Year 1619.* Vol. 8. Richmond, Va.: J. and G. Cochran, 1821.

Hershkowitz, Leo. "The Troublesome Turk: An Illustration of Judicial Process in New Amsterdam." *New York History* 46, no. 4 (1965): 299–310.

Heuman, Gad J. *Between Black and White: Race, Politics, and the Free Coloreds in Jamaica, 1792–1865.* Westport, Conn.: Greenwood, 1981.

Heywood, Linda M., and John K. Thornton. *Central Africans, Atlantic Creoles, and the Foundation of the Americas, 1585–1660.* New York: Cambridge University Press, 2007.

Higginbotham, A. Leon, Jr. *In the Matter of Color: Race and the American Legal Process; The Colonial Period.* New York: Oxford University Press, 1978.

Higginbotham, A. Leon, Jr., and Barbara K. Kopytoff. "Racial Purity and Interracial Sex in the Law of Colonial and Antebellum Virginia." *Georgetown Law Journal* 77, no. 6 (1989): 1967–2029.

Hobbs, Allyson. *A Chosen Exile: A History of Racial Passing in American Life.* Cambridge, Mass.: Harvard University Press, 2014.

Hodes, Martha, ed. *Sex, Love, Race: Crossing Boundaries in North American History.* New York: New York University Press, 1999.

———. *White Women, Black Men: Illicit Sex in the Nineteenth-Century South.* New Haven, Conn.: Yale University Press, 1997.

Hodges, Graham Russell. *Root and Branch: African Americans in New York and New Jersey, 1613–1863.* Chapel Hill: University of North Carolina Press, 1999.

Hodges, Graham Russell, and Alan Edward Brown, eds. *"Pretends to Be Free": Runaway Slave Advertisements from Colonial and Revolutionary New York and New Jersey.* New York: Garland, 1994.

Hoff, Henry B. "The de Vries Family of Tappan, New York: A Study in Assimilation." *American Genealogist* 72 (1997): 345–52.

Hoffman, Ronald, Mechel Sobel, and Fredrika J. Teute, eds. *Through a Glass Darkly: Reflections on Personal Identity in Early America.* Chapel Hill: University of North Carolina Press, 1997.

Hollinger, David A. "Amalgamation and Hypodescent: The Question of Ethnoracial Mixture in the History of the United States." *American Historical Review* 108, no. 5 (2003): 1363–90.

———. *Postethnic America: Beyond Multiculturalism.* 10th anniversary ed. New York: Basic Books, 2006.

Holt, Thomas C. "Marking: Race, Race-Making, and the Writing of History." *American Historical Review* 100, no. 1 (February 1995): 1–20.

Holton, Woody. *Forced Founders: Indians, Debtors, Slaves, and the Making of the American Revolution in Virginia.* Chapel Hill: University of North Carolina Press, 1999.

Horn, James. *Adapting to a New World: English Society in the Seventeenth-Century Chesapeake.* Chapel Hill: University of North Carolina Press, 1994.

Horne, Gerald. *The Counter-Revolution of 1776: Slave Resistance and the Origins of the United States of America.* New York: New York University Press, 2014.

Horsmanden, Daniel. *A Journal of the Proceedings in the Detection of the Conspiracy Formed by Some White People, in Conjunction with Negro and Other Slaves, for Burning the City of New-York in America, and Murdering the Inhabitants.* New York: James Parker, 1744.

Howard, John Henry, ed. *The Laws of the British Colonies, in the West Indies and Other Parts of America, Concerning Real and Personal Property and Manumission of Slaves.* Vol. 1. London: William Henry Bond, 1827.

Huggins, Nathan I., Martin Kilson, Daniel M. Fox, and John Morton Blum, eds. *Key Issues in the Afro-American Experience.* New York: Harcourt Brace Jovanovich, 1971.

Humboldt, Alexander de, and Aimé Bonpland. *Personal Narrative of Travels to the Equinoctial Regions of the New Continent.* London: Paternoster Row, 1826.

Hurd, John Codman. *The Law of Freedom and Bondage in the United States.* Vol. 1. Boston: Little, Brown, 1858.

Ingersoll, Thomas N. "'Releese Us out of This Cruell Bondegg': An Appeal from Virginia in 1723." *William and Mary Quarterly* 51, no. 4 (1994): 777–82.

Ipsen, Pernille. *Daughters of the Trade: Atlantic Slavers and Interracial Marriage on the Gold Coast.* Philadelphia: University of Pennsylvania Press, 2015.

Jacobs, Harriet. *Incidents in the Life of a Slave Girl.* Edited by Jean Fagan Yellin. Enlarged ed. Cambridge, Mass.: Harvard University Press, 1987. First published 1861 for the author (Boston).

Jobson, Richard. *The Golden Trade or a Discovery of the River Gambra, and the Golden Trade of the Aethiopians.* Edited by Charles G. Kingsley. Teignmouth, UK: E. E. Speight and R. H. Walpole, 1623.

Johnson, D. Andrew. "Displacing Captives in Colonial South Carolina: Native American Enslavement and the Rise of the Colonial State after the Yamasee War." *Journal of Early American History* 7, no. 2 (2017): 115–40.

Jones, Bernie D. *Fathers of Conscience: Mixed-Race Inheritance in the Antebellum South.* Athens: University of Georgia Press, 2009.

Jones, Hugh. *The Present State of Virginia.* London: J. Clarke, 1724.

Jones, Trina. "Shades of Brown: The Law of Skin Color." *Duke Law Journal* 49, no. 6 (2000): 1487–557.

Jordan, Winthrop D. "Historical Origins of the One-Drop Racial Rule in the United States." Edited by Paul Spickard. *Journal of Critical Mixed Race Studies* 1, no. 1 (2014): 98–132.

———. *White over Black: American Attitudes toward the Negro, 1550–1812.* Chapel Hill: University of North Carolina Press, 1968.

Kaplan, Sidney. "The Miscegenation Issue in the Election of 1864." *Journal of Negro History* 34, no. 3 (1949): 274–343.

Karras, Alan L. *Sojourners in the Sun: Scottish Migrants in Jamaica and the Chesapeake, 1740–1800.* Ithaca, N.Y.: Cornell University Press, 1992.

Katzew, Ilona. *Casta Painting: Images of Race in Eighteenth-Century Mexico.* New Haven, Conn.: Yale University Press, 2004.

Keen, Benjamin, ed. *The Life of the Admiral Christopher Columbus by His Son Ferdinand.* New Brunswick, N.J.: Rutgers University Press, 1959.

Kemble, Frances Anne. *Journal of a Residence on a Georgian Plantation in 1838–1839.* New York: Harper and Brothers, 1863.

Kennedy, John Pendleton, ed. *Journals of the House of Burgesses of Virginia, 1761–1765.* Richmond: Virginia State Library, 1907.

———, ed. *Journals of the House of Burgesses of Virginia, 1766–1769.* Richmond: Virginia State Library, 1906.

Kercheval, Samuel. *History of the Valley of Virginia.* 3rd ed. Woodstock, Va.: W. N. Grabill, 1902.

Klingberg, Frank J. *An Appraisal of the Negro in Colonial South Carolina*. Washington, D.C.: Associated Publishers, 1941.

Knight, William K., ed. *General History of the Caribbean*. Vol. 3, *The Slave Societies of the Caribbean*. London: UNESCO, 1997.

Koger, Larry. *Black Slaveowners: Free Black Slave Masters in South Carolina, 1790–1860*. Columbia: University of South Carolina Press, 1995.

Kolodny, Annette. *In Search of First Contact: The Vikings of Vinland, the Peoples of the Dawnland, and the Anglo-American Anxiety of Discovery*. Durham, N.C.: Duke University Press, 2012.

Kopelson, Heather Miyano. *Faithful Bodies: Performing Religion and Race in the Puritan Atlantic*. New York: New York University Press, 2014.

Kulikoff, Allan. *Tobacco and Slaves: The Development of Southern Cultures in the Chesapeake, 1680–1800*. Chapel Hill: University of North Carolina Press, 1986.

Landers, Jane. *Black Society in Spanish Florida*. Urbana: University of Illinois Press, 1999.

La Vere, David. *The Tuscarora War: Indians, Settlers, and the Fight for the Carolina Colonies*. Chapel Hill: University of North Carolina Press, 2013.

*Laws of the State of Delaware*. Vol. 1. New Castle, Del.: printed by Samuel and John Adams, 1797.

Lawson, John. *A New Voyage to Carolina: Containing the Exact Description and Natural History of That County; Together with the Present State Thereof*. London, 1709.

Lefroy, J. H. *Memorials of the Discovery and Early Settlement of the Bermudas or Somers Islands*. Vol. 2. London: Longmans, Green, 1879.

Lemay, J. A. Leo. *The Canon of Benjamin Franklin 1722–1776: New Attributions and Reconsiderations*. Newark: University of Delaware Press, 1986.

Lent, John A. "Oldest Existing Commonwealth Caribbean Newspapers." *Caribbean Quarterly* 22, no. 4 (1976): 90–106.

Lepore, Jill. *The Name of War: King Philip's War and the Origins of American Identity*. New York: Vintage Books, 1999.

———. *New York Burning: Liberty, Slavery, and Conspiracy in Eighteenth-Century Manhattan*. New York: Vintage Books, 2006.

Leroy-Beaulieu, Paul. *De la colonisation chez les peuples modernes*. Paris: Journal de Économistes, 1874.

"Letter from John Rolfe to Sir Thos. Dale." *Virginia Magazine of History and Biography* 22, no. 1 (1914): 150–57.

Lewis, Jan Ellen, and Peter S. Onuf, eds. *Sally Hemings and Thomas Jefferson: History, Memory, and Civic Culture*. Charlottesville: University of Virginia Press, 1999.

Ligon, Richard. *A True and Exact History of the Island of Barbadoes*. London: printed for Humphrey Moseley, 1657.

Livesay, Daniel. *Children of Uncertain Fortune: Mixed-Race Jamaicans in Britain and the Atlantic Family, 1733–1833*. Chapel Hill: University of North Carolina Press, 2018.

Long, Edward. *Candid Reflections upon the Judgement Lately Awarded by the Court of King's Bench, in Westminster-Hall, on What Is Commonly Called the Negroe-Cause, by a Planter*. London: T. Lowndes, 1772.

———. *The History of Jamaica, or, General Survey of the Antient and Modern State of the Island: With Reflections on Its Situation Settlements, Inhabitants, Climate, Products, Commerce, Laws, and Government, Vol II*. London: T. Lowndes, 1774.

Makinson, David H. *Barbados: A Study of North-America-West-Indian Relations 1739–1789*. London: Mouton, 1964.

Maury, Ann. *Memoirs of a Huguenot Family: Translated and Compiled from the Original Autobiography of the Rev. James Fontaine*. New York: George P. Putnam, 1853.

Maxwell, John Francis. *Slavery and the Catholic Church: The History of Catholic Teaching concerning the Moral Legitimacy of the Institution of Slavery*. Chichester, UK: Barry Rose, 1975.

McCleskey, Turk. *The Road to Black Ned's Forge: A Story of Race, Sex, and Trade on the Colonial American Frontier*. Charlottesville: University of Virginia Press, 2014.

McCord, David J., ed. *The Statutes at Large of South Carolina*. Vol. 7, *Containing the Acts Relating to Charleston, Courts, Slaves, and Rivers*. Columbia, S.C.: A. S. Johnston, 1840.

McCusker, John J., and Russell R. Menard. *The Economy of British America, 1607–1789*. Chapel Hill: University of North Carolina Press, 1991.

McDowell, William L., ed. *Documents Relating to Indian Affairs, May 21, 1750–August 7, 1754*. Columbia: South Carolina Archives Department 1958.

———, ed. *Journals of the Commissioners of the Indian Trade, September 20, 1710–August 29, 1718*. Columbia: South Carolina Archives Department, 1955.

McIlvenna, Noeleen. *The Short Life of Free Georgia: Class and Slavery in the Colonial South*. Chapel Hill: University of North Carolina Press, 2015.

———. *A Very Mutinous People: The Struggle for North Carolina, 1660–1713*. Chapel Hill: University of North Carolina Press, 2009.

McIlwaine, H. R., ed. *Executive Journals of the Council of Colonial Virginia*. Vol. 3, *May 1, 1705–October 23, 1721*. Richmond: Virginia State Library, 1928.

———, ed. *Journals of the House of Burgesses of Virginia, 1659/60–1693*. Richmond: Virginia State Library, 1914.

———, ed. *Journals of the House of Burgesses of Virginia, 1695–1696, 1696–1697, 1698, 1699, 1700–1702*. Richmond: Library of Virginia, 1913.

———, ed. *Journals of the House of Burgesses of Virginia, 1702/3–1705, 1705–1706, 1710–1712*. Richmond: Virginia State Library, 1912.

———, ed. *Legislative Journals of the Council of Colonial Virginia*. Vols. 1 and 3. Richmond: Virginia State Library, 1918–19.

Merrell, James. "Coming to Terms with Early America." *William and Mary Quarterly* 69, no. 3 (2012): 535–40.

Meyers, Debra, and Melanie Perreault, eds. *Colonial Chesapeake: New Perspectives*. Lanham, Md.: Lexington Books, 2006.

Mihalyka, Jean M., ed. *Loose Papers and Sundry Court Cases*. Vol. 1, *1628–1731, Northampton County, Virginia*. Eastville, Va.: Hickory House, 1997.

———, ed. *Loose Papers and Sundry Court Cases*. Vol. 2, *1732–1744/5, Northampton County, Virginia*. Eastville, Va.: Hickory House, 2000.

Miller, Helen Hill. *Colonel Parke of Virginia: "The Greatest Hector in the Town."* Chapel Hill: Algonquin Books, 1989.

Miller, Lee. *A Kingdom Strange: The Brief and Tragic History of the Lost Colony of Roanoke*. New York: Basic Books, 2010. http://site.ebrary.com/lib/unlv/reader.action?docID =10392426.

Miller, Perry. "Errand into the Wilderness." *William and Mary Quarterly* 10, no. 1 (1953): 3–32.

Milteer, Warren E., Jr. "The Strategies of Forbidden Love: Family across Racial Boundaries in Nineteenth-Century North Carolina." *Journal of Social History* 47, no. 3 (2014): 612–26.

*Minutes of the Provincial Council of Pennsylvania.* Vol. 2, *Containing the Proceedings of Council from December 18, 1700, to May 16, 1717*. Harrisburg, Pa.: Theophilus Finn, 1838.

Morgan, Edmund S. *American Slavery, American Freedom: The Ordeal of Colonial Virginia.* New York: W. W. Norton, 1975.

Morgan, Jennifer L. *Laboring Women: Reproduction and Gender in New World Slavery.* Philadelphia: University of Pennsylvania Press, 2004.

Morgan, Philip D. *Slave Counterpoint: Black Culture in the Eighteenth-Century Chesapeake and Lowcountry.* Chapel Hill: University of North Carolina Press, 1998.

Mörner, Magnus. *Race Mixture in the History of Latin America.* Boston: Little, Brown, 1967.

Morris, Thomas D. *Southern Slavery and the Law, 1619–1860.* Chapel Hill: University of North Carolina Press, 1996. http://site.ebrary.com/lib/unlv/detail.action?docID =10202633.

Morton, Richard L. "The Reverend Hugh Jones: Lord Baltimore's Mathematician." *William and Mary Quarterly* 7, no. 1 (1950): 107–15.

"Mottrom—Wright—Spencer—Ariss—Buckner." *William and Mary Quarterly* 17, no. 1 (1908): 53–59.

Mullin, Gerald W. *Flight and Rebellion: Slave Resistance in Eighteenth-Century Virginia.* New York: Oxford University Press, 1972.

Namias, June. *White Captives: Gender and Ethnicity on the American Frontier.* Chapel Hill: University of North Carolina Press, 1993.

Nash, Gary B. *Forbidden Love: The Hidden History of Mixed-Race America.* 2nd ed. Los Angeles: University of California Regents, National Center for History in the Schools, 2010.

———. *Forging Freedom: The Formation of Philadelphia's Black Community, 1720–1840.* Cambridge, Mass.: Harvard University Press, 1988.

———. "The Hidden History of Mestizo America." *Journal of American History* 82, no. 3 (1995): 941–64.

Nash, Gary B., and Jean R. Soderlund. *Freedom by Degrees: Emancipation in Pennsylvania and Its Aftermath.* New York: Oxford University Press, 1991.

Nelson, William E. *The Common Law in Colonial America.* Vol. 1, *The Chesapeake and New England, 1607–1660.* New York: Oxford University Press, 2008.

Nevill, Samuel, ed. *The Acts of the General Assembly of the Province of New-Jersey.* Philadelphia: William Bradford, 1752.

Newell, Margaret Ellen. *Brethren by Nature: New England Indians, Colonists, and the Origins of American Slavery.* Ithaca, N.Y.: Cornell University Press, 2015.

Newman, Brooke N. *A Dark Inheritance: Blood, Race, and Sex in Colonial Jamaica.* New Haven, Conn.: Yale University Press, 2018.

Newman, Harry Wright. *Charles County Gentry: A Genealogical History of Six Emigrants— Thomas Dent, John Dent, Richard Edelen, John Hanson, George Newman, Humphrey Warren.* Baltimore: Genealogical Publishing, 1971.

Newman, Simon P. *A New World of Labor: The Development of Plantation Slavery in the British Atlantic.* Philadelphia: University of Pennsylvania Press, 2013.

Norris, John. *Profitable Advice for Rich and Poor: In a Dialogue, or Discourse between James Freeman, a Carolina Planter, and Simon Question, a West-Country Farmer; Containing a Description, or True Relation of South Carolina, an English Plantation, or Colony, in America.* London: J. How, 1712.

Northrup, A. Judd. *Slavery in New York, a Historical Sketch*. Albany: University of the State of New York, 1900.

O'Callaghan, E. B., ed. *Laws and Ordinances of New Netherland, 1638–1674*. Albany, N.Y.: Weed, Parsons, 1868.

Olwell, Robert. "Becoming Free: Manumission and the Genesis of a Free Black Community in South Carolina, 1740–90." *Slavery and Abolition* 17, no. 1 (1996): 1–19.

Omi, Michael, and Howard Winant. *Racial Formation in the United States*. 3rd ed. New York: Routledge, 2015.

Palmer, Jennifer L. *Intimate Bonds: Family and Slavery in the French Atlantic*. Philadelphia: University of Pennsylvania Press, 2016.

Parent, Anthony S., Jr. *Foul Means: The Formation of a Slave Society in Virginia, 1660–1740*. Chapel Hill: University of North Carolina Press, 2003.

Patterson, Orlando. *Slavery and Social Death: A Comparative Study*. Cambridge, Mass.: Harvard University Press, 1982.

Peck, Douglas T. "Lucas Vásquez de Ayllón's Doomed Colony of San Miguel de Gualdape." *Georgia Historical Quarterly* 85, no. 2 (2001): 183–98.

Pencak, William. "Benjamin Franklin, Trickster." *Trickster's Way* 3, no. 1 (2004): art. 2.

Pérez-Mallaína, Pablo E. *Spain's Men of the Sea: Daily Life on the Indies Fleets in the Sixteenth Century*. Edited by Carla Rahn Phillips. Baltimore: John Hopkins University Press, 1998.

Peterson, Mark A. "The Selling of Joseph: Bostonians, Antislavery, and the Protestant International, 1689–1733." *Massachusetts Historical Review* 4 (2002): iv, 1–22.

Phillips, Edward. *The New World of English Words: Or, A General Dictionary*. London: E. Tyler, 1658.

———. *The New World of English Words: Or, Universal English Dictionary*. Edited by J. K. Philobibl. 7th ed. London: printed for J. Phillips at the King's-Arms in S. Paul's-Church-Yard, 1720.

Plane, Ann Marie. *Colonial Intimacies: Indian Marriage in Early New England*. Ithaca, N.Y.: Cornell University Press, 2000.

Portes, Alejandro. "Social Capital: Its Origins and Applications in Modern Sociology." *Annual Review of Sociology* 24 (1998): 1–24.

Price, William S., Jr., ed. *The Colonial Records of North Carolina*. Vol. 5, *North Carolina Higher-Court Records, 1709–1723*. Raleigh: North Carolina Department of Cultural Resources, 1977.

Raboteau, Albert J. *Slave Religion: The "Invisible Institution" in the Antebellum South*. Updated ed. New York: Oxford University Press, 2004.

Ramsey, William L. *The Yamasee War: A Study of Culture, Economy, and Conflict in the Colonial South*. Lincoln: University of Nebraska Press, 2008.

"The Randolph Manuscript: Virginia Seventeenth Century Records." Pts. 1 and 2. *Virginia Magazine of History and Biography* 15, no. 4 (April 1908): 390–405; 17, no. 3 (July 1909): 225–48.

Rappaport, Joanne. *The Disappearing Mestizo: Configuring Difference in the Colonial New Kingdom of Granada*. Durham, N.C.: Duke University Press, 2014.

*A Report of the Record Commissioners of the City of Boston*. Vol. 8, *Containing the Boston Records from 1700 to 1728*. Boston: Rockwell and Churchill, 1883.

*A Report of the Record Commissioners of the City of Boston*. Vol. 12, *Containing the Boston Records from 1729 to 1742*. Boston: Rockwell and Churchill, 1885.

Reséndez, Andrés. *A Land So Strange: The Epic Journey of Cabeza de Vaca*. New York: Basic Books, 2009.

———. *The Other Slavery: The Uncovered Story of Indian Enslavement in America*. New York: Houghton Mifflin Harcourt, 2016.

Rogers, George C., Jr., and David R. Chesnutt, eds. *The Papers of Henry Laurens*. Vol. 9, *April 19, 1773–Dec. 12, 1774*. Columbia: University of South Carolina Press, 1981.

Rogers, Woodes. *A Cruising Voyage round the World: First to the South-Seas, Thence to the East-Indies, and Homewards by the Cape of Good Hope*. London: A. Bell and B. Lintot, 1712.

Rothman, Joshua D. *Notorious in the Neighborhood: Sex and Families across the Color Line, 1787–1861*. Chapel Hill: University of North Carolina Press, 2003.

Rountree, Helen C. *Pocahontas's People: The Powhatan Indians of Virginia through Four Centuries*. Norman: University of Oklahoma Press, 1990.

Rucker, William C. *River Flows On: Black Resistance, Culture, and Identity Formation in Early America*. Baton Rouge: Louisiana State University Press, 2008.

Rugemer, Edward B. "The Development of Mastery and Race in the Comprehensive Slave Codes of the Greater Caribbean during the Seventeenth Century." *William and Mary Quarterly* 70, no. 3 (2013): 429–58. https://doi.org/10.5309/willmaryquar.70.3.0429.

Sachs, Honor. "'Freedom by a Judgement': The Legal History of an Afro-Indian Family." *Law and History Review* 30, no. 1 (2012): 173–203.

Salley, Alexander S., Jr., ed. *Narratives of Early Carolina, 1650–1708*. New York: Charles Scribner's Sons, 1911.

Saunders, William L., ed. *The Colonial Records of North Carolina*. Vol. 1, *1662–1712*. Raleigh, N.C.: P. M. Hale, 1886.

———, ed. *The Colonial Records of North Carolina*. Vol. 2, *1713 to 1728*. Raleigh, N.C.: P. M. Hale, 1886.

———, ed. *The Colonial Records of North Carolina*. Vol. 3: *1728–1734*. Raleigh, N.C.: P. M. Hale, 1886.

Schwartz, Philip J. *Slave Laws in Virginia*. Athens: University of Georgia Press, 1996.

Sewall, Samuel. *The Selling of Joseph: A Memorial*. Boston: Bartholomew Green and John Allen, 1700.

Sharfstein, Daniel J. "Crossing the Color Line: Racial Migration and the One-Drop Rule, 1600–1860." *Minnesota Law Review* 91, no. 3 (2007): 592–656.

———. *The Invisible Line: Three American Families and the Secret Journey from Black to White*. New York: Penguin, 2011.

Sharp, Granville. *A Representation of the Injustice and Dangerous Tendency of Tolerating Slavery*. London: printed for Benjamin White and Robert Horsfield, 1769.

Shurtleff, Nathaniel B., ed. *Records of the Colony of New Plymouth in New England: Court Orders*. Vol. 6, *1678–1691*. Boston: William White, 1856.

Sluiter, Engel. "New Light on the '20. and Odd Negroes' Arriving in Virginia, August 1619." *William and Mary Quarterly* 54, no. 2 (1997): 395–98.

Smith, Abbott Emerson. *Colonists in Bondage: White Servitude and Convict Labor in America, 1607–1776*. Chapel Hill: University of North Carolina Press, 1947.

Smith, Daniel Blake. "Mortality and Family in the Colonial Chesapeake." *Journal of Interdisciplinary History* 8, no. 3 (1978): 403–27.

Smith, John. *The Generall Historie of Virginia, New-England, and the Summer Iles*. London: I. D. and I. H. for Michael Sparkes, 1624.

Smits, David D. "'Abominable Mixture': Toward the Repudiation of Anglo-Indian Intermarriage in Seventeenth-Century Virginia." *Virginia Magazine of History and Biography* 95, no. 2 (1987): 157–92.

Sobel, Mechel. *The World They Made Together: Black and White Values in Eighteenth-Century Virginia.* Princeton, N.J.: Princeton University Press, 1987.

Sollors, Werner. *Neither Black nor White yet Both: Thematic Explorations of Interracial Literature.* New York: Oxford University Press, 1997.

Spear, Jennifer M. *Race, Sex, and Social Order in Early New Orleans.* Baltimore: John Hopkins University Press, 2009.

*The Statutes at Large of Pennsylvania.* Vol. 4, 1724–1744. Philadelphia: Clarence M. Busch, 1897.

Steiner, Bernard Christian, ed. *Archives of Maryland.* Vol. 36, *Proceedings and Acts of the General Assembly of Maryland, July 1727–August 1729.* Baltimore: Maryland Historical Society, 1916.

Steiner, Bruce E. "The Catholic Brents of Colonial Virginia: An Instance of Practical Toleration." *Virginia Magazine of History and Biography* 70, no. 4 (1962): 387–409.

Stevens-Acevedo, Anthony, Tom Weterings, and Leonor Alvarez Francés. *Juan Rodriguez and the Beginnings of New York City.* New York: CUNY Dominican Studies Institute, 2013.

Sussman, Robert Wald. *The Myth of Race: The Troubling Persistence of an Unscientific Idea.* Cambridge, Mass.: Harvard University Press, 2014.

Sweet, James H. "The Iberian Roots of American Racist Thought." *William and Mary Quarterly* 54, no. 1 (1997): 143–66.

Takaki, Ronald. *A Different Mirror: A History of Multicultural America.* Boston: Little, Brown, 1993.

Thornton, John. "The African Experience of the '20. and Odd Negroes' Arriving in Virginia in 1619." *William and Mary Quarterly* 55, no. 3 (1998): 421–34.

Tomlins, Christopher. *Freedom Bound: Law, Labor, and Civil Identity in Colonizing English America, 1580–1865.* New York: Cambridge University Press, 2010.

Tortura, Daniel J. *Carolina in Crisis: Cherokees, Colonists, and Slaves in the American Southeast, 1756–1763.* Chapel Hill: University of North Carolina Press, 2015.

Townsend, Camilla. *Pocahontas and the Powhatan Dilemma.* New York: Hill and Wang, 2004.

"Trans-Atlantic Slave Trade—Estimates," Slave Voyages, www.slavevoyages.org/assessments/estimates.

Twinam, Ann. *Purchasing Whiteness: Pardos, Mulattos, and the Quest for Social Mobility in the Spanish Indies.* Standford, Calif.: Stanford University Press, 2015.

Tyler, Lyon Gardiner, ed. *Encyclopedia of Virginia Biography.* Vol. 1. New York: Lewis Historical, 1915.

U.S. Library of Congress. *The Thomas Jefferson Papers.* Ser. 8, *Virginia Records, 1606–1737.* Vol. 6, *Charters of the Virginia Company of London, Laws, Abstracts of Rolls in the Offices of State, 1606–92.*

Vesey, Francis, ed. *Reports of Cases Argued and Determined in the High Court of Chancery, in the Time of Lord Chancellor Hardwicke, from the Year 1746–7, to 1755.* 3rd ed. Vol. 1. Philadelphia: Robert H. Small, 1788.

Walker, Alice. *In Search of Our Mothers' Gardens: Womanist Prose.* New York: Harcourt, 1983.

Walsh, Lorena S. *From Calabar to Carter's Grove: The History of a Virginian Slave Community*. Charlottesville: University Press of Virginia, 1997.

Warren, Wendy. *New England Bound: Slavery and Colonization in Early America*. New York: Liveright, 2016.

Washington, Scott Leon. "Hypodescent: A History of the Crystallization of the One-Drop Rule in the United States, 1880–1940." PhD diss., Princeton University, 2011.

Webber, Mabel Louise, ed. *The South Carolina Historical and Genealogical Magazine*. Vol. 23. Baltimore: Williams and Wilkins, 1922.

Wells, Robert V. *The Population of the British Colonies in America before 1776: A Survey of Census Data*. Princeton, N.J.: Princeton University Press, 1975.

White, Deborah Gray. *Ar'n't I a Woman: Female Slaves in the Plantation South*. New York: W. W. Norton, 1999.

Whittington, John B. "The Origin and Nature of African Slavery in Seventeenth Century Maryland." *Maryland Historical Magazine* 73, no. 3 (1978): 236–45.

Wiecek, William M. "The Statutory Law of Slavery and Race in the Thirteen Mainland Colonies of British America." *William and Mary Quarterly* 34, no. 2 (1977): 258–80.

Wilkinson, George Theodore. *An Authentic History of the Cato-Street Conspiracy*. London: Thomas Kelly, 1820.

Williams, Kim M. *Mark One or More: Civil Rights in Multiracial America*. Ann Arbor: University of Michigan Press, 2006.

Williams, William H. *Slavery and Freedom in Delaware, 1639–1865*. Wilmington, Del.: Rowman and Littlefield, 1999.

Williamson, Joel. *New People: Miscegenation and Mulattoes in the United States*. New York: Free Press, 1980.

Windley, Lathan A., ed. *Runaway Slave Advertisements: A Documentary History from the 1730s to 1790*. Vol. 2, *Maryland*. Westport, Conn.: Greenwood, 1983.

———, ed. *Runaway Slave Advertisements: A Documentary History from the 1730s to 1790*. Vol. 4, *Georgia*. Westport, Conn.: Greenwood, 1983.

Winters, Lisa Ze. *The Mulatta Concubine: Terror, Intimacy, Freedom, and Desire in the Black Atlantic*. Athens: University of Georgia Press, 2016.

Wood, Betty. *Slavery in Colonial Georgia, 1730–1775*. Athens: University of Georgia Press, 1984.

Wood, Peter H. *Black Majority: Negroes in Colonial South Carolina from 1670 through the Stono Rebellion*. New York: W. W. Norton, 1975.

———. *Strange New Land: African in Colonial America*. New York: Oxford University Press, 2003.

Wright, J. Leitch, Jr. *The Only Land They Knew: The Tragic Story of American Indians in the Old South*. New York: Free Press, 1981.

Zug, Marcia. "Lonely Colonist Seeks Wife: The Forgotten History of America's First Mail Order Brides." *Duke Journal of Gender Law and Policy* 20, no. 1 (2012): 85–125.

# INDEX

*Page numbers in italics refer to illustrations.*

Abda (Hartford), 99
Accomack County, Va., *xv*, 52, 116, 221
African, Africans: "country born," creole, 160, 212, 224–25; "saltwater," 201, 212, 225; slave trade, 11, 12, 35–36, 41, 44, 64, 95, 96, 97–98, 100, 101, 103, 107, 108, 109, 117, 118, 119, 127, 241, 267n54, 268 n69. *See also* "black"; demographics
agriculture: barley, 62–63; cereal grains, 62, 98, 110; coffee, 6; corn, 29, 53, 55, 63, 86, 89, 94, 104, 110, 117, 229; cotton, 38; indigo, 6, 38, 241; livestock, 53, 54, 55, 56, 62, 63, 108, 110, 112, 117, 213, 224; oats, 63; peas, 117; potatoes, 117; pumpkins, 117; rice, 6, 94, 104, 117, 118, 224, 238, 241; sugar, 6, 38, 39, 40, 98, 104, 111, 129, 206–8, 238; tobacco, 1, 6, 30–31, 36, 38, 39, 52, 55, 56, 58, 59–60, 62–63, 69, 73, 78, 86, 87, 98, 104, 176, 178, 179, 221, 222, 229, 238, 62; wheat, 62, 104, 225, 229
Alabama Fort, 205
Albany, N.Y., 103
Albemarle (region), Albemarle Sound, *xv*, 105–7, 112–13, 123, 196, 265n34
Albemarle County, Va., 220
Algonquin, 13, 97, 99, 100
Allen, Doll, 147
Allen, John, 236
Allen, Richard, 186
Amelia County, Va., *xv*, 228, 236
Amos (Va.), 20
Anglican Church (Church of England). *See* Protestantism
Ann (Westmoreland County, Va.), 186
Annapolis, Md., *xiv*, *xv*, 1, 72, 77, 84, 163

Annas (Northampton County, Va.), 228, 286n68
Anne Arundel County, Md., *xv*, 78, 133–34, 270n14
Anthonio, Anthony (#1, Middlesex County, Va.), 51, 52
Anthonio (#2, Middlesex County, Va.), 52
Antigua, *xii*, 46, 173–74, 212, 241, 255n46
anti-intermixture. *See* law, laws: anti-intermixture
Antoine (Charlestown), 156
Apalachees, 110, 120
Appalachian Mountains, *xv*, 204
apprenticeships, 55, 65, 132, 134, 167, 217, 284n39
*Ark* (ship), 37
Arnold, Ann, 135
Ashley River, 107, 110
Attanoughskomouck, 29, 32. *See also* Tsenacommacah

"backcountry" (Indigenous territories), *xii*, *xiv*, *xv*, 97, 111, 140, 154, 157, 202, 204, 205, 206, 226
Bacon, Nathaniel, Bacon's Rebellion, 34, 50
Bagwell, Edward, 116
Bahamas, *xii*, *xiv*, 180
Baker, Henry, 216
Baltimore County, Md., *xv*, 178, 251n39, 277n41
Banks, Elizabeth (European), 89
Banks, Elizabeth ("Mallato"), 90–91, 262n79
Banks, Hannah, 89–90, 262n79
Banks, Mary, 89–91, 262n79

Banks family, 89–91, 262n79
baptism. *See* Christianity
Barbados, *xii*, *xiv*, 7, 38–40, 41, 42, 44, 46,
    77, 82, 96, 101, 106–7, 109, 110, 111, 123, 129,
    131, 140, 171, 172, 173, 206–7, 209, 212, 213,
    215, 278n55, 282n23
Barnwell, John, 116
Bass, John, 33, 57
Bass, Keziah (née Tucker), 33, 57
Bass, Sarah, 54
Bass, William, 33
Bassett, Burwell, 159
Bass family (Norfolk County, Va.), 33–34,
    54, 57, 253n20
Bass family (Somerset County, Md.), 54
"bastard," "bastardy," 38, 46, 56, 59, 60, 64,
    67, 68, 69, 70, 72, 73–74, 75, 76, 77, 78, 86,
    87, 89, 90, 91, 98, 105, 115, 116, 124, 145, 168,
    178, 179, 180, 186, 187, 218, 220, 260n41,
    268n79, 278n49
Batts, Nathaniel, 106
Beaching, Catherine. *See* Scott, Catherine
Beaching, John, 168–70
Beaufort, S.C., 157
Bee, Isaac, 152
Ben (N.J.), 226
Ben (Va.), 229–30, 231
Berkeley, William, 34, 55
Berks County, Pa., 158
Bermuda, *xii*, *xiv*, 4, 38, 40, 46, 48, 109, 110,
    111, 147, 167–68, 180, 212, 259n16, 275n13,
    278n49
Bertie County, Bertie Precinct, N.C., *xv*,
    196, 216
Bess (Baltimore County, Md.), 178–79,
    277n41
Bess (Chowan precinct), 112
Bess (Suffolk County, Mass.), 98
Bestick, Dorothy, 56
Betty (Ashley River), 110
Betty (Barbados), 39
Betty (#1, Charlestown), 20, 224
Betty (#2, Charlestown, *South-Carolina
    Gazette*), 115, 266n50
Betty (Conn.), 99
Betty (S.C.), 93–94
Bible. *See* Christianity
Billey (St. James Parish, S.C.), 153

Billy, Will (Prince George County, Va.), 229
"black" (race), blackness: descriptions of,
    7, 8, 18, 22, 43–44, 57, 81, 174, 238, 243,
    255n41, 264n17. *See also* blood
Blackall, Abraham, 216
Blackamore, 147–50, 272n48
"Blackemore," "Blackmore." *See* Moors
Blacknall, John, 185–86, 279n60
Bland, John, 199
Bland, Theodorick, 152
Blisland Parish, Va., 175
blood (race), 8, 9, 14, 19, 22, 25, 35, 50, 80,
    81, 95, 100, 102, 126, 130, 146, 149, 153, 154,
    155, 157, 173, 182, 183–84, 188, 203, 209, 215,
    239, 242, 243–44, 249n19, 264n17, 272n51,
    280n73. *See also limpieza de sangre; sang-
    mêlés*
Board of Trade (British), 143
Bolling, Jane (née Rolfe), 57, 58
Bolling, John, 57
Bolling, Robert, 57
Bolzius, John, 194–95
Bond, William, 178–79, 277n41
Bonny, Hannah, 98
Boston, Mass., *xiv*, 40, 51, 52, 95, 97, 98, 135,
    140, 152
Brazil, *xii*, 100, 202, 277n29
Brent, Giles, Jr., 34
Brent, Giles, Sr., 34
Brent, Jane, 159
Brent, Mary (née Kittomaquund), 34
Bright, Delaney, 217
Britain, 9, 139, 146, 147, 171, 194, 199, 206, 214
Brown, Jack, 226–27
Brown (Gibson), Mary, 196
Bunch, John, 175–76, 177
Burke, Edmund, 244
Bushrod, Thomas, 48
Buss, Edward, 85, 86
Butler, Eleanor, 53, 134
Byrd, William, II, 175, 188

Caesar (Conn.), 99
Caesar (New York City). *See* John Gwin
Caesar (S.C.), 205
Calvert, Charles, 45, 53
Calvert, Leonard, 24
Calvert County, Md., *xv*, 76, 132

Canada, *xii, xiv*, 188, 203
Canary Islands, *xiii*, 37
Cape Fear, 106
Cape Verde Islands, *xiii*, 37
Carolina, Carolinas. *See* North Carolina; South Carolina
*Carolina* (ship), 107
Caroline County, Va., *xv*, 221
Carr, Mark, 196
Carroll, Peter (Baltimore County, Md.), 251n39
Carr's Field, Ga., 196
Cassity, Catherine, 75–76
*casta, castas*, 14, 15
Catawbas, 113
Catherina (Charlestown), 222–23
Catholic, Catholicism, 12, 13, 14, 24, 25, 34, 37, 64, 133, 134, 136, 200, 203, 205, 206, 208, 240, 241. *See also* Christianity
Catillah, William, 56, 257n69, 262n79
Cato (S.C.), 266n50
Charles (Hanover County, Va.), 236
Charles (N.J.), 157
Charles, "Negro Charles" (Md.), 53, 134
Charles City, Va., 286n81
Charles City County, Va., *xv*, 236
Charles County, Md., *xv*, 68, 73–75, 83, 88, 159
Charlestown, Charles Town, S.C., *xiv*, 20, 94, 95, 106–7, 108, 110, 111, 113, 117, 118, 119, 120, 121, 122, 149, 151, 152, 188, 189, 214, 221, 222, 224, 241, 280n70
Charlestown Harbor, 107, 108, 109, 118, 156
Cherokee, Cherokees, 113, 116, 155, 205
Chesapeake: location of, *xii, xv*, 47. *See also* Maryland; Virginia
Chesapeake Bay, *xv*, 24, 25, 29, 132, 169
Cheshire, James (Jim), 226
Cheshire (Chowan precinct), 112
Chester County, Pa., *xv*, 104, 156
Chesterfield, Va., 236
Chickahominy, 31
Choctaw, Choctaws, 110, 114, 120, 141
Chopstick, Jack, 147–48
Chowan County, Chowan precinct, N.C., *xv*, 112, 185, 196
Chowanocs, 28, 107, 112
Christian, Christianity: baptism, 12, 30, 33, 43, 49, 50, 64, 89, 115, 133, 136, 140, 242; Bible, biblical scripture, 30, 33, 100, 102, 133, 136, 138, 139, 140, 141, 142, 242, 250n19, 253n20, 264n17; churchwardens, 46, 67, 76, 86, 124, 125, 137, 216; education, 89, 111–12, 116, 134, 139, 167; faith, 25, 30, 31, 32, 33, 34, 43, 48, 51, 84, 89, 90, 91, 101, 102, 104, 111, 112, 129, 133–34, 136–41, 142–43, 185–86, 239, 242, 255n46; godparents, 30, 42, 111–12, 133, 270n15; Jesus, 136, 138, 140, 141; as race, 133–34. *See also* Catholicism; Protestantism
Christmas (Fredericksburg), 231–32
Clark, Daniel, 68–69, 71, 260n26
"Cleopatre" (Powhatan), 33
*Code Noir*, 12, 208
Codrington, William, 213
Codringtons (family), 173
Colón, Cristóbal (Christopher Columbus), 9, 27
colorism, 146–50, 243, 272n45, 272n47, 273n52
Concord, Mass., 233
Connecticut, *xiv*, 94, 97, 99, 104
Continental Congress, 235
convict labor, 72, 104, 145
Cooper, Will, 21
Copley, Lionel, 1
Cornelius (Yorktown), 235, 238
corporal punishment: branding, 205, 220, 221, 222, 226, 228, 236; dismemberment, 1–3, 71, 222–23, 278n49; evidence of, 52, 122, 152; execution, 222–23, 285n53, 285n54; hanging (gallows); 103, 129; iron collar, 222; shackles, 120, 222; whipping, 36, 60, 68, 73, 74, 89, 90, 98, 124, 142, 143, 178, 179, 182, 205, 221, 222
Courtney, Mrs., 1–2
Courtney, Thomas, 1–4, 71
Coxey, William, 262n68
Creek, Creeks, 113, 119, 120, 122, 205
creole, creoles, 51, 111, 156, 157, 160, 212, 224–25
*criollos*, 14
crops. *See* agriculture
Cuba, *xii, xiv*, 207, 208
Cudjoe (S.C.), 151
Cullee (Barbados), 39

Index : 309

Cumberland County, Va., 219, 226
Cumbo, Daniel, 286n81
Currituck County, Currituck precinct, N.C., *xv*, 124, 185

Damall, Henry, 133
Dancer, John, 232
Daniel (Lancaster County, Va.), 168–70, 276n19
Daniel (Va.), 158
Daniell, Martha, 118
Daniell, Robert, 118
David (Dinwiddie County, Va.), 285n64
Davis, Ann (née Hailey), 196
Davis, Captain, 192–94
Davis, Hugh, 36
Davis, Joanna, 167
Davis, John, 167
Davis, Mary, 132–34, 270n14
Davis, Penelope (née Strange), 167, 168
Davis, Rose, 132–34, 136, 270n15, 270n17
Davis, Thomas, 133–34
Davis, William, Jr., 196
Davis, William, Sr., 196
Davis family (Ga.), 196, 198
Davis family (Md.), 132–34
Deadfoot, Peter, 225
Delaware, *xiv*, *xv*, 94, 99, 101, 102, 104, 123–24, 127, 152, 165, 181–82, 204, 240, 278n49
Delaware River, *xv*, 94, 99, 100, 101, 105, 155
Delaware Valley, 100–101, 102, 124, 155
demographics: African, "Negro," 36, 40, 96, 103, *119*, 188, *210*, *211*, *214*, *230*; European, "white," 12, 13, 31, 36, 40, *41*, *210*, *211*; "Indian," Indigenous American, 109, 113, *119*, *214*; manumission, *214*; runaway, *119*, *230*; servant, slave, 36, 40, *41*, 52, 103, 104, 109, 113, 117–19, 209–14, *230*, 238; mixed-heritage people, free people of color, 40, 52, 76, 77, 95, 103, 118–19, 123, 200–201, 202, 207–14, *230*, 281n5, 282–83n23, 283n28, 286n82
Dennis, John. *See* John (S.C.)
Dent, William, 68–69, 71, 73, 75, 260n26
de Sorogosa, Francis, 157
de Soto, Hernando, 28
de Sousa, Mathias, 24–25, 37–38

de Vries, Jan, 103
de Vries, Johan, 103
Diana (S.C.), 120–21
Dinwiddie County, Va., 141, 152, 285n64
Dircks, Adriaentje, 103
Doll (Ashley River), 110
domestic labor. *See* occupations
Domingo (Calvert County, Md.), 132–34
Dominica, *xii*, *113*
Dorchester County, Md., *xv*, 68
Douglass, Frederick, 285n49
Douglass, William, 174
*Dove* (ship), 37
Duckenfield, William, 112
Ducket, Richard, 101
Dunmore, Lord, 233
Dutch, 11, 14, 18, 35, 96, 99–101, 103, 104, 155–56, 203, 207, 264n18
Dutchess County, N.Y., 155
Dutch Reformed Church, 103
Dutch West Indian Company, 264n18
Dyson, James (Jem), 160
Dyssli, Samuel, 188–89

Earl of Dartmouth, 173
Eastern Shore, 54, 55, 77, 116, 141, 221
"East India," "East Indian," 20
*Eastward Ho!* (play), 28
Ebenezer, 194
Edenton, N.C., 185
Edmonds, Elias, 67
education, 30, 39, 116, 134, 139, 145, 146, 147, 171, 191, 214, 242
Edwards, Bryan, 191–92, 280n73
Egyptian, 138, 141, 249–50n19
Elizabeth City, Elizabeth City County, Va., *xv*, 77
Ellis, Mary, 222–23
Eltham, Va., 158
Elwick, John, 180
Endecott, John, 51
endogamy, 67, 71
England, *xiii*, 9, 13, 28, 29, 31, 36, 42, 43, 66, 69, 71, 84, 106, 107, 132, 133, 136, 140, 144, 173, 185, 260n26
England (Goose Creek), 120
Estwick, Samuel, 215

310 ⋮ Index

ethnicity, ethnoracial: defined, 22, 23, 248n9
etymology (mixed-race), 8, 9–10, 19, 37, 43–44, 69, 203, 208, 249–50n19, 250n20
exogamy. *See* intermarriage

field labor. *See* agriculture; occupations: field hand
Finns, 100
Flora (Charlestown), 224
Flora (S.C.), 21
Florida (La Florida), *xii, xiv,* 13, 28, 106, 120, 192, 196, 205–6
Fontaine, Peter, 187, 188, 279n65
Fordyce, John, 140
"fornication," 36, 46, 56, 64, 89, 98, 101, 105, 186, 187, 195, 203, 258n5, 278n49, 281n81
Fortuna (S.C.), 111
Founding Fathers, 218–19, 235
Fountain, Mary, 74–75, 260n37
Fountain, Thomas, 74–75
France, *xiii,* 203, 206
Francis, George, 56
Francis, James, 204
Francisco (Chesapeake), 254n29
Frank (Accomack County, Va.), 52
Frank (S.C.), 20
Franke (Johns Island), 151
Franklin, Benjamin, 147–49, 272n48
Frederick County, Md., 228
Fredericksburg, Va., 231, 232, 235
Frederick Town, Md., 199, 228
French, 8, 12, 13, 14, 16, 19, 96, 106, 154, 156, 174, 188, 198, 200, 202–5, 206, 207–9, 213, 240, 279n67
French Revolution, 209
*Friendship* (ship), 156
furs, fur trade, 13, 97, 109, 169, 203, 206

Galloway (New York City), 155
Garcia, Antonio, 101–2
*gens de couleur* (people of color), 19, 208, 209
George, "Negro George" (Prince George's County, Md.), 86, 87
Georgetown, S.C., 140
Georgia, *xiv,* 192, 194–96, 198, 205, 206, 258n11, 280n67, 281n81

German, 96, 113, 156, 197
Gibbs, James, 86
Gibson, Agnes, 196
Gibson, Edmund, 136
Gibson, Gideon, Jr., 196
Gibson, Gideon, Sr., 196–97
Gibson, Tom, 196
Gibson, William, 196
Gibson family (S.C.), 196–97, 198
Gilbert, Elizabeth, 196
Gilbertson, Anne, 93, 262n1
Gilbertson, James, 93–94, 262n1
Gilbertson, Mehitable, 93, 262n1
Ginny (Ashley River), 110
Glen, James, 154
Glover, Jonathan, 88
Goddard, Francis, 220
Gooch, William, 143–46, 147, 150
Goodwin, James, 89
Goodwin, Martin, 89, 90, 91, 262n79
Goodwin, Peter, 89, 262n79
Goose Creek, S.C., 120
Graves, Elizabeth, 163–64, 179. *See also* Pearl, Elizabeth
Great Dismal Swamp, 107
Great Migration (Puritans), 97
Green's Savannah, S.C., 213
Greensted, Elizabeth. *See* Key, Elizabeth
Greensted, Elizabeth (daughter of Elizabeth Key), 57
Greensted, John, 57
Greensted, William, Jr., 57–58
Greensted, William, Sr., 43, 57, 167, 255n39, 257n73
Greenwood, John, 135
Griffin, Aaron, 220
Griggs, Robert, 52–53
Griggs (family), 173
Grimes, Elizabeth, 78
Grimes, Moses, 226
Grimes, Susanna, 78
Grinstead, John, 257n73
Guales, 110, 120
Guayaquil, 114
Guinea, Guinea coast, *xiii,* 36, 100
guns (arms), 34, 57, 108, 126, 152, 153, 154, 183, 203, 205, 233

*Index* ⋮ 311

Guy. *See* James (Chester County, Pa.)
Guy, Bridget, 186–87
Guy, Joseph, 186–87
Gwin, John (Caesar), 103, 104

Hailey, Ann. *See* Davis, Ann
Hailey, Mary, 196
Haiti. *See* Saint-Domingue
Haitian Revolution, 209
Hannah (Chowan precinct), 112
Hannah, old (Chowan precinct), 112
Hanover County, Va., *xv*, 236
Harman, Simon, 221
Harry (Charles County, Md.), 159–60
Harry (Dinwiddie County, Va.), 152
Hartford, Conn., 99
Harwood, Thomas, 83
Hasellwood, Anne, 74
Haudenosaunee (Iroquois), 113, 154
Hayly, William, 196
Haynes, Lemuel, 104
Helyar, Cary, 171
Helyar, William, 171
Hemings, Sally, 276n14
Hercules (Ashley River), 110
Hermitage, Samuell, 110
Higginson, Humphrey, 42–43
Hispaniola, 207
Hobson, Peter, 77
Hollyday, Colonel, 78
Hood, William, 236
Hoskins, Captain, 260n37
Howell, Samuel (Sam), 219–20
Howell, Simon, 219–20
Hudson River, Hudson River valley, *xiv*, 94, 99, 155
Hugill, George, 152
Hugill, William, 152
Hunt, Rose, 133
Hunting Creek, Md., 132
Huntziger, George, 156
Hutchins, John, 75, 76
hybrid, hybridity, 9, 10, 241–42, 249n19, 259–60n26, 264n17
hybrid degeneracy, 241–42
hyperdescent, 176, 180
hypodescent, 7–9, 16–17, 18, 26–27, 41–45, 48, 49, 50, 52, 54, 56–58, 61–62, 71, 75,

80–81, 88, 91–92, 95, 96, 98, 102, 105, 122, 123, 127, 131, 132, 134, 136, 137, 139, 143–45, 157, 162, 163, 165–66, 173, 174–76, 180, 182, 183–85, 187, 193, 200, 209, 215, 216, 218, 219, 220, 227, 233, 237–45, 249n14, 249n15, 263n9

Iberians. *See* Portuguese; Spanish
Igbo, "Eboe," 141, 251n41
indentures. *See* law, laws: servant and slave
"Indian-Land," 226. *See also* "backcountry"
"Indians." *See* Indigenous Americans
"Indian Wench" (St. James Parish, S.C.), 153
"Indian woman" (S.C.), 111, 112
"Indian woman" (N.J.), 153
Indigenous, Indigenous Americans ("Indians," Native Americans): defined, 20, 248n9; slave trade, 95, 107, 108, 109–14, 117–18, 119–20, 241, 266n39
*indios*, 11, 12
intermarriage (racial exogamy), 13, 14, 28, 29, 30–31, 33, 34, 43, 46, 53, 57, 58, 60, 61, 64, 65, 77, 78, 79–80, 81, 97, 100, 101, 103, 106, 126, 132, 134, 142, 144, 158, 162, 163–66, 167–71, 175–76, 177, 179, 180–81, 185–86, 188, 189, 191–92, 195, 196–97, 198, 203, 208, 214, 215, 242–43, 244–45, 275n9, 275–76n13, 279n60. *See also* intermixture; law, laws: anti-intermixture
intermixture: multigenerational, 35, 56–58, 81, 159, 165, 166, 174–76, 183–85, 188, 189, 196–97, 214–15, 227, 231, 233, 239, 241, 249n15, 257n73, 261n53; sexual, 8, 9–14, 16, 17, 27–29, 33, 36, 38, 42, 46, 56, 58, 60, 61, 64, 77, 86, 97, 98, 100, 101, 102, 103, 105, 111, 126, 162, 164–66, 168, 170–71, 172–74, 177–80, 186–89, 203, 212–13, 238–39, 240, 244–45, 279n62, 279–80n67. *See also* intermarriage; law, laws: anti-intermixture
interracial mixture. *See* intermarriage; intermixture
Ireland, Irish, *xiii*, 2, 38, 273–74n73
"Irish Nell." *See* Butler, Eleanor
Iroquois. *See* Haudenosaunee
Isaac (Va.), 152
Islam, 10
Ivie, George, 80

Jack (Chowan precinct), 112
Jack (N.J.), 226
Jack (Pa.), 21
Jack (Salkehatchie River), 157, 206
Jacob (N.J.), 20
Jacob (New England), 257n69
Jacobs, Harriet, 272n47, 276n14, 285n49
Jamaica, *xii*, *xiv*, 6, 7, 14, 39, 40, *41*, 42, 44, 46, 82, 101, 109, 110, 123, 131, 143, 146, 147, 149, 171–72, 173, 184–85, 189, 191, 194, 207, 208, 209–10, *211*, 212, 213, 214, 276n24, 286n81
James, Guy (Chester County, Pa.), 104
James River, *xv*, 29, 35, 77, 79, 178, 196
Jamestown, Va. (James Fort, James Town), *xiv*, *xv*, 29, 31, 33, 36, 42, 72, 79, 106, 175, 178, 222, 252n12
Jansen, Anthony, 100
Jasper (Suffolk County, Mass.), 98
Jeany (S.C.), 111
Jefferson, Thomas, 276n14, 286n2
Jeffries, Timothy, 104
Jem. *See* Dyson, James
Jemmey (Charlestown), 119–20
Jemmy (Williamsburg). *See* Williams, James
Jenkins, Captain, 124
Jesuits. *See* Catholicism
Jewish, Jews, 35, 249–50n19
Joan (Suffolk County, Mass.), 98
Joanna. *See* Davis, Joanna
Joe (S.C.), 206
John, Philip, 205
John (Barbados), 213
John (S.C.), John Dennis, John Poppeay, "Virginia John," 225–26
John (Va.), 222
Johns Island, S.C., 151
Johnson, Catherine, 158
Johnson, James, 158
Johnson, Nathaniel, 241–42, 287n13
Johnson, Robert, 197
Johnson, Thomas, 167
Jones, Hugh, 151
Jones, Morgan, 110

Kate (Chowan precinct), 112
Katherine (Essex County, Mass.), 98

Kaye, John. *See* Key, John
Keatty (S.C.), 93–94
Kelly, Mary. *See* Taylor, Mary
Kemble, Fanny, 272n51
Kenney, John, 152
Kent County, Del., *xv*, 204
Kent County, Md., *xv*, 204
Kerry, Peggy, 103, 104
Key, Elizabeth, 42–44, *45*, 49, 57, 134, 167, 168, 257n73
Key, John, 44
Key, Thomas, 36, 42–43, 44
Kimbundu, 36
King and Queen County, Va., *xv*, 232
Kingdom of Kongo, 36
Kingdom of Ndongo, 36
King Charles II, 106
King George I, 138
King George's War, 204
King James I, 29
King Philip's (Metacom's) War, 98, 99
Kingston, 147
Kittomaquund, Mary, 34. *See also* Brent, Mary

Lady (Charlestown), 224
Lancaster County, Pa., *xv*
Lancaster County, Va., *xv*, 52, 67, 75, 76, 168, 169, 276n19
Lane, Joe, 20
languages: African, 36, 111; Dutch, 18, 104, 155; French, 156; German, 156, 194; "Indian," Indigenous, 25, 31, 34, 97, 99, 100, 105, 106, 112, 154; "Negroish," 159–60; Spanish, 157; stuttering, 121, 229; Swedish, 156. *See also* etymology
Laurens, Henry, 215
law, laws: absence of, 43, 108, 123, 126–27, 181–82, 189, 197, 240–41; anti-intermixture, 25–26, 44–50, 65–69, 71, 81–82, 102, 107–8, 126, 168, 175, 179–80, 181–84, 188, 195, 244–45, 255n46, 258n11, 259n16, 259n20, 260n26, 260n30, 268n79, 270n17, 281n81; baptism and manumission, 49, 50, 101–2; of England (common law), 36, 43, 45, 46, 64, 69, 71, 144, 255n42, 260n26; enslaving European women, 45–46, 53, 260n26; free people

of color, 103, 143, 183, 184, 195, 286n81, 278n55; inheritance, 184–85; lacking enforcement, 46, 72–73, 74–76, 168, 181–82, 240–41, 259n16, 274n86; servant and slave, 2, 45, 47–48, 53, 60, 67, 68–69, 70, 71, 82, 96, 97, 98–99, 105, 114, 115, 123–24, 125–26, 137, 176, 182, 212, 217–18, 254n29, 255n42, 259n21, 260n30, 263n12, 270n17, 284n39, 285n53, 285n54; tax, 122, 126, 183, 219; witness, 144, 183, 268n77, 278n55. *See also* Mulatto, Mulattoes; tax, taxes; vote, voting

Lawson, John, 112
Lee, John, 38–39
Lee, Richard Henry, 218
Leeward Islands, *xii, xiv*, 40, 109, 123, 173, 212, 241
Left (Northampton County, Va.), 142, 144
Lettice (Jamaica), 280n70
Lexington, Mass., 233
Lewie (Va.), 21
*limpieza de sangre*, 35, 50, 239
literacy, 51, 91, 125, 128, 128–29, 136–39, 217, 232, 242, 286n81
livestock. *See* agriculture: livestock
Lloyd, Thomas, 84
Lloyd, William, 84
London, England, 29, 31, 42, 128, 132, 136, 138, 215
Long, Edward, 14, 189, 192, 193–94, 208, 214–15, 276n24, 280n73
Longo, Anthony "Tony," 54–56
Longo, Hannah, 54
Longo, James, 55–56
*loro*, 10, 249n19
Louisiana, *xiv*, 12, 13, 208
*Loving v. Virginia*, 244
Lowcountry, "Low Country" (described), 95
Luckett, Samuel, 88

Mackewn, James, 121–22
*malaet*, 99
"Malatto Girl" (Md.), 1–4, 71
Mall (Chowan precinct), 112
*mamaluco*, 10, 250n19
Man, William, 169, 276n19
Mandingo, 141, 280n70

Manena, Hannah. *See* McKenney, Hannah
Manhattan, 100
Manuel, Benjamin, 20
Manuel (Va.), 48–49, 256n50
March (S.C.), 121
Marea (Ashley River), 110
Marshall, Anne (née Pearl), 163–64
Marshall, William (Md.), 87
Marshall, William (Va.), 163–64, 179
Mary (Santee), 152–53
Mary (Surry County, Va.), 178, 277n39
Maryland: location of, *xiv, xv*, 47; origins of, 24–25, 31, 37
*Maryland Gazette*, 230
*Maryland Journal and Baltimore Advertiser*, 230
Mason, Christopher, 98
Massachusetts, Massachusetts Bay Colony, *xiv*, 94, 95, 97, 98, 102, 104, 105, 108, 181, 233, 263n12
Massachusetts Bay, 97
Matoaka, Matoaks (Pocahontas, Rebecca Rolfe), 30, 31, 32, 57
*mawallad*, 10
McCollins, Catherine, 67, 259n20
McKenney, Anthony, 180
McKenney, Hannah (née Manena), 180
Mecklenburg County, Va., 152
"Mellatto Boy" (N.C.), 124
"Mellatto" son (Currituck County, N.C.), 124–25
Mercer, James, 231, 232
*mestiçagem*, 8
*mestiço*, 10, 208, 250n19
*mestizaje*, 8, 11, 14–16
*mestizo, mestizos*, 10, 11, 13, 14, 15, 16, 28, 35, 56, 114, 115, 192, 195, 196, 203, 208, 249–50n19, 266n50
*métis*, 13, 203
Michael (Va.), 21
Middlesex County, Va., *xv*, 34, 51, 52
Mike (Baltimore County, Md.), 251n39
militia, military (service), 34, 57, 126, 183, 196, 204, 206, 233
Miller, John, 156
Mingo, Lewis, 83–84, 270n15
Minson, Henry, 236
"miscegenation," 5, 244–45

Mississippi River, *xiv*, 13, 206
"mixed blood." *See* blood
*mixticius*, 249n19
Mobile, La., 205
Mocamas, 110, 120
"molatters" (Va. group), 128–29, 136–39, 141, 269n4
"Mollato wench" (Norfolk, Va.), 177
Molley (Lancaster County, Va.), 52–53
Molly (S.C.), 93–94
"mongrel," "mongrels," 14, 69, 147, 173, 241, 259–60n26
Montserrat, *xii*, 173
Moors, Moorish, 10, 11, 35, 50, 157, 175–76, 239, 259n26
*Moriscos*, 215
Morris, George, 167
Morris, Sarah, 185
Moses (Va.), 222
Mottrom, John, 42, 43
Moycum, John, 20
*muellad*, 10
Muirhead, John, 236
*muladi, mulado*, 10
*mulato, mulatos*, 10, 13, 14, 15, 28, 35, 38, 208, 249n19, 250n20, 259n26
*mulâtres, mulâtresses*, 13, 208, 209
"mullatter boy" (St. Paul's Parish, N.C.), 216
Mulatto, Mulattoes: defined, 7, 10–11, 16, 18, 20, 21, 37, 56, 80–81, 176–77, 183–85
"mulatto escape hatch," 88–89, 174–76, 185, 241, 277n29. *See also* intermixture: multigenerational; passing: as "white"; whiteness
"Mulatto Man" (Chester County, Pa.), 156
"Mulatto Servant" (Savannah), 192–94
"Mulatto sweetheart" (Jamaica), 191
*mulo*, 10, 250n20
Mustapha (Chowan precinct), 112
Mustee, Mustees: defined, 18, 21, 95, 114–16, 117, 127, 176, 241, 266n50; "Mustee Negro," 120–21, 267n63
"Mustee Boy" (Cherokee trading post), 116–17
"Mustee Wench" (Stono River), 121–22

Nanny (Albemarle County, Va.), 219–20
Nanny (Ashley River), 110
Nansemond, 33–34, 54, 57
Nany (#1, Chowan precinct), 112
Nany (#2, Chowan precinct), 112
Narváez, Pánfilo de, 28
Nat (Chowan precinct), 112
Native Americans. *See* Indigenous Americans
Neabsco Furnace, 229
Ned (Chowan precinct), 112
*négresses*, 208
"Negro." *See* African, Africans; "black"
"Negro Fellow" (Prince George County, Md.), 181
*negros*, 12
Nevis, *xii*, 173
New Amsterdam, 103
New Castle County, Del., *xv*, 152
New England, *xii*, 13, 52, 62, 92, 94, 95, 97–98, 99, 102, 104, 105, 114, 127, 165, 168, 181, 257n69, 266n39. *See also* Connecticut; Massachusetts; New Hampshire; Rhode Island
New Hampshire, *xiv*, 94, 266n39
New Jersey, *xiv*, *xv*, 94, 99, 101, 103, 105, 127, 153, 155, 156, 157, 165, 226, 228, 240
New Netherland, 14, 99–100, 103, 155, 264n18
New Orleans, La., *xiv*, 13, 149
Newport, R.I., 40, 97
New Providence, Bahamas, 180
New Kent County, Va., *xv*, 158
New Spain. *See* Nueva España (New Spain)
Newton, Abram, 180–81
New York, *xiv*, 40, 94, 99, 100, 101, 103, 115, 127, 155, 165, 240
New York City, N.Y., *xiv*, 95, 97, 103, 104, 152, 155
Nimrod (Plymouth Colony), 98
Nisbet, James, 140
Nittewegas, 154
Norfolk, Va., 59, 80, 177, 221
Norfolk County, Va., *xv*, 33, 59, 60, 77
Norris, John, 117, 122
Norse, 9
Northampton County, Va., *xv*, 141, 142, 227
North Carolina: location of, *xii*, *xiv*, *xv*; origins of, 105–6, 107–8

Index : 315

Northumberland County, Va., *xv*, 42, 57, 58, 257n73
Nueva España (New Spain), 14, *15*
Nutus, John, 160
Nutus, Thomas, 160

occupations: accountant, 193; barber, 199; blacksmith, 224; butcher, 224, 225; carpenter, 55, 197, 204, 206, 224, 236; carter, 224, 225; child care, *135*, 223; cook, 117, 121, 224; cooper, 39, 204, 224; dairymaid, 117; doctor, 151; field hand, 59, 94, 117–18, 223–24, 229; gambler, 151; horse keeper, 221; housekeeper, 59, 104, 117, 121, 151, 177, 223, 224; iron founder, 229; laundress, 117, 121, 223; mason, 55, 229; merchant, 100, 193; miller, 229; millwright, 224; planter, 86, 197; plowman, 224, 225; pilot, 25, 223, 224, 225; prostitute, 103, 189, 280n70; mechanic, 147, 224; sawyer, 206, 225; scythe man, 225; seamstress, 59, 121, 224; shoemaker, 160, 206, 225, 236; tanner, 206; tax collector, 34; waiting man, 160, 231–32; wet nurse, *135*
Oglethorpe, James, 196
"one-drop rule," 7, 8, 22, 81, 237, 238, 242, 244, 245, 249n15
"Opecancanough," Opechancanough, 33
orphan, orphans, 57, 103, 104, 217, 284n39
Otho (Eltham), 158–59

Palmer, Anthony, 105
Pamlico River, 118
Pamlicos, 107
*pardo, pardos*, 10, 35, 249n19
Paretree, Elizabeth, 111
Paretree, James, 111
Parke, Daniel, 173–74, 276n25
Parker, Elizabeth, 98
Parthena (S.C.), 213
*partus sequitur ventrem*, 45, 53, 212, 255n42
Parvin, Silas, 153, 154
Pasquotank River, 106
passing: as free, 158–62, 201–2, 206, 219, 221, 223–33, 235, 242, 274n78, 286n81; as "Indian," 153–54, 160–61, 226–27; as free Mulatto, 223–27; as "white," 56–58, 131,

158–60, 161–62, 201, 229, 231, 233, 242, 272n47, 274n78, 274n85
Paul, Martha, 185–86, 279n60
Paul (S.C.), 121, 267n64
Pearl, Anne. *See* Marshall, Anne
Pearl, Daniel, 163–64, *165*, 179
Pearl, Elizabeth (née Graves), 163–64, 179
pegge (Ashley River), 110
Peggy (Chowan precinct), 112
Pendarvis, Brand, 213
Pendarvis, Elizabeth, 213
Pendarvis, John, 205, 213
Pendarvis, Joseph, 213
Pendarvis, Mary, 213
Pendarvis, Thomas, 213
Pendarvis, William, 213
Penn, William, Jr., 102
Penn, William, Sr., 101
Pennsylvania, *xiv*, *xv*, 20, 21, 94, 101, 102, 104, 105, 123–24, 127, 151, 156, 158, 160, 165, 181–82, 205, 226, 240
*Pennsylvania Gazette*, 147
Pequot, Pequots, 97, 257n69
Pequot War, 98, 114
Perrie, Mr., 276n25
Perth Amboy, N.J., 105
Peter, "Yellow Peter" (Va.), 233
Peter (Amelia County, Va.), 228
Peter (Caroline County, Va.), 221
Peter (S.C.), 206
Peyre, Rene, 153
Philadelphia, Pa., *xiv*, *xv*, 18, 40, 95, 97, 101, 104, 140, 147, 149, 151, 152, 156, 157, 226, 235
Pindar, Thomas, 110
Piscataway, Piscataways, 24, 25, 34
Plymouth Colony, 97, 98
Pocahontas, "Pokahuntas." *See* Matoaka, Matoaks (Pocahontas, Rebecca Rolfe)
Point Comfort, Va., 35, 36
Poole, John ("Molattoe Jack"), 151
Pope (Savannah), 193
Poppeay, John. *See* John (S.C.)
Port Royal, 107
Portugal, *xiii*, 10, 157
Portuguese, 8, 10, 11, 12, 14, 29, 35, 37, 100, 157, 158, 202, 215, 239, 249–50n19
Potomac River, *xv*, 65, 77, 132, 186
Powell, William, 177

Powhatan, Powhatans, 29, 30, 31, 32, 33, 36, 252n12
Poythress, Jane, 257n71
Primus (S.C.), 251n41
Prince (Goose Creek), 120
Prince Frederick's Parish, S.C., 140
Prince George County, Va., *xv*, 79, 81, 181, 222, 229
Prince George's County, Md., *xv*, 78, 86, 163, 179
Priscilla, Priss (Accomack County, Va.), 116
Priscilla (St. George's, Bermuda), 180
Priss. *See* Priscilla, Priss (Accomack County, Va.)
Prize, Elizabeth, 111–12, 117
Prize, Richard, 111
Prize, Sarah, 111–12, 117
Prosper (Goose Creek), 120
Protestant, Protestantism, 12, 13, 33, 34, 64, 67, 84, 97, 101, 134, 136, 138, 140, 185, 186, 194, 200, 239, 240. *See also* Christianity
Puerto Rico, *xii, xiv,* 207, 208
Pulton, Ferdinand, 25
Puritans, 12–13, 97, 102, 168
Pye, Edward, 68, 73, 74

Quakers (Friends, Society of Friends), 101, 102, 104
"Quasheba," 147
Queen Anne's County, Md., *xv,* 186

racial passing. *See* passing
Randolph, Henry, 220, 236
Randolph, John, 220, 236
Rappahannock River, *xv,* 51, 169
Redman, Ann, 84, 85
Redman, Jane, 84
Reed, Elizabeth, 186–87
Reyniers, Grietse, 100
Rhode Island, *xiv,* 94, 97, 99
rice. *See* agriculture: rice
Richmond County, Va., *xv,* 84, 140
Rise, Roger, 59, 60
Roanoke, Roanoke Island, 28, 29, 106
Roanoke River, 196
Robbin (Chowan precinct), 112
Robin (Nansemond), 33
Rockaways, 100

Rodriguez, Juan, 99–100
Roetty (Chowan precinct), 112
Rogers, Woodes, 114
Rolfe, Jane, 57
Rolfe, John, 30–31, 35, 57
Rolfe, Rebecca. *See* Matoaka, Matoaks (Pocahontas, Rebecca Rolfe)
Rolfe, Thomas, 31, 33, 34, 57, 257n71
Rolfe-Bolling family, 57, 58
Rose, David, 104
Rose, Mrs., 104
Roxbury, Mass., 98
Ruecastle, Francis, 189
Russells (family), 173
Ruston, Margaret, 68, 73–74
Ruth (Charlestown), 221
Ruth (S.C.), 93–94
Rutland, Edward, 227–28

Saffin, John, 52
Saint-Domingue, *xii, xiv,* 13, 205, 206, 207, 208–9
Salkehatchie River, 157
Sall (Yorktown), 235, 238
Sally (Georgia), 272n51
"saltwater" Africans. *See* Africans: "saltwater"
Salzburgers, 194
Sam (Amelia County, Va.), 236
Sam (Frederick Town, Md.), 199
Sam (N.J.), 153–54
Sambo (Ashley River), 110
Sambo (Chowan precinct), 112
Sampson (N.J.), 153–54
San Agustín (St. Augustine), *xiv,* 28, 192, 196, 205–6
Sandy (Va.), 286n2
*sang-mêlés* (mixed-bloods), 19, 203, 209
San Miguel de Gualdape, 27
Santee, S.C., 152
Santo Domingo, *xii, xiv,* 207, 208
Sappho (Jamaica), 189, 191
Sarah (Accomack County, Va.), 56
Sarah (Ashley River), 110
Sarah (New York City), 104
Sarah (S.C.), 220
Sarah (Va.), 230
Sarah (York County, Va.), 83

Index : 317

Saunders (S.C.), 21
Savage, Thomas, 142
Savannah, Ga., 192, 193, 194
Savannah River, 194, 226
Scandinavian, 100
Scarborough, Edmund, 55
Scots, Scottish, 38, 104, 185
Scott, Catherine, 168–70, 276n19
Seewee Bay, 107
*Selling of Joseph, The* (Sewall), 102
Senecas, 154
"Settlement Indians," 108, 121
Seven Years' War, 199, 204, 205, 206, 218
Sewall, Samuel, 102, 264n22
Sharp, Granville, 19, 247n7
Shawnees, 154
Sherwin, Samuel, 228
Simons, Ann, 276n13
*skrælingjar (skræling)*, 9
slaves, slavery: de facto, 69, 71, 90, 125, 134, 137–38, 215–18. See also African, Africans; demographics; Indigenous Americans; law, laws: servant and slave
Slayden, Sarah, 175, 176, 177
Smart (Ashley River), 110
Smith, John, 31
Smith, Sarah, 88
Smithers, Godfrey, 158
Smyth, John, 110
Snelson, John, 152, 236
Society for the Propagation of the Gospel in Foreign Parts, 140
Society of Friends, Friends. See Quakers
Somerset County, Md., *xv*, 54, 116
Somers Islands (Bermuda), 38
Somers Isles Company, 38
South Carolina: location of, *xii, xiv*; origins of, 106–7, 108–9
*South-Carolina Gazette*, 114, 115, 119, 147, 205
Southwark Church parish, Va., 178
Spain, *xiii*, 9, 10, 14, 203, 206
Spanish, 8, 9–14, 15, 27–28, 29, 35, 37, 51, 101, 105, 106, 108, 114, 157, 192, 198, 200, 202, 203, 205–8, 209, 213, 239–40, 241, 249–50n19
Sparrow, Elizabeth, 59–60
Sparrow, Mary, 59–60, 258n1
Speke, Mrs., 44

Spence, Patrick, Jr., 259n15
Spencer, Elizabeth, 169
Spencer, Thomas, 185–86, 279n60
Squire (#1, Chowan precinct), 112
Squire (#2, Chowan precinct), 112
Stafford County, Va., *xv*, 225
Stamp Act, 218
Statira (S.C.). See Tira, Statira (S.C.)
St. Augustine. See San Agustín (St. Augustine)
Steendam, Jacob, 100, 264n17
St. George's, Bermuda, 180
Stirling, Charlotte, 185
Stirling, Robert, 185
St. James Parish, S.C., 153
St. John's, Antigua, 174
St. Kitts (St. Christopher), *xii*, 173
St. Lawrence River, *xiv*, 13
St. Mary's County, Md., *xv*, 1, 71, 76, 133
Stone, Thomas, 260n37
Stono, S.C., 152
Stono River, 121
St. Paul's Parish, N.C., 216
Strange, Penelope. See Davis, Penelope
Strengwits, William, 100
Suffolk County, Mass., 98
sugar. See agriculture: sugar
Sukee (Chowan precinct), 112
Surry County, Va., *xv*, 79, 80, 178
"Susquehanna," Susquehannock, Susquehannocks, 25, 160
Swan, Thomas, 125
Swann, Ann (née Wall), 77–78, 261n45
Swann, John, 77–78, 261n45
Swann, Thomas, 77–78, 261n45
Swann (Juan), 77–78
Swart anna (Upland), 101
Swartinne (New Amsterdam), 103
Swedes, 100
Sweet, Robert, 36
Swiss, 96, 113, 188

Tappan, N.J., 103
Tate, Elizabeth, 65–66
Tate, Hester, 65
Tate, James, Jr., 65–66
Tate, James, Sr., 65
Tate, Jane, 65–66

Tate, William, 65–66
tax, taxes, 34, 55, 101, 103, 122, 126, 183, 184, 197, 209, 219, 264n18, 278n53
Taylor, Elizabeth, 86–87, 262n68
Taylor, Mary, 86, 262n68
Taylor, Sarah, 86
Taylor, William, 51
theata (Ashley River), 110
Thistlewood, Thomas, 189–90, 280n70
Thomas, James, 98
Thomas, Mary, 119
Thomas (Barbados), 213
Thomasina (Bermuda), 167
Thomson, Stevens, 115, 175–76
Timucuas, 110, 120
Tira, Statira (S.C.), 21
tobacco. *See* agriculture: tobacco
Toby (Kent County, Md.), 204
Tom (Chowan precinct), 112
Tom (Dutchess County, N.Y.), 155
Tom (Pa.), 160
Tom (Prince George County, Va.), 222
Tom (St. James Parish, S.C.), 153
Tom (Va.), 20
Toney, Peg, 181
Tony (Ashley River), 110
Tony (Chowan precinct), 112
Topp of the Hill, Md., 133
Totty (Chowan precinct), 112
Townshend Acts, 219
Treaty of Paris (1763), 206
Tsenacommacah (Attanoughskomouck), 29, 30, 31, 32, 36, 62
Tucker, Keziah Elizabeth. *See* Bass, Keziah (née Tucker)
Turtle River, 196
Tuscarora, Tuscaroras, 113–14, 120, 141
Tuscarora War, 113–14, 118, 120, 121

United States, U.S., 4, 5, 7, 8, 58, 233, 235, 237, 238, 244–45, 257n73, 274n73, 274n85, 277n29, 281n2. *See also* U.S. Revolution
Upland, 101
U.S. Revolution, 16, 18, 199, 204, 219, 227, 238, 244, 261n41

Vanhon, Stephen, 178, 277n39
Venus (Williamsburg), 151

Verrazzano, Giovanni da, 27
Vikings. *See* Norse
Violet (Frederick Town), 228
Virginia: location of, *xiv*, *xv*, 47; origins of, 27–29, 30–31
Virginia (Chowan precinct), 112
Virginia Company, 29, 30, 31
*Virginia Gazette*, 158, 232, 235, 236, 251n36
"Virginia John." *See* John (S.C.)
Virginia Resolves, 218, 284n42
vote, voting, 37, 38, 127, 129, 143–45, 149, 183, 184, 195, 208, 278n55

Wadsworth, Joseph, 99
Wahunsenacawh ("Prince Powhatan"), 30, 32
Wainwright, Thomas, 86
Wall, Ann. *See* Swann, Ann
Wallop, John, 52
Wampanoags, 97
Wan (Perth Amboy), 105
Wando River, 118
Warner, Mr., 276n25
Warro, Silvanus, Jr., 98
Washbourne, John, 55
Webb, Abimeleck, 142–43, 144
Webb, Daniel, 142
Webb, Jane, 141–42, 143, 144
Webb family, 141–43, 144, 146
Weech, Henry, 191
"wench," 5, 43, 104, 115, 121, 122, 151, 153, 177, 219, 220, 221, 223, 228, 255n40, 280n70
West, Richard, 143
West Africa, *xiii*, 36, 37, 118, 155, 224
Western Hemisphere, 3, 4, 9, 10, 11, 12, 23, 27, 35, 108, 131, 248n9
West Hartford, Conn., 104
Westmoreland County, Va., *xv*, 65, 85, 86, 186, 259n15
Westos, 110
Wenyam, James, 204
Wharton, Henry, 83–84, 133, 270n15
whipping. *See* corporal punishment: whipping
White, Andrew, 24, 37
White, Blake Leay, 267n64
White, John, 54
"white" (race), whiteness: descriptions

of, 8, 18, 22, 57, 264n17. *See also*
 blood; demographics; intermixture:
 multigenerational; "mulatto escape
 hatch"; passing: as "white"
Whitefield, George, 194, 195
*White Lion* (ship), 35
Whittacre, William, 48, 49
Wilkinson, Thomas, 186
Will (Ashley River), 110
Will (Caroline County, Va.), 221
Will (Philadelphia), 18
Will (Prince George County, Va.). *See* Billy,
 Will (Prince George County, Va.)
William (Accomack County, Va.), 116
William (Barbados), 213
Williams, Ann, 142
Williams, Col., 276n25
Williams, James (Jemmy), 141
Williams, Moses, 156–57

Williamsburg, Va., *xv*, 79, 141, 151, 152, 219
Williamson, David, 147
Williamson, Sarah, 124–25
Wood, Thomas, 276n13
Woodward, Henry, 111
Wormeley, Ralph, 52
Wragg, Joseph, 120

Yamasees, 113, 119, 120, 122
Yamasee War, 119–20
Yeopim, Yeopims, 106, 107
York County, Va., *xv*, 46, 83, 89, 90, 91, 196,
 235, 262n79
Yorktown, Va., 235
Young, Elizabeth, 180–81

*zambaigo*, 10
*zambo, zambos*, 10, 35